# CLOSE ENCOUNTERS

# WITH SIRENS

PAPERBACK ISBN: 979-8-9922051-3-8
EPUB ISBN: 979-8-2319528-2-3

\*\*\*

WRITTEN BY ROBERT KONSTANTY LEŚNIAKIEWICZ
PUBLISHED BY ROYAL HAWAIIAN PRESS
COVER ART BY TYRONE ROSHANTHA
TRANSLATED BY ANDRZEJ NOWAK
PUBLISHING ASSISTANCE: DOROTA RESZKE

\*\*\*

VERSION NUMBER 2.00

# CLOSE ENCOUNTERS
# WITH SIRENS

Robert K. Leśniakiewicz
Miloš Jesenský
Stanisław Bednarz

*Bunny*

# Table of Contents

*Credo quia absurdum  n o n  est!*

*Stanisław Lem*

*You will not see aliens in space.*

*You will see Them when you go down into the depths of the seas.*

*Ray Dalio, Akwanauta*

# EDITOR'S NOTE, OR ABOUT PURE AND APPLIED SEA MONSTROSITIES

I started to be interested in sea monsters since I was a child, since my Grandfather gave me the book "About Fairy Tale Dragons and Real Dragons" **by Anna Bańkowska** and **Kazimierz Greb**, and my Mother brought home **Daniel Jarząbek's** "Lost Landscapes", in which the authors described, m.in other things, legendary land and sea monsters, about which European cosmographers such as **Olaf the Great** called **Olaus Magnus, Conrad Lycosthenes** and **Konrad Gessner**. The illustrations from their treatises ignited the imagination! Of course, I knew that dragons and other monsters were gone, but who knows if they weren't hiding somewhere in the depths of the ocean?

*Sea monsters and animals from Konrad Gessner's
"Book of Fish"*

Let's just look at the map drawn by Olof the Great – bishop
of Uppsala – on which he showed various strange creatures
inhabiting the seas and the Atlantic. When we strip them of
their robes of extraordinariness and fantasy, we will see the
animals we know today: whales, sperm whales, orcas,
dolphins, sturgeons, crayfish, narwhals, crabs and others.
There's also the huge Kraken and the terrifying Sea Serpent
from sea legends. By the way, these two monsters are still
unknown to science...

Albert Rosales, an American ufologist and
cryptozoologist from Miami, Florida, is one of the
researchers of humanoid beings appearing on our planet in
the company of Unknown Flying Objects – UFOs. He has an

extensive record of Close Encounters with humanoid cryptids from all over the world, and especially from the United States. His file contains several thousand accounts of such meetings; he collected them for at least thirty years!

I completely agree with the author's final conclusions, we are dealing with Sea People, whose origin is still unexplored. Unexplored because official science does not deal with this issue at all – in fact, it ignores it!

And this is a mistake. On the other hand, knowing the mean and perverse mentality and the demoralization of some representatives of the Homo species (supposedly) sapiens, I realize that there would soon be some messed up person who would try to use the Sea People for his nefarious purposes, or – even worse – He would turn Them against other people. I'm satisfied with what was done with dolphins and other intelligent marine mammals in the marine laboratories of the US Navy and the Black Sea and Northern Fleets (and others too, let's not be fooled...), where dolphins were trained not only to fish for mines and torpedoes, detect foreign submarines or sensitive divers, but also to murder people...

To what Albert Rosales gave, I could also add the Warsaw Mermaid from the Vistula, Zielenica – the daughter of the king of the Baltic murdered and buried in Trzęsacz, and the beautiful Świetlana from Lake Wicko Wielkie. This is our contribution to his material.

What is the Sea People? Perhaps they are representatives of the human race that has returned to the ocean. It could also be an artificially bred species of aquatic man – some *Homo sapiens aquaticus* or even *subaquaticus*, which was supposed to wage war underwater? And why not? It could have been done in Atlantis or Mu in the distant past. And history likes to repeat itself and does it as many times as we let it!

I hope I am wrong...

*Traditional image of the Mermaid ("Secret of the 20th Century")*

Let's start with an encyclopedic definition:

A mermaid is a hypothetical aquatic creature with a human head, arms, and a female torso and a fish tail. The male version of the Syrena is known as merman (which has no equivalent in Polish, which could be translated as Syren) – and in general, both of them are the so-called "sea people" – the nation of the Sea People. Mermaids appear in folklore and literature as well as in pop culture in many countries of the world. However, many of them are based on real events that took place in the past or even the present.

And this is what Dr. Miloš Jesenský writes about it:

## 0.1. When Fish Sing: Mermaids in Culture, Art, and Psychology

*Once upon a time, there lived a fisherman on a cold, rocky shore. He lived alone, for he had never managed to persuade a woman to share his bleak home with him. Above all, he loved the sea, and so he never married. Women can see into a man's soul more than he would wish. And though he loved the cold drops falling on his face and the clouds rolling across the horizon, he still longed to meet someone to whom he could give his heart. One evening, at the end of a very long day, he pulled his net from the water and found a woman in it – or rather, she looked like a woman. She had black hair and eyes as gray as the sky before a storm. But instead of legs, she had a fish's tail.*

These sentences begin "The Siren" by American writer Christina Henry (*1974), a magical novel about the complicated fate of an extraordinary woman who came to the human world from the sea. But these words also fit into a whole series of stories, told and written since the dawn of time. Since ancient times, people have imagined what might lie beneath the surface of seas, lakes, and rivers. One of the most evocative images has been and still is female aquatic creatures – Rusalkas, Sirens, Water Nymphs, or Selkies. In literature, these figures have evolved from demonic death lures to tragic heroines longing for love, freedom, or a soul. How has their image changed from Romanticism to the present day? And what does it tell us about the human desire for otherness, depth, and the incommensurability of worlds?

## 0.2. Beauty that will knock you down

In Eastern European folklore, water is not only a source of life but also a place where the shadows of past tragedies and unspoken sorrows hide. It is from these mysterious depths that Rusalkas emerge – mysterious, ethereal, and often dangerous beings that defy simple labels. They are not classic mythical beauties waiting to be rescued – they are water spirits, drowned souls, vengeful fairies who have become symbols of pain, betrayal, and unfulfilled death.

Their roots are ancient and diverse. In Slavic cultures – especially in Ukrainian, Belarusian, Russian, but also Polish and Balkan traditions – Rusalkas embody girls who died tragically, especially at a very young age. Most often, these were girls who drowned before marriage – either by their own hand out of despair, due to the betrayal of a loved one, or due to social pressure or shame. A woman who died in childbirth, was raped, or did not experience desired love could also become a Siren. In some versions of legends, Rusalkas are also children who died without baptism – impure, rejected souls who could not find peace. According to tradition, these women could not go to heaven – they no longer belonged to the living, but death also rejected them. So they wander between worlds, tied to the places where they lost their lives – to lakes, rivers, swamps, or deep springs. They most often appear at night or at dawn, their bodies have a translucent paleness, and their hair is long, wet, often green or entwined with aquatic plants. In some descriptions, their eyes resemble wells – deep, dark, mesmerizing. Their laughter is resonant, childlike, but behind it lies a deadly call.

*Film Sirens from "Pirates of the Caribbean"*

According to legend, Rusalki lure men into the water – most often shepherds, fishermen, or young pilgrims who dare to approach the water at night. They lure them with singing, dancing, or seductive hair play. Those who followed them rarely returned. Death could be silent – drowning without a scream – or terrible – dancing to death, madness, or disappearing without a trace. However, some versions of the story say that if a man was not afraid of a Rusalka, but approached her with respect, she could spare him, or even help him. The line between malice and compassion, however, was always unclear for these creatures.

A special period, mentioned especially in Ukrainian and Belarusian traditions, is Rusalka Week – usually falling in June, at a time when nature turns green and water comes to life. It was then believed that Rusalki emerged from the water, danced in fields and meadows, played in trees, and lured people to them. Villages would then bring them gifts – ribbons, cakes, flowers – tie trees with green branches, and avoid bathing. Breaking the rules during this period threatened punishment by drowning or madness. Children were not allowed to play near the water, women were not allowed to look in the mirror after dark – as it was believed that a Rusalka might appear in it.

*Modern Rusalka ("Arguments and Facts")*

In the Czech Republic and Slovakia, similar beings appear in the form of wild women, water women, swamp women, or water nymphs, all sharing the same motif – a tragic death, a connection to nature, and a certain melancholy. Slovak legends also feature, for example, "left-sided lake girls" who appear before a storm, with long hair and a glassy gaze. In some villages, stories were told of young people who disappeared on summer nights by the river and were never found – supposedly abducted by the one who was still searching for her wedding.

Rusalkas also left a strong mark in literature. Russian poet **Alexander Sergeyevich Pushkin** (1799–1837) wrote about them in a romantic-tragic spirit, and his literary colleague **Nikolai Vasilyevich Gogol** (1809–1852) in the short story "May Night" (1831) depicted Rusalkas as beautiful but dangerous creatures in the Ukrainian countryside. **Adam Mickiewicz** (1798–1855) placed them on a symbolic level between life and death in his "Ballads and Romances". German Romanticism added a layer of sadness and melancholy to them – these are women who seduce, but only because they themselves long for a love they never experienced.

And so, Sirens emerge from the misty shores of our collective memory as archetypes of desire, loss, and punishment. Their stories remind us that water is not only a place of purification and rebirth, but also a place where invisible pain accumulates. Perhaps these are just old stories, full of metaphors and symbols – or perhaps warnings about what lies beneath the surface. For the depths have their memory – and the women who fell silent within them may still be waiting.

# 0.3. Hair like eyelashes, eyes like death

Ever since humans dared to venture out to sea, they began to ask themselves: what lies beneath the surface, in that dark, boundless depth, which can be as calm as it is deadly? The answer came in the form of legends – and these, on different continents, surprisingly often spoke of the same thing: a mysterious creature, half woman, half fish. A mermaid.

Mermaids, or Rusalki, have appeared in the collective imagination for centuries – as seductresses, guardians of water, but also as unfortunate victims of a curse. Their existence is not only linked to European folklore – legends of similar creatures can be found in Mesopotamia, Africa, Japan, among the Inuit, and in Polynesia. Isn't that strange? As if all humanity needed to personify the power of water in a female form that combines beauty and danger.

One of the oldest known legends comes from ancient Assyria, where the goddess **Atargatis** jumped into a lake to escape the shame of unrequited love and was transformed into a half-fish. Greek mythology, in turn, knows Sirens who lured sailors with their singing – and although the ancient poet **Homer** describes them as bird-like creatures, in later European iconography they took on the typical appearance of a mermaid with a fish tail. In fact, in the Middle Ages, Sirens and Water Nymphs merged into one archetype – a beautiful woman who is both seductive and mortally dangerous. In Irish legends, for example, we find the sea creature merrow with webbed fingers and a red cap, thanks to which she can move between the human world and the sea. If someone stole her cap, she remained trapped on land. In some versions of the story, the Rusalka falls in love with a fisherman, marries him, and lives with him for years – until she rediscovers her origins and disappears back into the sea with her children forever.

In Slavic mythology, the Rusalka – the spirit of a girl who died a violent death, often by drowning – is a common sight. She appears near rivers and lakes, has long hair, and moves with grace, sometimes as an innocent fairy, sometimes as an avenger. In many versions of the story, Rusalki lure men into the water to drag them down with them – not out of love, but out of pain and sorrow that they have nowhere else to express. Similar ideas can be found in Norwegian legends of havfruer, French tales of Ondines, or Irish and Scottish tales of Selkie – women who transform into seals and live between two worlds.

In Japanese folklore, there is a creature called ningyo – a fish-like woman with a monkey's face and golden scales. Catching her was said to bring storms, but her flesh gave the gift of immortality. The story of the girl **Yao Bikuni**, who ate a piece of ningyo and lived for 800 years, became known throughout Japan.

*Baltic Mermaid ("Secret of the 20th Century")*

In some cases, mermaids are also described as dangerous demonic creatures. Medieval bestiaries often depicted them as a symbol of temptation and sin, reminding that beauty can be a lure to perdition. In iconography, mermaids sometimes held a mirror and a comb – signs of vanity. However, in another sense, they were also prophetesses who foretold storms, or water spirits to whom sacrifices were made.

Their transition into folk folklore and maritime superstitions is also interesting. For example, some sailors swore they had seen a mermaid. A well-known case mentions the explorer of America, Christopher Columbus (1451–1506), who in 1493 recorded three mermaids off the coast of present-day Haiti – they were probably just manatees (Trichechus manatus), but imagination prevailed over reality. Mermaids as harbingers of misfortune or death were perceived similarly to banshees in Celtic tradition. Their appearance was supposed to signal an impending ship disaster or the death of a crew member.

An interesting phenomenon is also the frequent association of Mermaids with lunar symbolism and tidal cycles – which further links them to the archetypal principle of femininity. In psychoanalytic, Jungian interpretation, Mermaids represent the anima – the feminine aspect of the soul, which is mysterious, intuitive, and often suppressed by conscious reason. Their image balances between tenderness and threat, between the call of home and eternal exile.

It seems, therefore, that Mermaids are not merely a mythical product of imagination. They are beings embodying collective fears and desires: fear of death, the unknown, the limits of the world; and longing for something that transcends us – for freedom or love that defies logic.

And perhaps that is why stories of mermaids remain on the surface of culture for millennia – never quite swimming away, they simply change their form. The form of water.

## 0.4. Where land ends and legends begin

While today's geographical atlases offer only blue expanses of ocean with ship routes and statistical data on sea depth, old maps were different. In their folds, one could get lost not only in determining location but also in imagination. Mermaids were an inseparable part of them – they swam on the margins of medieval portolans, sat on rocks on Renaissance maps, and gazed from engravings in port books. Usually depicted with a human torso, a fish tail, and a mane of hair, they looked more like an element of nature than a fantasy. Some even had ornate head coverings or crowns, thus acquiring the characteristics of mythological aristocrats of the deep. In 1539, on the famous Carta Marina map by the Swedish geographer and bishop Olaus Magnus (1490–1557), mermaids appear in the North Sea and off the coast of Iceland – exactly where today we would expect oil rigs, not mermaids. From the 15th to the 17th century, mermaids appeared not only on maps but also on ships – in the form of carved figures on the bows. It was believed that their presence provided protection at sea. Some sources claim that wooden images of women with fish tails were meant to appease the wrath of sea deities or calm storms. At the same time, however, stories circulated that anyone who saw them was doomed to die. They were a symbol of both seduction and destruction. One of the earliest European accounts of a Mermaid comes from an English chronicle from 1403, which records the appearance of a "sea woman" off the coast of East Anglia – she was allegedly caught by fishermen, did not speak, and after several months escaped back to the sea.

The first known description of a Mermaid sighting probably dates from the 2nd century AD, and its author is the ancient naturalist Pliny the Elder (23–79). In his "Natural

History," he recorded stories of "half-human, half-fish" creatures washed ashore by waves. But Pliny was not alone – the Greek historian Pausanias (115–180) and the Roman writer Gaius Julius Solinus at the turn of the 3rd and 4th centuries also recorded mysterious aquatic creatures in the Mediterranean Sea. Some accounts suggest that people perceived Mermaids as harbingers of storms or misfortunes – a kind of aquatic equivalent of an ominous comet sign.

Let's move on to the golden age of explorers. As mentioned earlier, in 1493, Columbus wrote in his logbook during a voyage in the Caribbean that he "saw three Mermaids that rose out of the sea, but they were not as beautiful as they are painted." He added that "they had masculine features." Modern scientists now believe that these could have been manatees or dugongs – peaceful herbivores that swim vertically and whose movements can stir human imagination when they "embrace" their young.

Mermaids also appear in the writings of Henry Hudson (1570–1611), the famous British explorer who, in 1608, while exploring the coast of northern Norway, claimed that his crew spotted a woman with a fish tail swimming in the North Sea. Her "white hair floated on the surface like a veil," and she had "the face of a woman with fish eyes." The entry is in the diary of Hudson's officer, Thomas Whittbourne, who described the scene with incredible calm – as if observing a common marine creature, not some mythical being. In 1739, the British newspaper "The Gentleman's Magazine" reported a case in the Hebrides, where locals allegedly caught a Mermaid and put her on display as proof of her existence. In other parts of Scotland and Ireland, such as Bantry Bay or Wicklow, Mermaids continued to appear in local folklore throughout the 18th and 19th centuries. Many claimed that these creatures could change shape, sing, or warn of floods. With the advent of the Renaissance and the Enlightenment, mermaids became not only the subject of myths,but also an object of public interest and curiosity. The famous showman Phineas Taylor Barnum (1810–1891) exhibited the so-called "Fiji mermaid" in his museum in New York in 1842 – a stuffed artifact combining the body of a monkey with the tail of a fish. The deception was exposed, but it did not deter the public. The desire to believe was stronger than common sense. Although "circus king" Barnum claimed it was proof supporting the theory of evolution, in reality, it was a skillful manipulation of human curiosity. Towards the end of the 19th century, "discoveries" of Mermaids also appeared in Asian ports, especially in Japan. Local fishermen made them from various parts of fish, monkeys, and land animals, and then sold them to European sailors as exotic souvenirs. One such specimen also appeared in the British Museum, and only after a detailed autopsy was it revealed to be a "creatively assembled" specimen of different species. In some cases, these exhibits were even considered proof of the biblical flood or the existence of paradisiacal creatures. From a biological perspective, the most common explanation for observations of alleged Mermaids is an encounter with manatees, dugongs, or seals. From a distance, their bodies resemble human ones, especially when they "stand" in the water and cuddle their young.

But after all... who today can say with certainty what the sailors really saw? After long weeks at sea, far from home, in the constant rhythm of waves and the monotonous hum of the wind, the senses begin to behave somewhat differently. Loneliness, fatigue, and especially human imagination – all this creates the foundation for images that no one else has seen, but their impact is all the stronger. Months without women meant that even an indistinct shape on the surface, a flicker of a body beneath the surface, or an unusual gust of wind could seem like something more. A lonely man at sea desires not only to see something beautiful, something different – not because he wants to deceive himself, but because he needs to believe. Those feminine silhouettes in the distance... long hair mixed with salty foam... a gaze that didn't have time to focus – but remained forever in memory...

## 0.5. Call of the Deep: Between Folklore and Novel

One of the first iconic mermaid figures in European literature was Undine, a water nymph from the novella of the same title by German Romantic writer and poet Friedrich de la Motte Fouqué ("Undine", 1811). This being, longing for an immortal soul, marries a knight, but after his betrayal, she must obey the laws of nature – and kill him. Undine is one of the first literary characters who uses her beauty not as a weapon, but as a means to achieve the desire for transcendence. The character of Undine became a prototype of the romantic idea of a woman as a bearer of mystery, love, but also ruin.

A similar theme was developed several decades later by Hans Christian Andersen (1805–1875) in his "The Little Mermaid" ("Den lille Havfrue", 1837). His Mermaid sacrifices her voice and suffers immense pain to walk on land in search of a prince's love – which, however, will not be fulfilled. Andersen models here a new type of tragic fairy tale – pure and at the same time dark, in which selflessness triumphs, but without a happy ending.

The Slavic world responds with its Rusalki – ambiguous beings, often demonic, sometimes sad and condemned. In Czech literature, this tradition gave rise to "Rusalka" in the titular poetic libretto from 1899, by poet and theater director Jaroslav Kvapil (1868–1950), made famous two years later in the opera by the renowned composer Antonin Dvořák (1841–1904). This Rusalka longs for a human prince and undergoes almost the same transformation as Andersen's heroine. She loses her voice, is betrayed by the human world, and ultimately becomes an instrument of death. The motif of a water creature paying for love with the loss of identity is combined here with the folkloric motif of impure souls. The character of Rusalka later appeared in the works of Russian authors, such as Nikolai Rimsky-Korsakov (opera "Rusalka", 1898), and in symbolist works.

In English literature, the British writer and one of the precursors of the science-fiction genre, Herbert George Wells (1866–1946), also played with the mermaid motif in his lesser-known novel "The Sea Lady" (1901). In this work, the mermaid appears as an elegant lady who interferes with the social life of Edwardian society. She is a seductive yet tragic figure – showing the contradiction between human desire and the impossibility of fulfilling it beyond the boundaries of one's own world.

Some authors were also inspired by Scandinavian or Celtic ballads. In his fantasy novel "The Merman's Children" (1979), the English writer Poul Anderson (1926–2001) follows the fate of the descendants of the merman king, who face Christian assimilation and the loss of their magical identity. The motif of transformation and survival resonates equally strongly in the fairy tale "The Mermaid and the Boy," written by the Scottish novelist and ethnographer Andrew Lang (1844–1912) in "The Yellow Fairy Book" (1894). In the fairy tale, the prince escapes the fate of sacrifice through magic and courage, which shifts the story from fatalism to reconciliation. Scandinavian themes are also present in the novel "The Mermaid" (2013) by Norwegian author Camilla Läckberg (*1974), which combines historical background with a psychological thriller, where the Mermaid motif functions as a metaphor for mystery and loss. Another well-known author who developed this theme into a magical historical novel is American writer Erica Ferencik (born 1958). In her book "The Ice Harp" (2024), she presents a sea creature in the inhospitable environment of the North Atlantic as a symbol of desire, memory, and survival. Her story is darker, rooted in the reality of human trauma and environmental issues.

Similarly poetic and socially engaged is the novel "The Mermaid of Jeju" by American author Sumi Hahn from 2020, which refers to the Korean tradition of haenyeo – women divers. The Mermaid motif here becomes a means of telling a story about cultural memory, of war and maternal strength.

In the 20th and 21st centuries, the image of sea creatures has undergone a fundamental transformation. Not only romantic desire or folkloric horror come to the fore, but also issues of cultural identity and psychology. The 2020 novel "The Mermaid of Black Conch" by British author Monique Roffey (*1965) is an excellent example of this: a Caribbean mermaid falls in love with a fisherman, but instead of a fairy tale, trauma, isolation, and finding a home in a world that does not accept her emerge. Roffey creates a poetic-social fresco about otherness, colonialism, and intimacy.

In the Americas, science fiction authors have also embraced a similar transformation. Rivers Solomon's (*1988) "The Deep" (2019) draws on genre Afrofuturism – drowned children of enslaved women become underwater creatures devoid of memory. The protagonist, Yetu, however, decides to retain these memories, which gradually opens up burning questions about collective trauma, identity, and community consciousness.

Adaptations for young adults have also gained popularity, in which mermaids appear as strong, sometimes dark, and sometimes romantic heroines. In 2018, the novel "To Kill the Kingdom" by British author Alexandra Christo (*1990) was published. The protagonist is a Mermaid who must kill a prince, but ultimately falls in love with him. "Mermaid, Witch, and the Sea" (2020) is a book by American writer Maggie Tokuda-Hall (*1984), which creatively combines ancient legends, magical realism, and contemporary trends. Her literary colleague Julia Ember, in turn, revives Norse mythology in "The Kiss of the Selkie" (2017), telling a story about the fateful relationship between a mermaid and a human.

This theme is further developed in the novel "Mermaid" (2018) by American author Christina Henry. The story tells of Amelia, a mermaid who falls in love with a fisherman and decides to leave the underwater world. Soon, however, she falls into the trap of human desire for sensation when the famous showman P. T. Barnum exhibits her in his collection of oddities as a "real mermaid." Henry masterfully intertwines 19th-century historical frameworks with fantasy elements and feminist commentary – Amelia is not only a symbol of beauty, but above all an object of resistance and independence. The story is deeply emotional and touches on themes of power, freedom, exploitation, and the commercialization of otherness. The author subtly interweaves magical, historical, and tragic threads, creating the character of Amelia – a strong yet vulnerable woman amidst greed and human curiosity.

A significant work in the modern subgenre of mermaid literature is "The Surface Breaks" (2018) by Irish author Louise O'Neill (*1985). This book is a powerful feminist reinterpretation of the classic tale of The Little Mermaid, focusing on themes of female self-awareness, courage, and the struggle against the oppression of patriarchal social structures. O'Neill creates a character who does not want to be a victim of fate or traditional roles, but instead becomes a voice of resistance and a search for her own identity in a world that often demands submission and silence from women. Her version of the mermaid is therefore not only a symbol of the desire for freedom, but also a critical commentary on issues of power and social expectations that are still relevant today.

It would also be worth mentioning here the novel "The Seal-Keeper" by Australian writer Lilian Darcy (2003) – a romantic story of a Mermaid living on one of Australia's coral reefs. It would also be appropriate to mention literary works that speak of the existence of entire underwater civilizations, such as Sir Arthur Conan Doyle's short stories "The Maracot Deep" and the Polish author Wiktor Żwirkiewicz's "Sindbad on RQM 57."

## 0.6. Painted on canvas, sculpted in stone

Sirens, Rusalkas, and sea nymphs belong to creatures that have continuously emerged from the depths of collective imagination since ancient times – even when no one believed in them anymore. Artists of all eras eagerly imagined them on the border between the real world and dreams, often as the feminine embodiment of water itself – fluid, elusive, dangerously beautiful. From ancient times to today, these mythical creatures have changed with aesthetics and what society at the time considered desirable, longed for, or forbidden.

Ancient artists already depicted goddesses and nymphs associated with water – especially the Naiads, guardians of springs, rivers, and lakes. In mosaics and reliefs, they are shown as naked or semi-naked women with pitchers from which a spring flows, sometimes accompanied by dolphins or tritons. In the Roman environment, decorative sculptures for gardens and fountains were popular, where water deities symbolized not only the beauty of nature but also its power – the moisture that gives life. For example, the famous Siren with a fish from Pompeii has been preserved, combining a realistic concept with a mythological motif. In the Renaissance, artists returned to these motifs, but in line with the new emphasis on the beauty of the human body. Sandro Botticelli (1445–1510) painted the famous Birth of Venus (c. 1486), which does not depict a siren in the true sense of the word, but the image of a goddess born from sea foam on a shell became an iconic archetype – a combination of water, femininity, and wonder. Similarly, Leonardo da Vinci (1452–1519) explored the forms of nymphs and aquatic creatures in his drawings as part of the natural order, idealizing them as beings of unearthly beauty. During the Baroque period, these creatures became a more frequent motif in sculpture – for example, Gian Lorenzo Bernini (1598–1680) created fountains in which water nymphs mingled with mythological scenes. Their smooth and shiny bodies gave the impression that they had just emerged from the water.

At the end of the 19th century, with the development of symbolism, sirens and rusalkas became popular carriers of ambiguous meanings. Gustave Moreau (1826–1898) painted ethereal female figures as the embodiment of temptation and mystery, often accompanied by fantastic fish or coral palaces. Arnold Böcklin (1827–1901), known for his melancholic painting "Isle of the Dead," also created "The Play of the Nymphs with a Centaur," in which the Sirens are playful and seductive, but their laughter has a chilling undertone. The Symbolist vision of these beings reached its peak in the work of Odilon Redon (1840–1916), who depicted them as dream creatures – half-women, half-products of imagination, often floating in an elusive space between darkness and light.

A special place in this iconography is occupied by the Pre-Raphaelites, especially John William Waterhouse (1849–1917), whose painting "The Siren" (1900) is one of the most famous depictions of a Siren. She sits on the shore, combing her hair and gazing into the distance – she is neither a phantom nor a purely erotic object, but a melancholic figure full of loneliness and longing. Similarly, "Hylas and the Nymphs" (1896) depicts a mythical scene in which nymphs draw a young man into the water – but the beautiful bodies and calm surface hide a dark depth.

*"Hylas and the Nymphs" by Waterhouse*

In Art Nouveau, aquatic creatures became a popular decorative motif. Alfons Mucha (1860–1939) depicts them as sensual women with flowing hair, surrounded by vegetation and aquatic motifs, often as if merging with nature. Gustav Klimt (1862–1918) creates an almost abstract rhythm of colors, gilding, and eroticism in his paintings ("Water Nymphs", 1899). Their faces and bodies become part of the ornament – beautiful, yet coldly inaccessible. In the 20th century, myths underwent a strong re-evaluation. Surrealists, such as Max Ernst (1891–1976) and Salvador Dalí (1904–1989), experimented with mermaids as oneiric beings – female figures that represent both desires and fears of the unknown. Their bodies are deformed, often with fish-shaped heads or fins, which shatters the classical ideal of beauty. Contemporary artists go even further – for example, the

British provocateur Damien Hirst (*1965) created "The Mermaid" in 2008, which depicts this creature as a hyperrealistic statue with all the details of the body – skin, scales, and gaze – placed, however, in a sterile display case as an object of biological research. Public sculptures of mermaids are no less interesting. Edvard Eriksen's (1876–1959) "The Little Mermaid", installed in Copenhagen in 1913, became a symbol not only of the city but also of melancholy and loneliness – a small, fragile figure sitting on a rock by the sea, reminiscent of Andersen's fairy tale of sacrifice and love. Similarly famous is the Warsaw Mermaid, a Polish mermaid with a shield and sword, which became a symbol of Warsaw – sculptor Ludwika Nitschowa (1889–1989) created it in 1939 as a monument of protection, not seduction. In modern cities, these statues have become part of identity – in Helsinki, London, Brisbane, and San Francisco, we can find fountains and sculptures in which aquatic creatures continue to live as artistic metaphors.

*The Little Mermaid by Edvard Eriksen*

Mermaids have never disappeared from culture. Neither from water, nor from canvas, nor from stone. Perhaps because their faces change like the surface of the sea – sometimes calm and seductive, sometimes dark and impenetrable. Or perhaps they are simply waiting for someone to look at them again.

# 0.7. From Pearls to Popcorn: Mermaids in Film

In the world of moving images, mermaids and related aquatic creatures have held a special place since the dawn of cinema – as an embodiment of desire, danger, romance, and unspoken melancholy. Just as the surface of water reflects the sky, so film reflects our shared dreams – and the dreams of creatures from the deep are among the most enduring.

One of the first appearances of a mermaid on screen was in the silent film "The Mermaid" (1904) by cinema pioneer Georges Méliès. Optical tricks and illusions created a magical image of a sea creature, but in reality, it was more or less a theatrical scene. It wasn't until the American film "Mr. Peabody and the Mermaid" (1948) that the first romantic story emerged between a man in a mid-life crisis and a beautiful, mute creature from the sea who appears to him during his vacation.

However, one of the most important milestones is Disney's animated film "The Little Mermaid" (1989), which, although it significantly softened Andersen's tragic tale, created a modern image of the mermaid as a rebellious and curious heroine, longing for freedom beyond the marine world. This model influenced several generations and still defines the visual stereotype of the mermaid – long hair, a shimmering tail, a naive but brave nature.

From a completely different perspective, the romantic comedy "Splash" (1984) presents a story where Tom Hanks meets a mermaid in the form of the beautiful Daryl Hannah. The film plays with the idea of what it would be like if an aquatic creature lived among us. Although it is a funny and benevolent film, the theme of longing for otherness and the inability of the ordinary world to accept something that goes beyond its rules emerges from beneath the surface.

Irish director Neil Jordan, in the film "Ondine" (2009), transports the theme of sea creatures to the harsher environment of Irish ports. The main character – a fisherman – pulls a woman from the sea who could be a Selkie (a Scottish-Irish shapeshifting sea creature) or simply a refugee. The film leaves the viewer in doubt: is she miraculous, or simply fragile and different? Guillermo del Toro's "The Shape of Water" (2017) also fits this trend, creating a modern "monster romance," a tribute to classic horror and a manifesto of empathy. A mute cleaning lady falls in love with a mysterious aquatic creature held in an American military base. Although the main creature is not explicitly called a Mermaid, the film addresses the same themes: otherness, isolation, love beyond rules, the desire to escape to another world.

Another fascinating adaptation of mythical creatures is "The Lure" (2015), a Polish musical horror film in the style of an art musical. In it, two mermaids perform in a cabaret club, where they sing, kill, and long for love. The film intertwines sexuality, violence, and ballet aesthetics – and although it may seem bizarrely grotesque, it provides a profound commentary on female otherness in a patriarchal world. Similarly non-classical is "She Creature" (2001) – a dark

Victorian horror in which the mermaid is not a passive victim, but a powerful force from the depths.

M. Night Shyamalan's "Lady in the Water" (2006) also introduces us to a peculiar world of magical realism. Although the main character, a narf, is not a classic Mermaid, she represents an interpretation of the same archetype: a quiet, mysterious creature from the water who enters the everyday world and reveals hidden truths and potential. The film plays with fairy tale structures, but at the same time leaves the viewer with many questions.

The melancholic film "The Lake House" (2006) also falls into the romantic genre, where no supernatural aquatic creature appears, but the lake and the lonely house by it become a symbol of desire, isolation, and love that transcends time. This is a more metaphorical approach to the theme of "water women," who seem unable to belong to the ordinary world, yet still fascinate us.

When it comes to pop culture influences, animated productions cannot be overlooked. Japanese Studio Ghibli created the film "Ponyo on the Cliff by the Sea" (2008), loosely inspired by "The Little Mermaid," in which water is not just a backdrop, but an entire element—unruly, playful, and dangerous all at once. Ponyo, a little fish who longs to become a girl, embodies both childlike imagination and the power of nature that transcends us.

Finally, it's worth mentioning bizarre and lesser-known films, such as "She Creature" (2001), a gothic horror in which a traveler kidnaps a real mermaid from Ireland to exhibit her in America. Of course, nothing goes according to plan—the viewer finds themselves in a terrifying story full of blood, lies, and revenge from the depths. The film portrays the dark side of the desire for sensation.

And what about Russian mermaids? Anna Melikyan's "Rusalka" (2007) is a modern magical-realist tale about a girl who may possess supernatural powers, but certainly has a strange, melancholic soul. The story of love, loneliness, and the desire to escape everyday life follows the poetics of classic Slavic tales—but at the same time offers a contemporary, sensitive perspective.

Television creators have not lagged behind. While films often emphasize romance and uniqueness, TV series offer space for greater psychological depth and myth development.

The most famous television phenomenon was the Australian series "H2O: Just Add Water" (2006–2010), in which three teenagers gain the ability to transform into mermaids. The series combines teen drama, ecological messages, and mythology—it became a cult hit among teenage viewers and launched an entire subgenre of "teen mermaids."

The sequel was the series "Mako Mermaids" (2013–2016), expanded to include "mermaids"—mermen, thus breaking the stereotype of a purely female, aquatic world. Both series maintained a light tone, but at the same time presented the myth in the contemporary language of pop culture.

*The likeable heroines of the Australian series "H2O: Just Add Water"*

From a darker barrel emerges the American series "Siren" (2018–2020), in which mermaids are not beautiful pop princesses, but evolutionary predators with their own society. The action takes place in a fishing town, where a mysterious woman, the mermaid Ryn, appears, looking for her sister.

The series addresses ecological themes (pollution, military tests, marine biology), but also issues of identity – mermaids are both strong and vulnerable.

It would also be worth mentioning here the Japanese fantastic film about Water People titled "Latitude Zero" directed by Ishirō Honda from 1969. There are no mermaids there, but there are people inhabiting the depths of the Pacific somewhere at the equator...

The Japanese anime "Mermaid Forest" (2003), an adaptation of Rumiko Takahashi's manga, develops a dark plot: whoever eats mermaid flesh gains immortality – but often at a terrible price. In this way, the anime thematizes the horror of immortality, guilt, and transformation.

The internet also offers another space for marine creatures: from short horror films on YouTube (e.g., "The Siren"), through independent series (Blue Moon, Mythic Mermaid), to documentary hoaxes such as "Mermaids: The Body Found" (2012), which pretended to be scientific evidence for the existence of mermaids and caused a wave of public questions in the USA, which we will now join.

## 0.8. In prime time

In the era of reality shows and pseudo-documentaries, the line between scientific knowledge and fantasy seems thinner than ever. In 2012, this invisible line was finally crossed by a television program that revealed the "shocking truth" about mermaids. Sounds like an advertisement? Yes. And yet: the documentary "Mermaids: The Body Found" won the hearts of millions of viewers and briefly convinced the world that creatures looking like us could live in the depths of the oceans – only with fins.

It all started with innocent television entertainment on the Animal Planet channel. Viewers, accustomed to educational programs about animals, this time sat in front of their screens, expecting something extraordinary. Instead of another documentary about dolphins or octopuses, they saw the captivating film "Mermaids: The Body Found". Filmed as a serious investigative documentary, it contained dramatic reconstructions, archival footage, "secret" research, and testimonies from seemingly real scientists. The film presented a theory according to which there is a secret government report on the discovery of mermaids – or rather, aquatic humanoids, who, after millions of years of evolution, have perfectly adapted to life in the oceans.

The film deliberately used the style of a so-called mockumentary – a fictional production that pretends to be reality. Despite minor warnings at the beginning and end of the program, most viewers believed it was a real documentary. And they shouldn't be surprised. The presented "evidence" – sonar recordings, bone fragments, video footage of mysterious creatures, and especially the testimonies of experts who claimed that governments were hiding the truth – seemed very convincing. Combined with dramatic editing, dark music, and references to real scientific theories, all of this gave the impression of a serious investigation. The viewer almost regretted that it wasn't true.

The strongest pillar of the entire hoax was the aquatic ape theory – a controversial hypothesis according to which human ancestors might have spent a certain stage of development near water, which would explain certain peculiarities of human anatomy: the ability to dive, hairless skin, subcutaneous fat, or the ability to swim from an early age. Although most scientists consider this theory marginal, the film presented it as a fundamental piece of evidence for the existence and survival of "water people" in the depths.

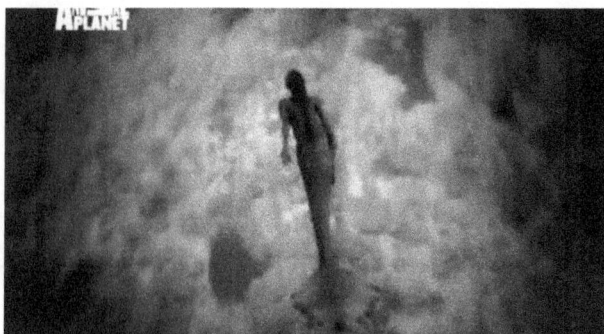

*Silhouette of a mermaid from the film "Mermaid - The Body Found"*

And as is often the case, a combination of a bit of science, a pinch of mystery, and a large dose of clever deception yields an explosive effect. After the film aired, American authorities were inundated with thousands of questions. Viewers asked: Where are the remains? Why is the government silent? Is it true? In a way, they managed to create a phenomenon – something on the border of a modern urban legend and media hysteria. Even NOAA, the renowned agency for ocean and atmospheric research, had to issue an official statement declaring: "There is no evidence of aquatic humanoids."

The public reaction was so strong that Animal Planet did not hesitate and released a sequel a year later – "Mermaids: The New Evidence." This time, new footage appeared, even more "credible" testimonies, blurry cell phone recordings, and mysterious deep-sea footage. There was even a case of "forbidden research" and "brave scientists" who risked their lives to get to the truth. Entertainment in the background. And at the same time, a psychological experiment that showed how quickly a new myth can arise.

The entire project became a model example of so-called infotainment – entertainment masquerading as information. Although the creators maintained an alibi about the fictional nature of the program, these were lost in the overall presentation style. The film sparked serious discussions among educators, scientists, and journalists about the need for media literacy – the ability to critically interpret images, information, and context. But in the eyes of many viewers, something else remained: the question: what if...?

In the end, even if it's a hoax, "Mermaids" fulfilled a deep human desire: the belief that the world still remains unexplored, that beings belonging neither to the realm of fish nor to humans might hide beneath the surface. Modern technology merely replaced old sea tales – sonar "echoes" of television documentaries replaced the once weary stories of captains. And perhaps those ancient sailors, like these modern filmmakers, simply looked in the same direction – into the darkness of the depths that never look back.

## 0.9. Beneath the surface of the subconscious

Mermaid and Rusalka are ancient figures that emerge from the depths of humanity's collective subconscious. In their seductive yet unsettling embrace, humanity's fascination with the element of water, the desire for otherness, unspoken dreams of transitioning to another world, and also the fear of one's own darkness, all meet. It's no wonder these creatures attract us so much – they are not only beautiful and elusive but also psychologically deeply symbolic. Their appearance in mythologies, literature, art, and popular culture is not accidental: aquatic creatures represent archetypal images, reflecting fundamental human desires and fears.

In the analytical psychology of the Swiss physician Carl Gustav Jung (1875–1961), water holds an important place as a symbol of the unconscious. And it is precisely aquatic creatures – especially female ones – that embody what emerges from the unconscious into consciousness as a warning, a desire, or a temptation. The mermaid is an archetypal image of the anima – the feminine aspect of the psyche, essential for a man to achieve wholeness, yet at the same time incomprehensible and dangerous. She is a being of two worlds – higher and lower, known and mysterious. Her fish tail refers to animal origins and deep instinctiveness, while the upper half of her body remains human, often very feminine and sensual. It is this duality that makes the mermaid a symbol of unintegrated psychic energy, which can be healing or destructive – depending on how it is treated. The Rusalka, the Eastern European equivalent of the Mermaid, has an even darker character. She is not a creature of the sea, but of rivers, swamps, and forest lakes – these freshwater mirrors, closer to the human world, yet somehow forgotten and wild. Rusalkas in Slavic mythology are not always just seductive women, but often the spirits of young girls who died a violent death, due to misfortune or unrequited love. Their existence is linked to death, loss, and unspoken sorrow. From a psychological perspective, it is the embodiment of suppressed emotions, suppressed desires, a suppressed voice. A Rusalka appears when something forgotten or suppressed tries to speak – often in dreams, stories, or in strange, melancholic feelings that we cannot name.

Both beings are united by their appearance at the boundary – between water and land, between life and death, between reality and myth. That is why they are so powerful – they represent a liminal space, a transition, a transformation. Whoever touches them can be changed – but not without consequences. Their song seduces, but also warns: look deep within yourself, listen to what your own depths whisper to you. Therefore, in many stories, whoever falls in love with a mermaid or a Rusalka cannot avoid pain, sacrifice, or even tragedy. Not because these beings are evil, but because they symbolize an encounter with what is most true, and at the same time most vulnerable, within us. Dreams of mermaids and Rusalkas can also be an escape – but not in a trivial sense. It is about the desire to touch something pure, primal, untainted, something that has not yet been completely domesticated. These creatures awaken in us a nostalgia for myth, for a world where things still had symbolic meaning. This is where their strength lies – in their ability to survive centuries, cultural changes, changing perceptions of body and soul. And when they appear to us today in literature, films, visual arts, or dreams, they are not merely reflections of water, but also reflections of ourselves, who look into this water and search in it for something that eludes us – a voice, love, death, or transformation.

*Sirens in the painting by Teofil Kwiatkowski*
*(National Museum in Krakow, public domain)*

## 0.10. Enchanted by Water

From the turbulent waters of esotericism and contemporary spiritual thought, Mermaids emerge not as mythical creatures from ancient legends, but as powerful archetypes of connection to emotions, intuition, and the deep currents of the feminine principle. For many practitioners of modern spirituality—from New Age to sea witches—Rusalkas and Mermaids symbolize the ancient bond between humans and the ocean, between the conscious and unconscious worlds, between nature and the magical order of the universe.

In this context, the Mermaid is the embodiment of the Water-Woman—unstable, enchanting, impenetrable. Her tail is a sign of her otherness, and her voice an invitation to dive into the depths of one's own psyche. In neo-pagan symbolism, she is associated with lunar cycles, emotions, dreams, but also with sexuality and the power of the female body. She stands on the borderland—not entirely human, not entirely animal, like a sphinx or a centaur. In some systems (especially Wiccan or eclectic magical traditions), she is classified as one of the "water goddess archetypes"— alongside ancient nymphs, Celtic water maidens, or Egyptian sea deities.

This peculiar mythology creates a framework for understanding the wild, untamed feminine archetype, whose aquatic version fully appears in later symbolic literature. Contemporary authors such as Lucy H. Pearce (*1978)— author of "Burning Woman" (2016), and Sophie Strand (*1992), follow this line, viewing the mermaid, or rusalka, as an image of "liquid identity"—a femininity that cannot be confined within rigid boundaries.

Within contemporary esotericism, a specific direction called sea witchcraft also emerges. Its adherents perform rituals on the coast, work with tides, and collect natural artifacts such as shells, pearls, sand, and pieces of wood washed ashore by waves. Here, the Mermaid becomes the patroness of intuitive magic, the guardian of secrets, and a guide in meditations that "penetrate the depths"—towards self-knowledge. Some claim that through contact with mermaid energy, they can heal old emotional wounds, reconnect with their feminine side, or discover their identity beyond conventional social frameworks, as in the novel "The Seal-Wife" by Australian writer Lilian Darcy—a romantic story of a Mermaid living in Australia.

*Rusalkas drag the fisherman into the watery abyss...*

An interesting phenomenon is the adoption of the mermaid archetype in contemporary New Age spirituality. Here, she is sometimes understood literally as an "otherworldly being," often in reference to the concept of water elementals or interdimensional guides. Books, channelings, and guided meditations emerge where sea creatures appear as bearers of ancient wisdom, teachers of harmony with nature, or as energetic beings that help awaken the inner voice. In some cases, these ideas blend with modern forms of spiritual feminism, where the Mermaid embodies uninhibited, sensual, and independent femininity – in contrast to traditional images of the "submissive woman."

For example, in her book "Mermaids 101: Exploring the Magical Underwater World of the Sea People" (2013), American writer Doreen Virtue (*1958) – before her conversion to Christianity – claims that mermaids are subtle beings from the fourth energy spectrum who communicate with humans through meditations, dreams, and "water portals." In spiritual literature, mermaids symbolize communication with other dimensions, are healers, or guides in personal transformation. This view, while bordering on esoteric kitsch, also reflects modern humanity's deep desire to return to a natural and intuitive way of being.

## 0.11. Mirror over the abyss

In a world of growing ecological awareness, even figures that were once exclusively the subject of myths and fairy tales are beginning to transform into bearers of an ecological message. Mermaids, Rusalkas, and other aquatic creatures are no longer just fascinating symbols of femininity, sexuality, or mysterious otherness. In recent decades, they have become iconic figures of the ecological imagination, embodying the natural world crying out for help.

*Rusalkas as sex goddesses...*

This change can be observed especially in visual culture – in films, art, campaigns, and advertisements. Once an object of desire or fear, the mermaid today often symbolizes endangered oceans, lost ecosystems, and the innocence of a planet destroyed by human greed. Her body – half-human, half-fish – becomes a metaphor for the fusion of humans with nature, but also for their inability to maintain this balance. In polluted waters, surrounded by plastic, oil, and dead fish, the mermaid no longer sings, but is silent – and this silence is an eloquent cry to conscience.

This symbolism appears increasingly in both animated and live-action films. Disney's "The Little Mermaid" (1989), though primarily a story of love and identity, is set in a world where the human world and the sea intertwine in conflict – and humans pose a threat to underwater life. Later works include "Blue My Mind" (2017), where a teenager's transformation into a mermaid is not only a metaphor for coming of age, but also a warning about the broken relationship between body, nature, and social norms.

A special case is the independent film "The Mermaid" (2016) by Chinese director Stephen Chow, which openly addresses the issue of environmental devastation. The main character – The Mermaid – is sent by a rescue colony to take revenge on a businessman destroying their living space. The film combines humor, tragedy, romance, and an ecological message, and became the highest-grossing Chinese film of its time – proof that ecological symbolism also resonates in the commercial sphere. Various NGO campaigns have also contributed to this shift in meaning, adopting the mermaid as a visual symbol of ecological catastrophe. For example, in 2017, the British advertising campaign for Sea Life London attracted attention, featuring a realistic "mermaid" – a performer who silently swam among plastic waste in an aquarium. The film generated a huge response on social media, especially among young people, for whom the character was associated with childhood and fairy tales. It was this moment of nostalgia in contrast to reality that acted as a strong emotional stimulus.

The symbolism of aquatic creatures is also incredibly strong in the context of the climate crisis. Water is one of the first elements threatened – rising ocean levels, melting glaciers, ocean acidification, shrinking coral reefs. As a being inextricably linked to the aquatic world, the mermaid begins to play the role of a symbol of the guardian of the ocean ecosystem. In many works of art – from street art to digital illustration – the mermaid is depicted as a dying, rescued, or transformed being that reveals a destroyed reality. If she once seduced, she is now more inclined to warn. Psychologically speaking, this development reflects a change in our consciousness. Where we once wanted to control, we now want to protect. The fantastic creatures that today represent nature act as mirrors of our own guilt, but also of hope. They show us what we can lose, but also what we can still save. Their eyes reflect not only fish and the deep, but also our own decisions. Nevertheless, the mermaid is not only a tragic victim. She is also a bearer of a new imagination, in which humans cease to be the rulers of the world and wish to live in harmony with water, not against it.

And now we will address this problem assuming that they do exist...

# CHAPTER 1. AMERICAN CE WITH SIRENS

And here is the more interesting Close Encounters with these cryptids. I present a list **of Al Rosales'** most interesting observations and CE with Sirens in the Americas, and so:

## 1.1. Meeting in the Atlantic

**Location:** Atlantic Ocean, Central American coast

**Date:** 9 January 1493

Time: Unknown

**Description of the event:** according to the chronicle of Father **Bartholome de las Casas**, the famous navigator **Christopher Columbus (Cristobal Colon)** reported the sighting of three Sirens on the high seas, but according to him – they were not as beautiful as they are said, they had male faces.

**Source:** "Cryptozoological Manual"

**Probable explanation:** Most likely they were manatees.[1]

## 1.2. Mermaid in the port

**Location:** St. John's, Newfoundland, Canada

---

[1] Translated from Spanish into English by Albert Rosales.

**Date:** 1610

**Time:** Morning

**Description of the event:** Captain **Whitbourne** relates in great detail the appearance of what he believed to be a mermaid in the port of St. John's in Newfoundland:

Now, too, I will not fail to relate something of the strange creature which I saw here in the year of our Lord 1610, early in the morning, as I stood on the side of the water in the harbor of St. John's, which was coming swiftly in its direction towards us, and which appeared to be a woman in face, eyes, nose, mouth, chin, cheeks, neck, and forehead. She seemed beautiful, and the proportions of her body were perfect, around her head there were strands like hair, running down her neck, of course it was not hair, as we had seen her for a long time, and another of my company, still alive, who was not too far from me, and saw it flowing towards me, I took a step back, and this came within a long spade's distance. When this strange creature saw me come out towards it, it dived shallowly under the water, and swam towards the place where I had landed; then I saw the arms and back halfway down, white and smooth like a man's back, and from the middle to the lower part of the body it was proportionately forked like an arrow; what it looked like from the front, I do not know. [...] So I think it was the Syrena. Now that divers talk a lot about Virgos, I think I saw one in Newfoundland.

But whether it was a Syrena or not, I don't know for sure, and I'll leave it to others to judge...

**Source:** George Eberhart – "Mysterious Creatures", London 1840, p. 111.

*Meeting with a Mermaid according to a 17th-century drawing*

## 1.3. Levitating Siren

**Location:** Lake Lacar, Neuguen, Argentina
**Date:** 1850
Time: Unknown

**Description of the event:** A creature similar to the Mermaid – apparently a half-amphibian – half-human was seen in this body of water. The mermaid was seen levitating above the water and most likely living in an underwater city. There are no other data.

**Source:** Fabio Picasso in "Strange Magazine" No. 10.

Translated from Spanish by Albert Rosales

## 1.4. Howling beauty

**Location:** Bahamas, exact place unknown

**Date:** 1869

Time: Unknown

**Description:** Six men canoeing across the bay spotted a beautiful Mermaid running aground, her bluish hair flowing down her neck and shoulders. Upon noticing the humans, the creature emitted a series of ghostly howl-like sounds and disappeared into the depths of the ocean before the men could approach it.

**Source:**

*http://www.grupoelron.org/temasextraterrestres/sirenas.htm*

# 1.5. The Mermaid at Cape Breton

**Location:** Cape Breton, North Sydney, Nova Scotia, Canada

**Date:** 1885

**Time:** afternoon

**Description of the event:** The fishermen of Gabarus experienced a moment of excitement at the appearance of the Mermaid seen in the waters by several people a few days ago. As Mr. **Bagnell** and several fishermen were in the boat, they noticed floating on the surface of the water, a few yards from the boat, what they at first thought was a human corpse. Approaching them in order to lift them aboard the boat and then bury them in the cemetery, the supposed corpse turned on its back, sat down and looked at it, and then disappeared. The face, head, arms, and forearms resembled those of humans, but the lower half was fish-shaped. The back of the head was covered with long hair resembling a horse's mane. The arms were almost exactly the same as those of a human, but the fingers of the hands were longer than those of humans. The color of the skin did not differ from that of humans. There is no doubt that the mysterious entity was none other than a Mermaid, first seen in the waters around Cape Breton.

**Source:** "Cooperstown NY Otsego Farmer" (no data)

## 1.6. Mermaid Dead on the Beach

**Location:** Quidnet Beach, MA, USA

**Date:** 22.VI.1898

**Time:** by day

**Description of the event:** Mr. **William H. Norcross**, fishing on Quidnet Beach today, found a small animal that died some time ago, and had the shape of a human – with eyes, mouth and nose exactly like those of humans. One of the old captains of the ships says that he once found something similar in the South Pacific Ocean that was also similar to a man, but was alive, but died in a short time, and said it was of Mermaid origin. Mr. Norcross plans to preserve this creature as much as possible and hand it over to naturalists for study.

**Source:** Jerome Clark in "Magonia" quoting the "Boston Journal" of June 23, 1898

## 1.7. CE with Siren

**Location** Redondo Beach, CA, USA

**Date:** May 1935

**Time:** by day

**Event Description:** The crew of a fishing boat saw a strange Mermaid 3 miles from the shore with shining eyes, a wide smooth forehead, dark hair on his head and beard. It was about 10-12 ft. (3.3-3.96 m) long; it shook its tail and disappeared into the water as anglers tried to approach it with their boats.

**Source:** Janet & Colin Bord – „Unexplained Mysteries of the 20th Century"

**Type:** E – CE with water humanoid

## 1.8. A mermaid with a sad voice

**Location:** Strait of Magellan, near Punta Arenas, Chile

**Date:** Circa 1936

Time: Unknown

**Description of the event:** A Scandinavian hunter (no further details available) encountered a mermaid with long green hair, radiant eyes and a sad voice in the Strait of Magellan. There are no further details.

**Source:** George Ebergart – „Mysterious Creatures"

## 1.9. Siren in the Mist

**Venue:** Mar de la Plata, Argentina

**Date:** 1953

Time: Unknown

**Description of the event:** Witnesses reported noticing a half-human - half-fish creature that appeared in a cloud of fog during siesta. There are no further details.

**Source:** Fabio Picasso – "Strange Magazin" No. 20.

**Type:** E – CE with lung or underwater breathing humanoid.

Strangeness: high – 8

Translated from Spanish by Albert Rosales

**Notes:** This account is the first contemporary account of a UAH meeting[2]

# 1.10. A mermaid in the glow of fireworks

**Location:** Vancouver area, British Columbia, Canada

**Date:** 31.XII.1969

**Time:** Night

**Description of the event:** During the New Year's Eve party at the seafront house, during which there was a fireworks display, **Bill Evans** and **Jack Scott** were outside while the rest of the guests returned to the house. Scott went out to admire the fireworks as Evans went down to the beach.

He justified himself by collecting oysters, but he wanted to walk alone. The flashes of fireworks were over and only the moon illuminated the beach. Evans had been picking oysters for 20 minutes when Scott looked down and saw his friend standing "as if paralyzed." Scott was greatly surprised to see

---

[2] Unknown Aquatic Humanoid.

this, and Evans beckoned him to him. When Scott came down to him, his friend looked strange. He didn't say anything. He walked a few steps and sat down, and still looking at the ocean he only said:

"I just met the Mermaid...

Scott, of course, thought it was some kind ofjoke, but Evans looked nervous. He continued:

"She went out into shallow water, and then she went ashore, to the beach, where we have mussels. She was beautiful. She had long, golden hair. They looked more like strands of seaweed, but they were much more beautiful. She had a long, green fish tail that was part of her body. I didn't know what to say to her.

Stunned by the story of his friend, who had never had a tendency to fantasize in the past, Scott noticed the euphoric expression on his face and took it seriously.

-What are you saying? He asked him.

Evans covered his confusion with a smile and continued his story of how he had asked the Mermaid:

- Aren't you cold?

She laughed and in her inhuman, but still human, low voice "like a sea breeze" she replied that she was not, that she was not cold.

She asked him why people gathered on the beaches, and he replied that they were welcoming the New Year with their friends. Evans thought he had talked to her for a few minutes. Scott asked him if he could describe her. Evans was a bit embarrassed. The mermaid was naked to the waist and he saw her extraordinary beauty and got the impression that there was some kind of interaction between them, so that he did not want her to think of him as an ordinary boor. He replied to Scott as follows:

"There was nothing there, not even some distant thought about her — you understand—but she didn't wear any clothes, and I felt a bit uncomfortable looking at her nakedness. I still saw her and she was absolutely beautiful. You can say breathtaking beauty. When I asked her where she lived, she pointed to the water and the path of moonlight on it. Then we noticed someone coming down to the beach, then she took my hand for a moment, then she slipped into the waters of the bay and swam away.

And Evans unconsciously pointed to the water. Scott noticed that it was still wet. Before his death, Evans requested that his ashes be scattered into the waters of the bay. And this despite the fact that he had never been a sailor and only had a small boat.

**Source:** *http://thebiggeststudy.blogspot.ca/*

## 1.11. Blonde Mermaid on the Rock

**Location:** Active Strait, British Columbia, Canada

**Date:** 1967

Time: Unknown

**Describing:** Passengers on the shuttle saw what they called the Siren sitting on a rock at the entrance to the Active Pass. Reports indicate that the Siren had long blonde hair, a lower body like a porpoise, and was sitting on a rock eating salmon. Photos taken by the pilot of the plane support the accounts of the passengers of the shuttle. The Times-Colonist published an article about the sighting and printed a photo, but unfortunately none of the passengers who saw the Syrena were asked to comment later.

**Source:** *http://www.pararesearchers.org/Cryptozoology*

## 1.12. Mermaid or joker?

**Location:** Sayward Beach, Cordova Bay, British Columbia, Canada

**Date:** 1967

**Time:** evening

**Event Description:** An elderly housewife who lived on the seashore was walking along the beach and noticed some "sunbathing girl" about 200 ft/66 m away from her. But then she noticed that the topless sunbathing girl had a fish tail instead of legs. The woman wanted to run closer, but the Mermaid noticed her and slipped over the stones and ran back to where she came from. Perhaps in order to preserve his sanity, the witness believes that it was not some kind of mermaid, but rather someone who simply made fun of her.

**Source:** *http://thebiggeststudy.blogspot.ca/*

Type: E

# 1.13. The Little Mermaid on a Tricycle

**Location:** Iberia Miraflores, akwen Rio Tahuamanu, Peru

**Date:** 1975

**Time:** varies

**According** to the statement of the main witness **Daniel Peinachi** (40), he and many other witnesses saw him catch a "small creature that looks like a Mermaid" in the Rio Tahuamanu River. According to his statement and that of Mr. **Albert Chitahuari,** the person who caught the "little Mermaid" exhibited her in the region and she was seen "riding a tricycle" on several occasions. Later, after it was seen in public, it returned to the water of the Rio Tahuamanu River in the Miraflores area. As it was said, the little Mermaid did not try to run away and looked content, regardless of the captivity.

**Source:** Victor Hugo Velasquez Zea – "The Sirens or Yakurunas and the Amazonian Cosmovision on Water Sources".

Translated from Spanish by Albert Rosales

## 1.14. The Mysterious Stranger[3]

**Location:** Rio Tampobata, region Chonta, Peru

**Date:** 1976

**Time:** evening

**Description of the event:** The main witness is a woman named **Elena**, who was sailing her small canoe on the river and suddenly a young woman also in a small canoe approached her. When the stranger swam up to the witness, she greeted her and sat down next to Elena, talking to her about several topics, and before she left, she told Elena that her name was **Rogelia** and that she would be back here tomorrow.

According to Elena's statement, this woman was very pretty, with very white skin, long blonde hair, and eyes of an intense green color. She was dressed in a shiny green outfit and indented, low shoes. At last Elena returned home, and the next day Rogelia did return, and Elena offered her breakfast, and after long chat, Rogelia went away again. From that day on, the visits became very frequent, all in the

---

[3] Yacuruna – a mythical human creature that lives in beautiful water cities, often in the mouths of rivers. The belief in their existence is especially strong in Amazonas. The name itself comes from the Quechua language, where "yacu" means "water" and "rune" means "man" – and therefore "water man", but not the Mermaid, who has a fish or dolphin tail in the lower part of her body.

morning. Elena's husband Heliodoro went to work in the fields every morning and never saw Rogelia, because she visited his house when he was not there.

One day, Elena told him about Rogelia and her visits, and that she wanted to meet him, but again they couldn't meet because he always left early for work and came back when she left. Heliodoro did not believe Elena and quickly forgot about it. One day, when Heliodoro returned from work, Elena told him that Rogelia had just left the house, but this only angered Heliodor, who made a scene for her.

One day, Elena's son was suffering from nasty diarrhea, and Rogelia came to visit. So, Rogelia told Elena that her mother was a "doctor" and that she could take her son to look at him. The two women went to the river and as Elena got into Rogelia's boat, the boat began to sink, which frightened Elena, who immediately jumped into her boat sailing next to Rogelia's canoe. Elena told Rogelia that her boat was too small and it would be best if she came the next day and then went home frightened. The next day, Heliodoro came home early from work, around 10 a.m., and found his wife apparently talking to an invisible person whom he was unable to see. Seeing this, Heliodoro threw his machete on the ground in front of his house, which apparently snapped Elena out of her trance, and she said to him:

"Helioda, you must be careful, you almost cut off Rogelia's foot!"

Apparently, the machete fell next to the foot of the invisible Rogelia. Heliodoro went home furious, and Rogelia told Elena that she had to go home. On another occasion, when the waters in the river were rising, Elena could see Rogelia in her little boat in the middle of the swift current, she showed her to Heliodorus, but he – of course – could not see her.

One day, when Rogelia was talking to Elena, she mentioned that she had just seen the young son of her neighbor **Ernestina** and... "She liked him so much that she was going to steal him from her." This caused Elena to visit her neighbor as soon as possible and warn her of the possibility of kidnapping and to guard him from strangers. On another occasion, Rogelia approached Elena and angrily told her that she had seen another neighbor who had been sitting in a canoe last night and defecating into the river, and apparently in the same boat Rogelia had accidentally left a small "beautiful machete." The next day, Elena went to look for the machete, but she only found a small and rusty machete in the boat, so she took it and gave it to Rogelia.

Rogelia had once told Elena about the river, and had told her that there were "new lands and homes, just like these here" under its waters. But Elena was skeptical and pointed out that she couldn't live underwater because she could drown, but Rogelia assured her that it wouldn't happen because "it's the same thing below as it is above."

On another occasion, Rogelia gave Elena a stone as a talisman, but never said where the stone came from. Elena has this stone to this day. One day, Rogelia said to Elena:

"Elena, let's make a pact between you and me, because I can't come here anymore.

Astonished, Elena asked her what kind of pact this should be between them? Rogelia replied that she would return here at midnight and whistle for her, so let Elena go out and confirm the pact. That night, Elena heard a whistle, but she was afraid to leave the hut. Later, in a dream, Elena saw Rogelia, who asked her:

"Elena, why didn't you come out then?" I didn't want to hurt you, and I don't want to bother you, I just wanted to seal a pact with you to make your life better. But don't worry, I won't haunt you anymore.

After this dream vision, Rogelia kept her word and did not pay any more visits to Elena. Later, Elena did a little investigation in the neighboring villages and towns, but no one knew who Rogelia was and no one saw her again.

**Source:** Victor Hugo Velasquez Zea – "The Sirens or Yakurunas and the Amazonian Cosmovision on Water Sources".

Type: E?

Translated from Spanish by Albert Rosales

Comments:

It all sounds very similar to "being bewitched by a fairy", which was apparently common to events in Europe, in the Middle Ages, and of course had many variations. According to this source, this is a case of CE with a kind of creature being a river nymph from European myths and legends. (This brings to mind a movie "The Woman in the Blue Water" directed by **M. Night Shymalana**, 2006.)

It also brings to mind all the stories about the Icelandic Alfurs (Elves) and Huddefolk (Hidden Men), who sometimes take care of human children and *vice-versa*. Rogelia's primary concern was for Elena's or Ernestina's child, whom she was going to kidnap – this was the "pact" she wanted to make with Elena. This is reminiscent of all the stories of abductions of small children or pregnant women that are told throughout Europe, regardless of nationality and religion, as described by Dr. **Miloš Jesenský** in his work "Gods of Atomic Wars".

## 1.15. Underwater CE with Siren

**Location:** A few miles off the coast of Florida, USA

**Date:** 1988

**Time:** afternoon

**Event Description:** Professional diver **Robert Froster** was diving alone in search of mysterious underwater formations when he noticed turbulence in the water. When he turned his eyes there, he saw a figure walking towards him. The water swirled around him and a cloud of clay was surrounded by it. When this creature moved towards it, it flowed with a serpentine motion, not glided in the water. When the strange creature was 20 yards away from him, he saw something strange in his appearance. The appendages seemed to be stretching out in his direction, and each of them ended in a hand with clawed fingers. Then he saw the creature in all its glory. He saw a pair of women's breasts, long wavy hair, smooth skin, and a fish tail from the waist down. She looked like a half-woman, half-fish. Froster said:

"I have never seen so much hatred in the eyes of any living being.

*The Unflinching Gaze of the Bermuda Triangle Siren*

*Reconstruction of the Siren from Robert Froster's account ("Secret 20th Century")*

Before the creature could reach him with its claws, Froster shot to the surface and swam as fast as he could towards his boat. He never saw it again.

**Source:** E. Randal-Floyd – „Great Southern Mysteries"

Type: E

**Comment:** It seems that the Orion Greys based here are not the only hostile beings on this planet. (Albert Rosales)

*Recreating the appearance of the Syrena from Robert*
*Froster's ("Most Amazing Top 10") account*

## 1.16. Married to Mermaid?

**Location:** Lake Tres Chimbadas, Madre de Dios region,
Peru

**Date:** 1992

**Time:** varies

**Description of the event:** there are reports that a strange
old man lives on an isolated stretch of the lake's coast, whom
the locals fear and avoid meeting him. He lived alone and
rarely spoke to his neighbors, and when he did talk to them,

he told them about "living in the lake" and that there was a "city" in the waters of the lake. He also told them that he was going to leave the earth to live under the waters of the lake, since he had "found someone there to marry." The locals remember that they could not catch anything in this sector of the lake, and this old man always had a full net, and he was not afraid to spend the night on the lake. It is not known what happened to him next.

**Source:** Victor Hugo Velasquez Zea – "The Sirens or Yakurunas and the Amazonian Cosmovision on Water Sources".

Type: X

## 1.17. Mysterious kidnapping?

**Location:** Breakwater, Tampobata River, Peru

**Date:** summer 1992

**Time:** 14:00 PET

**Description of the event:** A group of students from Puerto Maldonado with their teachers came to the river to refresh themselves and swim during the great heat that took place there at that time. The students dispersed to different places on the river bank and the group of girls decided to separate from the main group. While they were playing on the shore, one of them decided to enter the water alone, unnoticed by anyone. A moment later, one of the girls named

**Ana** heard her hysterical cry for help. She told Ana that something "grabbed her and started to pull her into the depths", and at the same time she started banging her hands on the water trying to scare it away. Ana ran up and jumped into the water to help her friend, but she couldn't do anything and watched in horror as her friend disappeared under the water. Despite a long search, neither the girl nor her body was ever found again.

**Source:** Victor Hugo Velasquez Zea – "The Sirens or Yakurunas and the Amazonian Cosmovision on Water Sources".

Type: X?

**Comment:** The unfortunate disappearance of this girl can be attributed to the Water People (Yacurunas), the Mermaids or just... anaconda. (Albert Rosales)

And the last case of the latest date:

# 1.18. Mermaid in the middle of the lake

**Location:** Lake Quistococha, Iquitos, Peru

**Date:** September 2007

**Time:** 12:00 PET

**Description of the event:** A group of more than 20 students from **the Maria Parado de Bellindo** school declared that a Mermaid appeared to them in the middle of Lake Quistococha and beckoned them with her hands. Kids aged

7-8 said that when they were bathing in the lake, a woman with a fish tail appeared in the middle of it and made gestures as if she were bathing: she took water in her hands and poured it over her head. When the Mermaid noticed that she was being watched, she made an inviting gesture, but the students were frightened by her unusual appearance and left the place, and the Mermaid dived underwater.

The students said that the Mermaid was very pretty. She had golden, wavy hair and very white skin, but no legs. Instead, they saw a very long fish tail.

According to them, the mermaid looked very nice and did not look dangerous. Locals say that seeing the Mermaid at noon is extremely rare, she usually appears on the surface of the lake at night, especially when the moon is reflected in the waters in the middle of the lake. According to their neighbors, her crying and sad voice can be heard then, melancholic – even tragic – and incredibly intense. This creature has never harmed anyone, and today it is treated as the guardian of this town.

**Source:** *http://www.cryptomundo.com/cryptozoo-news/xtrox/* quote from „Pro & Contra Journal" (no further details)

Type: E

A truly terrifying event with a similar type of entity occurred one afternoon in 1988, a few miles off the coast of Florida in the Atlantic Ocean.

# 1.19. Once again about UAH in the Bermuda Triangle

The strangest events occurred in 1992, when I was informed of an afternoon incident on Playa Media Luna, Vieques Island, Puerto Rico, which brought to mind the events of the Twilight Zone:

Mr. **Anibal Perez** and his young nephew came to the beach with their grandmother and were happily bathing in the sea and sun, when suddenly, and apparently directly from the depths, a boy of perhaps 12 years emerged and approached the witnesses. The stranger did not betray any ill intentions, on the contrary – it seemed as if he was looking for the company of people. Witnesses asked him who he was, but he did not answer, but made sounds similar to the squeaks of dolphins. Suddenly, the boy dived vertically down in the deep water, only to resurface a moment later with a handful of sand in his hands, which he offered to the astonished witnesses.

Apparently, he wanted people to eat the sand, but they refused. They were even more amazed when it turned out that the boy was eating this sand like normal food. They described the alien as a complete human being, thin with black hair and dressed in yellow swimming trunks. When the witnesses were swimming, the Alien tried to imitate their movements. He plunged into the depths again, and this time he came out, carrying out some seaweed, which he also offered to the witnesses. Making strange noises like dolphin squeaks, he tried to communicate with people.

After the witnesses tried to question the Alien, the Alien tried to repeat their speech, repeating everything they said to him. After a while, he seemed to be able to repeat it in an orderly manner and said that it came "from the bottom of the ocean". A few minutes later, he waved goodbye to them and said something like, "Goodbye, people!" – then he dived in and that's all they saw of him. They did not see him again.

And this automatically begs the question: are there undersea civilizations, or only undersea alien bases?

# CHAPTER 2. ANECDOTAL ENCOUNTERS WITH UAH

## 2.1. Mermaid on Mindoro Island (Philippines)

Another, perhaps even more bizarre account came from Sablayan on the island of Mindoro, Philippines. This event took place on the night of June 21, 1978. Filipino fisherman **Jacinto Fetalvero** recounted how on a moonlit night he met a beautiful mermaid with "brilliantly shining eyes, red cheeks and green spots on her tail". She helped him halfway. Apart from him, there were three other fishermen there. Later, however, Fetalvero did not want to say anything about this event.

Encounters with strange-looking amphibious humanoids or beings continued in the 1980s, sometimes under such unexpected circumstances as in this case from the Indian Ocean, which occurred shortly after midnight on an August day in 1986:

## 2.2. Siren on board the steamer

On board the SS *Uelen* – a steamer with a home port in

Odessa on a cruise to Singapore – sailor **Viktor Tanygin** had just returned from the watch and, tired, lay down on his berth with a book in his hand. Suddenly, he felt someone looking at him. He looked into the porthole and saw an unknown female face staring at him. Her hair was dark in color, her skin was very tanned, her eyes were blue, but much larger than those of a human. For a few seconds they both looked at each other, and then Wiktor jumped out of his bunk and ran out of the cabin, shouting that he ran into the cabin of his friends. He gathered them around him and told them that he had seen some strange, unknown being. They searched the ship, but did not find an unknown creature (which probably returned to the ocean). But Victor was afraid to sleep alone in his cabin and went to sleep in another cabin with his friends.

## 2.3. UAH from Crimea

The next report of an encounter with a completely different type of amphibious creature or humanoid came from Crimea, Ukraine. On August 18, 1991, at approximately 11:30 p.m. EEST, the following event took place in Batiliman near Cape Aja:

**Vyacheslav (Slava) Tertes** – the leader of the rock band "Oreol" from Sevastopol was taking a solitary evening bath in the area of Cape Aja, between Sevastopol and Foros. Being a good swimmer, he bounced about 100 m from the rocky coast in the south-west of the Crimean Peninsula. The Black Sea was completely silent and calm in the light of the full moon. Admiring the beautiful view, Vyacheslav swam slowly with the sea current. Suddenly, he felt something touch his shoulders, he immediately turned around, but he did not notice anyone behind him, but he heard the splash of water. He thought that surely one of his friends wanted to play a joke on him and swam towards the shore. Suddenly, he felt a touch again, and then a kick in the shoulder. He turned to see the face of a young woman with long hair clearly visible in the moonlight. Her eyes were much larger than those of a human and seemed to emit a phosphorescent light. The witness was frightened and threw away her hand with which she was touching him, and then fled towards the shore as fast as he could. He didn't hear a splash behind him and didn't turn around. When he finally reached the shore, he felt a strong stab in the back again, and when he finally turned around, he saw the face of the woman behind him, who seemed to be "disappointed", but he did not stop, but ran out of the water to the shore and began to scream. His colleagues rushed up and saw something shiny and silvery in the narrow strip of moonlit water, and they also heard the splash of water. Vyacheslav calmed down only a few hours later, as soon as he drank vodka. However, after a while, he felt the desire to see the Mermaid again, and he visited the place several times and swam alone at night in the Black Sea, but never met her again. He had dreams about her, how she called him to her.

## 2.4. UAH in the Gulf of Finland

Another case of high strangeness took place on a summer day in 1997 in the Gulf of Finland, near St. Petersburg (formerly Leningrad) in Russia:

An officer of the Russian Navy – submariner, **Nikolai M.,** who is an amateur diver, was diving in the shallow water of the bay when he noticed a strange, oblong object in the shape of a cucumber. Thinking that it was some fragment of the wreck of some old ship or vessel, Nikolai tied a rope around the object and tried to bring this "something" to the surface. However, he did not succeed, so he decided to tie the nib to this object and retrieve it with a car winch from the waters of the bay. So he came to the surface to take the equipment necessary to perform this task. He took a pneumatic auger to drill holes to attach the nibs. Nikolai dived to the bottom and tried to drill holes. Suddenly, a dark liquid similar to petroleum gushed out of the hole and hit him in the face. But Nikolai nevertheless increased the pressure in order to enlarge the hole. Suddenly he heard a dull bang inside the "cucumber" and saw a blood-like liquid in the water. The object released bubbles of gas and jerked as it moved closer to it. At the same moment, Nikolai saw a strange creature, apparently humanoid, with unnaturally white skin, which appeared to have been wounded in the back by an auger. The wound was bleeding.

The creature's face was twisted by pain, terror. The creature looked at Nikolai with hypnotic eyes, silently opening and closing its mouth. Nikolai tried to push the "cucumber" away from him in the direction of the strange creature, but the Alien grabbed his hands. His hands had claws, very sharp, that had dug into Nikolai's hands and wounded them. Defending himself, Nikolai took a pneumatic drill with his free hand and aimed it at the alien's chest. At that moment, he most likely lost consciousness. He was pushed out of the water and saved his life, but he lost part of his arm. No traces of the object or the humanoid were found. Apparently, the "cucumber" was some kind of cocoon for the Alien, in which the latter resided at the bottom of the Gulf.

The next four reports come from Africa, specifically from Zimbabwe, near the city of Charmwood and happened in January 2000:

## 2.5. Mermaid in the Hunyadi River, Zimbabwe

Mr. **Marko Batau** was walking from the direction of the Chawarura Shopping Center, and as he approached the

Hunyadi River, he saw what appeared to be a white woman sitting in the sun on a rock, half submerged in water. The woman was naked, and Mark was amazed by this fact. And then he was even more surprised to see that the woman had no legs, but a fish's tail.

The mermaid did not notice him at first, until he made a noise trying to approach her through the bushes. When he did, the mermaid disappeared into the water.

A few days later, his curiosity grew as he walked the same way home. To his utter amazement, the mermaid was once again on a stone, and moreover, there was laundry lying next to her, which was also drying on the bushes nearby. Unfortunately, either out of emotion or fear, he did not notice what was actually drying there – whether it was clothes or some rags. And again, he came closer to see better. Suddenly, his gaze crossed with that of the Mermaid, who chained him to the ground. Then the mermaid disappeared under the water.

The following week, Marko deliberately took a shortcut home. And again, he saw the same mermaid in his place. This time she had a child in her arms, which she was bathing. Again, as before, Marko tried to approach the Siren to get a closer look, and again hearing his footsteps, the Siren disappeared under the water with the child.

In March 2005, I was reported of a series of similar incidents on the shores of the Caspian Sea, particularly from the Astara and Lenkoran areas of Azerbaijan:

## 2.6. UMH from the Caspian Sea

Residents of several cities on the shores of the Caspian Sea in Iran and Azerbaijan claimed to have seen an amphibious man who was seen swimming among large schools of fish. Rumor had it that the waters in which this Siren swam became crystal clear. Recently, it was seen by members of the crew of the Azerbaijani fishing vessel MV *Baku*. According to the statement of **Gafar Gasanov**, the captain of this trawler, this creature sailed on a course parallel to the ship for a long time. At first, they thought it was some kind of large fish, but they noticed the hair on its head and found its outward appearance unusual. The front part of the body was equipped with arms. Shortly after their report was published in Iranian newspapers, there were many witnesses who described their own observations of such a being.

Readers have pointed out that fishermen have seen the creature many times in the sea and on shore shortly after the activation of the undersea volcanoes in the Babolsera basin in February [2005] and oil extraction became more intense in the Caspian Sea.

All these accounts speak of a marine humanoid. His height ranges between 165 and 168 cm, he has a flat stomach, fingers and toes fastened with webbing. His skin is pale. His hair looks black and green. His arms and legs look shorter than those of average-sized people. Besides, it had a kind of dorsal dolphin fin. Nothing is known about his ears. His eyes were large and round. The mouth of this creature was large, the upper jaw overlapped the lower one, which smoothly transitioned into the neck. No cheeks were found.

The Iranians call this creature "Runan-shah" or "Lord of the seas and rivers". Other accounts say that the waters of the sea become crystal clear when this creature is in them for a long time. Fishermen say that the fish know that this creature is approaching them and makes a gurgling noise. There is a theory that this creature is not alone and has its kinship or family here, which hides from people, and which is doing some mission here... – solving environmental and ecological problems in the Caspian Sea.

The matter is not insignificant, because the reproduction of flora and fauna in the Caspian Sea has significantly decreased due to increased oil production and underwater volcanic activity, which is especially true for the western and southern parts of this body of water. Astrakhan fishermen have a serious problem due to a decrease in sturgeon catch. [No caviar...]

To sum up all the reports about CE0 with amphibious and aquatic beings from my file are repeated, and I would like to end my report.

What can we say about these strange encounters? Is it possible for such things to happen at all? Even if only one or two of the accounts quoted here are true, it must be said that there is some underwater civilization or some cryptids in the oceans and inland waters! Are they aliens? Or are they the inhabitants of Earth who have been here for millennia before humans appeared on our planet? I don't have an answer to that, just more and more questions...

## 2.7. UAH from Israel

As recently as July and August 2009, in the coastal village of Kiryat-Yam (Israel), its inhabitants recorded several encounters with these creatures. According to the account of **Schlomo Cohen** – one of the first people to come into contact with the Syrena, it happened like this:

"I was just a friend when I suddenly saw a woman lying in a strange position on the sand. At first, I thought she was sunbathing, but when we got closer, she jumped into the water and swam away, disappearing into it. We were all shocked because we saw that it had a fish tail.

*Mermaid vs. Cannibal Crustacean*

## 2.8. The Girl from the Caspian Sea

A much earlier and even more astonishing testimony of an encounter with a Siren or some other humanoid sea cryptid can be found in an old work by the well-known writer **Caforni** entitled "Agaub El-Malkowkat", in which we read that:

In the year A.D. 894, a fish was caught in the Caspian Sea, which was opened and shown to the Prince of Salem, for inside the fish was a "sea girl." She wore a kind of pantaloons made of human-like skin, reaching to the knees. From time to time, she raised her hands to her face and hair. She was breathing heavily and lived only a few moments.

- and there is no other information about it.

## 2.9. UAH in the East of England

One of the earliest reports of CE with the Siren was recorded in Orford, East Anglia in the British Isles in the year 1204. One day, a few English fishermen or anglers caught something large and heavy in their nets. As they pulled the nets aboard their boats, they saw what they thought was some large creature that was jerking violently inside them.

They were most surprised to find that when they pulled the net out on deck, they saw a man lying there looking at them furiously. They described him as being naked, but his body was hairy, he had a long beard, and the top of his head was completely bald. They tried unsuccessfully to communicate with him, finally tied him up and took him to the city. The mermaid was taken to Orford Castle, where its resident Sir **Barthomolew de Gladville** imprisoned him. He and the prisoners tried to communicate with the Siren, but it only made strange sounds. They also noticed that when he ate raw fish, he squeezed water out of it on his clasped hand and drank it. Bartholomew de Gladville was irritated by his silence, so he began to torture him by hanging him upside down. Despite this, the Siren was still silent (why?) and was finally left alone.

Barthomolew de Gladville then took him to the nearest church, but it was evident that the creature had never been to church or attended the service before. One day, the Syrena was delivered to the port. Nets were stretched across the port exit so that he could not escape. The mermaid jumped into the water and immediately swam towards the net, and then easily swam under it towards the open sea with joy, making circles on the water. He was never seen again. And the interesting thing is that this Mermaid did not have a fish tail!

## 2.10. Female UAH from Edam

Another historical testimony is the account of Edamu in the Netherlands. It was in 1403. Two girls walking with milk met a strange creature on a muddy shoal in the Edam Canal. According to an account from old chronicles – the strange, female creature was hairy and covered with moss and small sea plants. She did not utter a word, but was later seen on several other occasions. This creature was written about in "The Purnermeer Mermaid".

### Siren in the Northwest Passage

Another case involving the crew members of another outstanding sailor and explorer **Henry Hudson** – **Thomas Hilles** and **Robert Raynar**, who on June 15, 1608, during Hudson's second expedition in search of the so-called Northeast Passage, spotted the Siren near the shores of Novaya Zemlya (Russia), almost at 75 degrees north latitude. She was the size of a man, had a woman's back and breasts, white skin and long and black hair. When she submerged, they noticed her mottled tail like a porpoise's.

### Mermaids of the Faroe Islands

Another case took place in the Faroe Islands (Denmark) in 1723. Members of the Royal Danish Commission investigating probable accounts of encounters with Sirens and similar-looking creatures in these waters observed a strange-looking creature approaching their ship. The creature would submerge violently and then just as quickly emerge to take a closer look at them. Within a few minutes of observing this creature, the ship began to rock violently, which forced the crew to sail away from this place. As they did, the Siren pouted his cheeks and let out a deep roar, then dove and disappeared from their sight.

**UAH from Wales**

Once, before 1791, on the shore near Castlemartin near Dyfed (Wales). **Henry Reynolds** was walking along the beach, and suddenly he saw someone who looked like a sixteen-year-old sitting in the sea. When he got closer, he saw that the creature had a large, eel-like tail, which the creature was moving all the time. His/her (???) shoulders seemed thin and short, and some brown ribbons protruded from his forehead, which hung over his back and went into the water. Reynolds observed this creature for a full hour as it swam near the rock at a distance of about 35 feet (10.5 m).

# 2.14. The Mermaid of Scotland

On January 12, 1809, early in the morning at Sandside (Caithness, north-east of the U.S. Army). Scotland), two women standing on the beach saw what looked like "a young woman's face, round and plump with a pink hue" in the sea. It appeared in the water, then disappeared and reappeared after a short while. Then they could see more details of her constitution, and they saw that she had nicely formed female breasts, and from time to time she raised her thin arm to brush her long green hair from her forehead.

## UAH from Lake Lacar, Argentina

Truly astonishing and at the same time anecdotal is a report from South America, more specifically from Lake Lacar in the province of Neuquen, Argentina, dating back to 1850. A creature similar to the Siren – some kind of half-amphibian, half-human – has been seen many times in this body of water. This mermaid, according to witnesses, had the ability to levitate above the water surface and – as it was assumed – lived in an underwater city. Unfortunately, there is no further information about these Close Encounters...

# 2.16. The Siren of the Bahamas

Somewhere in the Bahamas, where exactly unknown, in 1869 six men sailing a boat into the bay noticed a beautiful mermaid in the shallows with bluish hair that flowed over her shoulders and hands. Noticing the humans, the creature let out an incredible howl and disappeared into the depths of the ocean before the men approached it.

## Mermaid of Deernees

In the summer of 1890, a series of sightings of a creature that was later named the Mermaid of Deerness took place near Deerness, Orkney, Scotland. A regular visitor to Newark Bay, the Siren was included in archival records that corroborated the sightings of hundreds of eyewitnesses giving their oath statements. These documents show that the Mermaid stopped at a distance from the shore, so that there is no clear description of her figure. But there is one exception that gives her an accurate description, not deviating from the archetypal descriptions of the Sirens in the books:

It was a creature 6-7 feet (1.8 – 2.1 m) long, with a small black head, neck, snow-white body and two arms, which it moved as people as it swam along. It seemed that sometimes she was slipping on the sunken rock, and sometimes she was waving her arms.

### Mermaid of Sandwood, Scotland

In 1900, a landowner in Sandwood, Highland, Scotland, heard his dog barking, and noticed a strange creature lying on a rocky ledge on the seashore a few paces away. He described this creature as feminine, with human dimensions, beautiful posture, wavy red hair, blue-green eyes, and arched eyebrows. This mermaid-shaped creature gave the witness a frightened and angry look, forcing the witness to come out of the water.

### Mermaid of Redondo Beach, CA

What happened is one of the first of the most recent sightings of the Sirens, and it occurred in May 1935, in broad daylight near the coast of Redondo Beach, CA. The crew of the fishing boat spotted an astonishing Mermaid at a distance of 3 miles (about 5.5 km) from the shore, which they then described as an individual with shining eyes, a wide and smooth forehead, dark hair on the head and a beard. Its height – or in this case, rather its length – was estimated at 10-12 feet (3.6-4 m). He flicked his tail and disappeared from their sight before they could get close to him.

### Mermaid of Island of Muck, Scotland

In 1947 – the same year that the modern Age of Flying Saucers began – 80-year-old **Alexander Gunn**, an angler from the Island of Muck (Highland, Scotland), spotted a mermaid off the coast of this island. This creature was a Mermaid, judging by its appearance, and was sitting on a wooden box floating on the water. She looked as if she was combing her long, blond hair. The mermaid jumped into the water as soon as she noticed that someone was watching her.

### Mermaid in the Zambezi

Another similar account comes from Chirundu, Zimbabwe, in late 1951:

16-year-old **Cleo Rosin** was walking with her mother to the Zambezi River to fetch water. When they came ashore, they noticed a canoe anchored near the school, so Cleo entered it in a somewhat risky way. When she sat down in it, she found that in the middle of the river there was a small circular island that was unusually wide from that point. And on this island sat with her body partially submerged in the water, a beautiful woman with long black hair. To Cleo's amazement, the woman was naked and her skin was white. Meanwhile, Cleo's mother filled buckets with water. Cleo shouted to her mother:

-Mom! There's a woman there!

The mother looked in that direction and said:

"Quiet, shah... You'd better keep quiet," and then she added, " Look back!"

But Cleo was looking at the bottom of the woman's body, which was a fish, and she was looking at it. When she looked back, as her mother had told her, and then looked back at the island, the woman was no longer there. Her mother forbade her to tell anyone about the encounter, on the grounds that the mermaid would come back and kidnap her.

## UAH from Lake Maracaibo

A bizarre incident with some species of underwater cryptids took place at Lake Maracaibo in Venezuela, on November 8, 1965. Three families reported sighting a strange aquatic animal that resembled a snake with three human heads. There are no other data on this.

## Siren with Active Pass, Canada

One day in 1967, in the area of the Active Pass Isthmus in British Columbia (Canada), the passengers of the ferry noticed what they later called the Siren sitting on the rocks at the entrance to the isthmus. Reports indicate that the Mermaid had long, fair hair, the underside of her body was a porpoise's tail and she ate salmon. Photos taken by a man flying there in a plane confirm the accounts of witnesses. The newspaper "Times – Colonist" published the information and photo along with eyewitness statements. Unfortunately, none of the witnesses was able to give an interview at that time. There is also – unfortunately – no other photo that would confirm their authenticity and source.

* * *

The incident with the Lady of the Lake in Peru

In September 2007, the following incident occurred in Lake Quistococha in Iquitos, Peru:

More than 20 students from Maria Parado de Bellindo claimed that a mermaid-like creature appeared to them in the middle of Lake Quistococha, and signaled to them by waving its arms. The kids, whose age ranged between 7 and 8 years, stated that when they were taking a bath, a woman with a tail instead of legs appeared in the middle of the lake and it looked as if she was washing herself by taking water in her clasped hands and pouring it on her head.

When the mermaid realized that she had been noticed, she began to make beckoning gestures to make the children approach her. However, the disciples were frightened by her unusual appearance and ran away, while the Mermaid submerged under the surface of the water. The children said later that she was very pretty. She had golden wavy hair and very white skin, but she had no legs, but they noticed a thin fish tail.

According to their statement, the Lady of the Lake did not look threatening and did not pose any danger. Locals say that seeing the Mermaid at noon is something unusual, as it usually comes to the surface at night, especially when the moon is reflected in the water in the middle of the lake.

Their neighbors add that she is often heard crying and her voice is sad, melancholic – even destructive – and extremely intense. The mermaid did not cause any harm to anyone and is currently considered the guardian of this town... (how do we Poles know this???)

\* \* \*

What can we say about these strange encounters? Is it possible for such things to happen at all? Even if only one or two of the accounts quoted here are true, it must be said that there is some underwater civilization or some cryptids in the oceans and inland waters! Are they aliens? Or are they the inhabitants of Earth who have been here for millennia before humans appeared on our planet? I don't have an answer to that, just more and more questions...

# CHAPTER 3. STRANGE ENCOUNTERS

## BETWEEN DIVERS AND MERMAIDS

The author of this material is **Brent Swancer**. One of the beings that has managed to weave itself into the lore and legend of different cultures is the Mermaid. Water Virgos are found in a vast area of folklore from all over the world, and in some cultures, such beings are considered more than just a myth, with some areas accepting them as real and obvious. Indeed, there have been many encounters reported with supposedly real Sirens, and this is one of the unknown cryptozoological phenomena. Here, we will delve into some of the reports of divers who have stumbled upon these mystical entities in a series of startling statements that are as intriguing as they are bizarre.

## 3.1. Meeting the Siren in the Deep

Some very bizarre reports come from the *Imaginarich website*, which deals with sightings of mermaids and unknown beings. In one account, a female diver was diving somewhere in the Caribbean when she heard a "haunting tune" that seemed to pull her into deeper waters. As she followed the ethereal melody, she finally came face to face with a "siren," the male type of Siren, and her report reads like this:

As the deep-sea diver descended into the mystical depths of the Caribbean, a haunting melody drove her deeper into the depths of the ocean, weaving a mesmerizing spell that captivated her mind. She was enveloped by the enigmatic charm of the underwater world, and as she followed the ethereal song, she encountered the mesmerizing beauty of the Caribbean Sirens. The Siren's enchanting presence was a testament to captivating legends that echoed through generations. Her iridescent scales shimmered like precious jewels in the sunlight that filtered from the surface, and her captivating voice resonated with otherworldly grace. The woman was drawn to the mermaid, her heart beating with a mixture of fear and amazement. The Siren's enigmatic singing kept her in a trance, her movements smooth and graceful as she danced through the azure waters. The woman could not help but be captivated by the hypnotic effect of the Siren, feeling a deep connection with the mythical maiden of the ocean. It was a moment of pure magic, where reality and fantasy intertwined in the most enchanting way.

What was happening here? Magic? Hypnosis?

*Dugong - a candidate for a mermaid?*

# 3.2. Meeting with UAH in the Indian Ocean

In another similar report, a diver in the Indian Ocean came face to face with a Siren whose report reads:

Amidst the rippling currents of the Indian Ocean, the deep-sea diver plunged into a captivating encounter with an otherworldly creature of unparalleled beauty and mystery. As he plunged into the depths of the ocean, the water around him seemed to shimmer with an ethereal glow, casting an enchanting aura over the underwater landscape. Suddenly, a specific figure emerged from the swirling sea mist, revealing the form of the mesmerizing Siren, her iridescent scales reflecting the ambient light in a breathtaking display of underwater charm. The diver's heart pounded when he saw the mythical creature, its presence evoking a sense of wonder. The silhouette of the Siren swam through the ocean, captivating the diver with its haunting melody. Hypnotized by this encounter, the diver felt as if he had stumbled upon a living legend, the essence of myth and magic that existed in the depths of the Indian Ocean. In that fleeting moment, amidst the hidden wonders of the deep, the divers' encounter with the mythical maiden became a precious memory, forever etched in the annals of deep-sea exploration.

## 3.3. Mermaids from the Great Barrier Reef

We also have an alleged encounter with the UAH on the Great Barrier Reef in Australia, where an unnamed diver came across not just one mermaid, but a whole group of them. The report says:

In the vibrant depths of the Great Barrier Reef, the diver was enchanted by a mesmerizing encounter with an otherworldly presence. As they sailed through the crystal-clear waters, they came across an enchanting sight – a group of ethereal Mermaids gracefully floating coral gardens. The diver couldn't believe his luck and immediately reached for the underwater camera to capture this surreal moment. The mermaids, with their shimmering tails and flowing hair, seemed to exude an aura of mystery and beauty that was truly captivating. In that fleeting moment, the diver felt a deep connection to the marine environment and realized the importance of protecting the sea. Meeting these mythical girls served as a reminder of the need to protect and preserve the fragile ecosystems of the Great Barrier Reef. As they swam alongside the Mermaids, the diver was filled with an overwhelming sense of wonder and respect for the underwater world. This encounter became a pivotal moment, igniting the will in the diver to advocate for the conservation of marine life and its habitats.

*Hylas and the Water Nymphs (Henrietta Rae)*

## 3.4. Mermaids from the Maldives

In a report directly related to me, a diver was diving in the azure waters of the Maldives when he claimed that three mermaids appeared out of nowhere and began to circle him. He described them:

- as having dolphin-like tails and humanoid upper body parts. The upper parts of the body were described as looking very androgynous, with no hair on their heads, smooth skin, and face, which were described as an "ill-fated look", with sharp teeth and black eyes like those of a shark. These creatures allegedly circled the diver for several minutes, seeming to study him, before looking away.

## 3.5. The Hawaiian Mermaid

Since April 1998, there has been a strange account of a diving master, 43-year-old **Jeff Leicher**, on the Hawaiian island of Kauai. At the time, Leicher was diving with a group of six other divers who were exploring the ocean floor about 20 minutes off the sunny coast of Kona, Hawaii. At one point, he saw what appeared to be a woman just 10 feet away, swimming with a pod of dolphins and keeping up with a fast pace, which Leicher found strange. Then it got weird when he noticed that the woman had a tail like a fish's. He said this about the amazing meeting:

I've heard about it before. Most of us who are in these waters regularly have heard these stories. But I never saw her until this morning. We were on our way to the point where a pod of dolphins started following the boat, playing with each other. Suddenly, one of the men on the port side starts shouting and pointing. I couldn't believe what I was seeing.

There, about 10 feet from the side, was a figure that looked like a naked woman. She had long, loose hair and one of the most beautiful faces I've ever seen. But there is no way that a human can swim that fast. She hung out with the dolphins. Then she jumped into the air and my heart almost stopped. Its entire lower half was covered in scales and narrowed back to a huge fish tail. She jumped once more, then disappeared beneath the surface.

About an hour later, we reached the point and dived. I photographed colorful fish with an underwater camera. Suddenly, I felt something graze my right leg. The siren shot at me like a streak of lightning, then turned and came back next to me, swimming the other way. I just pointed the camera and started taking pictures. I was still photographing as she surfaced and swam away.

You can see the alleged photos here, but many have pointed out that they could easily have beenfaked, despite Leicher's claims that the photos were studied and authenticated by experts. What do you think?

# 3.6. A mermaid off the coast of Northern Ireland

Another photo of the alleged mermaid was taken by free-diver **Hanno Windisch**, who was diving in the quaint seaside village of Ballintoy in Northern Ireland when he had his strange experiences. The report of the Causeway Coasts and Glens visit reads:

Hanno initially thought he had spotted a large fish or seal. However, upon closer inspection, he realized that it was a creature with the upper part of a human body and the tail of a fish, basking near the rocks. The mermaid, described as having long hair and an iridescent tail, seemed as curious to Hanno as he was to her. He claims that the creature sat on the rocks for about five minutes before plunging back into the cool waters of the Atlantic. The mermaid reportedly stopped for a few moments, closing her eyes, with a diving instructor who is originally from Germany, before diving back into the depths of the sea, leaving a trail of shimmering water in his wake. As an SSI Level Two of Freediving instructor, Hanno tried to follow the mermaid's path, but it was too fast, even for his years of professional diving.

You can see a photograph of Hanno here, but it is ambiguous to say the least.

## 3.7. About Terrorist Sirens

Not all mermaids seem beautiful and kind. In 2012, work at the Gokwe Dam in the Midlands and the Osborne Dam in Manicaland, on reservoirs near the towns of Gokwe, Manicaland and Mutare, Zimbabwe, was suspended when workers refused to go to work because they claimed they were terrorised by the Sirens that lurk there, which were supposed to look like pale skinned people with black hair and fish tails. Initially, workers were supposed to repair and install water pumps there, but they got scared when some people in the area mysteriously disappeared and others reported being attacked or chased by these entities. Things with the stalled bill have gotten so bad that Zimbabwe's water resources minister, **Sam Sipepa Nkomo**, appeared before a parliamentary committee to explain the situation. Nkomo said that the white workers were brought in because they had no knowledge, but even they claimed to have spotted the creatures, and also refused to return to work. The Minister of Rural and Urban Development, **Ignatius Chombo**, also made arrangements for the tribal chiefs of the area to perform rites and rituals to appease the creatures, if only to calm the minds of the workers.

According to tribal leaders who were consulted, many of the lakes and reservoirs in the region are inhabited by Mermaids, and the dams appear to be a favorite place for congregants, although they have been said to be typically attracted to larger dams than those that have been harassed, such as the huge dam at Lake Kariba, which is a hotbed for such sightings. When faced with the question of whether they believe these creatures really exist, they have been unanimous and adamant in their claim that they do. When asked if the

Mermaids of the Zimbabwean Lakes are real, one of the bosses **Edison Chihota** of Mashonaland East said:

- As a guardian of the traditional one, I have no doubts. For anyone who questions this, there is also questioning yourself.

For his part, Nkomo was more worried about the workers refusing to return, and he only went through rituals to dispel fears. He was skeptical that their problems were caused by literal mermaids, blaming them for a mixture of superstitions perhaps combined with optical illusions and dangerous water currents. He said about the matter:

In Mutare, I think what happens is that there has to be an empty space underneath that creates a hole, and the water will swirl violently so that if you fall in, you don't come out, even if you have an oxygen mask.

Dangerous currents or sirens? Who knows?

## 3.8. UAH in Thailand

This rather strange report comes from Reddit user **One-Amphibian-5831**, who claims to have had an encounter while diving with his family off the Phi Phi Islands in Thailand. He says about the experience:

To paint this picture a little better: at this point, me and my brother were diving into the water just below the floating island, while the others in our group were a little further away from this island. This island was like a piece of land that stretched down into the water, not on a sloping slope. Suddenly, our dad called us, someone from our group saw a little shark and everyone gathered to see it. My brother was swimming there, but for some reason I stayed and watched the different fish that were swimming so close to me.

Then something caught my attention. There seemed to be smaller caves beneath the shore, and I saw something slowly coming out of there. It was similar to a human head, pointing downwards towards the ocean floor. I completely froze and am still staring. "Someone" came out of the cave, never returned to the surface, and did it really slowly. None of this person (whom I saw) moved. At this point, I could see the back of my head and most of my back. The person facing again had sparse black hair, sprinkled on his scalp. Their skin looked gray and their spine was extremely pronounced. I was so sure that I looked at the corpse and froze again. I couldn't breathe or move. Time passed slowly, as if it was standing still. The person was still swimming out of the cave and that's when I started to see his tail. The tail was dark and looked like the stereotypical tail of a mermaid. I blinked repeatedly, convinced that I was hallucinating, but I kept seeing it. I never believed in the supernatural, but it was only a few meters below me and I could see it so clearly. I felt danger, I knew I shouldn't see it, and I was terrified that he would see and attack me. But what it has never faced. After leaving, he

111

turned on his side and found himself near the island and disappeared into another cave.

After a few seconds, I snapped out of it and quickly swam to my dad and brother. I broke down in tears and frantically told them that we had to get back to the boat immediately. Dad asked me what was wrong and I told him what I had seen. Of course, he didn't believe me and got mad at me for "lying". When we got back on the boat, I told them again, and stood by that I wasn't lying. My father told me that he really hoped it was either a lie or that I was crazy and had to be locked up in a mental hospital. I knew how it all sounded and to be honest, I didn't even believe myself. I decided to tell him that I had made everything up. From that day on, I tried to convince myself that I made it all up, but I never experienced any hallucinations and I know what I saw. Ive told the others, but of course most of them thought I made it up. It's such an insanely frustrating feeling to be stunned by the whole world and I hope someone out there will believe me.

## 3.9. … and in the Andamans

Another Reddit user named **mencho 14** also has a bizarre encounter with a Syrena. At the time, he was on a very dangerous dive off North Sentinel Island, which is part of the Andaman Islands, an Indian archipelago in the Bay of Bengal. North Sentinel Island is best known for its unexplored tribe of ferocious natives, but it may now be known as a place where Mermaids may exist. The witness says:

*So, one day I went on a diving adventure off the coast of North Sentinel Island, it's a pristine island known for its vibrant marine life and untouched coral reefs. As an experienced diver, I wanted to explore the underwater wonders that this remote location had to offer. I descended into the crystal-clear waters, accompanied by the soft sound of my own breathing apparatus. Sunlight pierced the water, creating a dance of light and shadow at the ocean floor. Flocks of colorful fish swim through waters undisturbed by my presence.*

*As I ventured deeper, navigating through intricate coral formations, something unusual caught my eye. Hidden in the shadow of a large, overhanging rock formation, it was a figure unlike any sea creature I had ever met. At first, I thought it might be a large fish or a sea lion, but as I approached cautiously, the figure became clearer. There, in a small cave, there was what seemed to be a Mermaid. It had the upper part of a human body, with long, loose hair that shimmered in the filtering sunlight, and the lower part of a fish, along with a graceful, tanned tail. Her skin had a subtle, pearly sheen, and her eyes were a deep, mesmerizing blue color, reflecting the ocean itself. I was stunned, my heart throbbing with a mixture of fear and amazement. The mermaid seemed equally surprised when she saw me. For a moment we looked at each other, frozen in time. Then, with a smooth and elegant movement, she swam closer. Her movements were smooth and effortless, a dance of grace and beauty.*

*Mermaid or beluga*

*She was hanging around me, her eyes filled with curiosity. She then reached out, gently touching my diving suit with delicate fingers. Her touch was light and cool, sending shivers through my body. I moved out as well, but just as my fingers were about to touch her, she quickly turned and disappeared into the depths, leaving a trail of luminescent bubbles. I was dumbfounded, my mind racing with what I had just experienced. The meeting was short, but it was profound and life-changing. The existence of the Mermaid, a creature of such extraordinary beauty and grace, challenged everything I knew about the mysteries of the ocean.*

What are we to do with such reports as we have reviewed here? Of all the mysterious beasts and creatures that have been spotted around the world, Sirens seem to be in the more unlikely range of the spectrum, as they seem to defy everything we know about the natural world, evolution, and fossil records – things that belong heavily documented in myth and legend. So, what did these people see? Were they figments of the imagination, some undiscovered human species, some interdimensional phenomena, or something else entirely? Whatever the case, these are certainly strange accounts, and point perhaps to something more to the mysteries of the ocean than we can imagine.

ᘉ

# Chapter 4. Mermaids in the
# Darkness of the Oceans

## 4.1. Sirens appear where mass cetacean suicides occur

During Christmas 2012 a.D., among the various crap offered to us by TV, the Animal Planet channel broadcast an extremely interesting film entitled "Mermaids – The Body Found", in which the Close Encounters of Man with Mermaids were shown in the form of a quasi-documentary, which were even filmed with mobile phones. In ufological nomenclature, these would be...

*Beached cetaceans in the USA (still from the film "Mermaids - The Body Found")*

## 4.2. RV/CE0/UAH

i.e. Technical Observation and Close Encounter of Zero Kind
with an Unknown Water Humanoid (cryptid). I have already
touched on this topic earlier on the website -
*http://wszechocean.blogspot.com/2012/05/jeden-powod-
wiecej-by-obawiac-sie-plaz.html.* This article is a
continuation of this topic. As I can see from the statistics of
visits to my blog, the issue of the existence of the Mermaids
aroused considerable interest. And rightly so, in my opinion,
because – unlike the Little Green Men – Mermaids can be
creatures of flesh and blood.

The film features scientists who were accidentally drawn
into a whirlwind of unusual events that started two events:
the shooting of an unusual film by two American boys on a
beach where whales washed up, and the detection by
scientists of unusual sound or ultrasonic signals, the pattern
of which did not match any known inhabitant of the Pacific.

## 4.3. Mermaid on the beach and mysterious signals

The video was taken with a mobile phone on a beach in
Washington state. It depicts whales lying on the sand and
what at first glance resembles a pile of algae. But from this pile
of algae comes an almost human hand. The boy approaches

her, nudges her with a stick and looks at the camera. Almost at the same moment, the head of some humanoid creature appears next to his head, with wide-open eyes and mouth. The boy, terrified, jumps away... UMH tries to follow him, but he can't because he has no legs.

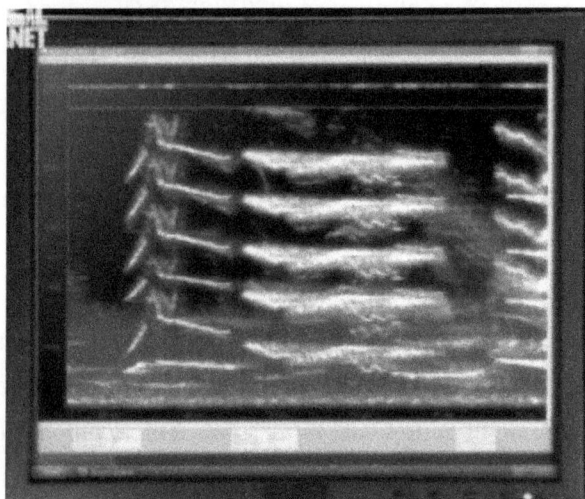

*Mysterious sonograms from the depths of the Pacific (still from the film "Mermaids - The Body Found")*

The second premise is the unusual sound signals picked up by scientists in the waters of the Pacific. Analysis showed that they did not match any known inhabitant of the oceans, and therefore they would be some new species of marine creature using ultrapisceans like cetaceans. What is most interesting – it was in those regions of the Pacific Ocean that

US Navy exercises took place and it is in these regions that mass suicides of cetaceans take place. Hence the idea that the USN and other fleets of the world were working on some kind of undersea sonic weapon.

There is no word about the principle of its operation – most likely it is about the production of strong ultrasonic waves in the water, which would be able to destroy targets in the vicinity of their own ships. This makes sense in relation to hostile divers-saboteurs who could swim up and mine surface and underwater vessels. Such weapons could be used against saboteur dolphins or sapper dolphins clearing their own sea minefields. But for this it would be enough to use an ordinary active sonar, which is able to create noise in the water with an intensity of >300 dB, which simply blows the heads of whales and dolphins! – and I remind you that the pain limit for humans is only 130 dB...

## 4.4. Metan i STD

I once hypothesized that whales and dolphins are poisoned in the sea by methane and hydrogen sulphide, which are deposited at the bottom of the ocean, see - *http://wszechocean.blogspot.com/2012/05/peru-rozwiazano-zagadke-dziwnych-zgonow.html*; *http://wszechocean.blogspot.com/2012/03/tajemnica-trojkata-bermudzkiego-wstep.html*;

_http://wszechocean.blogspot.com/2012/03/czy-to-eksplozja-metanu-zrujnowaa.html_ and this is because methane is a staggering gas that affects the sense of orientation. Whales and dolphins can poison themselves with methane from exhalation and then wash up on beaches with known results. In the light of what this film presented, this seems to be only part of the truth and cetaceans died not only from methane poisoning, but also from escaping from excessive noise.

## 4.5. The remains of a mysterious creature and its weapons

The third premise was the remains of a mysterious Creature devoured by a shark found in South Africa. Everything indicated that this creature had two arms, but instead of legs it had a strong tail ending in a rhomboidal fin like a manatee's. Interestingly, in addition to her remains, an artifact made by her was also found: a weapon in the form of a goad or harpoon made of long, straight bone and ending with a venomous stingray spike. And this suggests directly that we are dealing with a rational being, possessing the ability to make tools, which can no longer be called an animal. This is completely obvious.

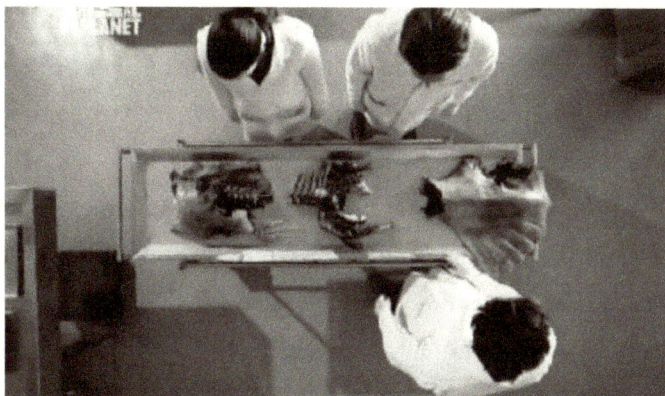

Alleged remains of a Mermaid (still from the film
"Mermaids - The Body Found)

Then there was other evidence that apart from humans,
there is a parallel intelligent race of Water People on this
planet, or if you prefer – Sirens. What is more, the filmmakers
of this film claim directly – and this already fits the
Conspiracy Theory of History – that the governments of the
USA and South Africa know perfectly well about their
existence and – what's more – imprison some of them in
order to conduct research and experiments on them related
to military techniques.

## 4.6. Water monkey and dolphins

Scientists claim that they have been living in the Global
Ocean for about 7 million years, since a certain species of apes

descended to the beaches on the African coast of the Indian Ocean – where they found a large amount of high-protein and easily digestible food in the form of fish, crabs, algae and other seafood, which had a positive effect on the development of their brain and accelerated the achievement of an upright posture, and after a few more millions of years, it caused the transition from the terrestrial environment to the marine environment. This caused them to lose their legs and develop a tail with a caudal fin. In addition, these beings had to adapt to the darkness of the waters of the ocean – hence their huge eyes, in which rhodopsin was replaced by chrysopsin, without which it would be impossible to see in residual light penetrating to a depth of about 300 m.

These creatures most likely – as deduced by scientists from the shape of her skull – have a sense of echolocation, like cetaceans, thanks to which they can orient themselves in water spaces. And then there's the issue of the ability to breathe underwater. It also had to be developed. These creatures either breathe air dissolved in water – like fish, or breathe, like cetaceans – atmospheric air. Observing seals in the Hel Seal Centre, I had the opportunity to see what they are capable of. And such a 100-kilogram gray seal (gray seal) is able to withstand 20-30 minutes submerged, so the Being should also be capable of something like this.

Aquatic People accompany whales and cooperate with dolphins. Thanks to this, they have the opportunity to protect themselves from marine predators. This is the case now, but it was not always so. This is shown in an interesting scene in which the male Mermaid sacrifices herself to protect her group from the attack of a megalodon – the largest shark of all time. I will devote a little more space to this issue later, because it is related to the mystery of the extinction of this species.[4]

## 4.7. Mermaids and people

The question of the interaction of mermaids and people. In the video, we see cave drawings from Lower Egypt in which people (probably) fight the Mermaids. Next to them you can see dolphins and whales. Were there fights between two rival species? Perhaps, or rather certainly, after all, both races fought for food sources and humans managed to push the Mermaids away from the coast. At least we think so...

So much for the film. Of course, I'm not mentioning issues that are already the domain of STDs, such as the fact

---

[4] The cause of the extinction of the Megalodons was most likely the explosion of a nearby Supernova star, as evidenced by the presence of the radioisotope iron-60 (60Fe) in the 2.6-million-year-old sediments of the bottom of the ocean, which is formed only in the course of nuclear transformations in the interior of stars.

that all materials were supposedly confiscated by the US and South African governments, which prevented scholars from studying this new cryptid. Although, on the other hand, it is impossible to keep secret what has not been a mystery since Antiquity. Homer and other ancient authors wrote about the Sirens. Legends are persistently told about Water People all over the world and in all cultural circles, so they are beings that really exist in our Reality. Another thing is that the military took away direct "hard" evidence of Their existence. The same is true of Aliens and UFOs.

## 4.8. Mermaids and Megalodons

And now on a different note: Mermaids *versus* Megalodon sharks. Megalodon – according to Wikipedia – is an extinct species of cartilaginous fish, a prehistoric shark, the largest of the known predatory fish. It lived 25–1.5 million years ago in the seas of the Oligocene, Miocene, Pliocene and Pleistocene.

Due to the cartilaginous structure of the skeleton, few fossils of this species have survived and it is known mainly from fossils in the form of huge triangular teeth with finely serrated edges, from which the species is named (from Greek *mégas*, D.-*megálou* – great + *odoús*, D.-*odóntos* – a tooth). In 1996, a Megalodon tooth measuring 16.8 cm in length was found, which was the largest known tooth of this shark at the time. Later, even larger teeth were discovered, which allowed the length of the entire shark to be estimated at over 18 m. According to an early reconstruction of the Megalodon's jaws by **Bashford Dean**, it could have exceeded 25 m in length, but this reconstruction was incorrect.

The megalodon was a predator probably hunting whales and other large marine mammals, it could also hunt other sharks, but these assumptions have not yet been confirmed. It was widely distributed in the Miocene seas.

The genus *Carcharodon* isolated in the Cretaceous is currently represented only by the great white shark. Megalodon has been classified in this genus as the presumed ancestor of the great white shark. Previous studies have not yielded conclusive evidence, and it is now debatable whether Megalodon is *Carcharodon megalodon* or whether it should be included in a separate genus *Carcharocles*.

The Water People protected the whales and *vice-versa*. They were forced to constantly fight with the Megalodons, which they eventually killed...

Now we see what the Water People had to face. Theoretically, Megalodons could live peacefully until the 21st century. In the ocean, they had good conditions for development, food in dirt... And yet they are extinct. Well, they could have been killed by the Mermaids. Of course, one Mermaid was lost in a clash with Megalodon, but in a clash with many Water People and dolphins cooperating with them, he would not be the winner at all according to the principle *nec Hercules contra plures...*

These monsters had strength and cunning. Humans and dolphins had cunning and intelligence, but also tools. The monsters acted instinctively, the Sirens deliberately. Well, it was enough to lure such a monster into the shallows, into some narrow bay, which limited its movements, and then killing it was not so difficult. The killing of the Megalodons was *a sine qua non for the* survival of the whales and the Water People associated with them.

## 4.9. Mermaids in the Bermuda Triangle?

And another issue – do the Sirens create a civilization in our understanding of the word? It is clear from the film that it is not. It is not a civilization of our type, a scientific-technical civilization. It seems that they have taken a different path – to adapt to the conditions of the Global Ocean as much as possible and thus – to use its biological capabilities to meet their needs. Therefore, they simply do not need complicated technology. This is somewhat reminiscent of the Aldebaran society from **Stanisław Lem's short story** "Invasion of Aldebaran" (Kraków 1959), which had biological technical means from plants and animals bred by themselves. In this context, there can be no question of the technical development of the Syrena in our understanding. Their tools are primitive and serve only to satisfy the simplest needs. Although...

The navies of several countries have live examples of Sirens in their laboratories. Will knowledge about them be directed against other people?

There is another version that claims that their technological development has long surpassed ours, which can be expressed by the events taking place in the Bermuda Triangle and the Dragon's Triangle. To this must be added UFO sightings and USOs in the waters of the Ocean – and especially UFOs of the NOTSUB-Id type, i.e. flying objects falling into the sea, or jumping out of it. Therefore, it may be that they are playing a delicate, intricate, but very effective disinformation game with us, which also includes this film and the "sensational" information it contains. Let's not forget that we only know about 3% of the surface of the ocean floor – which covers 70.8% of our planet's surface with a layer of water that is on average 3729 meters thick. Suffice it to say that our gray Baltic Sea is 21,721 $km^3$ of water, and yet the Baltic Sea is only 2% of the total area of the ocean...! What is happening in these waters we can only guess. And who knows, maybe we are not being spied on and controlled by our older and wiser cousins who survived all the cataclysms hidden in the waters of the World Ocean?

## 4.10. Sirens and cataclysms

Assuming that they have been around for 7 million years, we must also assume that they have experienced at least two terrible cataclysms, which were the volcanic supereruptions of the Yellowstone supervolcano – about 640,000 years ago and the Toba supervolcano – about 70,000 years ago. Both of these events were cataclysms that claimed hecatombs of victims – especially in North America, which was buried under a layer of volcanic ash and tephra many meters. On the other hand, the Toby super-explosion almost led to the extinction of the human race in general! As you can see, the Sirens went through both of these storms with flying colors. The waters of the Global Ocean saved them from the consequences of these volcanic cataclysms.

Speaking of volcanism, it is also associated with the destruction of Plato's Atlantis 12,000 years ago. Atlantis was the most developed and civilized country on the planet. And who knows if the Sirens – and other creatures known from Greek, Chaldean, Babylonian, Hindu and other mythologies – were not sometimes the products of Greek genetic engineering? Why do I think so? – It's simple. So far, no one has been able to unearth any fossilized remains of the Syrena, which would have to be found in marine sediments from 5-7 million years ago and younger. So these beings could have been younger and only arose a few thousand years ago as a result of genetic manipulation. To find such fossils would be evidence of their existence. I don't believe that all the Sirens were eaten by sharks and other Megalodons and that some had to be buried in the clay and mud of the bottom of the World Ocean. The creation hypothesis of these UMHs is – in my opinion – as legitimate as the others.

I hope that soon we will learn more about the Water People, because the seed has been thrown and the fuse has been lit – so it is only a matter of time before it germinates or explodes...[5]

---

[5] Source - _https://mysteriousuniverse.org/2024/09/Bizarre-Divers-Encounters-with-Real-Mermaids/?fbclid=IwY2xjawFI_4NleHRuA2FlbQIxMQABHXWR44Akt_Bung2l2ikKm77tHQc_yv-Hmh-Q-gk4I-xppMLluqDibw90ug_aem_5taIWEYj51wWEA-AyzEN4Q_

# Chapter 5. Mermaids sit on branches...?

This material is by **Vasily Miturov** and talks about mysterious creatures in the ocean. And here is the article:

**Nadya Vessie** from New Zealand is disabled; both of her legs have been amputated. Without looking at it, Nadya is a swimmer. Some time ago, a company made an artificial tail for her, like the fairy tale Mermaid.

\*\*\*

Do you think that Water nymphs are only in fairy tales? No! Documents have been preserved in the archives, according to which these mysterious creatures – half-woman-half-fish – really existed. So, we will take responsibility for saying: judging from everything, they really exist. But contrary to well-known poems, they do not sit on branches, but inhabit the seas and oceans to this day.

*"Sirens - At night naked women weave wreaths in the river" by Konstantin J. Makovsky (Internet)*

## 5.1. The Enigmatic Fugitive

From ancient times to this day, there have been plenty of testimonies about encounters with Water Nymphs *aka* Mermaids, or as they now call them – Water People (*Homo sapiens aquaticus*). There are testimonies about encounters with these beings on the territory of Russia – in the Black Sea, in the lakes of the Northern Belt, Siberia and also in the Caucasus. These Water People, according to the descriptions of witnesses, look different – height from 0.5 m to 3 m, the tail can be smooth like a dolphin's or covered with scales like a fish's.

In the mid-sixteenth century, English fishermen fished out a human-like creature with a fish's tail with a net and put it in the castle living near the lord. The creature was male, quite bald, but with a thick long beard. This Water Man survived in the castle basin for several months, then he was carried to the seashore to breathe fresh sea air, and he escaped. The most interesting thing is that the fugitive returned to the castle, where he lived again for some time, and then escaped again, definitively.

## 5.2. Water Man Roast

The famous sailor **Henry Hudson** wrote in his diary that two of his sailors observed the Siren on June 15, 1608, off the shores of the New World. She was a woman with bare breasts, black hair down to her shoulder blades and a fish tail, covered with black dots like those of a mackerel.

In 1739, an English newspaper published information about how sailors from the ship *Halifax* fished out several Sirens near the coast of the island of Mauritius. They baked them and ate them. Later, they said that their meat resembled tender veal.

In 1758, the live Mermaid was shown at a fair of curiosities in Paris. The painter **S. Gautier** made a drawing from nature. This drawing has survived.

## 5.3. Mummies and skeletons

Most biologists believe that mermaids/water nymphs actually existed some 200-300 years ago. But then they disappeared like ghosts. A number of skeletons resembling human skeletons were found, but with a fish tail instead of legs. Two mummies of nymphs were in King's *College Medicine* in London. But during World War II, his building was hit by a German aerial bomb – and the entire collection was destroyed. Fortunately, photos of these mummies remain. Mummies and skeletons of the Mermaids have remained in the collections of the Royal Museum of Scotland and the National Museum of Ethnology in Leiden, the Netherlands.

In the local museum of the American town of Tomstone, in a large glass window, there is a skeleton of a creature, the outer part of which resembles a human. Its chest has well-developed ribs, and this means that this creature breathed atmospheric air. The underside of the skeleton ends in a fish tail.

## 5.4. Brutality of the underwater inhabitants

Not so long ago, the secrecy clause was finally lifted from the events that took place in 1982, in the western part of Lake Baikal. There were exercises of military divers from the

Trans-Baikal MD. After the divers dived to a depth of 50 m, they often encountered creatures at least 3 m tall. The heads of these beings were like spherical helmets, but they did not have any scuba or other breathing devices underwater. These creatures swam very fast and followed the actions of our divers.

Unfortunately, these meetings ended tragically. An order came from the command to capture one of these Beings. Seven scuba divers commanded by an officer tried to catch one of the Beings in the net. In an instant, some force threw all seven to the surface of the lake. As a result, everyone developed caisson sickness due to the pressure difference. Three of them died within a few days, the others became disabled...tags. Nevertheless, these extraordinary inhabitants of the deep were not Rusalki. Who, then, were they? You can fantasize about it as much as you want, and let's continue our story.

In August 1992, fishermen from the village of Key Beach, (FL, USA), at a distance of one kilometer from the shore, noticed "half-human seals" lying on the water with large human-like heads, large eyes and long arms, ending in webbed hands. The creatures, seeing the barge approaching, circled around it and swam away into the deep. After an hour, the fishermen pulled out the net and found that it was cut in several places.

## 5.5. Time to get acquainted!

Employees of the US *National Oceanic and Atmospheric Administration* (NOAA) claim that women with fish tails, whose cave drawings appeared at the end of the Stone Age (about 30,000 years ago), exist even now and in all bodies of water in the oceans.

Recently, an international conference on the issue of Mermaids took place on the island of Tahiti. The main topic of the conference - a hybrid of a humanand a fish, or maybe a dolphin and a dolphin, inhabits the depths of the sea anyway. According toexperts – most of the population of Nymphs/Mermaids inhabit the warm waters of the Mediterranean Sea and the Caribbean Sea basin. They have also been seen in the Pacific Ocean and the waters of the South Atlantic.

In the USA, 7 mermaids supposedly live in a special aquarium. Where it is – the authorities carefully hide it. American media report that President **Obama himself** saw these nymphs and was amazed to see them. For now, there is a mania for keeping everything secret in the States and Rusalki – as you can see – are now particularly inaccessible.

*Syrena in the deep sea ("Secret of the 20th Century")*

# 5.6. They eat biscuits!

About a year ago, the tiny coastal city of Kiryat Yam/Kiryat Yam – N 32°50'45" – E 035°04'00" became famous throughout Israel. The mayor of the city officially stated that Sirens have been observed in the bay more than once and that bathers, especially children, should be careful and should not approach them. The press and TV from this town are constantly receiving reports and reports about people's encounters with Mermaids – both female and male, and children even offer them biscuits!

The authorities stated that they would pay NIS 1,000,000 (₪) or approximately PLN 660,000 to anyone who provided irrefutable evidence of the existence of the Water People. Boats sail around the bay, and further from the shore ships equipped with sonars and satellite observation means depart. However, the promised million shekels have not yet been paid to anyone...

... Scientists believe that the underwater world of seas and oceans is much worse explored than the space around the Earth. So, we will have to learn much more about this mysterious world.

CR

# CHAPTER 6. UNDERWATER
# HUMANOIDS

The author of this article is USAF Maj. **George A. Filer III** (MUFON). He writes as follows:

There are many reports that UFOs are flying out of underwater bases and several types of alien Sumerian fish-like gods exist.

Most of them assume that they came from other planets, but they lived on Earth and developed an underwater civilization and high-tech vehicles. Perhaps they are sapient species or Sea People inhabiting the oceans. They look like people from the waist up, but like fish from the waist down. They also have something like legs to move around on land. These amphibious creatures can operate in water and on land like turtles or alligators. Space races may have come to Earth from some aquatic planet and adapted to the conditions of our planet. In fact, we have thousands of reports of sirens and UFOs entering and flying into and out of the water.

It doesn't matter if you're a fan of the TV series "Ancient Aliens" or a fan of strange theories about the origin of man, you've probably heard of the Sumerian aliens. Their role in Humanity has become a subject of great controversy, and it is difficult to ignore the evidence found in the old Sumerian records. Who were the Sumerians and what were the Sumerian aliens doing here on Earth?

*Aquatic beings similar to the Sumerian Oannes*
*(according to Olaus Magnus)*

## 6.1. Sumerian Aliens from the Ocean

Sumer (Shumer) is also known as the "land of civilized kings", it was a flourishing civilization located in present-day Iraq (formerly known as Mesopotamia) around 4500 BCE.

The Sumerians had an advanced civilization with their written language and sophisticated writing. They also had extensive knowledge of the Solar System, astronomy and mathematics. Today, we use exactly the same mathematical, calendual, and time-sharing system that the Sumerians used. On top of their advanced language and understanding of the Cosmos, the Sumerian civilization cultivated advanced agriculture and irrigation systems.

In addition to a developed language system, the Sumerians had their comprehensive religious system, divine cosmology, and rituals. The Sumerians claimed that their gods came from outer space or from the depths of the ocean. According to their texts, every Sumerian city had its divine patron. Men and gods lived together, and men served their gods. Ancient Sumer was not only the home of his gods, but also home to the Nephilim described in Genesis:

And in those days, there were giants on the earth, and also later, when the sons of God drew near to the daughters of men, they bore them. So, they were those mighty men who had a reputation in those old times – Genesis 6:4. And:

And they said to them, we have gone to the land to which you have sent us. It is indeed a country flowing with milk and honey, and here are its fruits. However, the people who dwell in it are strong, and the cities are fortified and very large. We also saw Anakites there. The Amalekites occupy the vicinity of the Negeb; the Hittites, the Jebusites, and the Amorites live in the mountains, and the Canaanites dwell by the sea and on the banks of the Jordan. Then Caleb tried to pacify the people against Moses, and said, "We must go and take the land, and we will surely be able to take it." But the men that were with him said, we cannot go against this people, for they are stronger than we are. And they proclaimed bad news about the land they had explored, saying to the Israelites, the land that we passed through to examine it is a land that devours its inhabitants. And all the people we saw there are tall. We even saw giants there - the Anakites are descended from giants - and in comparison, with them we appeared to ourselves like locusts, and so we were in their eyes - Num 13:27-33 and:

In the twelfth year of the first month, on the fifteenth day of the month, the Lord said to me, Son of man, lament over the people of Egypt, and command them to come down into the underworld, to them and to the daughters of the mighty peoples, to those who have gone down into the pit. Who have you surpassed in virtues? Come down and lie down among the uncircumcised. They will fall among those who are slain with the sword; The sword has been handed down: Take him and all his people. Then the mighty heroes from the midst of Sheol will say to him, "They will go down into the pit with their helpers, and they will lie among the uncircumcised, with those whom the sword will smite." There is Ashur and all his troops around his tomb - they are all slain, fallen by the sword. Their graves are in the deepest pit, and his troops are around his grave - these are all the slain who fell by the sword, those who spread terror in the land of the living. There is

Elam and all his multitude around his tomb - all the slain, the slain by the sword, who have descended uncircumcised into the underworld, they who have spread terror in the land of the living, suffer shame with those who have descended into the pit. A lair has been prepared for him among the beaten, and there are plenty of him around his grave. All these are uncircumcised, beaten by the sword, for fear of them was widespread in the land of the living, and now they suffer their shame with those who have gone down into the pit, and have been placed among the slain. There is Meshech, Tubal, and a multitude of them around their tombs, all uncircumcised, slain with the sword, for they spread terror in the land of the living. And they do not lie with the heroes who fell in ancient times, who descended into Sheol in full armor of battle, and their swords were put under their heads, and their shields on their bones, because they were a terror to the heroes of the land of the living. And you will be cast among the uncircumcised, and you will have to lie among those who have been slain with the sword. There is Edom, and his kings, and all his princes, who, in spite of their heroic deeds, have been placed among those who have been slain by the sword, and they are lying with the uncircumcised, with those who have gone down into the pit. There are all the rulers of the North, and all the Sidonians who descended with the slain, disgraced in spite of the fear which their heroic deeds spread; now they lie uncircumcised with those who were slain with the sword, and suffer their shame with those who have gone down into the pit. Pharaoh will see them and console himself with all his multitude. Pharaoh and all his army will fall by the sword, saith the Lord God. Because he spread fear in the land of the living, they will cast him to lie among the uncircumcised, with those who fell by the sword, Pharaoh and all his multitude, says the Lord God, Ezek 32:17-27.[6]

Ancient Sumer was not only the home of these gods, but also the home of the Nephilim described in the Book of Genesis. There are several clay tablets collected at Sumerian archaeological sites, but one of them states that Earth is the SEVENTH planet (including Pluto).[7] How could a civilization from 6000 years ago know about Pluto? Many believe that the Sumerians received this knowledge from the gods and believe that these gods came from the Cosmos. Nammu is the Sumerian goddess of the primordial sea and later the depths, the mother goddess. She is also the goddess of Babylon with the same name, which is associated with fresh water, but is slightly less divine.

---

[6] All quotations according to the "Millennium Bible", Pallotinum, Poznań 2003.

[7] I don't think it's Pluto, which is too small to be considered a full-fledged planet. Perhaps it is a hypothetical 9. A super-Earth planet located deep in the Kuiper Belt or perhaps even in the Oort Cloud.

- Enki and Nammu are presented as the parents of humanity. Myths begin with the act of creation of humans and Humanity. And from then on, the gods begin their work.

## 6.2. Enki: the god who saved humanity

Enki, the epic god of water, helps humanity and plays a major role in the Akkadian, Babylonian, and Mesopotamian history of Atrahasis, which is the Mesopotamian version of the Great Flood. In this myth, Enki was responsible for creating those who were to serve the gods. The gods were overworked and needed help. Enki and Nammu created the human race. This race of humans multiplied rapidly, and Enlil, the chief deity, became irritated. He had a very compassionate character. His desire to educate people and favor their side over the gods, as well as his tendency to resolve conflicts rather than start them, counterbalanced his lustful deviances.

Enki was originally the patron god of the city of Eridu, believed to be the first city ever to be founded, according to ancient Sumerian beliefs. Although he was first recorded as an Akkadian god, from about 2600 to 2350 BC, temples to Enki were found that date back to 5400 BCE! In the "Enuma Elish," a Babylonian creation myth found on ancient tablets, the Universe was originally in a state of chaos. Chaos split into freshwater, a masculine principle called Apsu, and saltwater, a feminine principle called Tiamat. Apsu and

Tiamat were the first gods and gave birth to Enki, their eldest child.

Akkadian/Babylonian mythology holds that the younger gods were created to do all the work to sustain creation and were tired of the daily grind. Like some of today's youth, they were looking for a way out of hard work. As a result, they created other beings to do the work for them: humans. Humans were created from the sacrifice of one of the younger gods. The gods were angered by the noisy nature of humanity, the explosion of populations, and sought to reduce their numbers. The main initiator of the extermination of humanity was the god Enlil. He tried to eradicate people first through drought and then through pestilence, but his plans were constantly undermined by Enki. Apparently, the gods are furious again at killing millions of human children and have caused great disasters.

The Sumerian Alien theory originated from a clay tablet found in Nippur, an ancient city founded in 5000 BC. According to mythology, the earth was ruled by extraterrestrials, similar to humans.

These beings were called gods and had the power to travel in the sky. Once on earth, these beings would dig into the soil of the planet to make it habitable and accumulate resources. Some say that the Sumerian gods were here simply to mine for gold. According to the text, Anu (who was the god of the gods) thought the work was too hard. By creating humans on

Earth, a form for life under water was created. Today, the remains of many cities are located under the ocean near Cuba, the Azores, the Bahamas, the Mediterranean, Greece, Egypt, India, Cambodia, China, and Japan.

Enki, his son, proposed to create a human being to help with the work. Enki and his sister Ninki worked together to put this idea into practice – literally. His flesh and blood were mixed with clay to create the first man - in the image of the gods. It is worth noting that...

## 6.3. Underwater cities

The Sumerians believed that Enki would come out of the sea for days and teach people to read, write, build cities, and develop mathematical rules. You may have heard the term Annunaki, which looks familiar given that the god of the gods was Anu. The Annunaki were Sumerian gods or those extraterrestrial human-like beings.

The Annuaki's theories of extraterrestrial origin are largely attributed **to Zecharia Sitchin**, and opinions on whether these theories contain truth are controversial. According to Sumerian myths, extraterrestrials, some of the wetter planets, inhabited this earth long before man.

Interestingly, the first man was created in Eden, which in the Epic of Gilgamesh and the Bible is described as the garden of the gods. It is believed to be somewhere between the

Euphrates and Tigris rivers. The first humans were unable to reproduce and were later modified by Ninki and Enki to allow reproduction. He angered Enili, Enki's brother, and started a conflict between the gods. According to Sumerian alien theorists, this conflict is the reason why the Annunaki abandoned Earth and left humans to fend for themselves.

The Sumerians were not the first civilization to speak of beings descending from heaven to earth. Many cultures around the world have similar histories, and often these beings have given these cultures invaluable knowledge.

According to **Robert Temple**, author of The Sirius Mystery, the CIA and other U.S. government agencies have been actively involved in suppressing the truth about the existence of amphibious humanoid extraterrestrials from the Sirius star system since at least the late 1960s, when Temple began investigating them. This cover-up was so careful that there is no record of the government's interest in amphibious humanoid extraterrestrials. This educational NOS Q&A website is the first direct evidence that the government is actively covering up all traces of strange frog people.

This conspiracy is extremely long-lasting. It began in ancient times when a conspiracy destroyed all the records of Babylon to try to suppress the Babylonian records of amphibious life, leaving us with only a small mention in Eusebius' dissertation of earlier discussions by Greek historians about the Babylonian priest **Berossus** (**Berossus**).

At that time, Robert Temple first showed in his book "The Sirius Mystery" the fact that the Dogon tribe of West Africa had knowledge of star systems that even the modern world has yet to confirm. This story is connected to their stories of beings from other worlds in this star system, it was proof for some that humanity was indeed visited in the distant past by extraterrestrial beings, who then started civilization as we know it, teaching the knowledge and wisdom of the Universe.

Throughout the history of sailing, there are still accounts, stories and testimonies of eyewitnesses – including renowned captains – talking about the Mermaids. To this should also be included the crews of warships of all the world's fleets.

## 6.4. Mermaids have fins...

Mermaids have tails equipped with fins to move through the water. Mermaids build coral-based cities on the ocean floor, and their homes have clam shell roofs that open and close with the current of the water. Mermaids look like humans, except for their tails, which can be worn like swimming fins. I've heard from Navy Seals that they encounter Mermaids as creatures swimming past them at high speed. Russian divers reported similar encounters.

In folklore, a mermaid is an aquatic creature with a woman's head and torso and a fish's tail. Mermaids appear in the folklore of many cultures around the world, including the Middle East, Europe, America, Asia, and Africa.

Mermaids are sometimes associated with dangerous events such as floods, storms, shipwrecks, and drownings. In other folk traditions, ships are often sunk in mysterious ways, with the crew claiming to have been struck by something powerful. Sometimes, within the same tradition, there may be benevolent or benevolent humanoids saving crews.

## 6.5. Something powerful sank the ship...

Although the traditions and sightings of male mermaids (*merman*) are less common than female mermaids, *it is generally assumed* that they coexist with their female counterparts. Men and women are sometimes referred to as men (*menfolk*) or I (*me*).

The concept of Mermaids in the West may have been influenced by the Mermaids of Greek mythology, which originally resembled half birds, but in Christian times they began to be depicted as half fish. Historical accounts of the Sirens, such as those reported by Christopher Columbus during his exploration of the Caribbean. Although there is no evidence that mermaids exist outside of folklore, reports of sightings of mermaids continue to this day.

Mermaids have been a popular theme in art and literature in recent centuries, for example in Hans Christian

Andersen's "The Little Mermaid" (1836). They were then portrayed in operas, paintings, books, comics, animations, and action films.

There are many indications that the Global Ocean is home to a race of intelligent beings that may be a side branch of the developmental line of the Homo *sapiens sapiens species* – and in such a case we would be dealing with *Homo sapiens aquaticus* or perhaps even *subaquaticus.*

There is another possibility promoted by the author that the Sirens are visitors from outer space who settled in the ocean. Such a possibility is also real, because we are still dealing with mysterious underwater objects known as USOs or UAOs.

There is also a third possibility, namely that the Sirens are the product of genetic engineering of a previous civilization (e.g. Atlantis or Atlantic), which has survived to our times. The mermaids were tasked with exploring the oceans and defending the Atlanteans from the attempts of their neighbors, which is reflected in the legends of the Sea People.

So far, all three hypotheses are equally justified, because we still have no evidence directly for their existence apart from legends, legends and witness accounts. Anyway, strange things are happening in the depths that we can't get over on a daily basis.

While writing a book about the mysteries of **the Titanic**, I suggested that perhaps it was the Sea People who contributed to its sinking by putting an iceberg in its way. The obvious goal is to change the reality that threatens them from our side. How realistic is it? As much as it is real to stop the development of our civilization heading towards self-destruction...

Let me make one more remark – who knows if the Mermaids are not leaving the Baltic Sea given the tense political situation in this region. From 2022 onwards, there too is threatened by the outbreak of criminal madness, threatened by incompetent politicians and haunted lunatics hiding behind "reasons" and "national interest"...

# Chapter 7: NOAA Declares – Sirens Do Not Exist

Information from July 2, 2012 The U.S. National Oceanic and Atmospheric Administration is NASA's ocean "sister".[8] It usually deals with hurricanes, tsunamis and atmosphere. She has just issued a statement on the Mermaids. The statement is titled "No Evidence of Aquatic Humanoids Has Ever Been Found." NOAA specialists note in it that the belief in Mermaids was born at the dawn of civilization. Magical women, living in water, appear already in Paleolithic paintings, and then in mythologies. But their existence has never been scientifically confirmed.

Okay, but why does NOAA even bother with this? And why now? After all, there are no dragons and dwarfs either, and no one has yet issued a statement on this matter.

---

[8] NOAA is the US National Administration for the Atmosphere and Oceans, which studies the atmosphere and hydrosphere of our planet. In addition, he speaks on all topics related to the atmosphere and the ocean. Its space counterpart is NASA.

## 7.1. Who is to blame?

The guilty party is the popular science channel Animal Planet, which in June broadcast a quasi-documentary program entitled "Syrena. A body has been found" ("Mermaids: The Body Found"). The authors showed what mermaids could look like and why they were hiding... until now. As the New York Times journalists commented, the program is "fiction, but built on elements of truth, so that it looks like a documentary. If you know the rules, it's fun."

The whole thing was a bit like "The X-Files", but for many people in the USA the program turned out to be very convincing. Americans simply believed in sirens. Therefore, the agency that is responsible for the world of mermaids had to speak out. Hence the NOAA statement.

It is worth reminding that the noble agency has already made similar statements. NOAA specialists have spoken, for example, about Atlantis and the Bermuda Triangle. U.S. government agencies don't just investigate. They have a mission to popularize science in their field. If there is a confusion in oceanography, NOAA will certainly speak out. (Polskie.Radio.pl). One more interesting fact:

## 7.2. "Bloop" - the secret of sea sound

"Bloop" is an underwater sound with an ultra-low frequency

of unknown origin. It was registered in 1997 by the American NOAA. At first, it was thought that these were sounds made by an animal, but the sound was too loud. Some have suggested that it could be a monster, aliens, or a sleeping Cthulhu. And what does NOAA say about it?

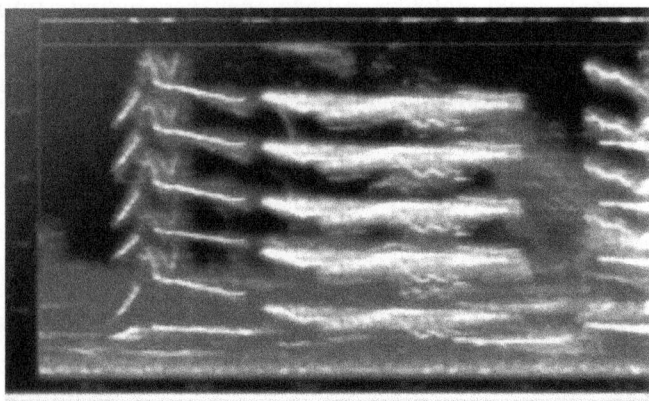

*Sonograms of the mysterious bloop sound recorded by NOAA*

The latest stance from the US government agency may be a bit disappointing. According to scientists, the "bloop" is the sound of disintegrating icebergs located off the coast of Cape Adare in Antarctica. Unfortunately, nothing of mystery – there is no monster in the depths of the sea. You can listen to the sound here.

However, fans of puzzles should not lose hope. There are a few more mysterious underwater sounds that NOAA cannot explain. Mainly it is about strange whistles against the background of low frequencies. They can be heard anywhere in the Pacific (check here and here). In addition, the American agency recorded other sounds of unknown origin, which were given the names Julia, Train and Slowdown. Is the time for the Great Old Ones to awaken soon? (Piotr Stępiński)

And one more article, from the source itself, from NOAA:

## 7.3. About Water Nymphs and Mermaids

Water nymphs, Water Maidens – these half-human, half-fish mermaids from the sea – are legendary sea creatures recorded in chronicles in maritime cultures since time immemorial. The ancient Greek poet **Homer** described them in the "Odyssey". In the ancient Far East, the Sirens were the wives of powerful sea dragons and served as trusted messengers between them and the rulers on the land. Australian Aborigines call them *yawkyawks* – a name referring to their mesmeric songs.

The belief in their existence was created at the dawn of our species. Magical female figurines first appeared in cave painting from the late Paleolithic, about 30,000 years ago, when the young human species was just appropriating land

and most likely began to sail the seas. Half-human beings called chimeras also abound in mythology – in addition to the Water Maidens, also wise centaurs, wild satyrs, terrifying minotaurs – to name a few.

But are these Water Nymphs and Aquarians real? No evidence of aquatic humanoids was found (where they even searched for?). Why, then, why do these beings still occupy a place in the collective unconscious of almost all seafarers? This question is better left to historians, philosophers and anthropologists.[9]

\* \* \*

Funnily enough, just a few days ago, on Wednesday, October 2, 2013, NOAA announced that it had at its disposal facts indicating that there are humanoid creatures similar to the legendary Sirens in the ocean. This statement was made by several radio stations. I looked for traces of this statement on the Internet and... - I haven't found any. As if this information did not exist at all!

This does not surprise me. I believe in science and rationalism, but when you mix science with money and

---

[9] See. http://www.polskieradio.pl/23/266/Artykul/637545,NOAA-oswiadcza-syreny-nie-istnieja -

http://www.geekweek.pl/aktualnosci/11111/bloop---tajemnica-morskiego-dzwieku http://oceanservice.noaa.gov/facts/mermaids.html

commerce, it doesn't work out such miracles! And there are enough examples of this: UFOs do not exist, and everyone can see them, the Loch Ness monster does not exist, and many people are looking for it, Hitler did not have an atomic bomb, and he ordered the construction of Riese and other research complexes (and fallout shelters) dealing with the atom by accident where there are deposits of uranium ores, etc., etc. The last hit is the delirium and deception of the so-called 'specialists' from the commission of Macierewicz in the matter of the Smolensk catastrophe, to which one of his so-called 'experts' admitted.

The same is true of the Mermaids. It is irrelevant that people have seen and met them since the dawn of time – as the "scribes" admit – and they have left behind accounts of both sailors and people living on the mainland (who can hardly be accused of any sexual deviations, as the so-called "scholars" eagerly explain it). The important thing is that some titled authority has issued a negative opinion and the whole thing either collapses or is ridiculed. Of course, it also works the other way around. First of all, how can you make this kind of opinion knowing that we have explored only 8% of the ocean floor? We know its photic zone quite well, but the euphotic zone and the abyssal are still almost a tabula rasa for us... Therefore, in this case, I DO NOT believe in the negative statements of scientists from NOAA – and any other ocean research agencies.

So, it seems that this information is either a journalistic duck – which is of course possible, but why on this and not another topic? – or someone from NOAA "blew the paint" and the news went around the world, and now it has been quickly withdrawn from all websites – this is also possible, after all, the NSA (as m.in. **Edward Snowden** has shown) has its tentacles very deeply let into the Web and deleting this information is a breeze for it. As far as I'm concerned, information about the observation of a *super-stealth aircraft* seen in our country in 2009, and several others, were deleted from the former CBZA blog without my knowledge and consent. Of course, this could have been done by the operator Onet.pl at the request of you-know-whom...

A critique of the view of the existence of Sirens and other similar sea creatures was presented by scientists from various oceanographic institutes, who were appointed in the fifth episode of the documentary series "Jurassic Warriors" (dir. **Kreg Lauterbach**, USA 2008) and tried to explain what happened to the Megalodons. I think they are wrong and they were killed by the Sea People...

I would like to draw the reader's attention to the book **by Ellen Prager** and **Dave Jones** entitled "Megalodons, Sirens and Hurricanes – Strange Questions and Scientific Answers" (*Wielka Litera*, Warsaw 2025). Well, the authors claim that there were no Mermaids, there are not and there will not be any mermaids. And slush. And of course, they cite a whole lot of arguments for NO. OK, so how to explain all these accounts, observations and stories of old men and captains? And here is their argument:

**Ariel** and **Aquaman** are fictional characters.

**Tom Hanks** never saved the real Mermaid in the 1984 film "Splash".

Manatees have never been mermaids, although it is pleasant to swim and dive among them.

Cave paintings depicting a human-dolphin hybrid **are not scientific proof** that Mermaids once lived.

No bones, fossils, photos, videos, or other real evidence of the existence of the Sirens have ever been found.

NOAA published a statement that reads: No evidence of the existence of humanoids living in the sea has ever been found.

Dr. **Shea Steingass** presented some important facts indicating that Mermaids – as we imagine them – would not survive in the ocean, and these are:

First of all, they would freeze to death, and this is because most of the water in the seas is cold. At a depth of 200 m or more, the water temperature is only +4°C, which is not conducive to life.

Humans and fish are evolutionarily distant from each other, so such a hybrid is genetically impossible.

The physique of the Mermaid poses many problems related to physiology.

A very interesting reasoning, but there is a small but, namely - if cave paintings do not constitute evidence for the existence of Sirens, then cave paintings also do not constitute evidence for the existence of, for example, mammoths. Typical wishful thinking of a "scholar". I'm much more worried about the problem of contamination of the Global Ocean with plastics and other waste, but more on that later.

Well, we'll wait to see what the Future holds for us, because the question is still open...

CR

# CHAPTER 8. WATER NYMPHS, WATER MAIDENS, MERMAIDS, OCEANIDS, ETC.

*They stand, and then they jump with all their might,*

*The drawbar broke at the very screw;*

*To stay in the field, alone and at night,*

*I like it, I said, I like it!*

*He barely finished until terrible necrosis*

*It flows out of the near waters of the depths;*

*Her white garments, like snow, white faces,*

*A fiery wreath on the temple.*

*I wanted to run away, I fell down in fear,*

*A hair stood on his head like an oak;*

*I will cry out: May Christ be praised:*

*"Forever and ever," he will answer.*

*"Whoever you are, good man,*

*Which he has preserved me from my torment,*

*Live to be happy and old age,*

*And peace to you and thanks."*

*"You see before you the image of a sinful soul, —*

*Soon I will boast of heaven;*
*For thou hast saved me from Purgatory*
*In one word: I like it.*

Adam Mickiewicz – "I Like It"

This is how our bard **Adam Mickiewicz** imagined a Close Meeting with a Water Maiden, or rather with a soul in purgatory, who was serving a punishment for ridiculing love for her and thus leading the boy to a suicidal death. From then on, she was supposed to frighten people passing by the lake where she was serving her sentence, and the condition for her release was the saying of the word "I like" by a man...

While searching the Internet for materials on intelligent beings in the ocean, I came across a poster entitled "Knowledge about Water Maids",[10] which presents a detailed study of the anatomy and physiology of these strange sea or amphibious creatures.

There is a plaque showing the anatomy of the Water Nymph aka the Water Maiden. Basically similar to human anatomy, except that instead of legs it has a fish tail. But it's not strictly a fish tail, but dolphins! The fish moves in the water wagging its tail from side to side, dolphins and other mammals wag their tails up and down.

---

[10] JIUFOTK (Amazon)

Then there is the distinction between Water Nymphs and Mermaids. And so...

# 8.1. Anatomy of the Water nymph and the Mermaid

Water nymphs are characterized by the fact that:

They have normal "human" teeth;

The tail is different from the tails of predatory species;

They are friendly to people;

They are naïve;

They are colorful;

They can't talk to Mermaids;

They do not use any magic.

Mermaids are characterized by:

Sharp teeth;

The tails are shaped like aquatic predators;

They are dangerous;

Sneaky;

Usually in green;

They do not leave the depths;

They use dark magic;

They manipulate people with the help of singing;

They have sharp gills;

And they are flirtatious.

## 8.2. 11 Amazing Facts About Water Virgos:

The earliest legends about the Water Nymphs come from Syria before 1000 BC. The original Water Nymph was **Atargatis** from Syria. Legend says that when it immersed itself in the lake, it became a fish, but only the lower half of the body was transformed.

Sea cows (manatees) were often confused with Water nymphs. They are large marine mammals and have often been mistaken for by sailors at sea. Christopher Columbus said that he saw "ugly and fat Water Nymphs". When I worked at the Seal Centre of the UG Marine Station in Hel, I came across this slogan: *Seals and manatees are the pets of Mermaids.* I am of the opinion that porpoises and dolphins too...

Water nymphs have 4 main powers:
- immortality
- the ability to see the future,
- telepathy...
- ...and hypnosis.

There are 4 types of Water Nymphs:
- traditional nymphs – living only in the sea;
- Irish Water nymphs that can shed their tail and have legs;

- shape-shifting – which can take on human form if necessary;

Sea People – amphibious vehicles that look like humans, which inhabit land and water. Many varieties of these creatures have been described in historical accounts and accounts.

Aquamarine (a blue-greenish transparent gemstone) is from the tears of Water Maidens. It was believed that these oceanic gems came from the tears of the Nymphs.

The word "Mermaid" means "woman from the sea". In Old English, "mer" means the sea, and "maid" means a girl, a woman.

Rusalka's kiss has the power to seduce. According to old legends, the kiss of the Water Nymph gives you the opportunity to breathe underwater.

The nymph (Merman) was the first. The water Babylonian god **Oannes** appeared 7000 years before Atargatis.

Water nymphs do not have strong, singing voices. The Sirens have strong and singing voices.

The most expensive nymph tail costs £10,000 GB. This hydrodynamic tail weighing about 17.5 kg is owned **by Linden Wolbert** from Los Angeles (CA), who has traveled the world as a completely professional *Merman*.

The color of the nymph's tail reveals her character. It reveals her momentary mood, as well as her personality.

## 8.3. My 3 cents

I didn't believe in the existence of the Sea People until one September afternoon, when I saw them in Lake Wicko on the shores of Wielki Krzek in 1987. There were several people who were bathing in the lake. Three or four – I didn't have binoculars to see them well. But I remember one detail, these people had no legs...

Let's not forget that somewhere in the old days, in this lake, lived a Water Maiden called **Świetlana**. On the other side, already in the Baltic Sea, Zielenica was caught, which people tortured in Trzęsacz... Is there anything in these legends? Of course – these are traces of meetings between people and Water People. Do they live in the Baltic Sea now? Perhaps, but rather they moved to the clear waters of the lake or to the Atlantic...

And what does it mean? Nymphs and Mermaids have become fashionable – as evidenced by series such as "H2O – All You Need is a Drop", films such as "Pirates of the Caribbean", "Syrena" and others. Let's not forget that the Mermaid – or rather the Water Miss – is in the coat of arms of Warsaw. In addition, there is a fashion for Mermaids – in flowing robes...

Why am I writing about these mythical creatures? Well, because they are not as mythical as they seem. We know only 10% of the surface of the bottom of our ocean, and the remaining 90% can be anything. In addition, I recommend a very interesting work by **Kevin Peter Hand** – "Extraterrestrial Oceans", in which he puts forward the thesis that in the oceans of gas moons and ice giants there can be life – even intelligent life! Why not? Could it have the forms we know from sailors' tales and legends? Possibly. Therefore, the study and search for such forms of aquatic life on Earth make sense, because we can also find them in space! As proof, I will cite an interesting account of the Close Encounters of the Zero Kind, which took place in Puerto Rico:

At the same Valle de Lajas farm, in 2012 at different times where the above ominous encounter took place, other workers reported encountering strange blonde women who sometimes approached the witness but did not allow anyone to approach them. They are described as being very tall and pale, with "shiny blonde hair". They are always seen wearing white, flowing tunics or robes that covered their feet and wrists, and which were buttoned around their necks. One night, two farm workers, including a security guard, saw two tall, pale figures of women standing on the path next to one of the barns. They described their hair as very thin "like strands of corn husks" but incredibly beautiful. Every time the men tried to approach the mysterious women, they withdrew, always keeping a very safe distance. One of the witnesses took four steps towards them, and they took four steps back.

One time, one of the men quickly approached, and they suddenly very quickly went sideways down a nearby slope towards a pond. They disappeared completely. According to the witness, they appeared to glide instead of running just above the ground.

Another witness from the area, Mr. Elmer Rivera, employed at the Western Hay Ranch, testified that he was sitting outside the house one night, about 3:00 a.m., enjoying the cool night breeze after a hard day's work. Fog or drizzle also hung over the valley. Suddenly, he noticed two white figures rapidly approaching him in a very strange way. Startled, Elmer stood up and asked who they were, but received no answer as strange figures continued to approach him. Concerned for his safety, Elmer armed himself with a pistol with only blanks and fired several shots over the figures' heads, asking them to stop. According to Elmer, these figures moved away at incredible speed, they did not run, but they hovered terribly close to the ground. They kept their legs stiff and straight. They disappeared in the vicinity of the pond. Elmer also testified that he had seen disc-shaped objects maneuvering over the area on various occasions.

What do you think? Another interesting fact from Crimea given by Dr. **Anton Anfalov**:

The famous bard, **Sergei Kurochkin**, director of the House of Culture and Recreation in Balaklava, on a September afternoon in 2020, was kayaking near the high rocks of Cape Aja (Ayya – N 44°25'38" – E 033°39'23") and in a place called "The Lost World" he saw three huge "people" standing on stones. Two of them were real giants, measuring 5 meters tall, and the third was about 2 meters tall (maybe it was a young man?). They wore tight-fitting silvery-blue jumpsuits, flippers on their legs, and webbed hands. Seeing the boat, they jumped off the cliff into the sea, entering the water without splashing.

And another interesting incident from the summer of 1997:

Diesel tractor operator **Vasily Ivanovich** was sitting on the rocky shore of the Black Sea near a large shoal under a desolate rock ledge east of Cape Aja. He prepared a few fishing lures, threw them into the water and watched them carefully. Suddenly, to his amazement, about 10 meters from the shore, he clearly saw two giants or giant humanoid beings with large heads. The giants were over three meters tall. The giant was talking among himself in some unknown language. Vasily could hear their speech and words, but he could not find any resemblance to any known human language. The giants slowly swam along the shore and talked to each other near the rocks. On their feet, Vasily noticed some kind of fins or fins. Both giants were dressed in shiny metallic silvery suits, tightly fitting to their huge bodies. Their eyes were larger than those of humans. Vasily was stunned and could not move for about 15 minutes, staring fearfully at the two floating giant figures. The humanoids were sailing towards Cape Aja and eventually disappeared from view. Apparently, they did not notice the terrified witness. As the giants disappeared behind the rocks, Vasily regained consciousness, grabbed his fishing gear, and fled back to the resort.

Cʒ

# CHAPTER 9. SIRENS REVEALED?

## 9.1. Beluga's smile

Scholars have explained why sailors occasionally encounter Mermaids, Water Nymphs, Naiads, Water Nymphs, Oceanids...

It is interesting to know where the legends about sea temptresses came from? Who do the sailors really meet? There are small cetaceans called belugas or beluga whales. Incredibly, but they are really similar to the Mermaids. In fact, it is one of the cetacean species.

*Beluga whale smile (Wikipedia)*

The Arctic beluga whale (*Delphinapterus leucas*) is an animal with a very interesting appearance that is hard to forget. They communicate with each other through sounds, as well as facial expressions – which allows them to maintain their status as very intelligent creatures. They are easy to tame and are widely shown in dolphinariums around the world.

The first mention of the Sirens as animals of flesh and blood, and not sea goddesses or their servants, can be found in the Spanish chronicle "Speculum Regale" from the 12th century.

With the development of shipping, the number of relations increased. And so, **in 1492,** Christopher Columbus noted that Mermaids „with rooster plumage and male faces" live on the coast of Cuba.

The famous sailor and geographer **Henry Hudson** (after whom a bay in Canada, a river and a strait are named), sailing near Novaya Zemlya, wrote in his ship's log:

This morning one of my companions looked overboard and saw the Siren. He started calling out to the others and another one came. The mermaid came very close to our ship and looked at them carefully...

After a while, the wave turned her on her back. From her navel up, her back and breasts were like a woman's... She had white skin, long black hair hanging from behind, and the underside of her body ended in a tail like that of a porpoise or a dolphin, but shiny like a mackerel. She was seen by the following sailors: **Thomas Heels** and **Robert Reinar**. Date: June 15, 1608.

*Isn't she like a woman?*

Well described? Could something like that happen, do sailors see such mermaids? By the way, despite the fact that beluga whales spend most of their time getting their own food (up to 16 hours a day), they are extremely playful animals.

Scientists have established that in addition to sounds, white whales are also characterized by touching two individuals.

In this way, they show their friendly attitude to each other, and touch is also used in the love game.

And also, about sailors. Perhaps the stress of being at sea for a long time and the influence of rum makes them see what they would like to see. Perhaps, but excess rum is out of place here: work and service at sea requires absolute sobriety, so the vision of drunken sailors is rather inadequate here.

## 9.2. In my opinion...

I agree with the author of the above article that beluga whales can resemble mermaids under certain conditions as we imagine them. OK, but then what about the creatures from legends, whose place is in inland waters that have no connection to the sea? And yet the Water Nymphs were seen there too!

I know from experience that seals can also resemble people in specific conditions: night, fog, lighting... This could have been the origin of legends about people's encounters with mermaids, but was it only? There are many indications that this is not the only one. Of course, "real scientists" claim that this is impossible and that Sirens do not exist and never have been. OK, so where did so many legends about the People of the Ocean come from?

**In his stories, Daniel Laskowski** puts forward a breakneck hypothesis: *Mermaids are the result of genetic experiments conducted in Atlantis. Their goal was to conquer the ocean by humans. It sounds unbelievable, but when you think* *about it, it's not that unbelievable. Opponents of the existence of the highly developed civilization of Atlantis claim that there are no traces of their technical devices. Yes, there are none, because they were not searched for. However, there are artefacts – e.g. the so-called Rhodes calculator – with which we do not know what to do. Besides, it is not at all said that the Atlanteans created a civilization like ours. They could, above all, use natural sources of renewable energy, geothermal energy, etc., and their civilization went in the direction of the development of biological sciences and was biological, not technical like ours. This is a fundamental difference. That is why this whole menagerie, which we know from Greek mythology and other peoples of the world, could have been created in Atlantis in order to perform certain works for its creators. After the destruction of Atlantis, Mu, Lanka, only strange hybrids remained of them, which were later killed. I think that Laskowski's hypothesis defends itself quite well! I present three of his sci-fi stories to the reader in the last three chapters of this book.*

And coming back to the Sirens, I think that they are only one link in a long chain of riddles from our Past, to which the "real" science has so far capitulated, so it ignores or ridicules them. Until then. There has never been a shortage of titled idiots in scientists' robes, but fortunately they will die out, as well as the pseudo-scientific nonsense they preach.[11]

*Merry children of the World Ocean...*

## 9.3. The strange fate of Hvaldimir

And *speaking of* beluga whales, recently the world has been told by the story of a beluga whale named **Hvaldimir**, which strangely found itself in one of the Norwegian ports. This is how **Sebastian Przybył** describes it:

*An Arctic beluga whale named Hvaldimir was not a spy for the Kremlin, according to the BBC. The tame animal was*

---

[11] Source -*https://obaldela.ru/tak-vot-pochemu-moryaki-inogda-vidyat-rusalok-eti-foto-obyasnyayut-srazu-vse-sushhestvuyushhie-domysly-2-video/* Also see- *https://youtu.be/WGPynVr9qsI*

*found a few years ago off the coast of Norway with a mysterious camera holder and a caption, indicating the Russian origin of the device. New facts about the cetacean were provided by Dr. **Olga Szpak**, who obtained information about the mammal from her former colleagues in Russia. Now she has revealed the details. The Cetacean Hvaldimir was supposed to be a spy for the Kremlin. A Russian researcher refutes the thesis that he was a spy. The history of the beluga whale went around the world in 2019, when it appeared off the northern coast of Norway, as if attacking the boat of local fishermen. - The cetacean began to rub against our boat. I've heard of animals who, when in danger, instinctively knew that when they needed help from humans, they should do it. I thought then that it was a wise cetacean - reported a fisherman who was on board at the time. The locals named it Hvaldimir - from the Norwegian word "hval" meaning whale and the name **of Vladimir Putin**.*

*The presence of the mammal raised eyebrows, as they rarely swim so far south. In addition, the animal was tame and wore a harness and a camera holder with the inscription in English: "Equipment St. Petersburg". It was then that suspicions of her "spying intentions" appeared. The authorities in Oslo took care of the cetacean, which was monitored and fed.*

*The beluga whale was not a Russian spy. Moscow has never confirmed or denied the use of the animal for military purposes. On Wednesday, however, the BBC portal pointed out that this theory was wrong. Dr. Olga Szpak, a Russian cetacean researcher currently working in the West, says that the beluga whale was trained by the Russians, but not to work for intelligence, but to protect a naval base. The Kremlin reacts to the American base in Poland. "Vladimir Putin was right." The expert based this information on her contacts with former colleagues from her homeland, but for security reasons she did not want to disclose the exact sources. The Russian Team, as soon as they heard about Hvaldimir, immediately knew that he was their protégé. The mammal was caught by the Russians in 2013 in the Sea of Okhotsk and then transported to a dolphinarium in St. Petersburg, where it was under the care of trainers and veterinarians from the Arctic military program. However, it happened differently, because the beluga whale was unruly.*

*They suspected that it was a Russian spy. The famous Hvaldimir cetacean has died. The beluga whale protected Russian bases. The animal died in September. After years of living close to humans, Hvaldimir or Andriuch, could not get food on his own. The Norwegians taught the whale this art, which is why the animal began to wander alone along the coast of the Norwegian Sea, also reaching Sweden - it was spotted there, among others, in May 2023.*

*The mysterious death of "Putin's spy". The results of the police investigation are in. Unfortunately, at the beginning of September this year, the Marine Mind organization reported that the famous beluga whale was found dead. One of the residents of the town of Risavika in southwestern Norway noticed the floating body of a cetacean. Environmentalists confirmed the death after reaching the place. Over the past five years, Hvaldimir has touched the hearts of tens of thousands of people, showing them the beauty of nature. His presence taught us about the need to protect the oceans," the group said. Hvaldimir was about 15 years old. The autopsy showed that the cause of death of the cetacean was choking on a stick.*[12]

The sad death of such an intelligent mammal. And by the way, it is extreme villainy to use these beings for the war madness of people supposedly created in the image and likeness of God. I cannot find enough insulting words against the warmongers who harness innocent animals for their nefarious ends.

**℃**

---

[12] Source: *https://wydarzenia.interia.pl/zagranica/news-tajemnicza-bialucha-arktyczna-nie-byla-rosyjskim-szpiegiem-z,nId,7854798#utm_source=paste&utm_medium=paste&utm_campaign=firefox*

# Chapter 10. Three famous sailors saw the Mermaids

Writes **Tomáš Chalupa**. Accounts of the Mermaids Mankind has known forever. **Homer** and **Hans Christian Andersen wrote about them**. They were seen by sailors and sailors, travelers and adventurers. Among them were the most famous: **Henry Hudson, John Smith** and also **Christopher Columbus** himself.

Henry Hudson became famous for being the first to swim across the river to its source. Now this river is called Hudson River and Hudson Bay. During his voyage, which he made in 1608, he wrote in the ship's log that some crewmen reported that Sirens were sailing next to the ship. According to them, they were creatures with breasts like women, but when they submerged under the water, a fish tail could be seen.

Similar observations were also noted by John Smith, a famous captain who sailed on many seas of the world. In 1611, he was sailing near one of the islands of the East Indies, and he saw a woman in the sea swimming in it with indescribable grace. She had long, green hair that was "pretty pretty to him." Surprisingly, he realized that the woman was a waist fish.

It is also not surprising that Christopher Columbus did not avoid meeting these sea girls. Namely, he saw as many as three Mermaids swimming together. It took place on January 9, 1493 on the shores of today's Dominican Republic. According to him, unlike Smith – Mermaids were not half as beautiful as they were described...

The question is not whether the Mermaids were beautiful or not, but who they really were. Specialists agree that famous sailors saw an aquatic animal called a manatee (*Trichechus manatus*). Of course, they have no breasts or green hair, but when they flash in the sea waves, they can remind sailors who have not seen a woman for months of time like a mermaid. After all, sailors in port inns and taverns heard stories about mermaids, while sea wolves did not talk about manatees. Human imagination created these imaginary sea women who have survived to the present day.

*Syrena from Gessner's "Book of Fish"*

In the Israeli coastal city of Kiryat Yam, dozens of witnesses reported sighting a siren swimming in the waves in 2009. It got so far that the city hall offered half a million dollars to anyone who would photograph the Mermaid. Unfortunately, this money has not been paid to anyone to this day, because no one came forward with a photo...[13]

# A handful of comments

Or maybe because people stopped trusting the offices? If someone had photographed Syrena, the offices would have done everything not to pay out this money, because the offices are there to take, not pay. That's one.

Secondly – if the offices had recognized the authenticity of this photo, a precedent would have been created: Mermaids exist, period! – because their existence would have been officially recognized, *ergo* they would have been recognized *de facto* and *de jure*. And this is what "real" scholars are afraid of like the devil of holy water, because they would have to change textbooks and cancel papers in which they proved that they did not exist...

---

[13] Source - Extrastory - *http://extrastory.cz/tri-slavni-moreplavci-historie-hlasili-ze-v-oceanu-spatrili-morske-panny.html?fbclid=IwAR38MRIX8zcUeNZ6e06_6O272F2R78hWxqjBa DKY6Zzws914U7M3P8FAs_M*

And finally – acknowledging the existence of the Sirens puts us in a situation in which we would finally have to confront the fact of the existence of other intelligent beings on our planet, inhabiting almost 3/4 of its surface! And this would be a very serious problem for philosophers, biologists, ethnologists, ethicists, politicians, military officers, and above all lawyers, who would have to adapt our laws to the fact of the existence of a parallel intelligent race in the ocean...

So as you can see from the above – there is a whole ocean in front of us... problems that we would have to solve no longer as individual states or blocs of states, but as Humanity. And it would not be easy. Hence it is obvious that if the problem cannot be solved, it must be ignored – just as in the case of the problem of the existence of UFOs and other strange things of this and not this world.

∞

# Chapter 11. Legendary UAH – do they really exist?

## Myths and legends of the Mermaid

The mermaid is found in folklore all over the world, especially in Asia, Europe, the Middle East, and Africa. The mermaid is a legendary creature: from the waist up she is a beautiful woman, from the waist down she is dressed in beautiful fish scales. Her whole body is beautiful and attractive, but thanks to it, she can escape quickly and easily. According to tradition, they do not have a soul like the sea, it is merciless, deceptive, vain, beautiful and cruel, experiencing love and despair, and many other feelings. Is this image true or false?

The latter images are of the mermaid supposedly caught, and they look too suspicious. There is no data on the circumstances in which these photos were taken.

According to scientists, 95% of things in the oceans are still undiscovered. This is not seen by human eyes. The global ocean is the largest part of the Earth; it covers over 70% of its surface. It is also responsible for regulating temperature and weather conditions around the world. The hydrosphere supports all living organisms on our planet. We saw only 5% of it, but most importantly, how much and where did we not see?

The mermaid, usually classified as a legendary aquatic organism, is characterized by its appearance – its upper body is human, the lower part is a fish tail, and their appearance is very different in general. Sometimes she will transform from a Water Virgo into a different shape. Mermaids, according to legends and fairy tales, emanate beauty, enchanting mainly women. Several studies suggest that in the beginning, the Sirens evolved from Australopithecus and chose an aquatic environment to live. Later, in the course of the development of Humanity, this branch of human evolution was forgotten and lives only in myths and legends.[14]

## Comments from my friends

As the matter seemed interesting to me, and the photos were authentic, although the place and time of their taking were not given, I asked my friends what they thought about it. And I received the following answers:

Eh, authentic mermaids should have nipples on their breasts so that their babies don't starve to death. It's a fake! – **Clas Svahn**, Sweden

---

[14] Source - *http://tw.gigacircle.com/1274658-1*

Thank you for the interesting photos and information. You brought up an old topic again. It is very important. Mermaids are our dream. This beautiful face reminds us of the beauty of the body. These photos show the entire Syrena and its fragments. They were made to show someone. They are astounding. But these photographs are not scientific if it is the body of a living being. In order to ensure scientific accuracy, zoom images should be taken showing the structure of the skin, the connection between both parts of the body and the tail, etc. – **Kiyoshi Amamiya,** Japan

This is a piece of decoration from the movie "Pirates of the Caribbean - On Uncharted Waters." (2007), see - *http://vk.com/wall-40188769_2251* - **Chen Li**, Tajwan

The photo is probably a fake, but well done, but just like you I believe in the existence of Mermaids and Water People, so I won't be surprised if one day someone finally takes a photo of a real Mermaid... - **Daniel Laskowski**, Great Britain

I checked on the website given to me by Chen Li and indeed – it is only a vision of the Mermaids from the film he mentioned. But like Daniel Laskowski, I believe in the existence of Water People and I will not let go of this matter as long as I can... - **Robert Leśniakiewicz**, Poland

**CR**

# CHAPTER 12. MERMAIDS – NOT SO BEAUTIFUL AT ALL!

*He walks by the water, he carries a wrong step,*
*With erroneous eyes he shoots:*
*Then the wind roared through the dense forest,*
*The water is storming and swelling.*
*It is storming, swelling, bursting sinks,*
*Oh, unheard-of phenomena!*
*Above the silvery Świtezi meadows*
*Virginal beauty squirts.*
*Her face, like a pale rose,*
*Sprinkled with a tear of dawn:*
*As a light fog, so light clothes*
*A blue figure was overflowing.*
Adam Mickiewicz – „Świtezianka"

Mermaids or Water Nymphs have been a very rewarding subject of stories by sailors, sailors, various researchers and novelists for centuries. They all describe creatures very similar to humans, most often female, with a fish or dolphin fin instead of lower limbs. Adam Mickiewicz depicted her as a complete beauty. Where did these legends about them come from? Or maybe there is some truth in them? – these are the questions asked by **Filip Appl**, the author of the following text.

## 12.1. Already the ancient Romans...

In different cultures, they have different names – Mermaid, Mermaid, Rusalka, Ningen, Kaaiman. When we turn to written sources, we find that the testimonies of their existence go very deep into history. As early as the first century AD, the Roman philosopher **Pliny the Elder** (23-79) writes about them about women with fish bodies who were found dead on the seashore.

*"I have this information from one soldier – a horseman, who says that he saw a sea man near Cadiz,"* he wrote. Such beings are also described by the Jewish rabbi **Shlomo Yitzchaki** (1040-1105) in the 11th century, or the English scholar **Bartholomeus Anglicus** (1203-1272) in the 13th century. The latter, admittedly, has somewhat departed from romantic descriptions and claims that the specimen found on the shores of Greenland is some kind of monster with a menacing face. Perhaps he was the closest to the truth?

# 12.2. Are African authorities also aware of them?

The number of witnesses is increasing in later centuries, and there are a number of well-known personalities. Mermaids were also observed by the Genoese navigator Christopher **Columbus** (1451-1506) and the English explorer **Henry Hudson** (1570-1611). A number of data come from the 19th and 20th centuries, for example, in 1947 a Scottish fisherman stated that he had seen the Mermaid near the shore. In 2008, a similar creature appeared near the village of Suubraak in South Africa.

- This character was identified as the legendary Kaaimana – half man – half fish. She was white in color, had long black hair and red eyes , wrote New Zealand journalist **Aldo Pekeur**. But the strangest case took place in 2012. Authorities in Zimbabwe also claim that the Sirens harass workers working on construction sites on dams on rivers. Was it someone's invention or further proof of the existence of these strange creatures?

## 12.3. Ghost or manta?

The Japanese people of the sea have their great experience with the Sirens, or rather with creatures called Ningen, which may be at the foundation of the legends of the Sirens. It all started in the 90s on the first Internet discussion forums, where Ningen were mentioned by sailors returning from sea voyages. They describe a large creature resembling a human in appearance, with limbs ending in fingers or fins, and having a nose and two small eyes on its face.

According to some cryptozoologists, the Ningens could be not only what is behind the legends of the Sirens, but also a Japanese spirit or an undersea UFO – USO or UAO.

*"There is also speculation that it could be a previously unknown species of a large, albino ray ray – manta ray,"* adds American cryptozoologist **Rob Morphy**. Could it be that it is only about observing some yet unknown species of aquatic creature?[15]

## 12.4. Feedback from the Space Contact Club

I also recommend

*https://zmiennoksztaltne.blogspot.com/2012/04/wodne-czarodziejki-czyli-obserwacje.html?fbclid=IwAR0ERbHv71r12ATfz677oV2xM*

---

[15] Source – Enigma Plus - *https://enigmaplus.cz/morska-panna-ke-krasce-z-pohadek-ma-nejspis-daleko/?fbclid=IwAR39cSZGMmCXQ777M6zio8V-nTRGw057reXgAfiWYFhcLTqta8PqAphRjEs*

_TRxnCFH1FGNt_NP4HafUM_VmqDq6mTOMyM_
(**Krzysztof Dreczkowski**)

Very interesting material, also by Krzysztof Dreczkowski. It seems to me that Sirens are real beings that really exist in the ocean, and I wrote about it in my literary blog some time ago. Best regards! (**Daniel Laskowski**)

☙

# CHAPTER 13. THE CORPSE OF THE MERMAID WAS FOUND

Author **Neil Genzlinger** writes: As if we didn't have enough beings to worry about. All over the world, people are looking for Bigfoot, chasing ghosts, looking for aliens. And now we'll have to add the Sirens to it, but...

Finally, we will take this information "The mermaid's corpse has been found" seriously. We should not do this. Screened on Saturday night on Animal Planet, the film is part of Monster Week – a fictional story based on facts and made into a documentary. If the reader knows these basic rules, he will watch it like watching the horror film "The Blair Witch Project".

This film, made by **Charlie Foley,** begins with the real fact that it is suspected that US Navy ships using sonar systems cause whales to escape to shore. By the way, underwater sounds known as Bloops were recorded, which were recorded in the Pacific Ocean in 1997.

*CE3 with the Siren ("Secret of the 20th Century")*

That is why in the movie "Mermaids" two well-known scientists are shown who want to show and tell us about secret government investigations aimed at proving the existence of the Mermaids. They say cetaceans aren't the only ones washing up on shore; two boys in Washington state filmed something else with a cell phone camera before authorities tracked them down and forced them into silence. Also, the remains found in the entrails of a shark caught in South Africa were decidedly mermaid-shaped.

An expert using these remains to reconstruct the Mermaid, who – unfortunately – is not as beautiful as **Ariel** from the Disney movie and does not have her flowing, long, red hair. But the public is not able to meet this model, because it is – as usual in such cases – secret.

"I feel like I'm a hero from Orwell's books," Paul, one of the scholars says with regret, "it was Big Brother, they copied the story exactly. This creature should not exist.

Mr. Foley finds a way to give us a hypothesis like the one about the expansion of aquatic apes, which assumes that human evolution split into two phases: one of them remained on land, the other went to seek happiness in the oceans. And – of course – the hypothesis about the reality of the existence of the Sirens has been supported by cultural references for centuries.

"Greek sailors described them," says the narrator in the film, "just like the Vikings, just like the Chinese during their long periods of exploration of the oceans. Records of meetings with them can be found in medieval manuscripts and even in the 19th century. So let's watch our beaches during the summer holidays, even though sonar exercises have scared them away.[16]

## 13.2. There is such a possibility, but...

The existence of a parallel intelligent race in the oceans of our planet would not surprise me at all. After all, it covers almost 3/4 of the planet's surface – 361 million $km^2$ to be precise, and its volume is 1.3 $Em^3$, or 1.3 x 1018 $m^3$ of aqueous solution of various salts and other chemical compounds. It is the largest

---

[16] Source - http://tv.nytimes.com/2012/05/26/arts/television/mermaids-the-body-found-on-animal-planet.html,
http://animal.discovery.com/videos/mermaids-world-premiere.html

environment of living beings on the planet, so why should not Reason develop in it?

The hypothesis of two parallel species (the aquatic ape hypothesis) makes sense, but whether it was? - it's hard to say. For now, there is no evolutionary evidence in favor of this hypothesis. That is why I think that there is one more possibility, namely – the Sirens were bred by genetic manipulation during the reign of one of the previous civilizations (Atlantis, Atlantic), which – attention! – wanted to conquer the ocean. It is not without reason that Plato wrote that Atlantis was dedicated to the god of the seas – Poseidon! The Atlanteans, as islanders, were naturally interested in the conquest of the Blue Continent and, consequently, in all means leading to this goal... Of course, this is just a hypothesis and nothing more.

But remember, Reader, Greek mythology or the mythology of Egypt, Assyria, Babylon, China, India, Japan, or the Americas in general. There are creatures that are hybrids of humans and various animals – which can be seen especially in Egypt. Were they not creatures artificially bred to achieve various goals of their creators? Did the Atlanteans not focus on the development of nuclear technologies (because they were up to their noses with geothermal energy), but on the development of biotechnology? Why not? Therefore, they did not have to mine anything and therefore there are no traces of mining activity. Only at the end did they start looking for uranium ores – hence the traces of mining these ores in Gabon, in the USA and in several other places in the world...

I think it would be worth considering such an approach to the mystery of Atlantis and its inhabitants.

## 13.3. And yet they exist!?

And the sensational news: The sea washed up the corpse of a mermaid! The Englishman **Paul Jones** found a dead "mermaid" by the sea. Judging by the images, the body discovered in Great Yarmouth (N 50°35'58" - E 001°43'41") is in an advanced state of decomposition. An unusual find was discovered on the shore of the North Sea in Norfolk County.

Not all commentators on the photos are convinced of the veracity of the discovery. There are accusations, m.in, of deliberately planting *a plastic skeleton with garbage bags pulled over the feet.*

Paul Jones also posted a video with the find on FB. You can see how the fin of the "mermaid" whirrs in the wind.[17]

---

[17] Show.
*https://www.facebook.com/100010512005438/videos/pcb.3076132695990 71/307611456265919/?type=3&theater*

If you look through Paul Jones' profile on FB, it is easy to see that he builds various Halloween spooks. Did you hope the mermaid was real?[18]

## 13.4. My comment

And yet it is not as funny as someone thinks, because there are many indications that Mermaids are not just a myth, but real, living beings inhabiting the ocean. Stories about them have been present in all cultures of the world and have been since time immemorial. So there is no need to laugh. Something like this can happen at any time and on any beach of our seas and oceans, and even inland waters.

After all, let's not forget that it is the Mermaid that is in the coat of arms of the capital of our country, and the legend about it is the founding myth of Warsaw!

**ରେ**

---

[18] Source - *http://www.o2.pl/galeria/a-jednak-istnieja-morze-wyrzucilo-zwloki-syreny-6044303377183361g/5*

# CHAPTER 14. UNDER FIRE OF CRITICISM

On March 25, 2014, I received an e-mail from the editors of "Unknown World", in which I read a letter from one of the readers, and it read as follows:

Dear editors,

I have been reading your monthly almost from the beginning and I come across various aspects of phenomena unknown to science. But please, for all the saints' sake, don't make fun of serious people by posting texts like "Mermaids in the Darkness of the Ocean End." I am literally terrified of Robert Leśniakiewicz's attitude, if not stupidity.

Well, the film, which the author uses so abundantly and excites about, was a provocation and a mystification. Such fake documentaries (so-called mockumentaries) are created, but at the very beginning the viewers are informed that these events are not true!! Below I attach some explanations and corrections of Animal Planet. Many people fell for it, but I would not suspect that Mr. Leśniakiewicz and you. The contents and alleged images and evidence contained in it were FORGERIES.

Geez, I'm really embarrassed to see something like this in the Unknown World. In an unknown world. [...] And Mr. Leśniakiewicz should be called to the carpet or should post a correction. And this is not the first time that he writes nonsense read on the Internet [...]

Here's how to do it:

http://www.dailymail.co.uk/news/article-2333515/Mermaid-hoax-How-mockumentary-gave-Animal-Planet-biggest-audience-EVER.html

http://articles.latimes.com/2013/may/30/entertainment/la-et-st-animal-planet-mermaid-hoax-special-record-ratings-20130530

http://www.businessinsider.com/animal-planets-mermaids-mockumentary-2013-5

http://abcnews.go.com/blogs/entertainment/2013/05/mermaids-mocumentary-stirs-big-ratings-for-animal-planet/

M. M.

Out of pity, I give only the initials of the author of this epistle. He is another "critic" whose attitude, and above all his lack of knowledge and imagination, also terrifies me. Let him watch one more movie about mermaids from the "Month with Beasts" series on Animal Planet, where, however, it turns out that not everything is a hoax and an invention. The AP has even broadcast it several times recently. So let this gentleman watch this film before he passes judgment on my stupidity. The films in question can be found on the Internet at:

U1 "Mermaids - Legend or Truth" [2012] "Mermaids the Body Found"

click *http://whitedevas.eu/?p=1485* online movie with voice-over (first window with the film), and

Part 2 "Mermaids - Mermaids the New Evidence" [2013] "Mermaids the New Evidence", it is online, but only with the original language track, click

*http://www.youtube.com/watch?v=OVhYo41FOY8*.

That's one.

Secondly - if the existence of the Sirens is stupidity and lies, because it was said so on the Internet, then all the accounts collected over the centuries - according to the author of this email - are also stupidity and lies? It's a pity that he didn't bother to read accounts of the Sirens and other creatures inhabiting the ocean, because then he wouldn't have written such authoritative words of criticism. Well, but this is his rogue right. Speaking *of* the Internet - since it contains only nonsense, it is logical that the denials contained in it, to which Mr. M. refers, are also stupid - in accordance with his logic. Colloquially speaking - referring to the Internet is a stick that has two ends. I think that Mr. M. should ask himself a fundamental question: if the existence of the Sirens is fairy tales and lies, why are such films made? What is their purpose? Ridiculing someone and something?

Or maybe just the opposite – telling the truth under the guise of mockery and mockery?

If Mr. M. had watched both videos on the AP channel, he would have known that scientists dealing with this issue were and are being dissected by the special services, which has been said clearly and several times. Just like m.in ufologists who dug up the truth about UFOs and several other interesting things and events. What does that mean? Namely, that forcing the special services to publish on the Internet materials showing the falsity of what was shown in these films is a piece of cake for them and is then a "proof" of the "truth" for such critics by the grace of God. And this is exactly what the services are after - obscuring and obscuring the truth with the help of the so-called "agents of influence" and "useful idiots". And why do the services do it? - It is obvious: they see it as a threat to national security and want to use it for their own purposes - most often and above all against other people. And it would be good if this truth – unfortunately the truth which I have often touched upon – would finally reach those who write various pamphlets and lampoons directed against those who want to reach the truth.

Therefore, there will be no correction. Simply because these creatures do exist, AGAINST THE WILL OF SOME PEOPLE AND SERVICES. And there is evidence for this, which I have already written about in the pages of "Unknown World", and which, as you can see, Mr. M. has not read. It was, m.in, about Mermaids from Japan and the United States. But I was convinced above all by Albert Rosales' materials, which were also published by me on the pages of "Unknown World".

And as for putting me on the carpet - hmmm, what a nice memory from "times rightly past", which I remember with fondness...

# CHAPTER 15. WATER PEOPLE

*Is there makani hema pa*
*The Manua of Kanoli Ikea*
*A kanaka ke kauahiwihoopii*
Clive Cussler – "Hawaiian Vortex"[19]

At the beginning of 2000, the first TVP program broadcast a collection of several amateur films under the common title "Undisclosed Secrets" produced in a French-German co-production. It is a set of seven films dealing with the disappearances of people that cannot be explained in any way by the known laws of physics.

Particularly interesting were the documentary records that concerned the sea. It was primarily about the mysterious disappearances of people by the sea, in the beach zone or from boats in the open ocean, and the paranormal nature of some of the presented cases could be discussed. The disappearance of a survivor from a lifeboat. In the video, we see a survivor of a Soviet ship that broke down and sank in

---

[19] When the south wind blows

Mount Kanoli seems to be visible

And the peak seems to be populated.

the Indian Ocean. We see a castaway who lives for days, in the tropical sun and in an open boat. Finally, he puts the camera on something and jumps into the water himself, swimming away into the distance, to finally disappear. It can be explained by the dysfunction of the victims' mental strength after a 40-day stay in an open lifeboat on the high seas, without water and food (another thing is that theoretically a person had no chance of surviving in such a psychophysical state and in such weather conditions for so many days). What did he see? – We don't know... Perhaps it was some kind of UFO or USO?

As for the diver from *the Zodiac*, he was kidnapped from an open pontoon during exercise by... - Well, by whom? It could have been the action of foreign (read: Soviet) special services, which – again theoretically – kidnapped (for what?) a diver of the NATO armed forces (such things did not happen). But what for? it is indisputable, however, that the diver was found on the beach AFTER a WEEK alive, but in such a condition that he had to be taken to a psychiatric hospital.

A real sensation in the good sense of the word turned out to be a film made by an anonymous American soldier stationed in Sicily. While the two cases mentioned above can be explained somehow, this one is a real mystery.

Here we see two beings in his film: a young woman in a swimming suit from the 1940s and a boy aged 10-12, who emerge from the waves, walk along the beach for a while, and then slowly enter the water and hide under its surface in an upright posture. What happened to them next – no one knows. Probably the American wanted to find out, and... Exactly – and he began to act irrationally. He puts his notebook and sweatshirt next to the film camera, and then, in his trousers and shoes on his feet – just like THEM, he enters the water in an upright posture – which is recorded by his film camera... Thanks to it, we see that the young man walks as if hypnotized into the depths of the Mediterranean... - and does not return from it – neither alive nor dead.

The whole sequence – let's face it – makes an extraordinary impression. It is especially about the abnormality of the situation; On the one hand, the incredible tranquility of the landscape: a sunny beach, clear sea, gentle waves, and on the other, footprints on the sand slowly washed away by the water. Normal traces of normal people...

So what happened on a Sicilian beach on August 18, 1943? Who or what did the young American see in the water near St. Antonio? Why is it that the battle-hardened soldier of the 7. General **Patton**'s Army did not make any note in his notebook (relying only on the film camera) – which he should have done, since the whole situation interested him so much that he decided to follow in the footsteps of the Beings...?

The answer to this question was once given by **Clive Cussler**, writing about an artificially bred race of human beings adapted to life in the oceans. Similarly, **Aleksandr Belyaev,** when creating the character of **Ichtiander,** pointed to the possibility of artificially adapting *Homo sapiens sapiens* to the aquatic environment. This topic has been exposed by many SF authors. The only question that remains open is whether such creatures appear only in SF novels?

*Ichthiander – a man with shark gills from A. Belyaev's novel (still from the film "Amphibian Man")*

If so, then Homer should undoubtedly be the precursor of all such fantasy writers. After all, it was he who described in the "Odyssey" the beautiful Sirens that lured sailors to their doom with their singing. Only the cunning king of Iraq – **Ulysses** called **Odysseus** managed to outwit them in a relatively simple way: he plugged the ears of his companions with wax stoppers, and he himself tied himself to the mainmast... - and survived this experiment. In light of what critics and researchers of Odysseus" migration routes later wrote; the Sirens inhabited the southeastern coast of Sicily. It was precisely there, where in the summer of 1943 the American 7. A and the British 8. A that drove the Germans and Italians away from *il Duce*.

But not only that, because the entire world mythology seems to suggest that the entire ocean is densely populated with various sea goddesses, to mention here the daughter of the king of the Baltic Sea, who was murdered in Trzęsacz and buried in the parish cemetery. Bałtyk claimed the earthly remains of its daughter – **Zielenica** – and washed the cliff shore with the parish church and the cemetery so that only the southern wall of the church remained there...

In the Mediterranean Sea lived the **Nereids** – the daughters **of Nereus** – an old man who always spoke the truth. Mermaids were also said to live in the cold and inhospitable seas of the North, frightening the sailors there: Slavs, Normans and Vikings.

And people can see them even today. And so, in the summer of 1890, a Scottish schoolteacher saw a mermaid in the sea near Caithness. In 1403, near Edam in the Netherlands, fishermen managed to capture the Mermaid, who later lived 15 years in Haarlem and then died. It was buried in a Christian way, but the sea claimed it and flooded the Dutch lowlands and depressions. On June 15, 1625, sailor **Henry Hudson** saw the Siren somewhere in the Atlantic. In a word, reports of encounters with strange aquatic creatures are recorded in all bodies of water in the ocean, and in fact, there is no place on Earth where their appearance has not been observed... Because they are also freshwater creatures!

And in our country? Of course, everyone knows the legend of the Warsaw Mermaid and the daughter of the King of the Baltic Sea, as well as of Świetlan from the Szczecin Lagoon. And yet in the waters of our rivers there are also Drowners – which, according to folk tales, drag people into the depths and drown...

Could it be that Drowners, Mermaids, Nereids mean different names for the same phenomenon? Well, the depths of the waters, and especially the oceans, are equally unexplored, less than the surface of the Moon! It is no coincidence that the topic of Water People returns so often in various cultures and civilizations. What is behind them? That is the question...

* * *

I wrote these words in 2000 and appeared in „Nieznany Świat" No. 8/2000 pp. 16-17, when it naively seemed to me that science would move forward and this puzzle would be solved in the near future. Unfortunately, nothing could be further from the truth! Science has sidelined the problem, and the question marks remain – nay! – there are even more!

The problem of Water People is marginalized, but only for a while, because as man penetrates more and more widely in the ocean, or sooner or later, inevitably there will be a meeting with these creatures and – what I fear most – a confrontation with the riches of the bottom of the ocean: metal ores, oil and natural gas, methane hydrates, biological resources and others. And I would not like the grim prophecy and warning of **Frank Schätzing**, which he included in his mare-like novel "The Revenge of the Ocean" (Wrocław 2006), and which I recommend to those interested in this issue, to come true. In any case, when you are on holiday hikes by the sea, look around carefully – maybe you will see a Water Virgo basking in the sun? And even if we fail, it is worth looking around for Baltic seals and porpoises, whose population is being rebuilt with such difficulty!

Water nymphs, mermaids – these are some of the most famous mythical personalities in our environment. Have you ever dreamed of becoming a mermaid with a fish tail and singing to yourself while sitting on a seaside stone? We wanted to believe in their existence so much that we believe in various mystifications, in which the Water Nymphs are supposedly pulled out of the water, but we give our imagination another chance.

ଔ

# CHAPTER 16. HOAXES

## 16.1. Old Skeleton

One of the most popular hoaxes is an old mermaid skeleton found on a beach in Sazabol, Bulgaria. According to experts, these remains date back to the time of Noah's Flood. Perhaps these remains convinced someone to the existence of the Water Nymphs, but people who thought a little more critically quickly grasped what and how. First of all, the assumed tail of the skeleton turned out to be a fake, and the photo showed a completely different skeleton from a different excavation zone. And in addition, the professor in the photograph was openly and not very skillfully "photoshopped". This photo is still circulating on social networks thanks to those who fell for it.

In addition, there is a whole series of artistic photographs entitled "Archaeological Finds 2013", in which there is a photo taken by artists who decided to bring the imaginary characters to life. And someone on the Internet decided to create an image of m.in. Rusalka and began to convince that these are real archaeological finds.

## 16.2. On a British beach

If photography is not enough to convince people of the existence of Mermaids, there are better ways to do it. At first glance, this "something" looks quite realistic, but the other way around. These photos were taken by a man named **Paul Jones** on a beach in the UK and posted on Facebook. The photos show a human body with a fish tail, but let's take a closer look at this mysterious picture. Look at the tail, which looks as if it was glued together from rubbish.

Of course, such a find could not be missed by the representatives of the media. However, those who saw it with their own eyes admitted that it was just a dead kitten. But those who believe certainly have no idea that Paul Jones is involved in the production of installations depicting mythical heroes, so this Rusalka became his next project. It was enough for him to take a photo to make it popular.

## 16.3. After the hurricane

Be more careful in your faith. With each passing year, video becomes more and more interesting and varied thanks to the use of more and more sophisticated F/X. Look, for example, at this video made by an anonymous author. According to its creator, it was taken down after the hurricane, but the beach looks quite calm and many people walked on it, as for the place where the hurricane passed. Rusalka herself looks as if she had been lying in the sun for a long time and had not put sunburn cream on herself. In addition, there should be a lot of different types of rubbish on the beach if a hurricane passes there

It's just a mannequin and its hair say so – it seems like the ocean didn't even tangle it. So, you can see that it is simply a wig. We give the author what he deserves for creativity, but Rusalka herself is unbelievable.

## 16.4. The cave

The man, known only by his *nickname* **Suertemalasuerte**, published a video in 2016 that he took while diving in Kankun, Mexico. When he swims underwater, he sees the silhouette of a creature that is half like a human and a fish from half. In the description of his video, he states that he filmed a real Mermaid. The video is indeed interesting, but it is too good to be true. There were a few more people with him in the cave, but he was the only one with the camera. How convenient! It would be good to determine where this provision came from and who is its real author.

Also in this case, we can say with conviction – it was not a Water Nymph. People who watched the video carefully said that it was just a girl who put her tail on her feet. There is interest in Mermaids in the world and it is not difficult to find such a tail. The girl in the video is called **Melissa** and she plays the Mermaid professionally. It turns out that this author simply stole the video from her YT channel.

## 16.5. Like in the cinema

Without looking at the huge amount of information we can get with one click, people turn out to be naïve as never before. It is even easier to deceive us through the excess of information. When you receive another photo or video with Rusalka from your friend, you simply enter its name into the search engine and she will show you the original, usually the photo that turns out to be the original one. One such photo turned out to be a still from the movie "Pirates of the Caribbean", but every time this photo is shown, people believe that they are real mermaids. For the sake of fairness, it must be added that these Water Nymphs look very likely and you have to give it to their creators.

## 16.6. Inspection of the cave

It was not only Mexican caves and *cenotes* that became the site of probable mermaids – this incident happened in the Philippines. In the frames of the photos, next to the divers, we see the silhouette of Rusalka, then in other frames we no longer see her, so that it was impossible to establish contact with her. Near the caves there is a hill called the Throne of the Mermaids (Sirena Trono/Trono de Sirena) and this is where Rusalka probably sat. Someone decided to verify this story and went to the scene, but found nothing.

## 16.7. The Zimbabwe incident

In 2017, two children drowned in Zimbabwe. This happened when they were chasing cattle past the dam. They supposedly saw a fish in the water and decided to catch it when the Water Nymph dragged them into the water. According to witnesses, she caught them and dragged them under the water, when the bodies of the children who were no longer breathing were pulled ashore, information appeared on the Zimbabwean information website with the same photo of the Water Nymphs from "Pirates of the Caribbean". In addition, the presence of Sirens was often observed in this zone.

And although everyone talks about the authenticity of this event, no one talks about the still from the film.

## 16.8. The Buffeljags River

Not too far from the town of Suurbraak, South Africa – Western Cape, flows the Buffeljags River. In its deep waters – as rumors say – it is common to see Water Nymphs and many locals confirm this, and these sightings have taken place during the lifetime of several generations. In January 2008, one of the local residents, **Daniel Coupido**, was relaxing by the water when he heard a splash. Intrigued, he headed in the direction where he heard the splash and saw a woman with long, dark hair. He decided to swim towards her and save her, but when he got closer, he noticed that she had red eyes and fell into a kind of hypnotic trance. His friends swam up and pulled him ashore, so they could see Rusalka.

If this is true, why did the news of such an event not spread around the world? Nevertheless, the locals believe in the existence of Water Nymphs, who appear there once every 10 years.

## 16.9. Activity

Mermaids seem  to appear all over the world and do not inhabit any particular place. Many claim to have seen Water Nymphs in British Columbia, Canada, and one of them was sitting on a rock near the bay. In 1967, passengers on the ship reported seeing a mermaid sitting in the seat eating salmon. A photograph even appeared in the local newspaper confirming this. The story sounded so amazing that one company set up a C$25,000 bounty for catching the Mermaid, but in the end, the whole story turned out to be a humbug. The passengers of the cruise ship had seen Rusalka, but it was a girl in a Mermaid costume. Her name was **Julia Allred**.

## 16.10. The corpse of the Mermaid has been found!

When we watch documentaries, we often see experts with animals or artifacts related to the subject of the film. We usually believe such facts and experts, and if such a video is broadcast on the Animal Planet channel, there is no doubt and there cannot be. And it was this TV channel that managed to fool the whole world thanks to the program "Syrena – the body was found". They showed a film that could convince a hardened skeptic of the existence of Rusalki – but when it turned out that the film was a fake, the channel's rankings plummeted. Then there was a sequel to the film, which could have improved the ratings. Both films featured actors who played experts and scholars. In the film, they talked about the evolution of Sirens from monkeys, m.in.[20]

## 16.11. My 3 cents

A film like a film – I also spoke about it on the pages of "Unknown World" and on this blog. Personally, I am in favor of the fact that there are humanoid creatures in the ocean, which have been seen many times in all its waters. So far, skeptics have not explained where the legends about the Sea People and meetings with them came from, and the fairy tales about drunken sailors longing for women's company are simply pathetic and embarrassing.

But that's how it is – if you can't explain something, you have to ridicule it. And to mock those who have come into contact with this or that phenomenon. I know this very well

---

[20] See also

https://www.youtube.com/watch?time_continue=18&v=OsldQGu6Z90
Source - HTTP://svnovsti.ru/nastyashiye-russalki-snatte-na-video/?utm_source=fb-mypage&utm_medium=fb-mypage-nastyashiye-russalki-snatye-na-video&um;utm_campaign=fb-mypage-nastye-russalki-snatte-na-video

from the times when I dabbled in ufology, when I had discussions on this subject with "real" scientists who were impermeable, petrified scientific concrete. They didn't get any arguments – there is no and that's it, and who claims that they are psychos. And the final. That is why I do not believe in such "explanations", because I know that "scientists" lie.

And so, as if à propos of scientists, I am reminded of a certain professor who – when it was possible to talk about Katyn – said the following: *I wrote 30 papers on Katyn proving that they were Germans (good that they were not Nazis – sic!), and not Russians, so I will not retract it now!*

Yet another luminary of astronomy rejected the very idea of matter exchange between planetary systems...

This is the mentality of "scientists" and "experts", which I leave without comment...

CR

# Chapter 17. Sirens and UFOs

## 17.1. Sirens, an old map and UFOs?

*An old map of America from 1562 shows a siren with a UFO!* – writes **Franco Lioy**. "The New and Most Accurate Description of America or The Fourth Part of the World" – a map made in 1562 by the Spanish cartographer **Diego Gutierrez** and the artist **Hieronymus**. This incredibly detailed map of the American continent consists of six well-folded sheets. It is 93 by 86 centimeters, so it remains the largest map of America in a century. It is the largest Spanish map printed in America before the mid-eighteenth century.

Drawings of parrots, monkeys, and an erupting volcano in Mexico are complemented by numerous sediments, rivers, mountains, and valleys.

The map correctly recognizes the presence of the Amazon and Paraná river basins, Lake Titicaca, the location of Potosi, Mexico, Florida, and several points along the coast. However, in addition to its significance and rich history, this old map illustrates many peculiar things.

In addition to representing cannibals, sea monsters, dragons, and giant sloths from Patagonia, the lower left corner of the map, near Tierra del Fuego, an archipelago at the southern tip of the South American continent, across the Strait of Magellan, illustrates what appears to be a mermaid holding an object resembling a flying saucer.

The mermaid, who stands in front of a ship sailing towards the coast of modern Chile, holds in her right hand an object that strangely resembles a disc-shaped object, with a bright dome protruding from the center.

It looks like what many people would say today is a UFO, a flying saucer.

But is that all it seems? Is it really a flying saucer?

Just above this mermaid, on the right side of the ship that travels to Tierra del Fuego, we see another mermaid looking at the ship and holding an oval object in her left hand. This object may be a mirror, as the mermaid is depicted by touching her hair while viewing what is likely a mirror.

Does this mean that the mermaid holding the supposed flying saucer does the same?

Whatever object the mermaid possesses, it remains a mystery, however, it is really interesting to see such elements on an ancient map of the American continent, as it clearly shows what people could have seen in America more than 500 years ago.

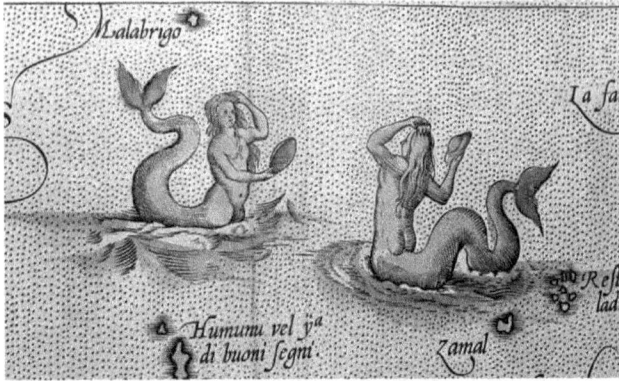

*Sirens and... UFOs?*

## 17.2. Commentary from the CCC

The thing looks really interesting. Perhaps these are mirrors, but the shape of the object held by one of the Sirens is indeed intriguing. The second holds an evident mirror, but what does the lower one hold? This "something" resembles either UAP or... hat? I know many accounts of mermaids, but I don't remember any of them parading around in a hat...

Sirens are representatives of an older underwater civilization, so naturally UFOs, USOs and other such phenomena may be of their origin. We must not omit this. It would be good to look through all the bestiaries of medieval and Renaissance cosmographers, who liked to draw such maps and loved to place images of beings on them, not only the existing ones. But why non-existent? There are thousands of accounts of Close Encounters with Them about the Mermaids, so there is more to it than a cheap fairy tale hatched in someone's half-baked head...

## 17.3. What happened in Shag Harbour?

UFO and USO researchers are puzzled by the incident in Shag Harbour (Canada), which took place in 1967. The incident itself is quite unusual: it looks like we are dealing with a UFO that fell into the water and became a USO – this can be classified as NL/NOTSUB. And this is how Wikipedia describes it:

The Shag Harbour Incident was an unexplained incident involving the impact of a large object on the ocean near Shag Harbour, Nova Scotia, Canada on the night of 4/5 October 1967.

Before midnight, a dozen or so villagers, independently of each other, noticed lights in the sky that had disappeared into the ocean. Thinking they were witnessing a plane crash, they informed the Royal Mounted Police. Despite the lack of information confirming any incidents or failures in the air and on the water, fifteen minutes after the incident, a search operation was launched with the participation of rescue boats and fishing boats.

According to the Library and Archives Canada, the only surviving original official account of the event is a memo made by the Department of National Defence. According to the Department of National Defence, the course of the event was as follows:

The author of the memo reported that on October 4, 1967, a corporal of the Royal Mounted Police (RCMP) and six other witnesses observed an unidentified flying object that descended sharply and then fell into the ocean. After this event, white light remained on the surface of the water. A police officer attempted to reach the facility, but it sank before the officer could reach the scene. The search operation in the air and on the water did not bring any results that could help identify the object.

The rescue operation did not bring any results, so the navy joined the search at the request of the Armed Forces Command in Ottawa. On 9 October 1967, the search operation was completed.

And that's it.

An interesting fact is that recently two grandchildren of the famous ocean explorer – Commander Dr. **Jacques Cousteau** – **Fabien Cousteau** and **Cèline Cousteau** – tried to investigate the case, who went to the site of the Incident and made several dives to the impact site.

They came to the conclusion that the case is indeed interesting, because in the testimonies of the witnesses of the impact, there was information about the surveillance of 6 ZOP escort destroyers, which cooperated with the SOSUS listening station located a short distance from Shag Harbour – on board HMCS *Shelburne*. There were 5 American destroyers and 1 Canadian destroyer, which were to protect this section of the Canadian coast from Soviet submarines.

Unfortunately – during these 55 years since the event, sea currents have erased all traces of him and the siblings have found nothing. Nothing material, but...

After descending to the impact site, at the site of the alleged crater on the seabed, communication problems began. Faddings appeared, and instead of the voices of the expedition participants, some strange sounds could be heard in the helmets, which were tried to be identified as "military transmissions".

Perhaps these were some "military transmissions", it is obvious, but... But they resembled something else, known from the Pacific basins – namely, we are talking about unusual sightings of strange sounds, which are attributed to the Water People.

Well, now there is nothing else to do but focus on those bodies of water where these creatures were observed. Because the Water People robot fits this whole thing best. And I think it's a job for people like the Cousteau siblings. I'm sure their grandfather knew more than he could tell.

But that's a topic from another ballad.

# 17.4. CE0/CE-III-E i B + NL (BOL) in Ukraine

In August 1995, several young men went to the local beach in Nikopol on a hot August day and returned to shore for a while after swimming. There they were stunned to see four beautiful young naked women coming out of the water. The young men asked them if they were nudists, but the answer was silence. They got the impression that the girls did not understand their speech at all, but one of the men knew 3 languages and asked the same question in German, French and English, but the reaction was the same. The girls returned to the water and when they started swimming, the young men noticed that the girls' movements were unnatural, they seemed to "slide" in the water. It also seemed that when they dived into the water, they seemed to stay dry. Strange women exchanged strange sounds resembling whistles. (Like dolphins?)

One of the men decided to approach one of the women and touch her, but when he did, he was hit by something that resembled an electric charge of such force that he was almost thrown 10 meters from the water.

The strange woman turned around, waved her hand and dived easily through several large waves; her friends did the same. Soon they reached the center of the Kakhovskoye water reservoir. Soon it began to rain, and the boys returned to the shore when suddenly a huge, luminous ball of light emerged from the clouds. It sank above the water and began to float directly above the place where the strange women were floating. Moments later, all four women rose to the sphere or were absorbed by the sphere. And then the ball quickly rose and disappeared among the clouds.[21]

## 17.5. My 3 cents

Unfortunately, as in many cases from the territories of the former USSR, there is no exact location of the incident and we are doomed to guesses. This is due to the mental inertia of the citizens of m.in Ukraine, who still believe that the West dreams of nothing else than attacking, robbing, killing, etc. This is the result of the communist brainwashing since 1917 and the historical lies of the nationalists. And that's a pity. Unfortunately, we will face such attitudes for a long time, especially now that there is a war with Russia in Ukraine. The chuckle and irony of history is that the threat there came not from the West, but from the East.

---

[21] Source: RIA "Novosti" (Russian news agency: "News") and "The Fourth Dimension and UFOs", Yaroslavl UFO Research Group Newspaper No. 1995 #11.

As for the CE itself, it is interesting that they were women. Although they did not have fins and tails, they could have been Mermaids – creatures from the Great Ocean that have been repeatedly observed in all the seas and internal waters of the world. After all, why not? If humans have conquered the land, why can't the Water People conquer the oceans?

## 17.6. USO in the Gulf of Mexico

Location coordinates: N 28°1.913' – W 083°4.032' (10 miles west of Caladesi Island, Clearwater Beach, Florida)

"I work on a research vessel. We recently completed a cruise researching bioluminescence in the Gulf of Mexico. Around 11:45 PM, we were conducting normal research when one of the scientific crew members noticed a strange light about a quarter mile off our stern.

We immediately moved towards the light. The intensity of the light was quite astonishing, and no one from the crew or scientific team knew what to make of it. Initially, we thought it was a sunken ship or a navigation buoy that had sunk.

We approached the light as closely as possible and eventually hovered directly over it. Our ship has a deep-sea window in the center, from which the crew and scientific team could observe the light directly from above.

We used a subsurface camera to try and capture what the object was. The team of scientists on board automatically ruled out the light being produced by bioluminescent phytoplankton.

This light source was 100% on the ocean floor, not floating in the water column. It was not moving with the current. The water depth at this particular location was 18 meters. While hovering over the light source, we used an EK-80 sonar to get an image of the ocean floor at that spot.

To our surprise, the object emitting the light had no physical shape that we could detect. It was invisible to our sonar. Sonar is also capable of imaging objects below the seabed (objects that might have been partially submerged in mud) and objects with a length/width of just 90 cm.

Any speculation as to what this object might have been? Consider the intensity of the light, which had to shine through 18 meters of water and was strong enough for us to observe it from a significant distance. There was certainly an arc of visibility that seemed to 'get brighter when viewed from a distance rather than from directly above'."[22]

---

[22] Source: Universe Science Mystery Technology Aliens UFO.

*Mysterious light in the depths of the Gulf of Mexico –*
*witness photo*

# CHAPTER 18. ARE MERMAIDS JUST A SAILOR'S INVENTION?

**Ajka**: If you believe in them, how do you explain their existence?

What do you think – are Mermaids creatures only from legends and fairy tales? Are they the product of the vivid imagination of sailors and old grandmothers? If you believe in them, you can prove your view. In some of the world's museums there are astonishing skeletons that, whether we like it or not, exactly resemble beauties with tail fin for legs.

All the finds we present to you have been the subject of serious scientific research, and they are one hundred percent convinced of their authenticity. And that would mean that all the stories about the Mermaids that we read to our children really come from real events? Did we hurt history when we didn't believe it?

## 18.1. Mermaid from the museum in Copenhagen

In a museum in Copenhagen, Denmark, there is a skeleton of a creature found by a farmer working his field near the village of Haraldskær (N 55°39'27" – E 012°35'31"; 33 m a.s.l.).

Using the radiocarbon method of determining the age, scientists came to the conclusion that there are traces of elements typical of Asian countries in the bones, where this creature was most likely born. This is also confirmed by the shape of her skull. The age of the bones indicates that the girl was about 18 years old and 180 cm tall. When she was found, she had long hair on her head and teeth with clearly sharp incisors in her mouth, with no signs of wear. The skeleton is missing one arm. It is believed that the farmer cut it off during ploughing.

How and when it flowed into Danish waters – this is not known.

*Seal and Mermaid – is there a resemblance? Perhaps many witnesses simply saw seals basking on the shore...*

## 18.2. The Fijian Mermaid

Around 1822, fishermen fished out a strange catch from the coastal waters of the island of Fiji – a man-fish. This creature – half humanoid – half fish, already interested the journalistic community and became the subject of trade on the black market. It changed hands many times, then it was exhibited by various museums. The last one in which the Syrena found herself burned down in mysterious circumstances and the find disappeared. After several dozen years – just as mysteriously – it was found.

This creature is currently on display at the Harvard University Museum of Archaeology and Ethnology in Massachusetts, USA. Specialists believe that this is what the creatures that we call Sirens in legends really looked like. With their seductive voice, they lured sailors to the rocky shallows, where men found cruel deaths.

## 18.3. The Mermaid of India

Another mermaid find is in the Indian city of Chennai/Chennai Madras (Tamiland state, N 13°05'00" – E 080°16'16"), but the museum curator refuses to display it to the public. Not because she is so beautiful... - and quite the opposite. It is not clear who and when fished it out of the sea – it is said that it was washed up on the beach by the tsunami. To this day, it is one of the most controversial exhibits in Indian museums.[23]

$\mathcal{CR}$

---

[23] Prepared on the basis of: _www.pinterest.com_, _www.travelingboomer.com_, _www.wikipedia.org_. Source - _https://zahadnysvet.sk/su-morske-panny-vymysel-ak-tomu-naozaj-verite-ako-by-ste-vysvetlili-toto/_

# CHAPTER 19. NINGEN: SIRENS OF ANTARCTIC WATERS

The author of this material is **Valdis Pejpinš**, who writes about the unusual Sirens of the icy waters of Antarctica. And here is the material.

The leaders in terms of the number of genes turn out to be daphnia – microscopic crays. There are 20-25 thousand genes in the human genome, and over 30,000 in daphnia! More than 1/3 of them have no analogues in other living organisms.

Over the past few years, there have been rumors in Japan about the existence of giant humanoids in the icy waters of Antarctica, which have been named **Ningen**. And although these stories are considered to be another sea legend, the information itself is very interesting.

## 19.1. Discovery of whalers

The story began when a Japanese WWW.2channel.jp forum posted several posts on the Internet with information that a blogger had taken from a friend of his, who in turn worked for the government's whale life research program. This program, called JARPA, was established in 1987, when Japan, under pressure from the International Whaling Commission, stopped industrial whaling in the waters around the Antarctic.

Opponents of JARPA claim that its real goal is to obtain whale meat for supermarkets and restaurants. In fact, the Land of the Rising Sun program kills more than 800 whales in Antarctica and the Pacific Northwest every year. And it is as if whalers disguised as scholars came across huge, mermaid-like creatures in high southern latitudes.

In November 2007, the editors of the Japanese magazine "Mu" devoted to the search for strange phenomena and cryptozoology, published an article on the possibility of the existence of unknown, gigantic cryptids in the waters of the Far South. And this is how this problem saw the light of day.

## 19.2. Whale-like mermaids

The word *Ningen* itself simply means man in translation from Japanese and – as eyewitnesses claim – in fact these creatures are similar to humanoid whales. Their description always includes a face, instead of legs they have a tail, and a whale's tail (with a fin set horizontally), and some also saw arms and hands in them. Those who have managed to observe the Ningen claim that their length is 20-30 m. Their skin is white and completely devoid of pigmentation. Encounters with these humanoids usually took place at night, and were very difficult to photograph. In some photos, Ningen resembles small icebergs, but on enlarged photos they can be seen exactly.

According to the crew of one of the ships who observed Ningen, they initially thought they were seeing a submarine. But when they got closer to it, it turned out that it was an object with a non-streamlined shape and not of artificial origin. The crew saw a huge creature that quickly disappeared under the water.

## 19.3. Were the Witnesses told to be silent?

On the Internet you can find several photographs of the Ningen. Some of them are reconstructions created by painters according to eyewitness accounts. Two extremely low-quality videos posted on YT:

*http://www.youtube.com/watch?v=c5QIMyK5DM0*
and *http://www.youtube.com/watch?v=5f2fUEiXlW0*
and a video from NHK:

*http://www.dailymotion.com/video/xfrmnu_alien-ningen-sighting-sagami-bay-japan-aug-23-2010_news*

in which, it is claimed, these mysterious inhabitants of Antarctica are located. In one of the images, Ningen was photographed from a high altitude in the southern Atlantic Ocean, off the coast of Namibia. As you can see, at a shallow depth is the huge body of a mermaid creature. Experts assess these photos and video recordings as unreliable. It seems that there are no photos with good resolution, or the Japanese have good photos, but they keep them secret, exposing themselves to attacks by cryptozoologists and the resentment of the general public. Conspiracy theorists also claim that the government not only keeps the data on the Ningen people secret, but also gags the witnesses.

Of course, it is premature to make any elaborate elaborations on this subject. Of course, this can be nothing more than a clever deception, for example with the use of a computer Photoshop program, and in this way, you can create such and other urban legends with the help of such fantastic photos. But for now, it cannot be ruled out that the Japanese have indeed discovered some giant cryptids in Antarctic waters. At the same time, they do not have to be humanoids and people simply look for humanoid features, as was the case of the manta ray from the Sea of Azov, which was also attributed with having hands. In short, if the information about the unknown cryptids is confirmed, it will become one of the greatest scientific sensations of the 21st century![24]

And now something extra about water giants. Here is the material from the Russian research society Kosmopoisk.

## 19.4. Chronicle of Soviet CE with underwater humanoids

Lake Baikal. The 70s–80s of the twentieth century

**July 1977. Naval base on Lake Baikal, Kabana region.**

During a training dive of a group of military divers (7 men) at a depth of about 50 meters, visual contact with three humanoid beings, at least 3 meters tall, was recorded. Witnesses described them as humanoid beings, dressed in silvery suits, with smooth, pale skin and large, rounded helmets. No breathing apparatus or means of communication were observed. The beings moved at high speed and, according to one instructor, "slid through the water without moving their limbs."

**July 17, 1977. An attempt at an approach.**

The next day, an attempt was made to approach these objects using deep-sea nets and two divers equipped with gripping devices. When they approached one of the creatures

---

[24] Source – "Tajny XX wieku" No. 38/2011

at a depth of about 5 meters, all participants experienced sudden decompression, even without violating the ascent protocols. Three died, three were hospitalized due to serious pressure injuries. The official cause: "a sudden change in pressure caused by an underwater micro-explosion of unknown origin". August 1982 Western Baikal, Cape Ryty. Border guard officers reported an object moving at depth, resembling "a man swimming about 4 meters tall". When they tried to track the object with sonar, it disappeared from range. Six minutes later, an unexplained increase in water temperature and a malfunction of the ship's communication equipment were reported. The report mentioned "unidentified underwater activity, unrelated to potential enemy technology."

**August 1982. Western Baikal, Cape Ryta.**

Border guard officers reported an object moving at depth, resembling "a man swimming about 4 meters high". When they tried to track the object with sonar, it disappeared from range. Six minutes later, an unexplained increase in water temperature and a malfunction of the ship's communication equipment were reported. The report mentioned "unidentified underwater activity, unrelated to potential enemy technology."

**1984. Secret report of the Central Naval Research Institute (TsNII WMF).**

According to unverified but indirectly confirmed data, after a series of incidents on Lake Baikal, a temporary department was established at the TsNII WMF to analyze unidentified underwater activity. One of the notes reads: "the observed objects with biological features do not seek contact, avoid aggression, but show the ability to manipulate the environment. It is recommended to stop voluntary approaches until the nature of the threat has been clarified."

Note from the Military Naval Review (1991, leaked edition).

A short article without an author described "the case of underwater giants in Lake Baikal" and suggested a connection with deep-sea geomagnetic anomalies recorded as early as the 1930s. The publication was later removed from all library collections, but a copy survived in the UFO archive "Svet-13".

Oral testimony.

Veterans of the diving school in Severobaikalsk recalled that any mention of "three-meter creatures" was cut out of training records, and superiors were punished even for talking. One instructor, on condition of anonymity, said, "These beings do not obey the laws of water. They know you're there. And you're in their zone."

Crimea and the Black Sea. The 60s–80s of the twentieth century

## June 1962. Cape Aja, the southern coast of Crimea.

During an underwater special force training at a depth of 30 meters, two soldiers reported seeing a "dark figure over 3 meters high" moving quickly among the rocks. Command attributed the report to stress and perceptual disturbances, but two days later, at the same location, a sudden impact deformed the metal structure of the training buoy. Witnesses stated that "it was as if something massive passed under us and emerged."

## August 1973. Laspi Bay.

The Soviet project "Depth-9", which explored underwater caves near Laspi Bay, encountered pressure surge anomalies and equipment failures while attempting to enter one of the caves. Divers heard "clicks and sounds similar to underwater speech, but without mouths." After one of the divers surfaced, microcracks were found on the helmet, as if caused by a directional acoustic impulse. Further immersion was prohibited.

## 1975. Secret operation "Topaz".

According to unconfirmed information, but mentioned in the archives of naval intelligence, a discreet attempt was made to intercept unidentified underwater objects near Sevastopol. Deep-sea steel nets dropped from two ships were used. The operation failed: one of the nets was torn apart by an unknown force, despite its calculated strength of 6 tons.

All monitoring devices showed simultaneous interference. The report, which was accessed by the coast guard officer, used the wording: "contact with a form of activity of an unknown nature, recommended suspension of further activities".

July 1980. Black Sea coast, Abkhazia.

A coastal patrol vessel detected unidentified objects at a depth of 50-70 meters at a variable speed of up to 80 knots. Eye contact was brief: dark, elongated silhouettes in an upright position. One officer reported seeing "a head with an elongated skull that turned towards us." This resulted in a report to the Central Intelligence Bureau of the Navy. The result of the investigation remains secret.

1982. Underwater naval training ground, Sevastopol Oblast.

During the exercise, two deep-sea probes disappeared without explanation. A diver involved in the rescue operation reported a "pale, webbed hand" that "emerged from the sand for a moment and disappeared". His mental state changed after the incident, and he had nocturnal epileptic seizures. Medical diagnosis: "acute stress reaction".

Testimonies of civilians.

Since the 1970s, residents of coastal villages near Balaklava have reported seeing "black figures rising to the surface on cloudless nights." In one case, teenagers claimed that "a giant with white eyes without pupils emerged from the water and stood motionless among the waves, not touching the sand."

Request of Soviet aquanauts (unofficial, oral).

Some retired officers in the early 1990s believed that there was a hidden network of underwater caves and tunnels in the Black Sea, leading to depths inaccessible to ordinary divers. That is where such beings were. The nature of their presence: observation and protection, not aggression — unless the balance of the depths is disturbed.

General analysis. An underground-underwater civilization and its observers?

A comparison of the Baikal and Black Sea incidents reveals a striking convergence in the parameters of the observed entities. Regardless of the geography – a continental lake or a sea area – they were humanoid forms between 3 and 4 meters high, with great maneuverability underwater, no breathing apparatus, the ability to interfere with equipment and, above all, a conscious avoidance of direct contact. These are not animals, nor drones, nor people. They are another form of intelligence, adapted to an environment in which people are only guests.

According to leaks from military agencies (including TsNII WMF, Coast Guard archives, and oral reports linked to the GRU), the following events have been recorded:

Four attempts to capture animals using nets and underwater devices, all unsuccessful.

– at least seven deaths among divers due to anomalies in physiological reactions in close proximity;

– located areas of equipment failure, overlapping with the areas where these entities were located;

– observations of precise movements, with monitoring of ships and objects – evidence of informed assessment.

Confidential reports link these phenomena to underwater zones of very ancient origin. Examples:

– Cape Aya geologically coincides with the collapsed vault, containing caves that have not been explored since the 30s of the twentieth century;

– sound anomalies and pseudo-echolocation signals were detected in Baikal, which were not produced by any known species.

Independent researchers such as **Vadim Chernobrov** and **V.I. Shemsuk** in the 1990s proposed the existence of a closed underground underwater system connecting lakes and seas — including the Kara Sea, Lake Baikal, Sayan Islands, Crimea, and possibly the Caucasus. This system would have been built by precivilization before the Flood, and the beings encountered by divers would have been the inhabitants or "patrolmen" of this complex, operating under a containment protocol.

From an esoteric perspective, these beings could be liminal guardians, connected to the planet's energy grid, reacting to the violation of critical nodes. They are not enemies, but they are not ready for open contact. Their mission: to observe, protect, correct imbalances, especially in times of pollution and underwater tests.

Their "inability to capture" does not reveal the limitations of human technology, but it does confirm that we are dealing with something more intelligent than we assume to be real. After 1985, almost all monitoring programs were terminated and references to them were removed from public records.

But they are still there.

And whoever wants to find them must come down not with nets, but with inner silence.

The water remembers. The depth listens.

And giants... also.

☙

# CHAPTER 20. THE ULTIMATE WEAPON OF THE GOD SHIVA

The largest artificial, material object on Earth can be considered to be the post-explosion mushroom after the explosion of the Soviet hydrogen bomb *AN-602* with the unofficial name *Tsar-bomba*, detonated in 1961 at the Novaya Zemlya training ground, writes Viktor **Mednikov in his article**.

**Darwin** and others lightly stated that life on Earth developed gradually – from lower forms to higher forms, from simple to complex. The culmination of evolution is man, who arose from primates that one day came down from trees to the ground, got back on their feet, learned to use fire and kill others like themselves. In the latter, the two-legged duopods had perfected replacing primitive javelins with thermonuclear warheads, making them like evil gods, capable of destroying the entire world. And contrary to the statements that our civilization is the first on Earth, the only and unrepeatable, the latest discoveries show that this is not true. Not so long ago, a joint project of French scientists and NASA was created, as a result of which it was concluded that

25,000 years ago on Earth there was... nuclear war! She threw Humanity back to the days of the stone not yet split.

## 20.1. "... like 10,000 suns at their zenith"

Echoes of this ancient global catastrophe can be found in the myths and messages of numerous nations in all corners of our planet. The African Pygmies, in particular, have the myth of "a great fire that came down from heaven." It talks about a powerful explosion and its consequences – nuclear winter. The Mayan "Code of Rio" speaks of a fire that raged "three days and three nights" and caused effects reminiscent of radioactive contamination. Those who survived it were approached by a dog that was hairless and its claws fell off (characteristic symptoms of radiation sickness).

In the ancient Indian epic "Mahabharata" written about 4000 years ago, the destruction of the city of Mohenjo Daro/Mohenjo-Daro (N 27°19′35" - E 068°08′15") – the capital of the Harappian civilization – is described:

And he unleashed the power of the angels' weapons, completely indefensible against them – even for the gods... Burned by strong heat, earthly creatures ran in fear, breathing heavily... Enemies fell literally like trees, burned by furious fire. And torrents of chariots fell to and fro. A projectile was released that had the power of the entire Universe in it. The eruption was as bright as 10,000 suns at their zenith.

In texts from ancient India, flying apparatuses called *vimanas* are described. They carried deadly weapons, the action of which is phenomenally reminiscent of nuclear strikes.

One of the main characters of the "Mahabharata" – **Arjuna** – received a powerful weapon from the god **Shiva**, with which he fought many enemies. But the god did not give an even more terrible "eternal weapon" to Arjuna. This is what Shiva said about her:

No man in the world should ever and will never fight it. When it falls into the hands of a weak man, it can burn the whole living world. It can be a protection against other weapons and it will deflect the attack of any other weapon.

- These are all fairy tales! – you will say, Reader – and where is the evidence???

There is a lot of evidence for this.[25]

---

[25] And once again, I would like to remind you that Hitler's and Himmler's scholars searched throughout the East and South America for evidence of the existence of these types of weapons of mass destruction. And perhaps they found such evidence. Perhaps they also found plans and construction sketches, descriptions of the production and use of air and nuclear weapons (today we would call them missile and nuclear weapons) used by the former inhabitants of India.

## 20.2. Mohenjo Daro – ancient Hiroshima

Scientists excavating Mohenjo Daro discovered the image as vividly reminiscent of the effects of the atomic bombing of Hiroshima and Nagasaki. The old city was destroyed suddenly and completely. The stones melted from the terrible heat. On top of that, the epicenter of destruction was in the very center of the city, and it diminished as it went to the outskirts – which refutes the version of a giant meteorite that would have hit the very center of the city. Many human skeletons were found on the outskirts of the city. At the time of the destruction of the city, many people held various objects and tools of work in their hands. Everything indicates that death caught up with them suddenly, when the townspeople were going about their business. The radioactive background of the ground in the city exceeded all standards by 50 times.[26]

Another ancient Indian city found between the Ganges and the Rajmahal/Rajmahal Mountains was apparently subjected to high temperatures similar to those produced by an atomic explosion. Its stone walls were immediately melted and a glassy mass was formed from them. Other cities were also destroyed by explosions of monstrous power, and their

---

[26] Other sources claim that the background in the city was 50 times higher than the radioactive background outside the city.

ruins are found in India. In the Indus Valley, in the Thar/Tar desert west of Jodhpur (N 26°16'53" - E 073°01'23"), many areas with traces of radioactive ashes have been found. All of this indicates that the Rama Empire in these territories was ravaged by nuclear war.

Traces of the nuclear war are also borne by stones from the Gobi Desert, the walls of the capital of the Hittite empire – Hattusa (today Boğazkale), Stonehenge, the former cities of Ireland, Scotland, France, Turkey, the walls of Babylon, excavations in Asia – that is, they are found all over the world.

## 20.3. Huge holes in the Earth

According to the scientists' estimates, published by scientists from the project mentioned above, more than 100 craters with a diameter of 2-3 km have been found on Earth, among which there are two huge ones: in South America – with a diameter of 40 km and in South Africa – with a diameter of 120 km. According to the official version, these craters were formed in the Paleozoic Era – that is, about 350 million years ago, as a result of the fall of meteorites. But in this case, there would be nothing left of them, because the thickness of the Earth's top layer increases by about 1 m/100 years. And the craters still exist today. According to scientists, they are the results of a nuclear war that took place 25,000 years ago and the energy of the explosion was 25 times stronger than the Hiroshima bomb and its TNT equivalent was 500 kt.

## 20.4. The Forgotten Old Rhythm

In the last century, Mayan calendars were found. According to them, the Earth's Day used to have 36 hours. So, what happened? As a result of these explosions, the water in the Global Ocean began to move like a water whirlpool, which in turn affected the position of the Earth's axis and the speed of its rotation. And what is extraordinary, the internal rhythm of the life of the human body is 36 hours! This is what scientists studying the biorhythms of closed people without the ability to observe the movement of the Sun have been able to determine. In such conditions, the human body switched from a 24-hour to a 36-hour rhythm of action. Physiologists believe that such information is found at the genetic level in human memory.

## 20.5. Are we children of mutants?

It is known that radiation causes mutations in organisms. Radiation changes the chains of chromosomes, and because of this, the form of a person changes. But mutations are different in different people. And that's why, soon after the nuclear catastrophe, the people who survived were even more diverse than they are now.[27]

Radiation causes mutations leading to cyclopism, which is currently observed in the offspring of animals and humans

---

[27] There is another possibly, which assumes that these mutations were created on purpose, through genetic engineering, which led to the creation of creatures such as cyclops, centaurs, mermaids and other monsters of mythical Antiquity, and which creatures were bred to perform specific tasks – e.g. in difficult terrain, underwater or in space, and which creatures could not reproduce and eventually became extinct. An alternative to them is... biological robots, cyborgs and other biological-mechanical robots, created precisely for the purpose of penetrating and exploring difficult environments by the people or aliens of the time.

living near the Chernobyl Zone. Many nations have legends about the existence of cyclops, with which people had to fight...

On Earth, in various excavations, the remains of giant skeletons with a double row of teeth are occasionally found. This is yet another piece of evidence for the influence of radioactivity – polyploidy – an increase in the number of chromosomes in cells leading to gigantism and duplication of certain organs: e.g. two hearts or two dental arches.

Mongolism – is also a consequence of radiation mutation. Currently, the race is the most widespread on our planet. It includes: Mongols, Chinese (Han), Inuit (Eskimo), Ural and South Siberian nations, and Indian nations of the Americas. Earlier, were also in Europe, Sumer and Egypt. Also, in Central Africa there are Bushmen with black skin, but other features. It would therefore appear that the spread of the race is due to the distribution of deserts and semi-deserts on Earth, where the centers of lost civilizations were once located.

Another evidence for the existence of radiation mutations is the birth of monsters and children with atavisms (return to ancestors) in humans. Survivors of thermonuclear war had many monsters, to the point where they were taken for granted. But Nature gradually regained what was her own, and the anomalies of organisms became less and less numerous. Nevertheless, today's Humanity can be called a descendant of mutants who survived the atomic apocalypse.[28]

*A sea monster on which the ship's crew had a picnic...*
*according to Olaus Magnus*

## 20.6. Who fought with whom?

There are many hypotheses. According to the most famous of them, a nuclear war, which almost sterilized the globe, resulted in the creation of two branches of Humanity – the Hyperborean (Aryans) and the distinct branches of the Atlanteans (those from the myth of the sunken continent). According to the second hypothesis, the indigenous inhabitants of Earth – the Asuras – good-natured and gullible giants – died as a result of an atomic attack by aliens-

---

[28]Aleksander Mora **writes on this subject** in his study "The Atomic War of the Gods" (in "Kamena", Lublin 1979) and Dr. **Miloš Jesenský** in his work "Gods of Atomic Wars" (Ústi n/Labem, 1998).

invaders, who after the victory over them proclaimed themselves gods. Today's Humanity is the descendants of these occupiers.

Aleksandr Koltypin, **Ph.D., of geological and mineralogical sciences** , believes that: *there have been not one, but at least seven nuclear wars on Earth.* (!!) it is difficult for us to judge the motives of these wars and their number. But one thing is clear: *Humanity has once again reached a dangerous period of its existence...*[29]

Sea monsters did not necessarily have to be large whales – they could have been artificially created mutants. They could also have been Ningens... (according to Gessner)

[29] Source – "Tajny XX wieku", No. 21/2015, pp.8-9

# 20.7. Opinions from the CCC

I wonder what type of civilization it would be, because, for example, type II civilization would only mean the management of system resources, which does not reflect the scale of the range. Ours, for example, type 0.7+, has gone beyond the atmosphere, conquered another celestial body (at least one that we know about), and we cannot control the entire spectrum of the Earth (despite such a possibility at our fingertips - the alleged orgone and orgone guns - vide e.g. YouTube). A type I civilization would be able to personally reach the limits of the system, but it would not rule it. The system rulers (type II) would probably be able to reach other systems, but not to rule them, etc., so whether it is advanced type I or II, and why not III?

Incidentally, we are touching on the subject of morality, because the management of civilizations is based on what we call spirituality and materialism, or rather on the functions just mentioned - are there civilizations of type II or III, which are moral but not for us, or immoral from every point of view? Are there any laws at play here?

**The Tsar bomb** was supposed to have 150 Mt TNT, but it was limited in terms of power for several reasons, e.g. technical and financial, first to 100 Mt TNT, then to 50 Mt

TNT (apparently it was a technical necessity resulting from the need for urgency).[30]

The Mahabharata is dated by some to several thousand years BCE and is supposed to describe times as distant as even 30 thousand years back. However, these are only legends, but are there messages of the ancients that are able to convince people from a different era than the time of their creation? Who knows, perhaps future thinkers will be playing about us in a few hundred thousand years, because we will leave such a strong impression on the face of our Mother Earth - unless these are too distant times for all kinds of archaeology, because then the wonders of technology will reveal a simple fact, unable to be the basis for a deeper interpretation. (Vide spheres from billions of years ago, hypersonic places of power in Africa, ancient statues in Africa, on islands around the Americas, mine artifacts and artifacts of unknown function from Africa, etc.). Could it be that nuclear wars really pushed our species (our species!?) back to a form, and the social system of that time enabled the survival of the most tribal groups, e.g. the white race, as the one that was not too insistently attacked?

---

[30] Nikita Khrushchev planned to detonate a Superbomb with a power of 0.5-1.0 Gt TNT. Fortunately, it would have a mass of 20 tons and there was no plane that would be able to lift and drop it.

By the way, the Vimans are not the only vehicles described in the epic.

Wasn't **Oppenheimer** looking for evidence to confirm his theses in the Mahabharata? Apparently, when he came across '10,000 suns', he knew that the fission of an atom was possible. This gave him the strength to continue pushing the project.

Mohenjo Daro and other cities were burned by an explosion well depicted in the movie Terminator II - at a certain height, variously given (from 20 meters to 500 meters), a burning charge detonated, even petrifying the bodies and building material of buildings.

**Tueasday Lobsang Rampa** describes giants like those mentioned in the article, who enjoyed life and had brown skin. I recommend his books, in my opinion he wrote from himself, because some of his books are just a confession like a biography, so it is not stuffed with miracles and invisibles.

Hmmm, seven wars with A/H/N BMR (even annihilation)? Why not - it was practically like that 7.5, 70 years ago. Mutations as a result of them? Why not. Thirdly, when I heard the term Mongolism for the first time, I immediately thought that maybe it was actually the effect of something, not a path per se. Since this is what radiation sickness is called, and I immediately associated it with what I had recently read (6th-8th grade of primary school), I coined this conclusion for my own use a dozen or so years ago (geez, how time flies...).

What's more - this pseudo-hoax about the appearance of aliens because of our WMD arsenal does not have to be a hoax. In the light of this article, such a working view is even permitted and subservient to logic as a modus operandi. Although... You can never be too careful, because thinking is one thing, and proclaiming your thoughts is another. Nevertheless, it is worth and necessary - people of good will understand everything in their own way, ergo - properly. (**Fireproof Dragon**)

Personally, I am convinced that a few or several thousand years ago some violent events took place, the traces of which we still see on Earth, but we do not understand them yet. If there really were astronaut gods, then traces of their presence will certainly be found on the Moon and other planets. This IS a mathematical certainty. Maybe it will be ruins, maybe it will be some remains of devices, or – as in the case of the Moon and taking into account the preservative properties of vacuum – whole and still working devices. And such devices would be worth looking for, but on the other hand – if we get to the Moon, will we need them? (**Daniel Laskowski**)

Thank you for this text. It is obvious that civilized life has "twisted" on this planet several times. How long does it take for it to recover from nuclear devastation? I think that 20-30 thousand years is enough. And how much is it in the scale of the Earth's life? NOTHING.

We are probably facing another collapse, the war will probably be preceded by the era of morons and morons, who are growing in front of our eyes. (**Hermocrates**)

ॐ

# CHAPTER 21. THE SEA DEVIL – MYTH AND REALITY

The depths of the sea hide the secret of the fish people, mermaids or simply Water People...

A.R. Belyaev – "Ichtyander"

The Danish naturalist **Erik Pontoppidan**, bishop of Bergen (1698-1774), described the Kraken – a sea monster the size of a floating island, supposedly able to engulf a large ship with its tentacles and pull it to the seabed, reports **Valery Kukarenko**.[31]

In 1928, Alexander Romanovich Belyaev's science fiction novel „**The Amphibious Man**" saw the world for the first time, which immediately became a bestseller. And in 1961, a feature film was released,[32] which was also a stunning success. Vladimir **Korieniev, who played the role of** Ichtiandr – a man who had shark gills implanted –

---

[31] This was exactly shown by the director of the second part of the adventures of Captain **Jack Sparrow** – "Pirates of the Caribbean: Dead Man's Chest" – **Gore Verbinski**, in which the Kraken wreaks havoc on the seas while chasing Captain Sparrow, who is indebted to **Davy Jones**.

[32] Polish title – "The Sea Devil".

immediately became an idol for millions of Soviet cinema lovers. In addition to the actor's extraordinary beauty and the many wonderful qualities of the character he played, there was another reason for the popularity of this film: the possibility of living in the depths of the oceans has always been one of the greatest dreams of Humanity...

*Sea devil according to Gessner*

## 21.1. From land to seabed!

Some scholars have actually tried to realize this dream and look for a solution to this task. Scientific and literary journals rarely published material on the subject, but their authors limited themselves only to theoretical considerations.

However, there were rare, as we would call them today, fanatics who wanted to move from the land to the aquatic environment, and in extreme cases – to put themselves under a surgical scalpel, so that, like Ichthyander, they would sew in his gills, fill their lungs with special mixtures – which, according to them – would allow them to switch to the second type of respiration... But all these experiments ended in misery.[33]

And yet it turns out that there was a real prototype of the legendary Ichtiandr, a literary character created by Alexander R. Belyaev! Its mystery has captured the imagination of historians for several centuries and has sparked heated disputes. This story once went around the world and brought fame to the boarded-up town of Liérganes near Santander, which later turned into a charming town in Cantabria, in the north of the Pyrenean Peninsula, on the shore of the turbulent Bay of Biscay (N 43°20'46" – E 003°44'28").

A highly learned man, the Benedictine monk Fra **Benito Geronimo Feiho y Montenegro**, at the beginning of the eighteenth century, with his sharp pen constantly fought against prejudices and superstitions, easily revealing various wonders and wonders presented by various fantasists and

---

[33] **Stanisław and Krzysztof Szymborski** in their work entitled "Wszechocean" (1981) state that for many years such experiments have been carried out with filling the lungs and bloodstream with special mixtures of fluids that conduct oxygen to tissues – including Teflon. The problem is that the experimental animals (e.g. dogs) lived in water with their lungs filled with water and a special mixture in the bloodstream, but the problem was and is the opposite, and the animals died while pumping water out of their lungs. So far, this problem has not been solved...

swindlers, until finally he wrote an encyclopedic work entitled "Teatrum krytyki universalnej" – in chapter VI "Teatrum..." he published the "Philosophical Review of Rare Events of Our Days", in which he described an unusual, fully real, case of human preparation for life in an aquatic environment.

The priests, scholars, and ordinary people who witnessed the transformation of **Francisco de la Vega Cassar,** the legendary fish-man who later lived five years in the depths of the sea, gave Fr Benito full information of this incredible event, and he found no lie in it.

## 21.2. Gone forever...

The Miera River flows through the town of Liérganes, on the bank of which the house of the de la Vega Cassar family was located. Already at the age of 5, one of the family members – Francisco – swam much better than his older brothers. Local residents watched with satisfaction from the bridge across the river, as the boy swims in the water, easily coping with the strong current and sometimes even large waves.

In 1672, Francisco turned 14 and went to Bilbao, where he wanted to learn to be a carpenter and worked for two years in a sawmill for the Basques. Every evening a company of carpenters went to the river to bathe after the hard and dirty work. Of course, our hero also walked with them.

And so, in 1674, on the eve of St. John's Day (23.VI), Francisco decided to sail down the river to a sea bay, which here cut deep into the land. Undressing, he jumped into the water, and the strong current carried him further. The carpenters knew that the young man felt like a real fish in the water, and they were not alarmed even when he did not return for dinner.

The next day, news of Francisco's disappearance reached his mother. Together with her sons, she searched all the rocks on the shore for his body, but all in vain. Francisco disappeared without a trace...

## 21.3. The Enigmatic Captive

Five years later, in February 1679, fishermen fishing in the bay of Cádiz in southern Spain saw a strange creature floating near their boats and nets, which they called the "sea devil." Despite the fact that there was a small depth, it was difficult to get a close look at it, but the fishermen quickly realized that this bizarre creature was stealing their fish and decided to catch it. The next day they made a bait trap out of the net, which consisted of bread and meat. But the strange creature scooped food out of the trap and quickly swam away.

It was many days before this sea wonder was caught. In front of the astonished fishermen appeared a tall young man with white, almost transparent skin and fiery-red hair. His fingers were connected by a transparent membrane, and from his throat to his lower abdomen there was a belt of fish-like scales. The strange prisoner roared like a wild animal. Ten fishermen could hardly hold it.

## 21.4. Escape

The mysterious creature stayed in the Franciscan monastery for three weeks. The Secretary of the Order for the Holiness of the Faith, Fra **Domingo de la Cantolia**, ordered a series of rites to be carried out to expel the devils from the fish-man, after which he summoned many interpreters who tried to extract some human words from him. At the end he said the word "Liérganes", which meant nothing to them. But one of the interpreters, who once came from that region, understood and said that it was the name of a small village in Cantabria, belonging to the bishopric of Burgos, to which all the settlements on the banks of the river Miera belonged.

To verify this information, Cantolia sent messengers to the town of Solares, which was located 10 km from Liérganes. There they found the hidalgo don **Dionisio Rubalcava**, **Gaspar Melchorro de Santiago**, Knight of the Order of San Santiago and Marquis **de Balbuena** – who went to Liérganes. Very quickly, Rubalcava learned the story of Francisco's disappearance.

In January 1680, the "fish-man" was transported across Spain to a Cantabrian village. Everyone wanted to know: Could this mysterious prisoner be Francisco the carpenter? The transport of the strange creature through the mountains was taken on by a monk – Father **Jose Rosende**.

It would seem that the prisoner began to get to know the area. Finding himself in the streets of Liérganes, the boy jumped down from the carriage and, walking at the head of the holy fathers, walked towards the house where the young carpenter lived. Old woman Maria recognized her son in him and with tears in her eyes she embraced him. The two brothers Francisco also recognized him.

The "fish-man" did not express any joy at meeting his family and remained silent during the next 2 years, which he spent at home under the supervision of hidalgo Rubalcava. Francisco walked through the fields and muttered something to himself, slept on the ground, ate raw fish and meat. Sometimes he starved for days without taking food, and on top of that, he was not interested in anything.

One evening he tensed up as if he had heard a distant call, and then ran to the bank of the Miera. The brothers tried to stop him, but he broke free from their hands, reached the shore in a few jumps, threw himself into the water and swam down the river at supernatural speed. Soon he disappeared from view, and this time forever.

## 21.5. The facts have been confirmed

Regardless of the arguments from the work of the Benedictine Benito Geronimo Feiho y Montenegro, many considered it to be some kind of invention, legend or fairy tale without any basis in reality and without evidence. And in our times, European scientists come to Liérganes from time to time to learn about the phenomenon of the "fish-man".

Some believe that scientists explain Francisco's appearance (if it was him, of course) not by an aquatic way of life, but by a disease – ichthyosoma/ichthyosis – during which scales appear on the skin, and his phenomenal swimming talent is included in the mythical part of his legend.

In 1997, the Spanish journalist and researcher **Iker Jimenez Elizari** tried to conduct another search for the truth. Driving along the roads of Cantabria, Iker, following the advice of Father **Antonio Fernandez**, went to the only place where the relevant documents could be found – to the convent of the Poor Clares (or Benedictines) in Santiliana del Mar. In order to get access to the church books of births and deaths of the parish of Liérganes, the journalist, hung like a Christmas tree with cameras, a notebook and a dictaphone, obtained a visit with the prioress, Sister **Emila Sierra**. The two of them quickly found the necessary records – documents shedding light on Francisco's life, real evidence of the existence of this unusual creature. According to the strict law of that era, it was necessary to wait 100 years before he was officially declared dead.

The facts confirmed that the "fish-man", Francisco de la Vega Cassar, lived in these places and his story cannot be considered a fairy tale.

And the possibility of human life in the aquatic environment still remains a dream. How the "sea devil" could live in the water is his mystery. It is a pity that the real prototype was far from the intellectual and romantic, literary and cinematic image of the sympathetic Ichtiandr...[34]

## 21.6. My 3 cents

When as a young man I served on the maritime border of our country, walking in the evenings on the Baltic beaches, I had the impression that I was standing on the border of two cosmos – the one above my head and the one in front of me – and it was obvious to me that in both of them there were living beings different from us, but close to us in Reason, who were maybe they even see me walking alone on the beach and looking for Them in the spaces of the Cosmos and the Ocean. And even today, when I have the seventh cross on my neck, I am still faithful to these dreams. That's why I deal with

[34] Source – "Tajny XX wiekua", No. 37/2015, pp. 22-23

strange things that happen to people from time to time and cause wonder, curiosity or even fear.

This is also the case with Sirens and other creatures inhabiting the oceans. The above story has an obvious connection with them and there is no need to delude ourselves that it is a phenomenon. It is not. There were and are more people like Francisco de la Vega Cassar. And who knows if the solution to this mystery of their origin should not be sought in Atlantis and maybe even earlier civilizations. Perhaps these beings were just one of many attempts to conquer the oceans? Why not?

Mermaids or Water People, or whatever else we call them, are not just a myth. Too many accounts, too many testimonies and eyewitnesses. Of course, as in the case of UFOs and USOs, in some of them these may be known but rare phenomena, but there are a whole lot of accounts of something that does not fit into the wide range of rare but natural phenomena and suggests that we are dealing with the All-Ocean Mind like the sentient ocean from **Stanisław Lem**'s novel – "Solaris", which affects us and our civilization like the inhabitants of the underwater city at Latitude Zero from **Ishirô Honda**'s film...

## 21.7. Readers' opinions

Yes Robert – I heard and read about the "Mermaid" of

Liérganes; it is a true and really strange story from the annals of medieval Spain. This man was apparently some kind of mutant who could survive underwater, but the question is, how? (**Albert Rosales**, Miami, FL, USA)

Can you imagine that Francisca's mother could be impregnated by a mermaid and from this union a child was born, who then returned to the sea? Somehow it reminds me of some Close Encounters with UFOnauts, doesn't it? Francisco could have been just such a hybrid of a man... also a man, but a water one. I can imagine that! (**Daniel Laskowski,** London, UK)

This is the legend of the fish-man. This man was found in the sea after disappearing from his home village and then re-established before disappearing again. Retarded? Madman? Who knows? See the link in Spanish –

_https://es.wikipedia.org/wiki/Hombre_pez_

and _http://yamato1.blogspot.com.es/2007/04/el-extrao-caso-del-hombre-pez-y-el.html_.

Unfortunately, I was not interested in it and I do not have more information on this subject. Yours sincerely, **Vincente-Juan Ballester Olmos**, Seville, Spain

## 21.8. The Devil of Devonshire

Another problem is from the nineteenth-century "X-Files", the case of the appearance of mysterious hoof prints of an unknown creature on the beaches, meadows, fields and gardens of the English Devonian county. Like many others, this case has not been resolved. And it was like this...

**Devonshire, England**

**February 8, 1855**

**07:00 GMT**

The winter of that year was severe in the British Isles, as well as in all Europe, and it afflicted the inhabitants terribly, so that it seemed to them that the merciful God had turned His face away from them. As a result of severe frosts, trees cracked[35], food supplies to human settlements were imprisoned, and predators waited for people in the forests. What happened that morning, when the sun shone on the snows that had traced the hoof prints, caused a great deal of panic and unspeakable horror at the visit of the devil himself *in persona*, and the frightened people did not even know how close they had managed to get to the truth, which will be discussed later.

The mysterious imprints that appeared on the surface of the thin snow cover were clearly different from the hoof prints and hooves of other animals known to man. They were similar to donkey hoof prints, 10 cm long, 7 cm wide, and 20

---

[35] Such a phenomenon is observed when the temperature drops below - 40 degrees Celsius.

cm apart. What was most interesting and at the same time the strangest was that these tracks ran in a perfect straight line and were certainly not left by a quadruped, but by a bipedal being. All the prints were the same size and looked as if someone had made them with a hot iron – the snow inside the footprint was not dented by the weight of the creature's body, but as if it had been evaporated from there, and so quickly that it did not melt!

This unknown "something" passed in a perfect straight line across the fields, through fences and roofs of houses, as well as mounds of hay over 3 m high, and everywhere it left traces as if burned in the snow. What's more interesting – the terrain obstacles did not affect the length of the stride in the slightest – it was always 20 cm! In one case, these tracks were seen on the gutter of a house in Whitycombe Raleigh, and in Marley they led along the window sill at the height of the first floor!

Of course, you can simply laugh at the whole problem and ignore it, but we should seriously think about – in our opinion – this riddle. And there is a lot to be over, because these traces stretched over large areas and the total distance covered by this unknown "something" was over 160 km. It remains a mystery, then, who or what left its traces in such a vast area, and to top it all off, crossed the mouth of the river 3 km wide!

# 21.8.1. The devil visited Devonshire.

If we are to describe the events that took place 147 years ago, we must refer to the testimonies of eyewitnesses of these events, which were published in the newspapers of that time. We learn from them that the search for the strange creature began just a few hours after finding its tracks. The armed groups of men followed a mysterious trail that started from Exmouth on the coast and headed north toward Raleigh and Bicton, then turned west to Woodbury and Topshan, toward the cove formed by the mouth of the Exte River. Then they reappeared south of Powdersham, and then turned towards Lusombe and Teignmouth, where they disappeared on the frozen surface of the bay, and then unexpectedly reappeared between Newton Abbey and Torquay, whence they headed through the roofs of houses, fences and snowy pastures to Totnes, where the trail ended.

The Reverend Pastor **G. M. Musgrave** tried to reassure his parishioners by claiming that these traces were left by... a kangaroo that escaped from the menagerie. It is possible that the words of the priest were a sufficient explanation for some of his sheep, but the rest were puzzled by the fact that this kangaroo had traveled a distance of over 160 km during a frosty night! Today, this hypothesis is indefensible, and it was already so at the time of its promulgation. The well-known chronicler of mysterious events of the nineteenth century,

**Charles Fort**, added his sarcastic comment to this "explanation":

This can also be explained by the fact that the snow in Devonshire was trampled by thousands of identical, one-legged kangaroos, and each of them had a small horseshoe.[36]

Others explained that these footprints were left by a lame hare, a frog, an otter, a huge bird from another continent, etc., etc. British biologist **Alfred G. Leutscher** published a hypothesis that it was about the tracks left by a forest mouse.[37] His hypothesis cannot be denied originality, his article entitled "Traces of the Devil: Solving the Mystery from a Hundred Years Ago" does not even have a question mark at the end of the title, not to mention a bit of self-criticism... It is really difficult to imagine the way in which forest mice jumped on roofs and left such strange hoof prints.

The set of animals accused of leaving these footprints is shocking with the stupidity of its creators – writes on the margin of this "explanation" the Czech researcher and publicist **Eng. Ivan Mackerle** – Most people associated these footprints with the footprints of a donkey, but no one was

---

[36] **Ch. Fort** – "The Book of Damned", New York 1919, chap. XXVIII – in Polish edition "Księga rzeczy wyklętych", Łódź 1993; chap. XXI.

[37] Journal of Zoology, No. 148, London, 1966. NB, another zoologist "explained" how the notorious grain pictograms were formed thanks to the mating dances of hedgehogs...

able to explain how a donkey could jump over a three-meter high wall, walk on the gutter without breaking it, and in addition walk over the window sills.[38]

A special group of hypotheses is the group of theories about the atmospheric influence on strange tracks in the snow. Paul **J. Willis is critical of them** in his article "Traces of the Devil", in which he poses a fundamental question:

[...] How could the atmosphere affect some tracks and not others at all? On the critical morning, fresh tracks of dogs, cats, hares, birds and people were clearly visible in the snow. What did the atmosphere have to do here? In one case, the trail led to water on the surface of which he could not hold, crossed it and appeared on the opposite bank.[39]

Willis's view is also supported by the statement of the author of the note to the British press about the mysterious events in Devonshire, who claimed that he had spent five winter months in Canada. According to his own experience and observations of tracks in the snow, he writes that:

... I have never seen clearer traces, or those that were so little distorted by atmospheric influences.[40]

---

[38] I. Mackerle – "Where Do They Come From?", Hořovice 1996, p. 36.

[39] **P. J. Willis** w **J. Bergier** – "The Book of the Inexplicable", Paryż 1972, p. 80.

[40] "Illustrated London News" of 24.02.1855, p. 214.

The group of hypotheses based on climate influences also includes the views of Exeter University researcher **Dr. Theo Brown**, who, at the request of the well-known writer and creator of the TV series "The Mysterious World of Arthur C. Clarke" **Arthur C. Clarke,** looked through the church archives of Devonian parishes and studied all historical materials from 1855 that concerned "devil's hoof prints". She interpreted this phenomenon in accordance with the research made by the Scottish scientist **James Renny**, the traces as artefacts created by the interaction of a warm air current with a cold snow cover. Needless to say, it had little to do with the traces of the "Devonian devil" and introduced unnecessary hype into the case. If such a phenomenon really existed, it would have to manifest itself more than once every winter and would be well known to people...

However, these traces appeared only once, on the night of February 7/8, and the panic due to the possibility of the return of the unknown creature lasted several weeks. Who was this unknown stranger and what did he actually want? The tracks looked like this, and were so arranged among the fields and buildings, as if this unknown "something" was looking for something. It is an interesting detail that will take on a dramatic sense the moment we get acquainted with the text of the French author **Richard Nolane**. The daughter of a minister from the town of Dawlish, Miss **Henrietta Fursdon**, described in a book from the late 1850s and early 1860s entitled "Riddles and Notes from Devon and Cornwall" the tense and heavy atmosphere that prevailed in the county:

The tracks appeared at night. As my father was a minister, other Anglican clergymen soon came to him and asked him his view of the traces that were seen all over Dawlish. They had a regular shape of a small hoof. In the hoof prints there were also claw prints. One row of traces running from the rectory to the sacristy door attracted attention in particular. The second row was heading towards the wall of the dead and appeared on the other side of it. Many similar traces were also found on the roofs of houses and in all parts of the city.

... To this day, I remember how large and clear the traces were, and also the fear I experienced at the time, because I thought it could have been done by big wild cats[41], and I was afraid that the servants forgot to lock the door at night...[42]

In the autumn of 1957, Tomorrow magazine published an article by Dr. Eric **J. Dingwall** entitled "The Devil Walks Again", which was analyzed by the American researcher of the Unknown, Vincent Gaddis, known m.in for his research

---

[41] "Big wild cats in the wild" – this is a beloved topic by the British during the cucumber season, next to UFOs, Nessie and the Exmoor monster, hence the concerns of the author of this report.

[42] **H. Fursdon** – „Devon and Cornwall Notes and Queries" w **S. Welfare** – "Arthur Clarke's Mysterious World", Londyn 1980 – wyd. słowackie Bratysława 1992, s. 45.

on the Bermuda Triangle. Dr. Dingwall, a former collaborator of the world-renowned anthropologist and psychology of sex Dr. **Alfred Kinsley,** is aware of the uniqueness of his article, but he says of its contents:

## 21.8.2. Of all the strange occurrences I have heard of, this was one of the strangest and least explained.

Its protagonist was a certain Mr. **Wilson**, who accused Dr. Dingwall of fraud, because he had read in some tabloid that the latter was involved in the study of paranormal phenomena. But when the two men got to know each other better, Wilson changed his mind. What's more – he told the following story about how in 1950 in one of the coastal towns of the Devonian, on a beach smoothed by water, he also found strange footprints resembling hooves. The tracks were very distinct and sharply contrasted with the sand smoothed by the waves—as if cut with a razor blade or some incredibly sharp tool—as he later recounted, which meant they were absolutely fresh. However, the distance between them was as much as about 180 cm, and the footprints were much deeper than those of Wilson, who weighed 80 kg. It was interesting that the trail came out of the water, but did not return to the water. Would Mr. Wilson have seen the "Devonian devil" with his own eyes if he had come to the beaches a minute earlier??? ...

The question in the epilogue to this event is: what aquatic or terrestrial animals will leave such traces on the beaches of the Devonian? How high was it and how long was its stride? Why are these marks so clear and hoof-shaped? And if it was a sea animal, why didn't it return to the sea? Perhaps he had wings?

Hmmm... Mythology knows such creatures: Pegasus – a flying horse, as well as sea horses from the chariot of Poseidon – the Lord Who Shakes the Earth. Could it be that one of them appeared on the beach in Devonian, and a foal from the same herd frightened the villagers in 1855?... Probably such events gave rise to some Greek myths about sea steeds and Pegasus!

This situation became a challenge for the French researcher Richard Nolane, who offered a new explanation for the phenomenon in an article entitled "Disturbing New News of the 'Devonshire Animal'", in which deep factual knowledge is mixed with imagination.[43]

## 21.8.3. The trail leads to Antarctica...

Nolane's first contact with the mystery of the "Devil of

---

[43] **R. D. Nolane** – "New disturbing news about the 'Devonshire Animal'" in "Ikaria" vol. II no. 3, 1992; pp. 50-53.

Devonshire" came in 1974, when as a 19-year-old he began to be interested in paranormal phenomena on the border of science and the Unknown. In June of the same year, he got his hands on the translation of "The Book of the Damned" by Ch. Fort and "The Morning of the Magi" by **L. Pauvels** and **J. Bergier**.[44] The inspiration for his search was a chapter in Fort's book. As the days passed, he found a great deal of information about similar events, which separated certain intervals of time and were scattered all over the globe, and were described by m.in. **Rupert T. Gould, Bernard Huevelmans,** and **Eric F. Russell**.[45]

Richard Nolane met with English science fiction writers and researchers of unknown phenomena at the World Science Fiction Congress in Brighton in August 1979 – in particular with Dr. **Manson Valentin** – an associate **of Charles Berlitz**, a well-known researcher of the Bermuda

---

[44] L. Pouvels and J. Bergier – "Le Matin des magiciens", Paris 1960; ed. Slovak: Bratislava 1991.

[45] The following cases of finding mysterious hoof prints on the beach or snow are listed there: Scotland - winter 1839/40 (source: "Times" of March 13, 1840), Kerguelen Islands on Oc. Indian in 1840 (we will return to this case later), Poland in 1855 (Illustrated London News of 17 March 1885, p. 242) – we will also return to this case, Belgium – 1945 (**E. F. Russell** in "Doubt" No. 20), Brazil – around 1954 (**B. Huevelmans** – "On the Trail of Unknown Animals", Polish edition: Warsaw 1963).

Triangle. During a backstage meeting, the following conversation took place between them:

" Exeter?" – I asked – I don't know anything about him, except the story of the "devil from Devon"...

- *Are you interested in this?* I shook my head in agreement.

"Can we finish this evening in my hotel room?" I have a bottle of Jack Daniels in there. And on top of that, some documentation about this... That thing that ran through the snow over 120 years ago...

Then, at the beginning of his research with his Bahamian friend and **David Sangster**, they adopted as their motto a sentence from **Colin Wilson's book** „Occult Mysteries," which reads as follows:

The footprints of the "Devil of Devonshire" looked as if this creature was looking for something. They wandered around the yards and roofs, as if their perpetrator did not know our habits.[46]

This text electrified Sangster, as did the paragraph two pages earlier:

One correspondent of the "Illustrated London News" points to a note by the British traveler Sir **James Ross** from May 1840. Ross anchored his ships off the shores of Kerguelen Island in Antarctica and was alarmed by hoof

---

[46] C. Wilson – "The Occult Mysteries", London 1979.

prints on the snowy shore. His scouting party followed this trail until he died among the rocks. On these islands there were neither pony horses nor other ungulates, which could leave such traces.[47]

Further investigation into the matter led Sangster to something even stranger – one of the members of Ross's expedition – a certain **Clark Perry**, after leaving the Royal Navy – settled permanently in Teingmouth in one of the coastal towns of Devonshire. Sangster had reached his papers and, to his surprise, found a daguerreotype of Clark Perry holding a large spherical object in his hand. The second such metal sphere was in a box that he had brought from the Kerguelen. And what did it turn out to be? It turned out that Ross had deliberately kept silent about finding these metal balls – and it also turned out that Ross and his sailors had not only found the marks of strange hooves – as described by the correspondent of the "Illustrated London News" – but two mysterious metal balls. One of them was whole, while the other was broken into pieces. What's more, these traces began with the remains of a broken sphere and headed straight for the rocks. Perry had no doubt that the bullets had fallen from the sky, and he had a nasty feeling that he and the other crew were still being watched by some curious eyes... Just before sailing to Hobart, Perry decided to take both balls

[47] C. Wilson – op. cit. s. 128.

with him. However, superstitious sailors preferred not to have otherworldly objects on board, and Perry went down with them in Hobart, Tasmania, and then took them with him to England, where he settled at Teingmouth, where he deposited the mysterious souvenirs in the cellar, where they lay in peace for 13 years, until February 3, 1855. As Richard Nolane describes it, on the critical evening, Perry returned home with "comrades from a wet quarter" and, under the influence of alcohol, they decided to open the mysterious ball. Together with five or six buddies, they began to hammer the surface. After about the tenth impact, a creaking sounded from the ball and a crack appeared on its surface. Perry sobered up immediately, dismissed his comrades and went to sleep. When he got up in the morning and got down to work, he found that the crack had widened and it could be assumed that it would open soon. Perry's manuscript ended on February 7, 1855, with the sudden statement that he would throw the bullet into the sea on Teingmouth Beach and spend the weekend with a friend who lived on the other side of the River Exte.

## 21.8.4. A Being Beyond Our World?...

Sangster, stricken with a sudden premonition, asked Perry's family about the date of his death. It turned out that Clark Perry died on the night of 8 to 9 February 1855 in Bicton –

the town where the 160-kilometer trek of the "Devonian devil" ended, starting on the beach in Teingmouth! Let's recall the motto from Wilson's book. Did this mean that the devil was looking for Clark Perry, the only man who died in Devonshire on that fateful night of February 8/9, 1855?

However, we still do not know why the creature from the bullet murdered the former sailor, how and what happened to it afterwards? A reassuring answer can be found to the first part of the question – it was most likely about the physical liquidation of an inconvenient witness who lifted the veil of secrecy on the unusual object. The second part of the answer is Perry's death certificate, in which it is written that he died of a heart attack caused by strong emotion. This medical blah-blah-blah, translated into human language, only means that the sailor died of fear when he was visited by a mysterious creature at night! Wilson answered the third part of the question in a story about his adventure with the footprints on the beach, which he noticed in October 1950. According to Sanster, it is one and the same creature that has grown up in the meantime, as well as other creatures of this species observed in different parts of the world – see note 11. According to his view, there were more of these "devils", "animals" or "creatures" from press reports and they represent a whole galaxy of otherworldly beings who have been traveling on our planet for centuries. Couldn't the fact that the alien orbs were found inspire **Herbert George Wells** to write The War of the Worlds?

Traces from the Devonian are still a mystery and at the beginning of the 21st century and to this day we do not know who or what left them behind, we only know that the "devil" was the killer. Will anyone solve this mystery? This can only be done by outsiders, for whom the Copernican motto is still alive: "man's task is to seek the truth", which has not become outdated in the 21st century, of which we are so proud. We think that there is a solution that is compatible with all the laws of physics, logic, etc., etc. – you just have to put them in a non-traditional order, and the puzzle will be put together.

## 21.8.5. The "Beast of Devonshire" and the Polish Issue

In this strange and confusing case, there are two polonica. And both are nice.

The first of these, mentioned in footnote 11, concerns an account in the Illustrated London News of March 17, 1855, in which there was a letter from a reader from Heidelberg, who had heard from a Polish doctor, that on the border of Galicia, but already on the Russian side, there was a hill called Sand Mountain, where similar tracks in the snow are found every year. sometimes they can be seen imprinted on the sand. The local population attributes them to the devil's frolics.

So much for Charles Fort, who quotes this without comment. The border of Galicia – that is, the Polish lands under the Austro-Hungarian partition – with the lands under the Russian partition was very long and after 1795 it reached from the junction of three borders near Sosnowiec to Chełm to the north-east, and then turned south-east to Kamieniec Podolski! A trifle – only about 1,500 km. And here is an appeal to the readers, has anyone heard anything about Piaskowa Góra, where devils organize their frolics, and strange tracks resembling hooves remain on the sand or snow, as in the attached illustrations?

The second polonicum is an excellent thrilling crime story written in the 60s by the famous – unfortunately deceased – **Joe Alex** or **Maciej Słomczyński** (1920-1992) entitled "You are only the devil", in which the insightful detective faced a criminal pretending to be... "the devil of Devon"! - And, of course, he solved the mystery of this crime.

The idea is excellent; the execution is excellent. What a pity that only once this novella was made into a TV show from the "Cobra Theatre" series, and yet it is material for an excellent film, much better than a Western production, in which shooting and beating after the murder goes for better with karate and kung-fu fights... Here you think!! – as in all Joe Alex's books – and that's why they're so cute! Maciej

Słomczyński – like **Jerzy Edigey** or **Kazimierz Korkozowicz** – wrote for thinking people, not for brainless "muscle-wings", whose adventures are so intoxicated by the contemporary mass television viewer. It's a pity that this is not noticed by our directors who make more and more idiotic series, modeled on Latino tearful scumbags, or American soap operas, not to mention the stories about our drunken defenders of the law, brandishing weapons at every opportunity and often loudly emitting religious shouts beginning with "k" and ending with "mać"... Sometimes you miss the "Cobra" from the old, but good 60s of the last centuries!

So, let's take a good look at the sands of the beaches and snowfields, because maybe we will see strange traces left by beings from other dimensions of our Reality. These beings are reality and they are among us – but we do not always want to see them, and even if we do, we try at all costs to inscribe them into the scheme of our everyday life, because in our naivety we think that in this way we will take the whole problem.

And this is a serious mistake...

**CR**

# CHAPTER 22. HOLLOW EARTH

Could these beings inhabit the oceans and the interior of our planet? This question is important due to the fact that while we have some knowledge about the Moon and the planets, almost none about the interior of the Earth, not to mention the Global Ocean.

I came across Hollow Earth in the sixth grade of primary school, when I read "Journey to the Center of the Earth" **by Jules Verne**. But even before that, my beloved Grandfather read to me at my pillow "Through the Land of People, Animals and Gods" by **Antoni Ferdinand Ossendowski**, which talks about the underground land of Agharti. I remember them well. Then, during my conscious search, I began to associate facts and legends. I figured that the thought that Sirens and other mythical and legendary creatures could originate from the Hollow Earth, Agharti, Caprona, Plutonia, Interterra or another Pellucidar...

## 22.1. The Agharta civilization exists!

Researcher **David Wilcock** claims that an inner-Earth civilization exists and reveals the secret of the Hollow Earth – as he knew before.

The concept of the "Hollow Earth" was first proposed to the modern world in the 17th century. The legendary scientist Sir Edmond Halley suggested that the Earth was hollow and that life was flourishing there. Later, his claim was challenged by other experts, and he also did not continue his research on it. However, in later years, the so-called Hollow Earth theory, which is talked about in several folklores and cultures, became popular. Now, ancient astronaut theorists argue that the Earth is hollow and that an unknown civilization lives inside.

In 2015, New York Times bestselling author **David Wilcock** stated in an interview with Coast To Coast AM radio that there is an alliance of ancient civilizations living inside the planet. These inhabitants had long called the inner Earth their home and had the intention of revealing it to humans, he added.

Wilcock firmly believes that over the course of our planet's long history, many advanced civilizations, such as the Atlanteans, have gone underground to survive the chaotic times that have ruled the surface of our planet. Finally, they decided to settle in their new underground environment.

According to his information, the human timeline seems to be branching out as the entire nature of matter, energy, and consciousness changes. While the negative timeline leads to Armageddon and the pole shift, the positive timeline is the ascension and progress of souls.

Quoting contactee **Corey Goode's testimony**, Wilcock claimed that the fragile relationship between the inner Earth people and those who live on the surface, who know of their existence, has recently splintered.

"This military-industrial complex has previously worked with these people and had treaties with them, and now they're trying to kill them," Wilcock said.

One group, known as the Nordics, presented themselves as ETs from the Pleiades to the U.S. government, when in fact they are descendants of the Atlanteans who have lived here all along, Wilcock revealed. This is why, according to Wilcock, these Inner Earth Civilizations have come together to respond to the great threat emerging in recent times, and are turning to interstellar beings in hopes of getting help in the fight against the forces that are trying to destroy them...

In the event that the underground societies complied with the request, he thought:

"I think we're going to find that the underground bases are much more extensive than we thought and much older.

Scientifically speaking, **Isaac Newton**, in his mathematical work on gravity, showed that nothing prevents astronomical bodies from having empty cavities inside. Newton did not object when **Edmond Halley** suggested to him that our planet might be empty. Even NASA seems to accept the possibility of hollow planets.

Wilcock explained that during the formation of all the aquatic planets in the universe, empty cavities form beneath the surface of the crust with their own biome with bacteria that are capable of emitting natural light. "It means that you can really live in caves on Earth that have visible light," he marveled.

## 22.2. Subterranean civilizations in folklore

The existence of underground tunnels and passages has been debated for centuries. Ancient civilizations around the world speak of these entrances leading to entirely new kingdoms, located deep beneath the planet's surface.

A good example of the underworld is the ancient city of Derinkuyu (formerly Melengübü) in Turkey, stretching to a depth of about 85 meters. It is large enough to provide shelter for up to 20,000 people with their livestock and food supplies. It is the largest excavated underground city in Turkey and one of several underground complexes located throughout Cappadocia.

The existence of underground tunnels and passages has been debated for centuries. Ancient civilizations around the world speak of these entrances leading to entirely new kingdoms, located deep beneath the planet's surface.

The underground city of Derinkuyu can accommodate up to 20,000 people, plenty of pets, and enough supplies to wait out the invaders.

The city was built during the Byzantine era when it was heavily used as a defense against Muslim Arabs during the Arab-Byzantine wars (780–1180 CE). The city was connected to other underground cities through many kilometers of tunnels. Some of the artifacts discovered in these underground settlements date back to the Middle Byzantine period, between the 5th and 10th centuries.

There are many deep believers who believe that there are many entrances to the underworld, such as the Pyramid of Giza, Iguaçú Falls, Gobi Desert, the Andes, the Himalayas, etc. (and in our country Babia Góra).

According to local legends, Shambhala (or Shamballah or Shambhallah, Shampullah, Land of d'Bus, Shangri-la, Land of Ui or Üi) is a realm of the gods that exists on both the physical and spiritual planes. There is also a mention of this mythical land in various ancient texts. In the writings of the Bön religion, there is a description of a closely related land known as the Tagzig Olmo Lung Ring.[48] In addition, the "Vishnu Purana," a sacred Hindu text, mentions Shambhala

---

[48] Tagzig Olmo-Luun-rin with Dr. **Ljudmila Shaposhnikova**.

as the birthplace **of Kalka,** the tenth and final avatar of the Hindu god **Vishnu.**

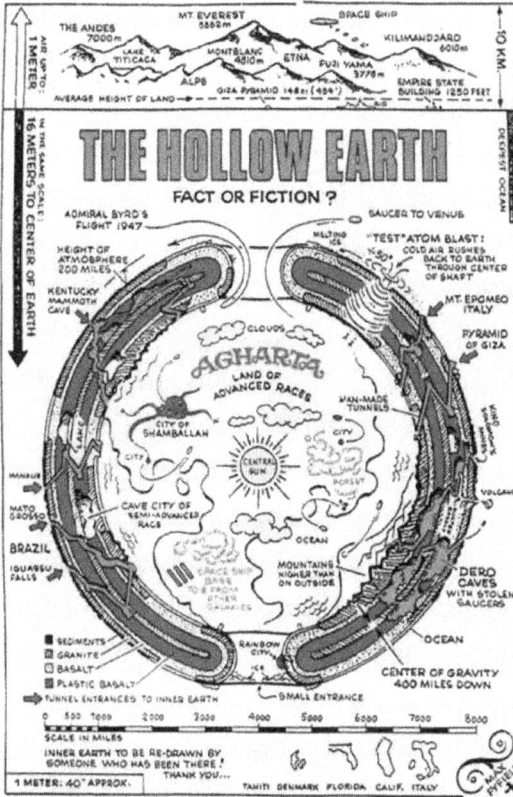

*The interior of the Hollow Earth according to esotericists. NB. in Poland, the entrance to Agharta is located somewhere on Babia Góra...*

Tibetans believe that the land of the gods is guarded by people with supernatural powers and has often been seen by locals. Tibetan lamas have been searching for Shambhala for centuries. Those who seek the kingdom never returned: they either found it or perished.

The most fascinating is the story of two Russian emigrants, **Nicholas and Helena Roerich.** The couple tried to reach Shambhala several times. At the end of 1923, they arrived in Darjeeling, India, with the intention of finding Shambhala.

Another incident that highlights the presence of Shambhala is the disappearance of the entire population of the Guge people. Archaeologists were stunned to find various tunnels in the town of Guge. Many theorists believe that these underground tunnels may have been a passage to Shambhala, and that the Guge people found them and decided to leave the surface. It is estimated that around 100,000 people have disappeared without a trace.

There is another legend about the Hopi Indians, when they were rescued by the so-called underground "ant people" during a fire, volcanic eruption, asteroid impact, ice age or strong coronal ejection from the Sun. During these two devastating events, the ant people civilization hid the Hopi people in their underground caves and provided them with food and water.

In the past, many conspiracy theories have shaped the tale of the underworld, but there are scientific discoveries that may support this theory.

## 22.3. Further evidence

The first scientist to assume that our planet was empty was the well-known English astronomer Sir **Edmund Halley** (1656-1742). In 1692, he wrote that the Earth is a crust 1000 km thick, and in its center, there is a core with the diameter of Mercury [4879.4 km], which heats and illuminates the inner part of the Earth's crust, so that it has its own unique flora and fauna. And one more, very interesting statement by this astronomer. Halley explained the effect of the polar auroras by the fact that the "subterranean" atmosphere, breaking outwards, began to glow into the "Earth" atmosphere. After 300 years, scientists looking at satellite images mention his theory.

## 22.4. Plutonia

In 1818, Congressmen, college presidents, and prominent scholars in the United States received a letter from **one D. K. Symmons**:

To the whole world!

I inform you that the Earth is hollow, inhabited in the center and having two holes at the Poles. (…) I need a hundred daring fellow travelers to leave Siberia at the end of the summer in a sleigh across the ice of the Arctic Sea. I promise that we will find warm and rich lands there, containing natural resources and game. (…)

The brave captain was denied a request to finance this daring enterprise, but his hypothesis of "holes at the Poles into which the waters of the oceans fall" was seriously considered, with some scholars giving it a positive assessment.

Renowned scientists are sensitive about their reputation, which is why they are afraid of publishing controversial theories about the existence of the Hollow Earth in scientific journals. Thus, instead of scientific articles, they published their crazy hypotheses in the form of fantasy and science-fiction novels. This is what Russian academician **Vladimir A. Obruchev** did. The scientist decided to convey his hypothesis about the underworld – Plutonia – in the form of *a sci-fi* novel. Obruchev assumed that in prehistoric times a giant meteorite fell on our planet and literally shot through it, tearing out a hole in the Earth's interior. And this void – as the scientist assumes – can be entered through the holes located at the Earth's poles.[49]

Obruchev's hypothesis attracted the attention of not only fans of SF literature, but even the leadership of the USSR. According to the views of researcher **V. Kriesławski**, the activity of Soviet Antarctic explorers in the 30s and 40s of the twentieth century was caused by nothing else than the desire to verify the "crazy" hypothesis of the famous academic!

## 22.5. Not only the Russians

But not only the Soviet government was interested in searching for entrances to Plutonia. Renowned political activist and Antarctic explorer **M. Serrano** expressed his belief in the existence of an underworld:

(…) It should be made clear here that all the arguments and theories here presented concerning the Hollow Earth are merely a repetition and development of old views which are expressed in ancient myths and legends of great and fundamental importance to Mankind, as I intend to clearly show and prove in this work. (…)

---

[49] In the novel, the travelers reached the center of the Earth – that is, Pluto – by entering it through an opening located on the mythical Nansen Land located somewhere near the North Pole.

The ground is pierced in two places and empty inside. There are two entrances to its interior, which are located near the Poles, in places above 83 degrees north and south latitude. On the other side of the earth's crust there could be continents, mountains, seas, forests and rivers, which are inhabited by a race that has come here for a long time, which we know as the Hyperboreans. (…)

Over the next decades, the idea of a Hollow Earth has been relegated to the mindless theories held by a handful of fanatics like Symmons, mystics like Serror, and fantasies of old academics like Obruchev.

## 22.6. And yet it exists?

The skeptical attitude towards the possibility of the existence of Plutonia changed at the end of the 20th century, as more and more new satellite photos and television images of polar and subpolar lands came in. In 1968, the American meteorological satellite *ESSA-7* transmitted strange images of the North Pole to Earth. With the complete absence of clouds, which is extremely rare in this type of photographs, there was a huge hole in the North Pole – the entrance. The fact that the photo was authentic – experts have proven it many times. Strange satellite images were also taken over

Antarctica. They are presented on the *Radarsat website*.[50]

Images taken by NASA's research satellites show that the auroras come out of the Earth's interior and form a kind of circle around the entrance to the Hollow Earth near the South Pole.

The American supporter of the idea of the Hollow Earth – **Jones Mac Libbly** cites three special types of premises confirming the existence of the underground land. Anyway:

In the photos of Antarctica, you can perfectly see a spot on one side, which can be interpreted as the entrance to the Hollow Earth, and from which fog is coming out. Where could it be there if not from the opening leading to the underworld?

From this part of the ice continent, where the entrance to the underground world is located, it is close to the shores of the ocean and it is from there that a lot of icebergs break off. This is related – according to his views – to the phenomenon of "ice escape from the dark and round area";

When we look closely at the directions of movement of air masses in Antarctica, we notice that they are moving towards the zone located near Queen Maud Earth located in the African part of Antarctica. Winds are created by masses of

---

[50] Other even more interesting evidence is presented on the website: *http://www.bibliotecapleyades.net/tierra_hueca/esp_tierra_hueca_24.ht m*, which shows satellite images of Antarctica with the South Entrance.

warm air flying out of the opening, which cause masses of cold, continental air to flow downwards.

## 22.8. Also other planets

Jones Mac Libbly also gives a more detailed explanation of the structure of the planets. He claims that the other planets of the Solar System are also hollow. The images of the planets show the same openings, analogous to Earth's, which are "obvious ventilation". As an example, he cites a photo of Venus taken in the thermal (infrared) radiation range found on the Internet. In this image, you can clearly see how the temperatures of gases from its atmosphere drop sharply in the region of the North Pole there, and then – completely unexpectedly – a "spot of heat" appears – and exactly at the place of the Venusian pole!

*Whales from Gesner's "Book of Fish" – but are they really? Or perhaps they are sea creatures from inside the Earth?*

The hollow planet hypothesis was unexpectedly confirmed during the exploration of the lunar surface during the *Apollo* program. Based on the data obtained, NASA employee Gordon McDonald managed to carry out calculations that showed that the Moon is a spherical celestial body hollow inside! But why didn't aviators flying over the Arctic and Antarctic notice a huge hole on the surface of our planet?

According to ufologists, there are two answers to this question. The first assumes that near these holes, the magnetic field lines turn and compasses point north (or south) and guide planes along the edge of this hole, not through it.[51]

The second answer is even simpler: many polar explorers from Germany, the USSR and the USA were associated with the military and pilots had no right to talk about the observed phenomena.[52]

Unfortunately, so far all these arguments for the existence of the Hollow Earth are a bunch of nonsense that does not correspond to reality in any way. I will not argue with them,

---

[51] Yes, it would be in the case of magnetic compasses, but for many years gyrocompasses or radio compasses and satellite navigation have been in use, or even the GPS system, which are not affected by magnetic fields.

[52] Source – "NLO" special issue no. 1/2010, p. 2

and I quote these materials only out of chronicle duty. It's a bit of a pity, but I can repeat after **Aristotle**: *Amicus Plato sed magis amica verita est.* And now let's consider another possibility, namely...

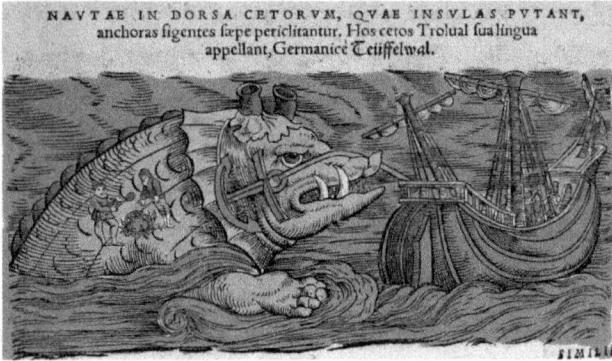

NAVTAE IN DORSA CETORVM, QVAE INSVLAS PVTANT, anchoras figentes sæpe periclitantur, Hos cetos Trolual sua lingua appellant, Germanicè Teiiffelwal.

*A whale as big as an island according to Gessner. However, zoology does not know of a toothed whale with huge tusks like the one in the drawing. Where did it come from in the Panthalassa?*

Back in the 80s of the last century, I was conducting a correspondence dispute (like in the good old days) with my journalist and writer friends. One of them, editor **Robert Jordan** from the weekly "Sea and Earth", consciously noticed that Humanity populated the sky with some Higher Beings, so the planetary underworld was also populated with human and non-human beings – including the inhabitants of

Agharta, Pellucidar and other lands. Was he right? – The future will show...

And as for the sensational photos from the *ESSA-7 satellite*, they show... regions not covered by the satellite's cameras, hence the impression that there is a hole to the center of the Earth. That's the whole mystery... – it makes my heart sad. And that is why I will repeat once again – *amicus Plato, sed magis amica verita est...*

Ⓒ

# CHAPTER 23. MERMAIDS AND ATLANTIS

Let's start with the fact that the legendary Atlantis is a hard, real fact. "Atlantis existed and we found it!" – geologists discover a lost world

Scientists have reportedly discovered the lost city of Atlantis off the coast of Lanzarote, Spain. When the discovery is confirmed, it will be a great discovery that will change our current understanding of history.

The Lost Continent is often hailed as the greatest myth ever told, taking on the dimensions of an actual historical event. It is considered by many to be a historical truth waiting to be confirmed. The lost city of Atlantis is one of the oldest such myths.

# 23.1. History of the Lost Continent

The story began with the ancient Greek philosopher **Plato** (427 – 348 BCE), who assumed the existence of an advanced civilization that flourished about 9000 years before his era.

He claimed that this civilization possessed technology far ahead of its time and was characterized by unusual architecture. According to him, they lived on a huge island lying behind the "Pillars of Hercules", now identified with Gibraltar.

Plato claimed that Atlantis did not survive the catastrophe that resulted in the entire island sinking into the sea in one day. It was widely believed that the island's collapse into the ocean was the result of the immorality of its inhabitants.

Although no concrete evidence of Atlantis has been discovered, numerous clues to its presence can be found not only in Plato's stories, but also in the myths of cultures east and west of the Atlantic Ocean. These reports include references not only to European nations, but also to the Mayans and Aztecs of present-day Latin America.

Plato was not the only ancient writer to refer to the island nations in the Atlantic Ocean. The historian **Theopompos** from the fourth century BCE described a vast continent inhabited by giants. The geographer **Marcellus** mentioned 10 divine islands. In the 17th century, the German scholar

**Athanasius Kircher** created a geographical map of Atlantis, which began the search for the mythical land of Atlantis.

Enthusiasts are looking for traces of Atlantis not only in the Atlantic, but also in the Arctic, near the northwest coasts of Europe and Africa, within the Bermuda Triangle and near Cuba, the Bahamas, the Azores and the Canary Islands, as well as nearby Sicily, Malta, Cyprus and Crete. Many researchers believe that the kingdom of Atlantis was not a single landmass, but rather a vast archipelago. Recently, it has been located on the continent of Antarctica, where ancient pyramid-shaped structures were reportedly discovered...

Myths and legends of almost all civilizations of both hemispheres of the Earth remember the founders of their cultures, who emerged from the depths of the ocean or from lands far beyond the horizon. These legends often speak of the homeland of these pioneers, which was destroyed by a catastrophic event.

# 23.2. We found her!

Scientists working on the IGME-CSIC Atlantis project in Spain believe they have discovered a place that inspired the entire myth of Atlantis. Using an underwater automatic submarine, they discovered a chain of sunken islands off the east coast of Lanzarote.

After descending to a depth of 2,500 meters, the submarine collected samples from the island's seabed, which probably sank millions of years ago.

Since then, they have christened this land "Los Atlantes" in honor of an ancient legend. Marine geologist **Luis Somoza** of the Spanish Geological Survey shared his findings with Live Science:

- This may be the beginning of the legend of Atlantis. We identified beaches, reefs, and dunes on the flat top of an underwater mountain. Somoza added: " In the past, these were islands that sank and are still sinking, as the legend of Atlantis goes.

Research suggests that the Los Atlantes archipelago existed in the Eocene, between 56 and 34 million years ago. Scientists have found that these sunken islands still retain features such as beaches, cliffs, and sand dunes. Some are only 60 meters below the water level. It is possible that during the last ice age, at much lower sea levels, wild animals may have lived in these areas.

The geologist stated that the extinction of volcanic eruptions led to increased solidification of lava, which contributed to the sinking of islands in the ocean.[53]

## 23.3. My 3 cents

And that's it, Czech brothers. It seems to me that Atlantis could indeed have existed in the location given by Aristocles-Plato in his "Dialogues", i.e. west of the Strait of Gibraltar. Let's look at the map – there are three oceanic hot spots – magma plumes that support three archipelagos on the surface of the Atlantic: Cape Verde (Cabo Verde), Canary Islands and Azores. This is where a large landmass – Atlantis – may have been located, which was held in waves by the pressure of the magma. According to the theory of plumes of heat from the Earth's interior, they can merge and separate, arise and disappear.

This could also be the case with Atlantis: it could be based on four plumes of heat from the inside of the Earth. Three of them are the archipelagos we know – the fourth was somewhere between them – exactly *vis-à-vis* the Strait of Gibraltar. And it was by displacement or disappearance that the stream of heat disappeared and Atlantis plunged into the

[53] Source "More Sprav" – www.morezprav.cz.

ocean. It left miserable remnants in the form of three archipelagos of volcanic islands and Madeira...

And most interestingly – it is there – in the middle of the Mid-Atlantic Ridge that there are mountains corresponding to Plato's description!

And one more issue, this time concerning the African continent, namely the Eye of the Sahara aka the Eye of Africa called Kalb al-Rishat (ar. قلب الريشات Qalb ar-Rīšāt, French: Guelb er Richât). It is an astonishing formation in the shape of concentric circles with a diameter of 50 km and is perfectly visible from space, which of course has resulted in a whole host of urban legends and conspiracy theories. It is here that their creators see Cerne – the capital of Atlantis.

Perhaps. But that doesn't bother her location in the Atlantic. The Eye of the Sahara does not have to be simultaneous with Atlantis – it could have been created earlier or later. Before or after the Cataclysm. Of course, "true" orthodox scholars reject the Atlantis hypothesis in favor of deliriums about a volcanic caldera, astroblem or regular weathering of the round dome of the Earth's mantle – whatever that means. The fact remains that no one knows what this Eye is.

At a distance of about 1000 km from Oko in the NW direction there is the Canary archipelago. A huge distance for an ordinary person, but for the Atlanteans it was an hour-long flight. 4000 km away is Egypt and its pyramids. It gives food for thought...

And what about the Mermaids?

Exactly – what does gingerbread have to do with a windmill? Well, it does. Mermaids have been known since Antiquity. Scientists claim that they never existed – that's right. For me, they were a product of evolution, but they could have become, assuming that there was a highly developed civilization of Atlantis, or Atlantica even earlier, a product of genetic engineering.

So, what were they? Biological machines used to conquer the Blue Continent and/or to defend the Atlanteans from their enemies. After the destruction of Atlantis, these bi0robots went their own way of evolution and became independent aquatic and human beings living in the ocean. That's the whole truth about Water people and their lives.

And now it will be about the possible interactions of people with them and more...

But their existence is threatened by our (mindless) activity and...

CR

# CHAPTER 24. MILLIONS OF TONS OF PLASTIC IN THE OCEANS (THE STATE OF DEFEAT OF REASON)

The lives of Mermaids and other sea creatures have recently been put to the test. This test is millions of tons of plastics and other products of human chemistry, which humanity carelessly disposes of in the ocean, hoping that they will decompose on their own. Yes, they decompose, but in time measured by centuries and in addition poisoning the environment and additionally contaminating it with the so-called microplastic, which is discussed below:

## 24.1. The largest dumpster in the oceans is twice the size of Texas!

The largest garbage dump in the oceans is getting bigger and bigger. The Great Pacific Garbage Patch is made up primarily of plastic, floating garbage halfway between Hawaii and California, which has grown to more than 600,000 mi²/1,553,900 km², as it stands in a recently published study. This is an area twice the size of the state of Texas!

*"Winds and convection currents collect this debris into one central location,"* says study author **Laurent Lebreton** of the Ocean Cleanup Foundation, OCF, the nonprofit that leads the study.

"It was first discovered in the 1990s that debris from these patches was coming from countries surrounding the Pacific Basin, particularly from nations in Asia, North America and South America," Lebreton said. It contains 1.8 trillion pieces with a total weight of 88,000 tons, which is the equivalent of 500 **Jumbo Jets**. But the new estimates are as much as 16 times higher than previous calculations. The results of the study — the most thorough study ever undertaken on ocean garbage patches — were published Thursday in the journal Scientific Reports.

"We were surprised by the large amount of plastic waste we encountered," said **Julia Reisser** from the Foundation. "We thought that most of this garbage was made up of small fragments, but these new analyses have shed new light on the nature of this garbage.

This study was based on three years of work carried out by an international team of scientists affiliated with OCF, 6 universities and an antenna sensor company.

"Our litter threatens fish in the deepest depths of the oceans. People have produced 18.2 x 1018 lb/8.4258 x 1012 tons, or 8.4258 Tt of plastics since the early 1950s. This is the equivalent of the weight of a billion elephants. The worst part is that this spot in the Pacific is not alone. The Great Pacific Garbage Patch is the largest of the five known dumps in the ocean, Lebreton said. Scientists work with ESA to take pictures of debris patches from space.

*Plastic beach in South America*

No government is doing anything to dispose of this garbage that is in international waters, so it is done by private organizations such as OCF, which are at the forefront of garbage and waste disposal.

"This is very urgent," says **Joost Dubois**, a spokesman for OCF. We need to fish it all out before it breaks down to a size that's too small to collect and also dangerous for marine life," he said.

Since plastics have been in common use since the 1950s, there's no way to determine how long it stays in the ocean. Left to itself, the artist will remain for decades, centuries or even longer.

"If we don't start extracting them, we can say that they will stay there forever," Lebreton said.[54]

## 24.2. Report: Plastic pollution in the Global Ocean reaches critical levels

The plastic infiltrates the ecosystem of the Global Ocean – from plankton to whales.

There are 5.25 trillion (5,250,000,000,000,000,000,000) fragments of plastic debris in the oceans, and each year 8,000,000 tons of plastic debris are added to this number. This is the equivalent of the contents of one city garbage truck washed up on the beach and thrown away every minute. (!!!) Thinking that the oceans would take all of this into their belly, the level of plasticization of the oceans began to approach a critical point: according to a new report by the McKinsley Center for Business and Environment's McKinsley Center for Business and Environment, the world's ocean will contain 1 ton of plastics for every 3 tons of fish by 2025.

All of this floating plastic debris – from microns to huge six-packs – not only disrupts the marine ecosystem, but also poisons global food resources.

---

[54] Source - Doyle Rice - https://www.usatoday.com/story/tech/science/2018/03/22/great-pacific-garbage-patch-grows/446405002/.

*Microplastics in the World Ocean*

"This has already reached crisis proportions," says **Andreas Merkl** of the Ocean Conservancy, "plastics break down into plastic particles that, like plankton, are eaten by all creatures – from plankton to whales." Plastics work like dirty, poisonous sponges in the ocean, and when animals eat them, they can just as easily poison them, because they act like poisonous pills.

The latest report calls for the introduction of control systems in the most developed countries, which are most responsible for plastic pollution of ocean waters. China, Indonesia, the Philippines, Thailand and Vietnam account for at least half of this pollution, as litter is conditioned by rapid economic development.

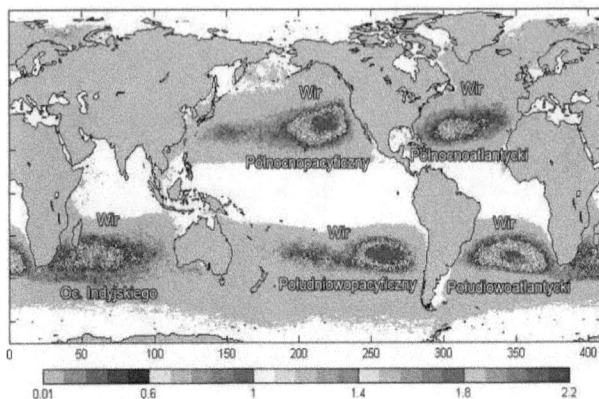

*Plastic Waste in the Global Ocean (according to NOAA)*

"We can focus on the places where plastics are being dumped into the ocean," says Merkl, "five countries can solve half the problem."

On average, about 40% of the garbage in these countries is collected and processed. But it is not this uncollected garbage floating around that is 3/4 of the problem, because it is this 1/4 of the ocean plastic that comes from this collected amount. And even if garbage companies collect garbage from land, the poor possibilities of its disposal will cause that this garbage will eventually end up in the ocean waters.

But how can these countries stop the flow of garbage into the ocean that is flowing from too many sources? The OCF report suggests five such "out there":

services collecting garbage and plastic waste,

Closure of leakage points without a plastic waste collection system

gasification and...

... incineration of plastics and

recycling of these.

The collection and accumulation of plastics in the countries of interest is about 40% - most of which ends up as rubbish. Thus, by expanding systems for collecting and closing plastic leaks in the waters of the Global Ocean, its pollution will be reduced by 50% by 2020.

This is not just a dream of ecologists. Coca-Cola and Dow Chemical, along with several other multinational companies, which we'll talk about later, have joined forces with the Ocean Conservancy to combat ocean pollution. A director from Dow Packaging and Speciality Plastics said at a press conference:

"We have joined together in order to fight for the future Omniocean free of plastics. Our companies will not produce plastics with the intention of ending ocean pollution, and we reaffirm that the industry must take a major role in order to completely eliminate plastic from the ocean by 2035.

Merkl said that countries that cannot recycle have no choice. Only 20% of plastic waste is worth recycling: the rest has to be sent to landfills or energy companies as fuel.

*"You have to concentrate on the basic handling of garbage,"* he says. And until the right infrastructure is built for this purpose, these countries will not be environmentally friendly. Here are the main problems with this:

1. Cleaning up the stains is difficult because of the size of the stains and because the areas of high concentration are constantly changing and any operations to collect them are difficult and no country will take responsibility for them.

2. We currently know five ocean vortices. They are formed when ocean currents meet each other and a system of eddies is formed. Most of the garbage in the oceans is pulled there and swirls, carried by currents.

*Local garbage patch off the coast of Central America*

3. These stains consist of pelagic plastic from plastic bags, water bottles, caps and polystyrene. **Plastics are not**

**biodegradable!!** The sun is grinding them into smaller and smaller particles in the process of photodegradation/photofragmentation, which makes it difficult to assess ocean garbage patches since the plastic fragments are not visible from satellites and aircraft.

4. Water striders (*Halobates sericeus*) lay their eggs on bird feathers, pumice stones, shells, and other insects, and these eggs are important for the marine food chain. The accumulation of microplastic particles forces them to change their eating habits, and they lay their eggs on drifting plastics that carry them outside their natural ecosystem.

5. Plastic garbage concentrates to a depth of 10 m of the water column. Then 70% of them sink and sink to the bottom of the ocean.

6. Plastic litter ranging in size from fishing nets to microparticles is found in waters. Garbage dumps from the east coast of Asia after a year or less end up in the Pacific gyres, where they go around in circles together with garbage from North America for 6 years.

7. 90% of the garbage rotating with the currents in the Global Ocean is made of plastic. Less than 5% of them are recycled.

8. These garbage stains also contain chemical compounds and other toxins. Plastics can absorb organic pollutants from seawater. Fish and birds eat those plastics that have broken into small fragments, which are then eaten by people.

9. North Pacific Eddies – subtropical convergence zone. The swirling ocean current of the North Pacific Gyres collects marine pollutants and slowly pulls them to their centers, where they accumulate.

10. Evaluated decomposition time of various anthropogenic objects:

a. Cardboard boxes – 2 months

b. Cigarette butts (filters) – 1-5 years

c. Plastic bags – 10-20 years

d. Styrofoam cups – 50 years

e. Styrofoam buoys – 50 years

f. Canned food cans – 50 years

g. Aluminium cans – 200 years

h. Plastic packaging for six-packs – 400 years

i. Plastic bottles – 450 years

j. Fishing line – 600 years

k. A glass bottle – we don't know.

11. 10% of the world's annual production of plastic mass of 200 Glb/~100 Gt is thrown into the waters of the ocean.

12. The size of the plastic patch is unknown, but it is estimated to be between 0.41% and 8.1% of the Pacific surface. Most oceania scholars believe that it is twice the size of Texas!

13. A typical cruise ship for 3000 passengers produces about 8 tons of solid garbage per week, most of which ends up in the ocean.

14. It is estimated that about 80% of all plastic garbage in the oceans got there from land watercourses (rivers and auxiliary water systems emptied in the sea) and the remaining 20% comes from ships and ocean sources (cruise ships, fishing vessels).

15. In many of the studied waters, the concentration of plastics was 7 times higher than that of zoo- and phytoplankton (algae).[55]

*Piles of plastic waste on beaches in Southeast Asia*

---

[55] Source - Claire Groden - http://fortune.com/2015/10/01/ocean-plastic-pollution/

# 24.3. How much does the consumption of plastics harm our oceans?

Whether we like it or not, art is part of our everyday life. Bags, sacks, containers, containers, kitchen utensils, various other items... - even clothes and shoes usually contain plastic parts. And why do we use them so often? The benefits of its use are threefold: plastics are versatile, durable, and above all else cheap, allowing them to be mass-produced at low cost. However, the proliferation of plastics causes a whole series of serious problems in the environment.

## 24.3.1. Ocean of plastic

The problem with plastic is the subject of many documentary materials. One of the latest is "A Plastic Ocean", directed by Australian journalist **Graig Lesson**. The video, which can be viewed on Netfix, shows the devastating, impact impact of plastic debris on the marine ecosystem in more than 20 places around the world. The film, produced by a group of scientists and activists, also shows the repercussions of underwater artists and the communities that live around these bodies of water.

The global environmental organization GREENPEACE also speaks repeatedly about the situation in our seas. She collects disturbing data in her report "Plastics in the Oceans", and so:

Every second, 200 kg of plastic enters the ocean;

Every year, 8 Mt of plastic garbage is dumped into the sea, which is the equivalent of the material from 800 Eiffel Towers;

The bottom of the ocean accumulates over 50 trillion pieces of plastic debris – according to estimates;

There are 5 "plastic islands" in the oceans of our planet: two in the Pacific, two more in the Atlantic and the last one in the Indian Ocean. Floating islands of plastic garbage contain so-called microplastics, i.e. plastic particles with a diameter of <5 mm;

If everything goes as before, the amount of plastic waste will increase by 900% in 2020 compared to the 1980 records. According to specialists, in 2050 there will be more plastics in the seas than fish;

And what happened in Spain? Every day, around 30,000,000 end-of-life containers and plastic bottles are discarded and pollute coastal waters, shores and coastal areas. On average, for every 320 products accumulated on every 100 m of beaches, as much as 70% are plastic products.

*A tangle of plastic nets threatening the lives of marine animals...*

## 24.3.2. Where do the plastics we throw into the sea come from?

When waste is properly managed, the plastics we leave in recycling bins end up in landfills, where they are incinerated and then recycled. However, there is a large amount of plastic waste that ends up in the sea in different ways:

Intentionally thrown into the sea;

Accidentally thrown from ships;

Wastewater (waste elements) from treatment units and wastewater treatment plants;

Municipal drainage and sewerage systems.

It is estimated that 80% of plastic litter accumulated in the sea comes directly from land, and the remaining 20% from activity at sea. Most of this marine debris has been found in coastal areas in densely populated areas: large cities and popular tourist areas. Another location of plastic marine litter are bodies of water where fishing is intensively practiced.

*Plastic beach in Southeast Asia*

# 24.3.3. The influence of artists on the life of the oceans

Plastics break down much more slowly in the sea than on land. Lower exposure to sunlight delays the process of decomposition of garbage, as well as contact with cold water. Although the influence of waves accelerates the decomposition process, the plastic breaks down into small particles that decompose chemically over a long period of time.

According to GREENPACE's estimates, it takes 500 years for a plastic bottle to disappear completely. Plastic cutlery needs 400 years, while plastic bags need 55 years. Plastic made of fishing ropes lasts even longer, which needs at least 600 years to completely disintegrate!

The devastating impact of plastic on marine life is multiple. Many fish eat plastic garbage and die by choking. But a special problem is the microplastics that float on the surface of the sea. These small shards, <5 mm in diameter, can be ingested by fish, crustaceans and plankton, which can cause their digestive systems to become blocked. Microplastics also accumulate chemical pollutants, which can then be eaten by humans at the top of the food chain.

# 24.3.4. Impact of marine pollution on the economy

The accumulation of plastic debris and waste not only harms marine fauna, but also has repercussions on the economy. The simplest and striking example we can give is what we call 'ghost fishing', where the nets and their mechanisms remain in the sea. These nets become a trap for many fish, which die, which reduces their number.

In Europe, cleaning up beaches and coastlines costs the administration €630 billion a year. The tourism sector also suffers the consequences: the presence of litter on the coasts gives a negative *image* to many potential holidaymakers and holidaymakers, and reduces its amount, which translates into a decrease in profits.

*Cleaning beaches of plastics – "Vac from the Sea" campaign (IOUG Hel Seal Sanctuary)*

# 24.3.5. What can we do for the ocean?

*Collecting plastic waste on the beaches of the North Sea (IOUG Hel Seal Sanctuary)*

The solution to the problem of plastic accumulation lies largely in the hands of governments. Effective waste management is essential, but other legal measures are also needed to prevent waste. Some are already underway, such as the obligation to pay for plastic bags in stores. Environmental organizations also demand the promotion of alternative materials for plastics.

Greater awareness-raising work that engages people in nature conservation is also important. Citizens also have a lot to contribute:

- Avoid using plastic bags and sacks: when buying, we should take home purchases in canvas or paper bags. Some supermarkets sell thick plastic bags that can be reused over and over again without the need to buy new packaging. Retrieving your shopping cart is another highly recommended option;

- Use of glass bottles instead of plastic bottles or cartons;

- Choose bulk products: there are now numerous stores that offer weight-based products such as soaps, shampoos, dishwashing liquids, legumes, etc. Establishments provide containers, but it is better to take them from home to avoid accumulating more plastics;

- Not using disposable packaging and containers: plastic cups, cutlery – especially at parties and celebrations – it is much better to use traditional dishes and cutlery. Even if we have to wash them off later, the effort is still worth it;

- Avoid buying products wrapped in plastics: do not buy fruit and vegetables wrapped in polystyrene containers. Buy eggs in cardboard packages, or buy them in bulk for your egg boxes.

- Replace your plastic jar containers or glass containers;

- Reduce or eliminate the use of film;
- Bring your own wrappers when you go shopping for food;
- Replace disposable razors with classic razors that allow you to change blades.
- Replace plastic lighters with ordinary wooden matches, or use reusable lighters;
- And – above all – put plastic waste in the right container.

The key is to shop rationally and adopt new habits. Adopting the 3R principle – reduce, recycle and reuse[56] is easier than we think, we just need to change our mentality to that of our grandmothers, who lived all their lives without plastics, without bakelite or polystyrene food containers.[57]

## 24.4. The problem of artists can be solved!

The series of articles aroused some interest.[58] In addition to phone calls and e-mails from my swimming or flying friends who had the opportunity to see this problem eye to eye, I

---

[56] W oryg. z ang.: *re-use*.

[57] Source - The Daily Prosper - *https://thedailyprosper.com/en/a/how-does-consumption-plastics-affect-our-oceans*.

[58] Na blogu Wszechocean – *www.wszechocean.blogspot.com*

received an email from Ms. **A.W.**, which read as follows:

*Dear Mr. Robert,*

*I've been reading your fantastic blog for years - there are not many such publications, so I don't look for better sources when I have the best ones. Since you have some knowledge, you also know many people, maybe I will learn something, without the disrespectful eyes of too serious mathematicians and contemptuous physicists with whom I wanted to talk.*

*I know that you deal with things that few do, and from what I sense from your blog, I have the impression that even the most absurd idea can interest you. This has been the case for many years, being a paper recycler, on the more scientific side of my work, but instead of spending time myself studying and looking for information, I prefer to ask if anyone knows, because they can read something somewhere. Of course, life does not give enough time for all the activities that we would like to do.*

*Could the solution to the problem of microplastics be gradual purification of water by evaporation? For some time now, I have been involved in the garden recycling of cellulose fibers, i.e. simply paper into usable forms - containers, lamps, furniture, acoustic coffers, picture frames, etc. I pour water into paper and dry it in the sun, the only thing I use is a drill and muscle power, I haven't had a chance to try a concrete mixer yet, but I will probably succeed next year. I wonder if such a beach action of grinding paper with water from the sea, performed by humanity, would have a positive effect on filtering the water, because plants may not withstand such a job. You could pour sand into a container with water, and mix the poured water with paper advertisements and dry it in the sun. The microorganisms will grow back in the remaining water, which will pour in cleaner from the sky. Instead of using energy, do something important. Instead of a rosary - next time he brings a bucket, a shovel, paper and purifies the water. Maybe there will be a new fashion for personally made items from paper that can be processed endlessly instead of producing new ones? Let us respect the lives of our beautiful brothers who gave us the lives of their trunks and branches, and let us carefully save every scrap of paper. I can hear them squealing as they lie in the street, mixed with mud. Let them also help to clean the water of the ocean.*

*Not to mention the fact that it's great fun. The kids leave the workshops as joyful as they can and beaming, relaxed, and the adults also join in willingly, how joyful and impatient they are waiting for the results!*

*I'm curious about one piece of information. How clean is the steam from water contaminated with printing ink, glue and hell knows what from the ocean or roof, because whenever I can I use rainwater, but mainly tap water, here terribly contaminated with chlorine and probably hormones. I am not a chemist, but I am very curious whether such particles of impurities will be fixed in paper objects and retained by this paper?*

*Paper can be as strong as wood, especially when combined with resin, polystyrene, I have already done experiments. However, such activity is related to filters in the paint shop, and I don't have one - I'm a 😨 vagabond. Paper can be like porcelain, durable and slightly brittle. It can successfully replace many plastics, but it does not electrify dust from the entire area, it is perfect for almost everything. I know because I use it. And if such an item gets boring, it won't become a plastic poison, which, despite recycling, is constant, how can you even drink water from a plastic bottle? Does it hurt so much to take a small glass bottle from home? What kind of jerk do you have to be to lug plastic garbage back and forth? From the store, with rubbish and so on. You really have nothing to do with time. I watch you people like this, and I cannot believe in your Collective Stupidity. In the shops, on the streets, everyone was hypnotized. It's time to turn on the Alarm Siren for Collective Stupidity – ha ha, I came up with the name of a punk band.*

*What would such measuring tools look like, where to examine the samples, could someone investigate the subject, make a measurement using seawater? Any calculation, would such an action make sense at all? I'm interested, for example, in the abstract number of people who would perform such a breakneck task, how many buckets would have to be sieved in how many days. Possibly robots, but here we would also have to calculate whether the ecological cost of creating such a robot will not exceed the benefits from it, but here we have to subtract the priceless aspect of working together, together for the greater good, and socializing children addicted to screens. Just an artistic curiosity about how many buckets of the ocean would take how many days for how many people. How much paper or other fibers?*

*It seems to me that we have to carry out this process of cleaning the ocean mechanically, genetically modifying organisms that build their bodies from plastic, it is better that it is out of the question, although it is probably already happening, if not spontaneously, then with the help of scientists.*

*I am curious about the fact how large a particle, or a nanoparticle of pollution, floats with water vapour? (Well, we played football with the boys in chemistry and travel books were also more important.) If someone explained it, preferably in a pictorial way ☺, it would be great.*

*Greetings to the Emergency Siren Team for Collective Stupidity,*

*A.W. and Paper Forms.*

And here is my answer:

*Madam*

*- Thank you very much for the good word.*

*I read your letter with interest and I agree with you that the waters of the Global Ocean need to be cleansed, this is a sine qua non condition for our survival as well! Plastics are a real threat that few people understand and appreciate. The worst thing is that human indifference and comfort have led to the emergence of situations that without radical steps on our part, will be a hopeless situation.*

*I don't think evaporation is a good idea. Of course, the larger fractions of plastics will remain, but the smallest and worst ones are unlikely to remain. They will be carried away by water molecules flying into the sky and will return to the ecosystem. Maybe I'm wrong, but I don't think it's the best idea.*

*Filtering will also be difficult, because very fine "sieves" are needed to stop the nanoplastics. They are the size of viruses, and as you know, viruses are difficult to filter...*

*Personally, I think that the best way will be to fight this filth biologically - apparently fungi have been discovered in the Amazon that devour plastics. There was also talk of GMOs, bacteria that feed on plastic - it would be an ideal solution.*

*You are right - we need to look for substitute solutions for artists, or artists that would be completely biodegradable. Well, as a businesswoman, you have more room for maneuver and resources to start cleaning up the world with your own company and spreading green technologies.*

*Let me include your letter (with some abbreviations) as a voice in the discussion.*

*Yours sincerely, R. Leśniakiewicz*

I would also like to add something that no one has mentioned in the materials I have translated, namely – nanoplastics, thanks to their small size, can also be a component of marine aerosol, which we inhale while at the seaside. I wonder if anyone has done research on this issue? And many more.

And something else from this shelf. Plastic-eating fungi really exist!

A team of biologists from the University of Michigan working in the Amazon rainforest on the border of Peru and Bolivia has discovered new species of fungi that are able to completely decompose plastic and turn it into organic matter.

The mushrooms, which were called *Petroleumvorous fungus*, were discovered in the Amazon forests, 400 km from the Peruvian-Bolivia border in the Del Manu natural reserve. The scientists made this astonishing discovery after their radio equipment was damaged by fungi that also fed on the crew's tents and synthetic clothing. The team had to be evacuated by helicopter in biological suits, because all their equipment and equipment had been devoured by mushrooms, which were not allowed to get to the surrounding towns. The scholars were escorted by Peruvian military and sent to quarantine at a military base near Cusco.

Government officials fear that these fungi will spread to surrounding cities and attack their entire infrastructure.

"The natives of the region told us about this mushroom before, but now we have concrete proof in our hands," explained Gen. **Horacio Mendez**, a Peruvian military officer.

"The discovery of a living organism that feeds on plastics like these fungi poses a serious threat to 'human civilization as we know it,', said Professor **Eduardo Chiapates** of the University of Mexico.

"These mushrooms will cost our civilization trillions of dollars for the destruction they will cause by spreading to our cities. This will cause massive damage to infrastructure, factories will be closed, cars will become unusable, and society as we know it will collapse – warns the scientist. – These simple fungi pose a threat to our civilization as we know it – he adds nervously.

This *Petroleumvorous fungus* also called the "doomsday fungus" can be used for a more constructive purpose, such as to get rid of plastic garbage around the world, or even to attack the Great Pacific Garbage Patch, but experts warn that these fungi should be in a "tightly controlled environment" and scientists are already working to find a potent selective fungicide. that would help keep these mushrooms under control.[59]

Hope? It would be good to have such a means to fight plastic waste. But this club has – as usual – two ends, because on the one hand it would be a salvation for the All-Ocean suffocated by billions of tons of plastics, and on the other hand, weapons from group B of the WMD triad, which could really annihilate the plastic civilization... Break it down into prime factors!

I hope that reason will prevail and it will be possible to clean our planet in the most ecological way possible. On the other hand, it should not be a problem for genetic engineering to produce GMOs that devour plastics and convert them into compost or hydrocarbons – gasoline or kerosene. That would be far more useful than glowing cucumbers or superweeds!

You can dream, but for now let's not throw plastics into forests and rivers, because we harm ourselves first of all. Let's start with bringing groceries in wicker baskets – just to start with. And until we start doing this, no fungi and bacteria will help us.

---

[59] Source - http://worldnewsdailyreport.com/plastic-eating-fungi-discovered-in-amazon-forest-danger-to-modern-civilization-believe-experts.

And the problem is growing, because it turns out that plastics also have an impact on the climate of our planet...

## 24.5. Ocean plastics have a significant impact on climate

Laguna Beach resident **James Pribram** holds plastic garbage in his hand that he found in the Atlantic Ocean 2,000 miles between Brazil and South Africa, in the South Atlantic Gyre in 2011. Although the burning of fossil fuels is a major cause of global warming, fossil fuels can also drive climate change through a completely different mechanism, in which plastic particles and small bioluminescent fish that inhabit hundreds of meters below the ocean surface play a role.

Glowing lighthouse fish or *Myctophis* (*Myctophidae*) are only a few inches long, but they are ubiquitous and make up almost half of the ocean's fish biomass. They are vital to the ocean's ability to absorb carbon, more than all the world's forests, during their migration in all seven seas.

During the day, lighthouse keepers avoid predators in deep water, from which they come to the surface at night, where they feed on carbon-rich plankton before diving back into deep water, where they in turn deposit their carbon-rich droppings. They also store carbon when they are eaten by larger fish. This migration ritual is the main opportunity to reduce the amount of CO2 produced by humanity and emitted into the atmosphere by – as it is estimated – 20-35%.

*The biggest threat to fish, birds, and marine mammals – plastic nets...*

So, whatever harms lighthouse keepers prevents the ocean from absorbing carbon. Alarming news that small crumbs of plastics resembling the favorite plankton food of lighthouse keepers can cause them problems and, consequently, climate change.

Most plastics are made from crude oil and natural gas and, for practical purposes, are not biodegradable, even if they break down into tiny and smaller fragments in water.

All marine plastic debris accumulates in circulating zones of ocean convergence called ocean eddies. Since the groundbreaking discovery in 1999 that plastic debris outweighs the amount of zooplankton in the surface waters of the North Pacific by a ratio of 6:1, it has been realized that tiny plastic debris can be confused by sea creatures that feed on plankton.

Subsequent research showed that more than a third of the stomachs of lighthouse keepers caught near the surface of the Pacific Ocean gyres contained pieces of plastic similar in size (1-3 mm) and color (transparent, white and blue) to local zooplankton.

The swallowing of plastics by lighthouse keepers explains the false results. Huge amounts of plastic disappear from the surface of the sea in all five of the world's largest whirlpools, especially those with a diameter of 2 mm.

Clogging of ducts, indigestion and starvation are obvious dangers resulting from eating plastic debris, which is believed to be associated with marine plastics and pose great dangers.

Petroleum contaminants that stick to the plastics are ingested and potentially join the food chain when small fish are eaten by large ones.

The threat also arises from blocks made of certain polymers. For example, polycarbonate plastic is derived from BPA (bisphenol A), an endocrine disrupting estrogen that can cause developmental disorders. In contrast, the basic components of polyvinyl chloride (PVC) and polystyrene are known as carcinogens.

The myriad additives that give plastic products the desired properties raise additional concerns, as they can get from ingested plastics into the body's tissues. Phthalate plasticizers and polybrominated flame retardants are typical additives that, for example, harm the endocrine systems of mammals.

Recent studies document the contamination of lighthouse keepers' tissues with chemicals that come from plastics and seawater.

In addition, the buoyancy of plastics can interfere with their stability and buoyancy during migration from the depths below the surface and *vice-versa*.

If the current trend continues until 2050, landfills and the environment will accumulate 12 Tt of plastic waste.

One of the earliest studies on how plastics enter the ocean annually from coastal communities indicates that there are between 4.8 and 12.7 Mt.

Depending on buoyancy, some plastics float and others sink and sink to the bottom, or move through water columns. Given the expanse of the oceans and the rate of influx of new plastics, open ocean clean-up programs are an unfeasible solution.

At the heart of the climate crisis is humanity's dysfunctional relationship to fossil fuels. If we continue to ignore it, this problem will grow faster and faster. The path we are following leads to increasing climate instability, which will manifest itself in increasingly severe storms and more severe droughts, the spread of human misery, mass extinction of species and social, economic and political upheavals.[60]

The need for a rational change from an economy based on burning fossil fuels as the primary source of energy to producing things based on renewable energy and producing

---

[60] For example, the migration crisis that we are witnessing in Europe, North America and Australia.

things that are recyclable and biodegradable. Eliminating single-use plastic items is a must.[61]

As you can see from the above materials – the problem of poisoning the waters of the Global Ocean exists and is becoming more and more serious. This applies to the entire biosphere of the Earth – not only its oceans – as well as all intelligent beings inhabiting it. This is obvious to every thinking person. Unfortunately, there are fewer and fewer rational thinkers and they are effectively silenced by *industrial lobbies*, for whom Nature conservation and ecology are a thorn in the side and interfere with the implementation of their interests. This is how it was, it is so and it will be so for a long time, so I am afraid that the gloomy vision of Humanity, which I presented in my work "UFOs and Time" (Tolkmicko 2011), will unfortunately become real, and sooner than we think...

ର

---

[61] Source - Sarah Mosko – „Los Angeles Times" - *http://www.latimes.com/socal/daily-pilot/opinion/tn-dpt-me-commentary-sarah-20171103-story.html*.

# CHAPTER 25. DANGEROUS WATERS OF THE BALTIC SEA

There is one more problem that I write about in each of my works – it is the problem of poisoning and contamination of the waters of our Baltic Sea. In order not to bore the reader, I will present him with my paper for the PHOENIX International Conference in Zázrivá, Slovakia - on September 17, 2022.

## 25.1. Report from Zázrivá

The Baltic Sea is a small, almost inland sea, occupying 0.2% of the entire Earth's ocean. Some even say it's a large lake. Its area is about 415,000 km², volume about 22,000 km³, the length of the developed coastline is about 22,000 km. Because it is surrounded by land on all sides, it is sometimes called the Mediterranean Sea of northern Europe. The Baltic Sea exchanges waters only with the North Sea – through the narrow and shallow Danish Straits: the Great and Small Belt, the Sound, the Skagerrak, the Kattegat. The total exchange of waters in the central Baltic Sea takes from 25 to 30 years. The Baltic Sea stretches widely from north to south for almost 1300 km, while from east to west it is more than half as long

– about 600 km long. The narrowest part of the Baltic Sea – the Gulf of Bothnia – is about 100 km long. At the same time, it is a young sea, because it is only 6000 years old. It was formed partly from ocean waters and from a melted Scandinavian glacier. It is a cold sea - its surface waters contain from 5‰ sodium chloride (NaCl) in the Gulf of Bothnia to 30‰ in the depths of the central Baltic Sea - east of the island of Bornholm and in the Danish Straits - Belts, Kattegat and Skagerrak. Deep waters are slightly sweeter and contain from 3‰ of salt in the gulfs of Bothnia and Finland, up to 8‰ in the south-west of the Gulf. Baltic Sea to 20-30‰ in Kattegat and Skagerrak.

The Baltic Sea has its own holiday – March 22 is the Baltic Sea Protection Day.

## 25.2. The Baltic Sea is home not only to birds, brown algae and fish

In the water of the Baltic Sea there are, m.in, pondweed (pierced or crested), seagrass (e.g. sea zostera), green algae (sea lettuce or tape, edible after cooking), brown algae (endangered bladderwrack), by the way, 30 years ago it was found on the Polish Central Coast, today it is no longer there – it can be found in the west of the Baltic Sea, red algae (forkwort, pinkflower).

There are plenty of mussels, the shells of which we collect on the beach (mussels, cockles, Baltic hornworts, sand mussels), crustaceans (gammarus, shrimps, barnacles and the largest – double great), as well as snails, e.g. Baltic waterflake. Jellyfish do happen. Most often the blue bowel, in winter – the water-footed bolt.

The Baltic Sea is home to both marine and freshwater fish (those most often in bays – perch, roach, zander, pike and bream) and the so-called bi-environmental fish, which spend part of their lives in fresh waters and part in salt waters (Atlantic salmon, European eel, sea trout, bellona).

We eat many of these fish every day. These are sprats, herring, cod, salmon and flatfish (flounder, plaice and turbot). Populations of some species are endangered, e.g. cod are overfished, as a result of which they cannot recover.

In the Baltic Sea there are also lesser-known fish, such as: devil hen (the only venomous species), foxtail, lumpfish, needlefish, snake warbler, sandeel and tobias. There are also two species of lampreys: the river lamprey and – very rare – the sea lamprey.

The Baltic Sea is inhabited by: the grey seal (grey seal), nerpa (i.e. ringed seal) and the common seal, as well as the only cetacean – the porpoise.

All these species are under protection. Among the birds nesting on the Baltic Sea, m.in are cormorants, auks, guillemots, swans, seagulls and ducks.

So much for the introduction, and now we will move on to the events that have taken place and are still taking place here.

## 25.3. UFOs over the Baltic Sea

Of course, there have been UFO sightings over this sea, and USO sightings in its waters. The first wave of UFO sightings over Scandinavia was a wave of sightings of "mysterious planes" seen there in the 20s and 30s of the twentieth century. These planes flew along the Scandinavian Peninsula from SW to NE directions. "Mysterious planes" were seen flying day and night. It was suspected that it was simply "illegal air traffic", especially smugglers smuggling alcohol into Sweden (where prohibition was already in force), but it was not possible to catch anyone red-handed and the whole matter was postponed ad acta. Today I am sure that the solution is training flights from Hamburg in the Third Reich to Murmansk and/or Arkhangelsk in the USSR and back, carried out under the ominous agreement of Rapallo of April 16, 1922.

The second wave of UFOs took place in the summer of 1946, when the echoes of World War II had already died down. During this period, strange objects resembling the shape of German *A-2/V-1/Fisseler Fi-103 missiles and* A-4/V-2 *ballistic missiles were observed over Sweden and other*

*Scandinavian countries*. The Swedes maintain that they were alien vehicles. Personally, I am of the opinion that these were German missiles that were fired from m.in Polish shores, where the training grounds for this weapon were located. These were tests of *V-1* and *V-2* missiles carried out by the Red Army, which seized a total of 22,000 units of these weapons. The aim was to learn about their capabilities and... intimidating the Scandinavian countries, which were to be the basis for World War III.

This is where it started, namely – with the fall of 1 *V-2* missile and 5 *V-1 missiles on Swedish territory*. They were carefully collected and transported to England, where they were thoroughly examined. Meanwhile, in July 1946, a strange phenomenon in the sky, the so-called July fireball, initiated the second wave of UFO sightings over Scandinavia...

The most interesting incident during the second wave of UFOs was the event on Lake Kolmjärv, into which a mysterious missile fell, exploded and covered people sunbathing there with shrapnel. Fortunately, no one was hurt. The strangest thing was that the bullet was made of a material resembling... plywood! As it turns out, some types of *V-1 missiles* were made of plywood and laminates, especially at the end of the war, and when exploding, they literally broke into sawdust!

Swedish ufologists estimate that 997 reports (as of 1987) on UFO sightings and incidents during that "rocket summer of 1946" have been accepted.

## 25.4. Also with us...

Mysterious balloon over Świnoujście. On June 27, 1985, between 8:30 p.m. and 11:00 p.m. CEST, a strange phenomenon was observed over Świnoujście. A strange "star" appeared above the western horizon, which moved very slowly over the city in an easterly direction. It was observed by soldiers of the Border Protection Forces and the Navy and soldiers of the National Air Defense Forces. It was determined that the object was moving at an altitude of about 7000±200 m and most likely it was a weather balloon released by the Royal Meteorological Institute in Drammen, Norway. But whether or not for sure, no one knows...

As a curiosity, I will add that we saw a similar object in July 1967 at the Szczecin Lagoon in the morning, during a cruise on the MS *Alina* cruise ship from Szczecin to Świnoujście. As in the above case, the object was visible for about 3 hours. It could have been a spy balloon released by NATO.

We also saw a similar "balloon" in September 1973 over the High Tatras. This object moved very slowly at an altitude of at least 10,000 m, had the shape of an isosceles triangle, and glowed white. It was observed from the Astronomical Observatory of the Jagiellonian University in Krakow by two professional astronomers: Prof. **Kazimierz Kordylewski** and Prof. Dr. **Zbigniew Dworak**. Both of these scientists claimed that this object could not have come from Earth.

In addition, such "balloons" have also been seen over Hungary, Bulgaria and Yugoslavia, and in these cases too, their nationality could not be identified. There is a possibility that these were American reconnaissance balloons, or – which is equally possible – Soviet balloons that are the equivalent of the American Farside program – launching ICBMs with the help of balloons that pulled the missile to an altitude of 30-40 km and flew to the target from this altitude. This program was abandoned at the end of the 70s.

Who fired at MF *Wawel*? This mystery is even darker, because to this day it is not known what happened in the waters of the northern sectors of the Pomeranian Bay on March 19, 1986. When the ferry was at the height of the Rügen cape Nord Perd, at 16:30 CET, three very high fountains of water shot into the sky on its port side and in front of the bow. Experienced crew members of the ferry estimated that they could have been artillery shells with a caliber of over 220 mm, fired from the shore of the GDR. After the ferry docked at the Sea Ferry Pier in Świnoujście, witnesses were interviewed, including the captain and two officers who saw the incident, and the case was set in motion.

R. Leśniakiewicz, M. Jesenský, S. Bednarz

The witnesses were questioned by officers of the Navy intelligence and the Security Service. No one admitted to shooting at the ferry. The case remains unsolved to this day.[62]

The first CE3 on the territory of Poland, which was recorded by the world ufology, took place on the island of Wolin on August 31, 1953. At around 19:00 CEST, 7 witnesses observed a saucer-shaped UFO landing with a turret. Probably, according to the Swedes, it was not the landing of an alien vehicle, but of a Nazi saucer-shaped *Haunebu V-7 flying vehicle*. Western authors claim that it was a German-built vehicle, but witnesses saw the letters CCCP and the coat of arms of the USSR on the side of the vehicle. It was flown in the area of Gdynia – more precisely in Babie Doły (Gotgenhafen-Hexelground), where the SS air training ground was located. The test pilot was to be Capt. pil. **Hanne Reitsch**, who was seen in a flying saucer in this area, which will be discussed later.

The second SS air training ground was located in nearby Władysławowo (Großendorf), and it was managed by SS-Brigadeführer **Otto Mazuw**. Flying saucers with pilots inside were also seen there.

---

[62] However, some facts related to the disputed issue as to the course of the GDR-PRL border in the Baltic Sea seem to indicate that it was the shelling of our ferry by the East German coastal artillery.

One of the surprises for the Allies that was being prepared there was the *Silbervogel rocket plane of* engineer **Eugene Sänger**, which, in theoretical assumptions, could bomb cities in the USA. This was possible thanks to its range and the ability to even orbit flight and *a payload* of 1000 kg. Fortunately, it was too small to carry atomic bombs weighing 4-5 tons, but dropping 1 ton of bombs with such expenditures as fuel + oxidizer made no sense. However, the rocket plane could carry 1 ton of usable mass into orbit and thus be a means of supporting the construction of an orbital station, which was to burn targets on Earth with the help of a large concave mirror.

This strange incident was classified as CE3 and even CE4. It happened in Szczecin, on April 23, 1983, at 19:30 CEST. The protagonist of the event is a woman who was telepathically abducted to the deck of a UFO. Fortunately, a friend of hers entered her apartment and the Ufits fled. It is particularly interesting that UFOs fulfilled the postulate of Prof. **J. Vallée** assuming that UFOs have a disintegrative drive. Annihilated air produces radiation and a vacuum zone in which UFOs move, hence CE witnesses have often been burned or even radiantly electrocuted.

The case of CE5 in the waters of the Gulf of Gdańsk. Two fishing boats *HEL-126* and *HEL-127* were attacked on August 23, 1979 by a glowing red BOL, which caused headaches and musculoskeletal pains, disorientation, changes in blood pressure, etc. unpleasant effects in the witnesses of this event. BOL also affected electronic equipment (radio, radar). Most interestingly, there were Soviet fishing vessels and a helicopter in the area, which approached the Polish cutters, which gave rise to the assumption that the Poles had been attacked with some kind of $\psi$ weapon that both superpowers were working on. The case has not been solved to this day.

This is one of the most mysterious and confusing UFO incidents on the Polish coast, the Polish Roswell. This is one of the strangest UFO incidents in the entire history of Polish ufology. On January 21, 1959, in the morning, a burning object fell into the port basin No. IV, which raised a cloud of water vapor. Later, on the city beach and in the Naval Port in Gdynia, some unusual creatures were found, which were first transported to the Academic Hospital in Gdynia, and then – after their death – under a convoy to the USSR. Witnesses of these events are still alive today, and NHK television made a film about this incident, in which the famous ufologist **Bronisław Rzepecki** participated.

So far, there is no explanation for this incident. I hypothesized that the Russians shot down the American biosatellite *SCORE (1958-Zeta),* which they extracted and transported to the USSR.

A typical incident with the Night Lights over the Bay of Gdańsk. The witnesses are young married couples from

Gdynia, who were going to Władysławowo in August 1994. Between Puck and Władysławowo, they noticed 7 objects glowing with yellow light over the waters of the Gulf of Gdańsk, which strangely "danced" in the air. Witnesses watched them for about 30 minutes, then got into the car and drove away. Unfortunately, they didn't have anything to take a photo with...

This incident took place in the first half of December 1991 in Jastarnia on Kosa Helska. Three witnesses observed a white light object hanging over the sea waters at a distance of about 2 km from the shore. This observation was also confirmed by Border Guard officers who observed the same object with their own eyes.

An exceptionally interesting case of **S. Theau**. This strange incident took place during World War II, and its protagonist is a French forced laborer/prisoner named S. Theau. On July 18, 1943. Theau worked in Gdynia as a butcher's assistant in the Babie Doły district – then Hexelgound. That day, on his way to work, he noticed a strange gray, metallic disk stuck in the sand at the foot of a seaside dune. Inside there was a pilot in whom he recognized the Nazi test pilot, Capt. pil. **Hanna Reitsch**. The woman told him to help her extract the disc from the sand, and then she got into it and flew in the direction of Władysławowo. At that time, the Polish coast was one large series of Nazi training grounds of the Wehrmacht, Luftwaffe and SS. It was there that the latest technologies were tested, such as V-missiles, *V-3 Tausendfüssler super-guns*, *V-7 Haunebu* and other flying discs, as well as Engineer Sänger's transatlantic suborbital bombers. This incident was described **by Jean Sider** in his book "Deux recontres de 3eme type prearnoldienes".

## 25.5. Falcon Millennium at the bottom of the Baltic Sea

A fantastic *Falcon Millennium* at the bottom of the Baltic Sea. This is one of the last mysteries of the Baltic Sea. Discovered in June 2011 by the Swedish team Ocean X, the rock formation at the bottom of the Gulf of Bothnia closely resembles the *Falcon Millennium* spacecraft from "Star Wars". So far, it has not been thoroughly explored by divers due to the fact that it is located at a depth of 90 m.

Personally, I think it could be a geological structure resembling the Devil's Tower (WY), which is the core of a volcanic chimney. A similar structure may be found at the bottom of the Baltic Sea, which was forced into the Earth's crust by the four glaciers of the Cenozoic.

Another possibility is a formation similar in shape to the mysterious structure of Yonaguni (Okinawa Prefecture), which may be a megalithic structure made by humans.

Mysterious Vineta – Baltic Atlantis? It has many names: Vineta, Jomsborg, Jumne, Jumeta, Yom... In the 9th and 10th centuries, the brave and valiant Jomsvikings lived there, who were feared on all coasts of the Baltic Sea. Later it was a populous, rich city, which – according to legend – sank into the waters of the Szczecin Lagoon as a punishment for immeasurable greed, promiscuity and debauchery. Today, on moonless nights, the bells of the sunken city can be heard ringing from the bottom of the Lagoon, and the ghosts of its inhabitants appear on the waves. The truth is that the city was sacked and destroyed by the armies of the Scandinavian jarls and never regained its importance.

Vineta is also a complex of fortifications and underground shelters from World War II. The history of the complex begins in the thirties of the last century. In order to effectively defend the Kriegsmarine's naval base, the German command decided to build a coastal artillery battery.

After the end of World War II, the post-German shelters were taken over by the Polish Army and then rebuilt into a backup command post. It was from this place that the units of the Polish Army were to be commanded during the attack to the west – in the direction of North Germany – Denmark. It was on this base that an order was to be issued that could end in the atomic annihilation of the entire world.

Today, on the site of Vineta, there is a Viking open-air museum in Ostrów Recławski, where in the summer historical and folklore events and shows of reenactment groups from Poland, Germany, Denmark, Sweden, Finland, Russia and the Baltic States take place.

Strange Ale's Stones or Ales Stenar or Swedish Stonehenge – a megalithic sanctuary. It is located in the village of Kåseberga near Ystad (11 km). It was built of 59 boulders weighing 5 tons each. The entire formation has the shape of an oval or a boat. It is not known who and why built it in the 6th century AD. There was probably a cult center or a heliophysical observatory there.

## 25.6. Poisons at the bottom of the Baltic Sea

Since the end of World War II, up to 50,000 tons of chemical weapons (chemical weapons from the ABC of Weapons of Mass Destruction triad) and 500,000 tons of conventional weapons – mines, bombs, artillery ammunition, etc. Thousands of shipwrecks also lie at the bottom of the basin, some of them in Polish waters – 415 objects of this type have been identified so far.

Almost a quarter of the units are located within the Gulf of Gdańsk, which is so important for the economy and tourism. Some wrecks pose a huge threat to the marine ecosystem. These are in particular the SS *Franken*, from which fuel is extracted, as well as the SS *Stuttgart*, whose remains contaminated 40 hectares of the seabed for many years. In other waters, these are the MS *Fu Shan Hai* and SS *Skitteren*, which contain chemicals and whale oil...

[…]

The photo shows a rusty barrel of mustard from the bottom of the Baltic Sea. From such barrels, Chemical Warfare Agents are released into the water, which penetrate into the water and contaminate the environment. In the last 20 years, there have already been 115 incidents with C-weapons. In the depths of the Baltic Sea there are poisons such as:

Sarin – $C_4H_{10}FO_2P$,

Soman – $C_7H_{16}FO_2P$,

Tabun – $C_5H_{11}N_2O_2P$,

Luisite A – $C_2H_2AsCl_3$,

Iperyt – $C_2H_8Cl_2S$,

Clark I – $C_{12}H_{10}AsCl$,

Clark II – $C_{12}H_{10}AsCN$ i inne.

Particularly dangerous wrecks are the SS *Skitteren*, which contains 500,000 liters of whale oil, and the MS *Fu Shang Hai,* with chemicals on board... Equally dangerous are the wrecks of the passenger ships MS *Wilhelm Gustloff*, MS *Goya* and MS *General von Steuben* sunk in the course of the German *Operation Hannibal*. Incidentally, the personnel of the V weapons training grounds on the Gdańsk coast, the cadets of the underwater weapons school in Gdynia and the personnel of the Torpedo und U-Bootwaffe Versuchenanstallt in Gotenhafen-Hexelground were evacuated on these ships. Therefore, even during and after the war, these wrecks were intensively penetrated by the Soviet intelligence services, which expected to find valuable scientific and technical documentation there. It was the Soviet equivalent of the American *Paperclip mission.*

## 25.7. The problem of pipelines on the bottom of the Baltic Sea

According to press materials, the NORD STREAM and NORD STREAM 2 pipelines are a real threat to the entire Baltic basin, as they run through areas of the bottom where C-weapons and explosives contained in bombs, mines and torpedoes were stored.

Gas pipelines threaten primarily Polish beaches and the Polish fishing zone as well as the Polish energy sector, which is why Poles are protesting against them so intensely. We already have the first results of work on the seabed – dead seal puppies found in Finland. They were killed by Chemical Warfare Agents from the bottom of the Baltic Sea.

A campaign codenamed *Vac from the Sea* carried out in the Scandinavian countries and Germany aimed at cleaning beaches of all plastic waste that poses a threat to all marine organisms – especially the so-called microplastics, which penetrate into the lungs of humans and animals along with sea aerosol!

## 25.8. Hel Seal Centre

At this point, I would like to pay tribute to the unfortunately deceased Prof. **Krzysztof Skóra** (1950-2016) – the creator and animator of the Hel Seal Sanctuary of the Marine Station of the Institute of Oceanography of the University of Gdańsk. On his initiative and under his leadership, in 1977 he began to transform the Institute's facility – the Marine Field Laboratory in Hel, established in the old smokehouse building of the fishing company, into a modern research building known today as the Marine Station, which was inaugurated in 1992. In later years, the complex was expanded to include accommodation and a Seal Centre. Work is being carried out there, m.in. to restore the population of grey seals on the Polish coast. During his ichthyological research, he also focused more and more attention on the observation of extremely endangered species found in the Baltic Sea, including seals and porpoises. Since then, the facility has been continuing research on the biology and ecology of marine mammals found in the Polish zone of the Baltic Sea, as well as inventory and analysis of threats in order to protect them as effectively as possible.[63] I had the honour to meet him in September 2012 and to work in 2013 as well.

The IOUG seal centre in Hel on Kosa Helska is designed to protect and restore the endangered species of grey seal - *Halichoerus grypus*, treat mutilated and sick animals, study their physiology and reproduction in order to restore their population to the state from before World War II, ultimately up to 100,000 animals.

In the Hel Seal Centre, the health and lives of not only grey seals are saved, but also ring seals – *Phoca hispida* and common seals – *Phoca vitulina*, as well as the local Baltic porpoise dolphins – *Phocoena phocoena*, whose population is now only 100 animals...

The seal centre is also a hospital for animals, where tests of the condition and health of seals are performed, as well as wounded, sick and poisoned animals by human activity are treated. Seals have problems with their eyes and mucous membranes of the mouth, which are particularly affected by harmful microorganisms, chemicals (especially petroleum derivatives) and BŚT from sunken containers, missiles and bombs.

---

[63] Wikipedia.

Preparing a wild seal for treatments: administering medicines, taking blood for tests, etc. Performing emergency medical procedures – applying eye drops with antibiotics... These procedures are performed by veterinarians together with IOUG specialists.

Unfortunately, even in the Seal Centre, there are deaths of seals – an example is **Krysia** the seal, which died as a result of poisoning with heavy metal salts after eating 697 coins with a total weight of 3.5 kg! There are many cases of these animals being run over by motorboats, jet skis or even *kite-surfs*, which leads to the death of these animals. Each corpse is carefully examined and described, some of them are disposed of, the rest are frozen for other examinations.

In addition to the Seal Centre, Prof. Skóra also intended to create a Porpoise Centre, where the Baltic porpoise species would be restored. So far, as part of this project, the House of the Porpoise has been created.

## 25.9. Guests from the Atlantic Ocean

From time to time, the Baltic waters are visited by whales from the Atlantic Ocean. These animals are driven by curiosity and most likely look for new feeding grounds and reservoirs for reproduction and care of their young. Unfortunately – the Baltic Sea is an inhospitable place for these giants and many of them die during these visits, most often as a result of collisions with fast-sailing ships, like the one found on the rocks near Swedish Gothenburg in 2012.

The Polish coast is also visited by these mammals, the remains of which we find from time to time on our seaside beaches. The photos show the remains of a whale in a state of advanced decomposition and the remains of a sperm whale that died in the Bay of Gdańsk in 2004.

A Greenland whale observed in Chałupy and a walrus that came to us in June 2022. And the last two whales that roamed the Polish shores in 2024.

## 25.10. Mysteries of the Western Baltic

The shape of the western Baltic Sea resembles quite closely a group of meteorite craters, post-impact astroblems. As you can see on the map – a meteor shower fell on this area some 100,000 – 1,000,000 years ago. The enchanting cliffs of Stevns Klint reveal a geological gulf between the Mesozoic and the Cenozoic – in the form of a thin layer of clay rich in iridium (Ir) – a trace of the Cretaceous/Paleogene catastrophe and the Saurocide. On the Polish coast, these traces can be seen on the island of Wolin, where there are several impact craters. This matter still needs to be thoroughly investigated, because the traces have been erased due to the action of glaciers.

# 25.11. And now it will be about mysterious disasters

The Polish rail-car ferry MF *Jan Heweliusz* sank on January 14, 1993 in a storm of 10-12 Beaufort degrees, the catastrophe claimed 55 victims. The wreck is located at N 54°36′58″ - E 014°13′16″. This place was often haunted by UFOs, which was observed in the 80s of the twentieth century. In addition, there was a German nuclear power plant Nord IV, which was very faulty. Conspiracy theories say that there was some kind of tref cargo on board the shuttle and the shuttle was deliberately sunk.

The explanation is simpler, namely – after the fire that broke out on it in September 1986, *Johannes Hevelius* was rebuilt, unfortunately defectively. The upper deck of the car was poured with concrete, which raised the ferry's center of gravity and completely changed its statics, and thus it became prone to capsizing in high waves and strong winds. This is how the catastrophe happened. The wreck lies at the bottom, but the black legend stubbornly circulates among the people...

The mystery of the sinking of MF *Estonia*. The sinking of the MF *Estonia* is still an unsolved mystery of the Baltic Sea, which claimed as many as 852 victims. There are a whole range of hypotheses about this tragedy – from the sinking in a storm to the deliberate, criminal sinking of the ferry... The cause of the catastrophe – according to the official version – was the tearing out of the bow gate onto the car deck and flooding the engine room. This version is unbelievable, to say the least. Witnesses who survived said they heard several explosions, and one noticed some bright, glowing white underwater object that rammed the shuttle and sailed away. This was confirmed by finding a large hole in the underwater part of the shuttle's hull.

The reason could also be the tref cargo transported through **Estonia**. It could be post-Soviet ultra-secret electronics, weapons for extremists – Swedish and Norwegian fascists or post-Soviet nuclear warheads. Nobody knows.

The atmosphere of mystery is deepened by the fact that the wreck of the ferry has been declared a marine cemetery and no one is allowed to dive into it. It is guarded by the Finnish Coast Guard...

## 25.12. The Cold War in the Baltic Sea

It all started on October 20, 1981, when a Soviet Whiskey-class diesel torpedo submarine with tactical number 137 ran aground at a Swedish naval base. This incident became the spark of a diplomatic war with the USSR until its end in 1991.

Legend has it that there were two submarines there, but one managed to escape and the Swedes did not capture it like a 137. The whole event was broadcast on TV, so the Soviets could no longer deny it. Officially, they claimed that it was all the fault of a navigational mistake. It was obvious that preparations were underway for the invasion of Scandinavia and then of NATO countries. Taking control of the Scandinavian Peninsula is *a sine qua non* condition for controlling the sea routes of the North Atlantic and, consequently, blocking American and Canadian supplies to NATO. And it is interesting that it was in the 80s that a wave of UFO sightings was observed over the Baltic Sea basin.

GLOOMY SEA OF PEACE – as the Swedish press called the Baltic Sea in the mid-80s of the twentieth century, at the very height of the Cold War. The article presents the balance of forces in the Baltic Sea basin and the activities of the Swedish radio intelligence and radio counterintelligence FRA. In 1986, the apogee of Soviet intelligence activity in the Baltic Sea occurred. It was carried out with the help of miniature submarines of the Maritime Spetsnaz Brigade of the GRU.

Many exercises of the Polish Navy and navies of NATO countries take place in Polish waters as part of the *Baltops* and *Anaconda exercises*. This is especially important now, in the state of threat of war and war in Ukraine.

## 25.13. The Baltic Sea and nuclear power

As you can see from the press materials, the Baltic Sea is surrounded by nuclear power plants, which present varying degrees of danger. The worst are the old post-Soviet nuclear reactors in the countries of the former USSR. An academic example of such a power plant is the GDR NORD IV EJ in Lubmin, which operated with a great risk of a Chernobyl-like disaster, i.e. INES 7. This power plant recorded 1211 accidents, 6 of which were only a degree lower than the disaster in the Chernobyl NPP, i.e. INES 6. The East German authorities effectively concealed what was happening there and the truth was revealed only in 1991, after the reunification of Germany and the liquidation of the GDR.

Its main problem was the transport of nuclear fuel and "ashes" after it was "burned out". Until 1989, it was carried out by rail, transit through Poland (the famous "glowing trains") from the border with the GDR to the border with the USSR. When in 1990 Poland banned entry to its territory, these trains were directed to the Mukran – Klaipeda ferry line, where they were transported by ferries serving passenger traffic, and only the intervention of the Americans forced the Germans and Russians to change.

We have a similar problem with Czech nuclear power plants, to which fuel is delivered by rail through Polish territory and the "ashes" are transported through the port of

Szczecin to the USA. This is the so-called *Operation Oklahoma*. This operation poses a great danger of committing an act of terror and is therefore surrounded by such secrecy.

## 25.14. The problem of cyanobacteria and cyanobacteria in the Baltic Sea

On the maps presented there, we can see the explosive development of cyanobacteria and algae blooms in the waters of the Baltic Sea. It is caused by overfertilization with artificial and natural NPK fertilizers, which, together with the effect of global warming, cause a rapid and massive bloom of water. Dead algae sink to the bottom, where they undergo anaerobic decomposition, releasing large amounts of poisonous hydrogen sulfide – $H_2S$ and methane – $CH_4$ – which is the worst greenhouse gas. The mixture of these gases is a toxic melange that causes, for m.in, loss of orientation, which may be the explanation for the washing up of cetaceans: dolphins, whales and sperm whales, which breathe atmospheric air contaminated by both of these gases.

Flood waters and sewage discharges are a particular threat to the Baltic Sea. In the press photos, we can see the outflow of flood waters to the Gulf of Gdańsk and the Vistula Lagoon. These waters are chemically and biologically polluted. They are the trophic basis for the development of algae and cyanobacteria, as well as the increase in the amount of greenhouse gases poisoning its waters.

These photos illustrate the impact of polluted waters of the Vistula River into the Gulf of Gdańsk... These are flood waters and waters contaminated with municipal sewage from Warsaw...

Green death causes suffocation and death of fish, which, by decomposing anaerobically, enrich the cocktail of H2S + CH4 with additional toxic organophosphorus decomposition gases such as phosphine – PH3 and its compounds.

The Baltic Sea is one of the busiest waters in the world – noise, vibrations from ship propellers, grease, oils, petroleum, faeces and other waste – all this causes further degradation of the marine environment...

*Whale attacking a ship from Olaus Magnus's book*

# 25.15. The Baltic Sea and Sea Monsters

As the Baltic Sea is a small and cold, poisoned sea, there are not too many monsters in it, such as those we see on Carta Marina by cosmographer **Olaus Magnus** *vel* **Olof den Storre** from 1539. We see many interesting things on it, m.in. Vineta *aka* Iulin at the mouth of the Szczecin Lagoon, the extent of the ice cover of the Baltic Sea, the third island in the Kattegat, which does not exist today (it has disappeared???), sea snakes and other monsters that today we can identify as sperm whales, whales, dolphins and sharks. But they were not in the Baltic Sea. On the other hand, if we are to believe the legends and tales, there were Mermaids here – beautiful and charming female creatures luring people with their singing. The Baltic Water Maidens did not murder or drown the unwary, but most often fell in love with them – often with reciprocity. And one of them chose the Vistula River as her apartment and even stood up for the settlement, which in time grew into the city of Warsaw. Today, we can see the Mermaid in the coat of arms of our capital city and on the monument in the Old Town near the Vistula River.

Mermaids and seals. It is said that Mermaids are nothing more than seals. And indeed, there is something to it, because seals standing in the water of the post are similar to humans from a distance and in unfavorable light conditions. The beautiful Mermaid from the fairy tale by **H.Ch. Andersen** is located at the entrance to the port of Copenhagen-Tuborg.

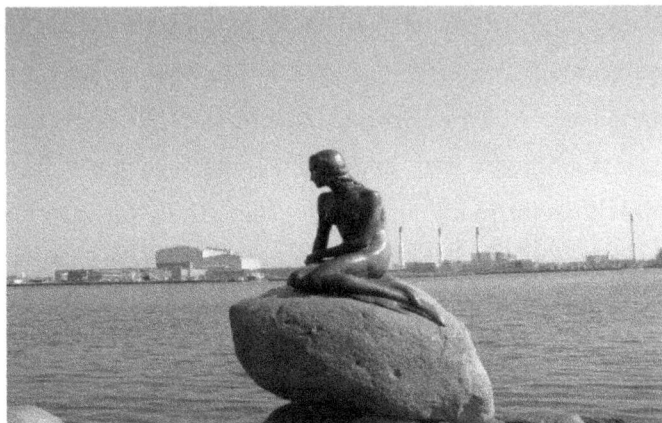

*The Mermaid from Tuborg Harbor*

Mermaids were also supposed to inhabit the waters around Kosa Helska from the side of the Bay of Puck and from the side of the Baltic Sea. And in these cases, it was probably seals lounging on sandbanks. The thing is that real mermaids sing with beautiful voices, and seals don't...

Another – this time the unhappy Mermaid – is Zielenica – the daughter of the king of the Baltic Sea. It was caught by a fisherman from Trzęsacz and transported to this town. The local pharoz imprisoned her and did not want to release her into the sea. Apparently, he fell in love with her, but Zielenica died of longing for the sea, father and playmates... She was buried in the church cemetery and since then the king of the

Baltic Sea, wanting to recover his daughter's body, washes the cliff shore, thanks to which only the southern wall of the church remains. Today, a monument was erected in Trzęsacz to commemorate these events.

In Western Pomerania, on the southern shore of the island of Wolin, there is Lake Wicko Wielkie. Rumor has it that a long time ago a Mermaid lived there – the beautiful Świetlana. And as it was, she fell head over heels in love with a local boy who deceived her and didn't reciprocate her feelings. It ended as usual – the boy married a peasant woman, and Svetlana disappeared forever in the lake. Although... The boy once went fishing, a storm broke out and the boy fell overboard of the boat. They say that it was Svetlana who claimed her beloved. A few years ago, a man saw a group of people (???) swimming at a considerable distance from the shore on Lake Wicko. Who were they, because they were definitely not divers? Sirens? Sea people?

Personally, I am convinced that the depths of the sea hide many secrets related to their existence.

## 25.16. And breaking news:

The poisoning of the Oder threatens to contaminate Lake Dąbie, the Szczecin Lagoon/Oderhaff and the southern part of the Baltic Sea. Despite the fact that the contamination of the river was found as early as the end of July, and the first symptoms of poisoning as early as May 2023, action was taken only when the poisoned wave reached the border with Germany, i.e. on August 9! Highly toxic mercury compounds (Hg++) and salts, including sodium chloride (NaCl) in huge concentrations, are most likely responsible for the contamination, which, given the low water level in the river, must have led to the complete destruction of biological life in the Oder. Stories about golden algae producing huge amounts of oxygen sound like fairy tales for good children...

And this is the end of the paper.

And also regarding contamination not only of the Baltic Sea, but of the entire World Ocean. It turns out that:

25.17. 200,000 time bombs (not only Americans)

Anamica Singh threw this information onto the Internet at the end of August 2025. It is so terrifying that I had to include it here. And here it is:

European countries dumped 200,000 barrels of radioactive waste into the ocean, and people may soon pay the price.

### 25.17.1. Key information

Radioactive waste of various kinds was dumped into the Atlantic Ocean for over 50 years, until 1990. Now, 35 years later, radioactive material threatens to contaminate marine life and enter the human body, causing a crisis.

A team of scientists found 3355 barrels of radioactive waste on the bottom of the Atlantic Ocean. The discovery was made at a depth of 13,000 feet (~4,300 m), hundreds of miles off the coast of France. This is only a small fraction of the actual number of barrels filled with radioactive waste scattered on the seabed. Between 1946 and 1990, European countries dumped over 200,000 such barrels, assuming this was the best way to keep people on land safe. These activities were carried out under the supervision of the Nuclear Energy Agency (NEA), a body comprising 34 countries, whose task is to ensure nuclear safety and waste management. However, there are now concerns that this waste could enter humans through the food chain. Scientists warn that this radioactive material could be absorbed by marine organisms, which could then enter marine organisms and then humans who consume contaminated seafood. This can cause long-term health problems, tissue damage, and increase the risk of cancer.

Barrels cannot store their contents indefinitely. They were designed to release radioactive material slowly but reliably. Their lifespan was 20 to 26 years, and that time has already passed. What next? French scientists are trying to understand what will happen to these barrels. In the first stage, they used sonar and the autonomous underwater robot DSV UlyX to map the Abyssal Plains. They found that most of the radioactive material in these barrels is weak and does not pose an immediate threat to humans because it is deep in the ocean. However, this does not mitigate the long-term effects, which include contamination of marine life and entry into the food chain. About one-third of the material in these barrels was tritium (3H*), the content of which is considered insignificant. The rest are beta and gamma emitters, which lose radioactivity, and about two percent is alpha radiation.

**25.17.2. Radioactive waste that can contaminate marine animals and humans**

However, some radionuclides still pose a problem. Strontium-90 (90Sr*), which is similar to calcium, can be absorbed by marine organisms, eventually entering the food chain. These unstable elements emit radiation as they decay and have different half-lives. Cesium-137 (137Cs*) persists for about 30 years, plutonium-241 (241Pu*) for about 13 years, and uranium-238 (238U*) can remain for over 4.5 billion years. This means there is a problem that needs to be addressed. The next stage of the mission will begin in 2026, when scientists will measure radionuclides in water, sediments, and marine organisms.

***

And how to live in such waters, where death lurks with every flick of the fin? I'm afraid that the Sea People have long since moved from the Baltic to the Atlantic, where the environment is not as polluted as here. I'm willing to bet that it is!

Now, what if? What if the Mermaids or the Sea People really existed and could operate on our planet. Not only in the oceans? If they were beings smarter than us? – So let's let our imagination and adventure run wild...

08

# Chapter 26. Rusalka: Love at First Sight

*Summer moved on and the way it goes*
*You can't tag along*
*Honey moved out and the way it went*
*Leaves no doubt*
*Seasons can't last and there's one thing*
*Left to ask*
*Stay, don't just walk away and leave me another day*
*A day just like today*
*With nobody else around.*
*(Paul Waaktar – Savoy)*

It happened shortly after my arrival in Calella. I was looking for seashells in the sand washed by the waves, with respect for the waves breaking against the rocks, having learned from the experience of the previous day, when an unexpected wave not only tripped me up and after two somersaults I landed on the shore with my swimming trunks pulled down below my knees, but also snatched from my teeth less than a third of a smoked Havana cigar, with which I had been strolling along the beach like a dandy. A little beyond the lighthouse, at the very end of Platja de Garbí, between the Rocapins bar, sadly looking up at the almost deserted beach by nudists with a boarded-up window before the end of the season, and the 666-kilometer national road leading to Barcelona high on the coastal cliffs. Just before sunset, I literally held my breath at the sight, although we had seen each other several times before. Although she didn't have a fish tail, she looked like a real mermaid. With her hair flowing, she emerged from the waves, slowly wiping away the water that glistened on her skin. And then she sat down, crossed her legs, wrapped her arms around them, and rested her chin on her knees.

A mermaid, a real mermaid.

Their world stretches between the seabed and the crests of foamy waves – Denisa Fulmeková poetically describes the homeland of mermaids. Here, in the unfathomable waters, there is supposedly a mysterious land, conquered by beautiful, long-haired creatures with whitish female breasts and a graceful fish tail. Just as in mythology they overshadowed their tritons, so too they maintained dominance in the matriarchal underwater society, where instead of monogamy they prefer to cultivate mischief and timeless beauty. They do not understand why the inhabitants of Earth cut their locks and cover themselves with clothes. Mermaids do not do such foolish things.

A mermaid with loose hair. She smiled. She smiled as she had before, in the city, in a cafe, but this time there was no doubt. There was no one to return her mysterious smile.

¡Qué día tan hermoso tenemos hoy!

I didn't understand Spanish, but I smiled. There was something like rebellious surrender in her gaze. A nymph from the Catalan coast. For a long time, we sat next to each other, watching the gulls flying low over the waves. Lingua sile, non est ultra narrabile quicquam. Her skin tasted of salt, and a delicate tattoo resembled a crown of thorns wrapped around her left arm, which I could touch without fear.

Rusalka, my Rusalka.

Love at first sight.

The mythological origin of rusalkas usually comes from water nymphs, belonging to the most numerous group of minor goddesses in ancient mythology – the naiads. In a broader sense, this also included the oceanids, daughters of the Titan Oceanus, of whom there were three thousand, and the nereids, of whom there were fifty or a hundred. In a narrower sense, naiads were nymphs exclusively of inland waters and, depending on their place of residence, nymphs of rivers, lakes, and individual springs, friendly to humans and spending their lives mainly in singing and dancing.

The sirens, who ignited the imagination of ancient sailors, were the daughters of the sea god Nereus and his wife Doris. They were considered minor sea goddesses inhabiting the "inner sea," on whose shores people lived, in contrast to the Oceanids, goddesses of the "outer sea," which, according to the Greeks, washed the inhabited world. While Homer mentions them by name as forty-four, and Ovid calls them "green daughters of the sea," Pliny writes of their bodies that "they are indeed as painters depict them," with the difference – as he adds piquantly – that "they are somewhat rougher and scaly, even in places where they resemble a woman." The Nereids lived in silver caves at the bottom of the sea near the rocky coast, inheriting a friendly nature from their parents and protecting the lives of sailors.

She was supposed to come that evening to meet us at Plaça de l'Església, just before our farewell on the beach. The slight anxiety I had felt since morning gradually grew. In the morning, few people entered the water because the waves had washed hundreds of jellyfish ashore – dangerous beauties of the deep, devoid of charisma, their glassy bodies helplessly floating in the waves, as if awaiting an approaching storm. I spent the afternoon sitting in a nearby bar in a wet swimsuit, with no chance of getting to my hotel room. The entire area was cordoned off, and police officers in bulletproof vests patrolled the streets – among dozens of men, I spotted a few women in uniform. Trying to break the language barrier, I formulated the address of my temporary residence as a question:

- Hotel Catalonia?

The senior police officer vigorously shook his head and replied without translating.

- El paquete la bomba. - ...aber ein Bier moge ich trinken? - I awkwardly blurted out another question in the ruins of my high school German, pointing to the shop on the corner where another policeman stood, momentarily holding a service dog by its collar. The carabiniere looked stern, the wolfhound panted with its tongue out in the heat that did not subside even under the stormy sky. A knowing, sincere smile appeared on the face of the sergeant with the gray mustache, and then he good-naturedly spread his arms, as if inviting me personally.

- Si, señor, si.

I wasn't listening to him very carefully; only thoughts of the mermaid swirled in my head.

Rusalka, my Rusalka.

Somewhere high above the sea, lightning flashed and thunder rumbled.

Mermaids are probably the heirs of ancient cults, over seven thousand years old, including the Babylonian fish-tailed god Oannes and the Syrian moon goddess Atargatis. Mermaids are also famous for their beautiful voices. This connects them with the sirens of ancient mythology, originally river nymphs, luring sailors to their doom with their singing, which is why in Western Sea tales, the appearance of mermaids is a traditional harbinger of a ship's sinking.

Most sailors described mermaids as attractive beauties with fish tails and long hair, often holding a mirror and a comb in their hands. The image of a mermaid on church coats of arms was the same as a warning symbol of sin, the embodiment of a femme fatale, a symbol of the vanity of female beauty, which, according to church dogmas, led men astray from the path of eternal salvation.

I managed to do it at the last moment. Although the bomb was found in front of the hotel entrance, at the base of a flowerpot, searching the entire building took several hours. It turned out that I had spared myself the pain of evacuation – waiting on a bar stool was more pleasant than involuntarily being on the roof, where rescuers had moved everyone. But it was understandable that I was very tense. In addition, heavy rain began to fall, so I had to go out into the evening city with an umbrella, which – given the previous situation – the reception gladly lent me.

I waited in vain; my fairy did not come to the meeting. Heavy rain drummed on the roof of the umbrella that the waiter from Cafetteria Delicia had kindly lent me. On the miniature table in front of me, my second coffee grew cold –

I preferred not to look at my watch. I passed the time deciphering a short report in the evening edition of the local newspaper with a striking headline – Desalojan oficina Correos Calella por paquete bomba similar hotel Catalonia. Opposite me, through the gray curtain of rain, I observed the weather-beaten faces carved on both sides of the portal on the facade of the Church of Saints Mary and Nicholas. On the left, I recognized the sad image of the eternal pilgrim James – streams of water gushed from the edges of his wide hat adorned with a shell," He stared at me with the blind gaze of his extinguished, stone eyes.

Rusalka, my rusalka.

Another cigarette butt went out in the ashtray.

Somewhere high above the sea, lightning and thunder erupted.

And water still poured from the sky.

In "The Little Mermaid," Andersen took up a theme that is part of the mythology of all nations, the story of love between a human and a nature spirit – wrote Emil Páleš about the most famous work of the brilliant Danish fairy tale writer, and one can only heartily agree with him. Although this story, first published in 1835, is largely a product of Andersen's imagination, combined with an intuitive knowledge of the esoteric laws of the supersensible world, we find in it a deep connection to Baron de la Motte Fouqué's novella "Undine" or to Renaissance tales of love for sea creatures.

When the Copenhagen city council erected a bronze statue of the sad little mermaid sitting motionless on the Langelinie pier and gazing at the harbor in 1913, they probably did not suspect that the sculpture would become the greatest tourist attraction in the Kingdom of Denmark, as well as the most photographed statue in the world. "Der Lille Havefrue" is rightly considered an immortal story and a model for other versions of fairy tales in which a fairy falls in love with a mortal under unusual circumstances.

That night I had a strange dream. I dreamt of an inhospitable coast, resembling a sea frozen solid, churned by the fury of the elements under the claws of storm clouds, obscured by a sky driven by winds. Stones enchanted in motion swelled like mighty, rocky waves, sharp-edged in places, and among them dozens, hundreds of shipwrecks, keeled over, capsized, or wedged between rocks, giving the impression that they were still wandering the stony ocean. Masts reaching dark clouds, tattered sails on yards.

A mermaid walking barefoot among the wrecks, boulders, and bones of ancient sailors on shattered decks.

To this day, I wake up from that dream drenched in fear.

In that dream, the mermaid did not find her prince, she had no chance to save anyone.

Rusalka, my Rusalka.

Somewhere high above the sea, lightning flashed and thundered.

And the wind blew.

"Why do we not have an immortal soul?" asks the sad mermaid from Andersen's fairy tale. "I would give all the years of life I have left to be human for just one day and then get to know the world of heaven!"

The desire for human love, which makes the soul immortal, is the main motif of Andersen's fairy tale. In my version, one hundred and seventy years later, I should look in the fairy tale for an answer to the question of what happens to the soul of a man into whose world a woman briefly enters directly from the foam of sea waves.

"Only if a certain man loved you so much that you were more to him than his own father and mother," the little mermaid learns, "if he clung to you with all his mind and love and placed his right hand in yours with a promise of fidelity here and for all eternity, his soul would enter your body and you too could experience human happiness. He would give you his soul, and keep his own."

On the last day of my stay, I knew she would not return. The fairy who entered my dreams from the waves. I guessed it before I waited in a cafe at Girona airport, exchanging the last euros from the translation of my new book for double cognacs on ice at an unfavorable rate and repeating to myself that my eyes were only stinging from sea salt. In less than an hour, I boarded the plane.

Mermaid, my mermaid.

Somewhere far, far away, lightning flashed and thunder roared. The wind blew; water poured from the sky.

And summer was over.

# Chapter 27. Kasia – Mermaid from the Seal Patrol

## I

Sand and sky.

Sand and blue emptiness, from which the heat pours onto my almost naked body, which is not cooled even by the sea breeze. The murmuring sea is a few steps away from me, but apart from the pungent smell of salt and the stench of a green carpet of algae decomposing in the sun, you don't feel its cool presence under your feet. Lazy waves run out onto the sand of the beach, here on the edge of the asphalt smooth as freshly poured, and then retreat into the turquoise water to run back onto the creamy sand. Sometimes it washes my feet and then I feel like it's like a warm soup. Brackish with greens. Am I hungry?

Hot air vibrates over the sands of the beach. The heat is increasing. The sun reaches the highest point of its path. The south – from somewhere the bells for the midday prayers sound – it is probably from Piaski.

I have a terrible desire to take off my bikini and walk naked through this sand because I liked to be nicely and uniformly tanned, but on the other hand I had to reckon with the elderly lowelas who looked back at me, smacking my lips and undressing me with their eyes. But the worst were the fat women who looked at me with cold hatred in their eyes. They envied my shapely, tanned despite May, athletic body, small but firm breasts and alluring butt, which I didn't have to turn my head to make men turn their heads when they saw me. Add dark, almost black straight hair, now in a bun, and eyes with an intense shade of cobalt. I was already walking the tenth kilometer along the shore, looking for our herd of seals, which we were taking care of. I was wearing a blue bikini and a name tag with the Seal Patrol logo pinned to the strap above my left breast. Dark glasses on his nose, covering almost half of his face. A backpack carelessly slung over his shoulder contained a mobile phone with a dictaphone, a camera, the Internet and something else, a professional camera with a telephoto lens, a wallet and a bottle of suntan oil, and a Motorola CB for communication with the Headquarters. I had to walk another five kilometers to Nowa Karczma or Piaski and the border, and then turn back to Krynica Morska, report to the headquarters and go to my room in the basement of a two-story villa. Eat something, stare at the stupefyer, talk to the landlady and go to bed. And so until the next day, which I spent at the pool or on the beach. And after two days again to sweep the beach. A rather boring job, because seals had their moods and moods and sometimes, they could be extremely unpredictable...

Behind the New Inn, the road ended and the border zone began, where few people were allowed to enter. Fortunately, the Seal Patrol headquarters had permission to move its employees there, so I didn't have to ask anyone for anything. As environmentalists, we were not very liked. Most often, people instigated by priests and local businessmen spat after us and made the sign of the cross. At first it irritated me, then I didn't pay attention to it anymore. They could not understand that every animal dying unnecessarily, every living creature was the Cosmos in itself and when it left this world, it also took a part of ourselves from it. But it was already a higher school of riding and all they needed was the gibberish of some drunken, unruly dresser, who thought that he had already won the rule of souls and could act as he pleased. Not with me. I didn't like their damp paws and the roving eyes they wanted to grope me with when I was still going to church and believing the fairy tales they preached. One of them took the measure and slipped his paw into my panties. I punched him in the face and when I returned home I told my mother that I would never go to church. I kept my word. The grief and shame are gone, and the disgust remains. Until today. Maybe that's why, despite being thirty years old, I was alone, which made my parents want to marry me at all costs. But I didn't want to anymore. Yes, in my dreams I saw myself by someone's side, but I couldn't imagine this "someone". I escaped to the other end of Polish and found a job at the Seal Patrol outpost. They paid meagerly, but I was free and independent of anyone. I had several offers to move to Gdańsk or even Warsaw, but the very thought of living in the city made me nauseous. After graduating, I wanted to leave Gdańsk as soon as possible and move to the provinces. Of course, I didn't find a bother—I mean, I had a few boyfriends, one of whom proposed to me. And it was a complete flop, because he was a crypto-alcoholic and on the day of the engagement he got so drunk that he ended up in bed. With another. The next day I left his life. And from Gdańsk. He wasn't even looking for me... Then someone else found me and it was a great love that ended so tragically...

I went down from the beach to the water because the sand burned my feet. I was immediately relieved. In front of me I had the beach in Piaski – the town itself was behind the forest on the southern side of the spit. The beach was almost empty, except for a few elderly couples who were lounging in the holes. It was so hot that no one paid attention to me.

The radio chirped.

- Switchboard to two – I heard Maciek's voice.

I took the motorola out of my backpack pocket and pressed the transmit button with my finger.

"Two to the Headquarters," I answered.

- Kasia, we got information about a dead seal. The Border Guard found her about two hundred meters from the border. Where are you now?

"In Piaski," I answered.

"OK, don't be in too much of a hurry," he said, "we're assembling a team and sending a motorboat there." Romek and Janka are already coming here. Rest, they will take you from the beach.

- OK, so cool! I replied with all the enthusiasm I could, because I didn't want to tread another four kilometers on the sand. – No pickup.

I put the radio back in my backpack pocket. I wondered which seal had died. I sat down on the sand, feeling my buttocks fry through the fabric of my panties. It could have been Bałtysia or Bronny, the oldest couple in this reservoir. Well, unless a younger one got under the ship's propellers – such things also happened. Although there was a border zone here and little traffic. Almost none.

We have been saving Baltic seals for several years. Porpoises too. Grey seals settled here, in the vicinity of Piaski, where the sea was still relatively clean and peaceful. Our flock of ten animals – Bronny, who was the harem of Bronny, hung around between Krynica Morska and Kaliningrad, and sometimes even sailed to the Saarema. At least that's what our Russian and Estonian colleagues told us. We tracked our flock with the help of GPS tenants implanted in the necks of Bałtys and Bronny. The tenants of the Central signaled their presence near the border, so it would be possible that one of our herd died... But why?

Everything was possible in the Baltic Sea. Since time immemorial, it has been the rubbish heap and wreckage of Europe. After the war, there were also sunken poisonous warfare agents – several hundred tons of mustard and luisite, clark I and clark II, and other nasty things – as unpleasant as the poisonous and stinging white phosphorus from Russian incendiary bombs... The sea also threw up lumps of mazut and other nasty things here. And algae. When washed ashore, they decomposed and smelled. In autumn, jellyfish appeared again – millions of blue jellyfish, which did not stink, but soaked into the sand and disappeared. That's good.

The heat was thickening and it was getting stuffy. There will probably be a storm – I thought. The sun has made me lazy. The sound of the sea was calming down, and you could feel the kilometers traveled in your legs. I struggled with drowsiness, but after a few minutes I was roused from my stupor by the sound of running engines. Janka swam as close to the shore as possible, and I got up and headed towards the motorboat in a warm algae soup.

-Hi! – I told Janka and Romek as I scrambled to the boat.

- Hello Kaśka – they replied.

They had been a couple for several months, which I sometimes envied them. Sometimes they discreetly hugged or kissed each other secretly and worked looking into each other's eyes. Both in love with each other and the sea. Enthusiasts. They liked animals and they liked them too. You could feel it. Janka was a veterinarian – almost because she had not yet finished her studies. Romek, on the other hand, was passionate about zoology. They ended up in the Headquarters and, just like me, they liked this place and this job.

Romek jerked the throttle and turned the bow of the boat towards the open sea. After a few minutes, we saw a blackish, motionless shape on the white and cream sand of the beach. She was there. Someone was standing next to her. We swam to the shore. Romek dropped the hook, which got stuck in the sand. We jumped out of the boat and swam to a sandy beach. When Sergeant Malicki saw us, he came up to us and shook hands with us.

"It's nice to see you," he said, "I suppose you're from your flock?"

Romek smiled.

"I'd rather meet you over a beer, not in such natural circumstances," he made an indefinable gesture with his hand...

Janka fell to the animal. A quiet cry of disbelief escaped her lips.

- Kaśka! Come here and look," she said quietly.

-What happened? I asked and looked at the lying seal. My voice froze, I didn't have to ask anymore.

Romek knelt next to the corpse and rubbed his eyes in disbelief with a rather comical face.

Malicki gave me a questioning look.

- Kasia, what's going on? He asked, calmly turning to me. "Something wrong?"

I raised my eyebrows.

"Everything is OK," I muttered, "except for the fact that it's a seal..."

"Uhm..." the sergeant nodded, "I can see it's a seal, so?...

- ... Which shouldn't be here," I said slowly, "because its lair is about eighteen thousand kilometers away. This is a Weddell seal...

## II

Malicki looked at us in amazement.

- Is that true? – he asked Roman.

"True," replied the other, "we have before us a specimen of a Weddell seal, if you prefer *Leptonychotes weddelli*." A young specimen weighs about a hundred kilos, and adults reach 350 – 450 kilograms of live weight. This is an Antarctic seal, resistant to cold like no other. And it can dive up to six hundred meters for an hour...

"Antarctic, you say?" Malicki reached for a notebook and a pen.

"Yes," Roman shrugged, "it lives in Antarctica, and it can also be found in South Africa, the southern headlands of Australia and New Zealand, and South America.

- Where did it come from? – asked Malicki – escaped from the zoo?

I shook my head.

"No, Sergeant," I said, "if that were the case, we would know about it.

"What are you going to do with it?" He asked, jotting something down diligently.

"The same as always, the examination, the autopsy, the analysis," I said, "we need to know what killed her.

"Why do you assume she was killed?" – he asked me another question. "You can't see any injuries.

"Did you turn it around?" Romek asked.

"I didn't touch it, I preferred to wait for you," Malicki replied.

We exchanged glances.

"Okay," said Janka, "then let's take a look at it."

I took my camera out of my backpack.

- First, photographic documentation – I said, taking the animal in the viewfinder of the DSLR camera and snapping.

A shot from the front, back, both sides and some general shots. I took out my phone and after a few seconds I had the coordinates - 54°27'22.25" north latitude and 019°38'04.99" east longitude. I noticed that Malicki also wrote them down.

"We can turn it around," I said, and together we turned the seal onto its stomach.

I expected some wounds from the propellers of a ship or a motorboat, or a wound inflicted by a crossbow or a harpoon, but I was disappointed. The seal's body was intact and showed no signs of violent death. I took a few photos again.

"Strange," Janka muttered.

- And what do you think was the cause of death of this animal? Malicki asked in an official tone.

- Hmmm... - Janka thought for a moment - if I had to bet, I would say poisoning, and a strong toxic agent at that. At the same time, it was certainly not a poison that acted on contact, because then there would be traces of it on the skin or in the mouth of this seal.

"So?" Malicki persisted, and I had the intuitive impression that he knew more than he showed us. And what's more, he knew perfectly well that this seal would be here...

"Food poison or inhalation poison," Janka replied. "Some toxic gas, smoke or aerosol.

- And the food one? Malicki asked again. "Some poisoned herrings or cod...

"It makes sense, but it had to be a poison with an fulminant effect – like cyanide – of sodium, potassium or another metal, or hydrogen cyanide.

"It's gas.

- Exactly, it can be used as a combat gas, or as the Germans did in Auschwitz: they locked people in a sealed chamber and poured Zyklon B, that is, hydrogen cyanide in diatomaceous earth, which released the gas when it was poured out of the can. The lethal concentration of HCN is 0.2 – 0.3 mg per liter of air. But there's a catch, Sergeant," Janka stood up and brushed her hands off the sand.

- What's the catch?

-Humidity. The higher the level, the less lethal the hydrogen cyanide, it happened that people were still alive in the gas chamber, Nyiszli writes about it. The seal is an aquatic animal, and killing it with hydrogen cyanide would be technically difficult. Well, unless some scuba diver sprayed a stream of hydrogen cyanide in her nose when she inhaled air, for example, after surfacing ... No, this is complete nonsense. It's not hydrogen cyanide.

- And on land? – Malicki consistently delved into the topic.

"Of course, it's possible, but wouldn't it be easier to shoot her with a firearm or stab her with a harpoon?" – Janka said the word 'stab' in such a way that, despite the heat, I felt icy cold.

Malicki smiled.

- You are right, of course it would be easier. So you still insist on food poisoning?

Janka nodded. I also agreed with that.

Malicki began to say goodbye.

"Allow me to say goodbye to you," he said, shaking our hand, "but if you find anything interesting or unusual during the autopsy, please let me know at the watchtower."

"Of course," I assured him.

I followed him with my eyes, and in the meantime he disappeared in the forest. After a while, we heard the whirr of his quad's engine. After a minute, everything fell silent. We were alone with a dead seal.

- You know what, girls? Roman asked. "I have the impression that he knew something.

We looked at each other. I nodded in the affirmative.

- I also had this impression - said Janka. "Come on, we'll load this meat onto the boat."

After ten minutes we were slowly sailing along the shore to Krynica Morska. I hoped to spend the rest of the day on sweet *dolce far niente*, but I was wrong.

And very much so.

Maciek first of all rushed us to work. I was supposed to perform an autopsy of this unfortunate seal. Janka was to help me.

- Let the girl learn – Maciek said commissioning me to do this job.

I wanted to show him my tongue – goodbye free afternoon... I didn't really like rummaging through the guts of various animals, but this case genuinely interested me.

"Come on, Janka, you're going to play Dr. House," I said to Janka, putting on my bikini apron, "we need to find out what killed her."

We entered a cool room. Someone set the air conditioner to fully cool, so after a minute I shuddered from the cold.

"Damn, you can catch a cold here," I growled, chattering my teeth. On the other hand, however, I preferred the cold and airy to the stuffy and hot atmosphere outside the room.

I started the autopsy. Janka gave me the tools, and I recorded what I saw on a dictaphone. First, I looked at the lungs. They were filled with water, as if the animal had simply drowned. This was already unusual, for these animals, by their very nature, could drown in only one case—if they were under the ice and found no hole before the oxygen supply in the air in the lungs was exhausted. In this case, these seals were able to bite out a breathing hole in the thin ice with their strong teeth. It was strange. After all, it was the end of May and there was a shortage of ice in the Baltic Sea. So...

I cut open the abdominal wall and peritoneum. The animal's foul-smelling entrails spilled out. Janka turned pale and swallowed.

- What, you don't like tripe? I asked jokingly.

"Not like that," she said, suppressing her disgust.

I wanted to laugh. Once, when I was still a student, I went with my group to a lecture on autopsies in the dissecting room of the provincial police headquarters in Gdańsk. An autopsy of a hanged man was carried out in front of us. Everything was OK until his stomach was opened, from where the smell of fermented alcohol and the stench of decay came out. Someone embroidered, someone fainted. But the best part was at the end, when the preparator took venous blood samples from the hands of the corpse – he did it with an ordinary soup ladle. Needless to say, I haven't touched the red borscht with dumplings for a long time. I kept seeing this scene.

I smiled.

- What amuses you so much? Janka asked.

"A memory," I said. "I'll tell you about them when we're done."

I started to check the intestines. They were almost empty, which in itself was unusual. They contained nothing but some solution that reminded me of nothing. It looked as if someone had starved the seal for at least two or three days... Her stomach, on the other hand, was filled and thoroughly. Swollen like a balloon.

- She ate quite a bit – commented Janka.

"I wonder what it is," I muttered and cut open the strong muscular sac of my stomach with my lancet. I took the edge of the cut and widened it to see what was inside. Unnecessarily – the stomach was tightly filled with small plastic bags tightly closed and protected against tearing.

- Oh shit! Janka blurted out.

I took out one bag and cut it open. Its content was a white, crystalline powder.

"Well, we know what happened," I said. "Go get Maciek."

Janka ran out of the studio.

## III

I reached for my camera and took a series of photos. Out of habit, I preferred to have evidence in my hand, just in case. This is what my difficult life has taught me. Besides, I realized that we had cut into someone's criminal activity and we were already on a road with no way out...

Maciek rushed in with Janka and jumped to the sliced animal.

-What is this? He exclaimed.

"Hera," I muttered, "or coke." White powder. Drugs, this seal poisoned herself with it. She was dying on a powerful high...

- Damn, Malicki knew something... - muttered Janka.

Maciek took out his cell phone and dialed the number to the watchtower.

Malicki appeared after a quarter of an hour with a small suitcase in his hand. He didn't look too surprised or interested. On the contrary – he gave the impression that he expected something like this. Janka was right.

"I had a feeling that we would meet today," he said from the doorstep. "Can you show me your find?"

Maciek pointed to the autopsy table. Malicki approached the seal and looked into the cut stomach. He took out one of the bags and cut it open with a springer. He smelled the contents, then took a few crystals on the tip of the knife and put them in his mouth. He rubbed his tongue on the roof of his mouth and spat into the sink.

We looked at it in silence.

- What kind of Bandudztwo is that? - searches Janka.

- Not coke and not hera, not crack either. It's some kind of synthetic. We'll investigate that in a moment.

He took out of his suitcase a few flat bags containing small ampoules with some solutions.

"Valtox?" I asked.

He looked at me appreciatively and shook his head.

- Something much better than Valtox. It has a much wider detection spectrum, and is much more accurate than Valtox. How do you know this?

"My dad was a volunteer and then served in the Border Guard," I replied. "I've seen and heard a lot...

Smiled.

He threw a few crystals into each bag and then crushed the ampoules. After several seconds, the solutions in some of them changed color.

"Strange," he muttered, shaking his bags.

- What surprises you? I asked.

- This is some rare filth and a cocaine derivative like *crack*. It is cocaine in the form of a free base, isolated by precipitation occurring during the boiling of a solution of cocaine hydrochloride and sodium bicarbonate. Compared to other forms of cocaine, *crack cocaine* is highly addictive, with an immediate, short-term effect of 5 to 10 minutes. The drug is taken by heating and inhaling the vapors. It was invented in the 80s in the States. But this is only similar to coca and *crack*. Here is something that the Swedes called the "Russian troika". This something is even worse than coca, crack, pervitin, or methylamphetamine. It seems that we came across a courier transporting it across the Baltic Sea...

- So it would mean that the "Russian troika" is produced in Russia? – asked Maciek – and smuggled by seals?

- This is what it looks like – answered Malicki. – And do you know what is the most interesting in all this?

We stood like three question marks.

- And the fact that we got a tip. Authentically – he said when he saw our astonished looks. "First, we received a notification from the Swedish police, whose narcotics department was working on the case of the appearance of small amounts of the "Russian troika" on the Swedish and Scandinavian market. The Swedes have come to the conclusion that this filth was invented in China as a chemical weapon for direct use. Säkerhetspolisen and Militära Underrättelse och Säkerhetstjänsten were involved in their investigation. And, of course, FOI.

-What? – we asked almost in unison.

"And yes," Malicki shrugged, "civilian intelligence and counterintelligence, as well as military intelligence and security service. And the defence research institute. After all, it is a chemical weapon with incredible firepower. Well, imagine that you are attacked by a regimental unit. And it is enough to fire three or four grenades with this substance and the soldiers, instead of attacking the enemy, abandon their weapons and let themselves be tied up like sheep, because they experience euphoria combined with visions, because after that you have visions like after mescaline and derivatives. Oh and one more thing – the action of the "Russian troika" is actually immediate! The reaction time is from 15 seconds to half a minute, depending on the individual immunity from the time of application of the effective dose.

- And what did they manage to determine? I asked, because I was consumed by curiosity.

- That the Chinese mafia stole the most closely guarded secret of the production of this shit, excuse me, and is beating the money out of it.

"So the Triad?" Janka asked.

- For now, the Triad, but I'm afraid that the Russian, Lithuanian, Latvian, Estonian mafias will too. And ours, of course. It is only a matter of time. It appeared on the market about a month or two ago. The Chinese will not let off steam until they get drunk and come up with something new. I think they will try to maintain their monopoly and for as long as they can. And this smells like a gang war...

"But, but," I said, "you were talking about some zinc?...

Malicki looked around for a chair and sat down.

"Yes," he replied, "we have recently received a letter signed with a name, surname and even an address. The thing is, we checked. There is no such person, and the address is also fake. In the letter, a woman signing herself as Jastra Wolińska from Gdańsk warns us against smugglers using seals and other large marine animals to smuggle ashes. And what is most interesting – a similar letter was received by our colleagues from the other side of the border, identical in content, and it was signed by Jastra Wolińskaja from Kaliningrad, or rather from Königsberg...

- Yes, did she sign? From Königsberg? – asked Maciek, astonished.

Malicki nodded.

- And what next? Janka couldn't help but be curious.

- And the fact that they also checked the address, which turned out to be outdated. I mean, there was one, but before the Second World War. Interesting, isn't it?

"Isn't it," I answered, "and what?"

- And we couldn't determine anything, until today... - Malicki got up his chair and reached for the phone. He talked to someone for a while, and when he finished, he turned to Maciek.

- I would like to ask for a copy of the report from the autopsy of this seal, because we are taking over this matter. A convoy will take her from here to Gdańsk. And one more thing: for your own good, not a word to the press, media, family, loved ones. For your own good. This transport is worth several hundred thousand euros and someone will be looking for it. Don't trust anyone, because anyone can be an emissary of the Triad and it doesn't have to be Chinese. This someone will probably ask about seals, so he can turn to you. The matter is very serious, so I warn you about it – and please inform us about such cases. Do we understand each other?

We nodded.

The case really looked awful. I remembered all the gangster movies that our TV fed us without order, composition and moderation. And the very fall at the mafia threatened with unpleasant consequences, of which drilling with a drill made knees or knocking out teeth a pleasure... Malicki was right. It was an extremely smelly thing.

## IV

I was slowly returning home hungry, mentally shattered and simply tired of the heat and stuffiness. Dark clouds were pulling from the side of the Gulf of Gdańsk. Somewhere there were rumblings of thunder. The storm was coming lazily, but mercilessly, like some kind of Nemesis. Or Ananke. In the brain crowded with impressions, thoughts flowed lazily. Or I didn't want to think – it was the same thing. I had the impression that my brain had turned into some kind of warm slush, in which something flashed from time to time.

I dragged myself home. I opened the gate to the garden and Kuki immediately fell on me. My hostess's mongrel He probably thought I had something good for him. Unfortunately, I didn't. He licked my hand courteously and chased me somewhere behind the rose bushes, which Mrs. Kubacka carefully tended during the day and watered with a hose in the evenings. After a while, an angry meow was heard from there. It was probably Brydzia, her cat, who played with Kuki like a puppy.

Next to my Fiat there was an elegant Mercedes with Swedish plates. Any guests? Anyway, certainly not to me. I didn't care much. I was fed up with today, and if I wanted anything, it was to end as soon as possible...

- How is Kasia? What's so late today? – Mrs. Kubacka asked me, sitting on a bench in front of the house and observing the traffic on the street. She liked to sit like this in the evening, chatting with other women. It was a real forge of gossip and an exchange of information exchange with the JPDP agency.

"I've had some work and a day is useless," I replied lazily, "it's going to be a storm."

"It's true," Mrs. Kubacka smiled a few degrees wider, "the atmosphere is so thick that you can cut it with a knife. But, but," Krystek Szmidt asked about you, "she lowered her voice to a conspiratorial whisper, and her gaze was fixed on my face.

Krystian Szmidt was one of her acquaintances, whom she wanted to match for me, as if I had nothing better to do. I didn't like standing over the pots and looking after brats. I didn't run away from Karpacz and Gdańsk to now...

-Truly? – I feigned surprise and masked my awkward yawn – to tell the truth, I want a lukewarm shower and a comfortable bed. And as for Krystek, he's not my type.

Anyway, as a lifeguard he will have a snatch during the season. Many will fly to him...

She smiled and lit a cigarette.

"We already have holidaymakers," she said.

- Oh, that's great – I hope not some troublemakers or drunks? Are they the Swedes? I nodded to the Mercedes.

Last summer we were unlucky enough to rent rooms to some shady "businessmen" from Łódź who did nothing but drink and sleep with some seagulls. They were disgusting. They drooled and smacked their lips when they saw me. One of them was picking on me, so without hesitation I punched him in the face and announced that I would kill him next time. Then I had peace of mind, because they knew that I could defend myself and I could defend myself effectively.

"No, no way," she replied, blowing a trickle of smoke, "it's a young woman from Gothenburg, maybe you can finally find a friend?"

- Maybe, we'll live and see – I answered. – Does he speak at least Polish?

- Oh yes, of course, and without an accent. Some nouveau riche, she has a lot of money and such a car...

Well, yes, money and a car, these are the measures of human value in Poland of the 21st century.

-Itself?

-Itself. A bit strange, isn't it Kasia?

"I'm alone too, and no one is surprised..." I replied in the most bored tone I could muster. "Have a nice evening!"

I shrugged and went home.

And Kuki follow me.

Kuki has been following me whenever he could, ever since I cured him of some nasty peritonitis. At night he would lie down in front of my door, and when I fell ill with some disgusting stomach flu and lay in bed for three days, he would not leave me. I think he was one of the reasons why I loved animals more than people. People were mean, they weren't. Someone once said that the better he knows people, the more he loves animals. I was able to sign off on it with all my limbs.

I went into my room. I unloaded my backpack and took off my dress, and then my bikini. I put on my dressing gown and marched to the bathroom. I took it off and jumped naked under the ink. I felt better right away. I left after a quarter of an hour quite satisfied with my life. I went to the kitchen, where I made myself a dinner – I threw two sheets of overgrown bacon into the pan, on which I cut two tomatoes and a pepper pod. I salted, and stewed. I didn't care about the warnings and advice of dieticians. If it were true what they say about LDL cholesterol, then my dad wouldn't have lived to be ninety, and my mom would have ended up having a heart attack and atherosclerosis in her fifties. Total nonsense – it all depends on outdoor exercise, not diet. You can eat anything and nothing will happen to you, provided that you work hard physically. And after the age of fifty, we will grow fat anyway, because these are the laws of biology that we will not overcome. I cut open a fresh-smelling loaf of bread and cut myself two large slices. I smeared it with butter and swept away everything that was to eat, down to the crumb. I was terribly hungry. The sea air has always whetted my appetite.

I washed, cleaned up the kitchen and went back to my room. I downloaded all the photos from the camera to my PC's hard drive and cleaned the card. For a moment, my eyes lingered on the DVD shelf, but then I gave up. I turned on the radio on pianissimo and looked for Radio Two. I liked classical music and it was the only program I could listen to over and over again. I didn't watch TV, because there was nothing to watch. Talking heads, game shows, quizzes, the gibberish of politicians and a never-ending festival of crime, violence and again the raving of various madmen, haunted half-brains and specialists in fixing the world. I lay down looking at the window, where the sky was darkening, but this darkness was brightened every now and then by the orange-purple glow of lightning. The thunder intensified. It was going to be a big storm. I also thought about reading something for the pillow. I had a choice between Baldwin and Shaw, but I waved my hand. Outside, there was almost a thick darkness. Thunder roared outside the windows, and when the first drops of thick rain fell to the ground, I fell asleep with the sleep of a righteous man...

# V

I woke up suddenly, as if feeling threatened. After a while, I realized that I was dreaming a nightmare. I looked at the window, behind which the clear night sky was already pale. It was half past four. A bright spark glided slowly across the sky. It was the ISS.

I was still under the impression of sleep. I dreamed of the impression of being in a dark, empty space. A cave or maybe just a deep valley or canyon where I heard voices. Many voices are saying something to me, or rather to themselves, talking to themselves in languages unknown to me. Some laughter, some chants of Gregorian chants. I guess this is what Christian Hell looks like - I thought.

I got up and walked to the window, then opened it. Fresh air smelling of the wet forest flowed into the room. Only now did I feel how hot and musty it was. That's where these hellish dreams came from," crossed my mind. I stood at the window for a few more minutes, feeling the cool streams of air wash over my sweaty body. The first birds spoke. Their chirping began to intensify. Nature began to welcome the rising sun. I liked such concerts to welcome the day. And I was surprised to find that the memory of the nightmare had vanished somewhere to hell. Nothing remained of the crushing memory of a bad dream. I breathed a sigh of relief and at the same time shuddered from the cold. I quickly jumped under the covers and closed my eyes. Maybe I'll be able to take a nap until six.

This time the dream had a specific shape, colors and sound. I was in some kind of crypt lit by a white-bluish light. The walls of the crypt reminded me of the walls of caves with dripstone formation, but they were some creatures like anemones or other animals from coral reefs. I slowly turned around. Hearing registered as if distant sounds of wave beats, but under water. Because I was under water and this room (???) too. Suddenly, I heard a sound behind me – no, I didn't hear it – I sensed it. I turned around and against the light background of the opening in the cave I saw a dark, as if feminine figure. I couldn't see her face clearly.

"It's me, Jastra," I heard my voice slightly distorted by the water, "you have finally come to me. I've been waiting for you for so long, Mermaid...

I wanted to say something, but I was overcome with fear and woke up screaming. Kuki, lying next to my bed, barked briefly and jumped to his feet.

I sat down on the bed, trying to collect my terrified thoughts.

- Hush, quiet, dog – I said to Kuki, stroking his head. He licked my hand and lay down again. And I was still sitting and thinking hard.

Jastra, Jastra... Where did I hear it? – I tried to remember. And I remembered – it was the name of the mysterious author (???) of the anonymous letter to the border guards. The one that warned against smuggling the "Russian troika" to Scandinavia. I was curious how they smuggled the money in the other direction? Probably not in the entrails of seals? After a while, I came to the conclusion that they were simply transferring it from the account of company A to the account of company B, which invested it in some profit-making ventures. The left money dissolved in the ocean of "normal" money and returned to company A. Classic washing of left money.

I looked at my watch—it was seven in three minutes. I got out of bed and went to the bathroom as I stood. A quick mascara, after which I wrapped myself in a wide terry cloth towel and walked to the dressing table. At first, I was surprised when I saw a second set next to my toiletries. I blinked my eyes blankly and remembered that we had another tenant. I quickly brushed my teeth and dried my hair. I did my ponytail and left the bathroom.

Kuki was not there – apparently he had gone to breakfast. But I wasn't alone. No longer.

She was standing in the corridor leaning against the wall. I was expecting – I don't know why – a squat, strongly built blonde with a Nordic type of beauty – some Frau Herta or Brunhilda. Meanwhile, opposite me stood a girl a little younger than me, with the ethereal beauty of an Irish Elf. Her face resembled a bit of Olivia Wilde's features – Thirteen

417

from "Dr. House" in a younger version. Her long, wheat hair flowed down to her shoulders. But the most amazing thing was her eyes – a large, intense green and green bathrobe perfectly matched their color. And I guess she didn't have chorea... From a heavy Fru she turned into an almost petite Fröken...

With one movement of her lithe body, she broke away from the wall and stood in front of me.

"Good morning," she said, looking at me closely. – Ms. Kasia, I suppose?

"Hi," I replied. "And you think right. Katarzyna Warzyńska, Kaśka for friends.

I reached out to her. She took it gently and gave it a light hug. A slight blush appeared on her dull cheeks.

"I'm sorry, I didn't introduce myself," she said shyly, "I'm Astrid Polanovskaya." But my friends call me Jastra. Like Easter.

I shook her hand.

Jastra. A mysterious name heard yesterday from Sergeant Malicki. A mysterious name that I heard in my dream. It was weird, even more than weird. I made sure that my face expressed nothing but kindness. Over the course of my life, I've learned to control my emotions, and if I played poker, I'd make a fortune...

"Nice to meet you," I said with a smile. – The bathroom is free and at your disposal. And maybe we'll go on a first-name basis anyway?

-Clear! Thank you," she said quietly and brushed her lips against my cheek.

And then she slipped into the bathroom.

And I went to my room. I quickly dressed in white shorts and a greenish top. It was going to be a beautiful day again. A crisp breeze was blowing from the sea at that time, but clouds hung over the land. There will be a storm again – I thought.

In the kitchen, I made myself a quick breakfast. While drinking coffee, I was thinking about what had happened to me since yesterday. First, the mysterious case with the Weddell seal – damn it knows where it got here from. Someone brought it from Antarctica and domesticated it or what? One thing is certain – she was trained. I was sure of that, because I couldn't imagine her swallowing everything they put in her mouth. On the other hand, I knew about seals from a certain zoo, which had to be operated on because they had a few kilograms of coins in their stomachs, which were thrown into their pool by reckless visitors... So it wasn't as big a problem as I thought?

- Is there a coffee spring here? I heard her voice above me.

I looked and saw Astrid standing with a cup the size of a small bucket in her hand. I was so lost in thought that I didn't notice her entrance. She did her ponytail and dressed almost identically to me. Only her feet slipped into white ballerinas, and I preferred Japanese zori flip-flops...

- There isn't, you have to make it yourself. You can help yourself – I said, pointing to the jug.

She poured herself a pour and sat down opposite me.

- What are you going to do on this beautiful day? –Asked. "I want to catch some sun, and you?"

In fact, her skin was so white as if it was whitened with lime. She looked pretty unhealthy, but her face was ruddy, so she couldn't be sick. Sweden hasn't had much sunshine lately, so she couldn't get a tan... Apparently, she did not recognize Sollux. Like me...

- Heh, heh, and I'm going to work right away and I'll be back at 3 p.m. It's unbelievable, but in this country you have to work to live somehow," I got up and walked to the sink. I washed the mug and put it on the dryer.

- If you want, we can meet on the beach or for dinner – I added.

- And where do you eat dinner? –Asked.

- In the "Fala" guesthouse, it's a stone's throw away – I replied going to get my backpack. "Mrs. Kubacka will tell you." My company's employees eat there, but you will have to buy some food. So the spatulas!

I slapped her lightly on the shoulder and I was gone.

# VI

At work, a surprise awaited me in the form of Sergeant Malicki. He was a civilian and if I didn't know him, I wouldn't recognize him. He looked like some bum dressed in a T-shirt greyed by the sun with the inscription POLISH-FINNISH PARTY OF DRUNKARDS and shorts made of old jeans that had been cut off with some blunt instrument. And spilling sneakers on bare feet. Only it didn't smell, on the contrary – it smelled of good aftershave. And he was damn handsome.

"What can I do for you?" – I asked after exchanging polite greetings.

"I would like to give you a warning," he said without preliminaries. "The point is that there are four of you here. Mr. Maciej is married, Mrs. Janka and Mr. Roman are together. Only you are lonely and therefore if someone wants to stick to you and snatch the secrets of your institution, they will look for access only through you. So watch out for lovers.

" Cave is a lover," I said, "OK.

He laughed, but after a while he became serious.

- The second thing, even more interesting. It turned out that your Wedel seal...

- Weddell – I corrected it automatically.

- … It doesn't matter. Whatever you call it. This seal was slightly radioactive. That is, its meat. And that would mean that she was either fed something that contained radionuclides, or she was kept somewhere where they were. For example, in some nuclear fuel storage, spent rods or uranium mine...

It was a revelation.

"Well, Sergeant, you shot me here," I said, "although on the other hand, it doesn't surprise me, because in the vicinity of Piaski or, if you prefer, the Old Inn, there is a deposit of uranium-thorium ores. The Ministry of the Environment and the Polish Geological Institute are interested in uranium deposits in northern Poland. What not so long ago would have seemed to be fantasy, is now taking on more and more concrete shapes. And all because of the nuclear plans of the government, which wants at least one nuclear power plant to be built in Poland by 2020. It is possible that it will be built near Żarnobyl, and uranium will be mined, m.in on the Vistula Spit. The Vistula Spit and the areas located up to about 100 km south of it are promising uranium deposits. Scientists estimate that their content in the area of the so-called Peribaltic Syneclysis for Krynica Morska and Ptaszków-Pasłęka is up to 2500 tons of uranium. These resources were found in the seventies of the last century. The uranium area discovered at that time reaches from Sopot to Tczew, and then its southern border runs east, towards Gołdap. The largest amount of uranium ore is in the area of

Krynica Morska and Pasłęk... And do you know what it means if it works out?

- Well, what? He asked, a bit intrigued.

"The end of tourism," I said. – Total filth of this corner of Polish by miners and heaps of radioactive soil... What the Americans want to do to us in Kuyavia is enough for me. Or what happened in May and June 2010, when there were inflows of chemically and biologically contaminated water into bays and lagoons...

He raised his eyebrows slightly and thought for a moment.

- Where did you get this information from? –Asked.

"From the Internet," I replied, "after all, that's what it's for.

"Well, yes, yes..." Malicki nodded. "I didn't think about it.

But I understood what he wanted from me. He came to me just for advice.

- I think that this seal could have been in some shaft or search adit. Or... - I thought for a moment, because the thought seemed equally tempting and smelling of interviews fights - ... or in some disused Russian nuclear installation in the Kaliningrad Oblast. They probably have this one there for a metre...

Sergeant Malicki nodded.

"Uhm," he said thoughtfully, "maybe you're right. On the other side, there's a hell of it, and I didn't think about it. Thank you for your help! Have a nice day!

And he ran out of my office.

A moment later, Maciek came to me.

"What did he want from you?" – he asked from the threshold.

He was clearly excited.

"He warned me about gangsters," I said truthfully, "and told me to watch out for all the guys who get in on me.

Maciek grimaced. If he could, he would be the first, but it was a specimen of a classic slipper. His wife and teenage daughter kept him short, and he couldn't have any "sides" unless he was a genius at time management. But it wasn't.

"And what are you going to do about it?" he asked, somewhat helplessly.

- Of course, I'm not going to worry about it – I said – after all, the seal is already in Gdańsk, and its tref goods too. I doubt they know about it, but I bet that they do, since the package did not arrive on time. On the other hand, we were seen with a seal, but whether it was this one, they cannot know. I doubt that those beachgoers who saw us reloading it from boat to car were able to recognize whether it was a gray seal or a Weddell. A calm skull.

- So why did Malicki warn you?

- Maybe he is in love with me? I replied. –Just! I added to myself.

Maja Malicka was a young, beautiful woman. It was strange to me that she married a sergeant and not a colonel. Then I understood that the colonels were men in their forties, and she was at most in her twenties and had an appetite for life. I saw them both running on the beach before bed or swimming in the sea. In winter, they rode cross-country skating and ice skating, and in general they were both athletic and bursting with the joy of life. Complete nonsense.

- And anything else? Maciek asked.

"Nothing," I shrugged, "this seal was supposedly radioactive. Maybe they fed her fish from Chernobyl or Kysztyn...

- Are you kidding yourself, Kaśka? He looked at me, completely disgusted.

"No," I said. "That's what he said. Now he is probably wondering with his superiors where they got these fish from...

I had peace of mind until the end of the working day. I wrote a report from the autopsy and sent it to the Seal Centre in Hel, and a copy to the Border Guard Watchtower. I sorted out my financial papers and looked through my bills. At half past three, Janka returned from a routine patrol on the beach. It turned out that our herd showed up somewhere near Piaski, but did not come ashore. Janka waited for them for some time, and then gave up and returned to the base. At three o'clock I got out of the headquarters and went to "Fala" for dinner.

The weather was pleasant, but the shortness of breath was growing again. Another storm was brewing, but it was still quite a long way off. I entered the dining room of the guesthouse and headed for the window where meals were served.

- Hello Kaśka – I was greeted by Ola, a blonde perkatonos who worked at "Fala" for her studies – today we have dumplings with meat and cabbage.

- It can be anything, as long as it's suitable for eating – I replied – I'm hellishly hungry!

I handed her a dinner voucher, which Ola had skewered on a nail sticking out of the counter, and after a while she came back with a plate piled with dumplings and a bowl of fragrant cabbage with cracklings.

- And strawberry compote – said Ola.

I looked around the dining room for someone I knew. After a while, my gaze stopped on the raised hand. I looked in that direction – Astrid waved at me with a raised hand. With a plate in one and a bowl in the other, I walked towards her.

-Hi! I said, "and how do you like it here?"

- Quite a meal, after so many years in Sweden I feel that I am Polish after all. It's in my genes," she said with a smile and pointed to a heaped plate of dumplings.

We enjoyed them for a few minutes.

I looked at her skin, it was slightly browned in the sun.

- Did you sunbathe? I asked.

- Yes, I fell asleep in the sun – she replied – but nothing hurts me...

- Well, we'll buy you suntan oil, because your skin is too fair. And here it is easy to get burns. Do you want to suffer all night?

- No, I tan quickly. What are you doing tomorrow? – Asked.

"I'm going on patrol," I replied, "back to the border." Twelve kilometers one way. Do you sign up for it?

- What patrol? She asked, opening her green eyes wide.

- We look after the local herds of seals: one local, and one on guest performances from Latvia.

- And that's interesting! – she was happy – can I go with you?

I nodded.

- Provided you don't melt the candles after two kilometers, OK.?

"OK," she assured me. "You can rest assured.

We ate the rest of the dish in silence.

# VII

We were returning home. The heat finally eased and it was more pleasant to breathe. The storm had gone somewhere to the south and – judging by the roar of thunder – it was tormenting Tolkmicko.

- What do we do with such a beautiful start to the day? – Asked.

"As for me, I have some work to do with the documentation," I said. "I finally have to organize the photos, describe them and put them in the archive. We have our website, which I run. If you want, you are welcome to visit me. You will watch it yourself.

"As for me, I'd rather lie in the sun..." she muttered.

- Tomorrow you will have the sun higher in your nostrils – I replied – we are going to the sun for the whole day.

Of course, it will have – I thought – twenty kilometers *per pedes apostolorum*. It's just good that the beach was smooth as asphalt and there are no vehicles to watch out for... Janka and Romek rode horses, Maciek Mountain bikes. And I was on my feet. It helped me stay fit and I could gorge myself on good things without risking unnecessary kilograms. And most importantly – I had peace of mind.

- How do you dress? –Asked.

"I go out at six in the morning, so I take a tracksuit and then undress for a beach bag," I replied, "and I advise you to do the same." Anyway, I undress after the first kilometer... Do you have a backpack?

-I.

- Well, OK. Get a good night's sleep.

We entered the garden and I found to my surprise that Kuki was not greeting me. The landlady also got lost somewhere and the house was empty and quiet. It was strange, but I thought that Kuki must have gone gossiping with his mistress and I didn't bother about it anymore. I went to my room on the way to my amazement and horror to see someone lying in the corridor.

I turned on the light.

Mrs. Kubacka was lying on the floor, and Kuki next to her. With a cry of terror, I jumped to her. I put my ear to her breast. My heart was beating faintly and almost imperceptibly, but it was beating. She was breathing poorly, but she was breathing. Heart attack or stroke? –I thought. Kuki howled, and I felt uncomfortable. I reached for the phone and called an ambulance.

After a while, I heard Astrid leave her room.

-What is going on? – she asked – what are these noises.

Kuki howled and jumped outside.

"He's dead?" Astrid looked at me and then at her.

"She's alive, I think she fainted and fell down, hitting her head on the floor," I said, pointing to the trickle of blood that was seeping from under her head. "I've already called an ambulance.

Astrid knelt next to her and patted her cheek gently. She rubbed her temples and finally gently shook her shoulders.

Mrs. Kubacka opened her eyes and moaned. We helped her to sit down.

"Don't move," Astrid warned her. "I think you have a concussion.

"I'm sick," she whispered, her body tormented.

"That's right," I muttered, "I'll put a compress on your head in a moment."

I jumped to the bathroom, dipped my towel and wrapped her head. She hissed in pain.

"You have a head contusion," I said, "how did it happen?"

Mrs. Kubacka thought about it.

- N... no... I don't remember..." she stammered in surprise.

"A typical symptom," Astrid said. "They'll come for you in a moment." A few days in the hospital will do you good.

"We will take care of the house and Kuki," I added.

- Kasia, please inform Lidzia – she asked.

Lidzia was her younger sister who lived in Braniewo.

"Sure," I replied and after a while I heard voices at the gate.

I went out and saw the ambulance team.

-What happened? – asked the doctor – where is the patient?

- Inside – please continue – I said, looking around for Kuki. He was not there. It was strange, because he barked at strangers like any normal dog, but not this time... - My landlady had an accident. I think she fainted and fell down, hitting the back of the head on the step.

"Well, she had more luck than brains," muttered the medic, "we're taking her."

And he entered the house.

After a few minutes, everyone left. I helped Mrs. Kubacka get into the ambulance. I caught Kuki, who wanted to run after the departing ambulance. We closed the gate and the back exit. We were left alone.

-Tea? I asked.

"Well, it would be," she answered. "Oh, where is that sister's number?"

We searched for a while and found it attached to the fridge with a magnet. I called. On the other side, Mrs. Lidka's nice female voice spoke. I told her what had happened and received an answer that she would try to come here to see her sister. So this matter was also settled.

I poured two cups of fragrant Earl Grey and carried it to my room. Astrid sat on the bed and stroked Kuki. The dog was lying next to her, hanging its head sadly.

"You became friends quickly," I said, handing her a cup of fragrant drink.

"I like animals too," she said. "You won't believe it, but I once wanted to be a veterinarian, but it didn't work out.

- Welcome to my world – I thought – many things in my life didn't work out for me either...

"I believe you," I said with a sigh, "I also have a different specialty, and I deal with seals.

- Funny, you and the seals. What do you actually do with them? Do you feed them?

"Eh, no," I replied, "we take care of them, treat them as they should, feed them with vitamins when they are weak, and so on, and so on..."

"Oh, that must be fascinating.

- If you want, look at the photos – I said – they are on your laptop.

For the rest of the evening, we looked at my photos from my work. And it didn't even occur to me to inform Malicki that there was someone who, like me, was interested in seals. And he has the same special approach to animals as I do.

And even more...

# VIII

The morning was beautiful. We walked along the beach towards the sun, which was already quite high in the sky. It was going to be another beautiful day. We walked on the still cool sand. A fresh wind from the sea was waking up and it was pleasant to breathe in the salty breeze.

"Wonderful, isn't it?" I asked Astrid.

"Wonderful indeed," she replied, exposing her face to the fresh breeze.

We walked in no hurry, because we had a lot of time. We only had to walk a certain section of the beach and look around the sand and waves to see if something new had happened in the flocks of seals that were under our care. For the time being, there was nothing new – "our" herd – if we are to believe the bearings of their GPS transmitters, kept to the Vistula Spit and was somewhere near Piaski. Slightly northeast of this village, on the border waters.

- Do you really love animals? I asked.

"Really, you can believe me," she replied.

"And that's why you wrapped Kuki around your finger so easily?"

She smiled in return with her charming smile, and I saw how much she fit in with her surroundings. To the Baltic sand and greenish water...

- How do you do it? I asked.

She thought for a moment.

"I'd like to explain it to you somehow, but I can't.

"Try it," I answered.

She shook her head.

"Wait, maybe I'll give you a little show.

433

I nodded curiously to the highest degree.

Astrid walked away from me for a dozen or so steps. She stood slightly apart, closed her eyes and raised her hands. She now resembled the figures that can be seen in Egyptian frescoes from Faras or the Valley of the Kings... And then it happened. A flock of seagulls flew in from the seaside, which first began to circle around the motionless girl, and then began to sit on her head and shoulders. All this took place in an eerie, unreal silence disturbed by the sound of the sea. The birds perched on every free patch of her head and shoulders, and she turned to me, a smile on her face. The seagulls sitting on it did not even react to her movements. Did she hypnotize them, or what? – a thought crossed my mind.

Astrid finally stirred, and it was as if someone had lifted the spell from the seagulls. They took off into the air and flew away.

"Now you believe me?" She asked with a sweet smile.

"I believe because I saw," I replied, "how did you do it?"

I just closed my eyes and called them. And they came. That's all..." Astrid shrugged, as if it was obvious to her.

We started patrolling the beach. I had already recovered from my amazement and was looking for rational explanations. I didn't believe in witchcraft, magic and other superstitions. I've always been an atheist and I've never hidden it. I inherited the principle of "nothing beyond reason" from my parents. In this case, too, there was a rational explanation, of which I was absolutely sure.

Astrid shrugged again.

"I don't know, and I have no idea how it happens. It's some kind of magic.

"We both know that magic doesn't exist," I replied.

-Yes? And then what is it? – she said with defiance in her voice. –Miracle?

"There are no miracles," I replied calmly, "there are only unexplained, as yet unexplained, phenomena of Nature. Nature, as you prefer. And this is one of them.

"Are you so sure?" I noticed something like irritation in her voice. Or maybe I just thought so.

"Of course," I replied, "no offense, but power over animals, or rather finding a common language with them, is the oldest skill practiced by humans. Shamans, priests or whatever you call them. In the old days you would have been a priestess of Wotan or Odin... It was not for nothing that Osthanes wrote his famous *he physea te physei terpetai, he physea te physei nika, he physea te physei kratei...*

- ???

"Nature rejoices in Nature, Nature conquers Nature, Nature reigns over Nature," I replied, "this means that Nature does not lie. Nature is honest and answers every question,

435

and the whole art of doing science depends on the ability to ask them. And you have to be able to ask the right questions.

- So you think that this has a natural explanation?

"Yes," I replied, "it's obvious. That's why the Inquisition exterminated people like you. They could not understand that such phenomena, although rare, were explainable and were attributed to "unclean forces".

- And can YOU explain it? – she asked with an emphasis on "you".

I shrugged.

"No, I can't," I replied honestly, "but I'm sure that if we examined your brain, we would learn a lot..." But, but – does your mind only work on dogs and birds?

"No, all the animals I come into contact with," she replied.

"Do you know what that reminds me of?" I asked.

"Well, what?"

"The Yenisei Canyon and the cave drawings of the 'mushroom people', who also had power over the animals," I replied.

Astrid's eyes flashed with curiosity.

"Have you been there?" She asked with interest in her voice.

- No, but I read the accounts of those who were there and photographed these petroglyphs.

"And you believe all this?" –Asked.

I laughed.

- You know what? Who's who, but you should know it best.

Around noon, we entered the beach sector where our seals were supposed to be. And indeed, at some distance from the shore, we saw some movement in the water.

"Can you summon them?" I asked.

- Yes, and you? – she answered the question with a question.

I nodded and took out my marmot. I took a breath in my lungs and whistled: long, short, long, short – a moment of pause and three long ones.

-What was that? - Zapytała zaintrygowana.

"Morse," I replied, "CO from *come on* ."

The seals heard the call signal and slowly, without hurry, swam our way. They swam up and slowly rolled out to the beach.

Astrid crouched down and reached out to the nearest seal.

- This is Pelasia – I introduced the animal.

Astrid smiled.

The seal crawled up to her without showing any concern, and Astrid stroked her head and then began to scratch her back. Pelasia was very pleased. Other seals surrounded her and wanted to be caressed too. I knelt next to Astrid and stroked and scratched our charges.

- And what? She asked with a smile. – Can I apply for a job with you?

"Of course," I replied, "you would be a great purchase..."

- So since when?

I turned to her.

- Who are you really? Because you're not who you say you are, I'm sure of that, so? I asked in a calm, firm tone.

"I am who I am," she replied equally calmly and with a slight hint of irony, "I will tell you a legend, then you will more easily understand who I really am.

"I sense that you think I'm some kind of spy or a female mafioso, but no, I can assure you that we're on the right side of the barricades.

Somehow, I swallowed it.

- What kind of legend is that? - Zappen ich.

We moved east again, because the second herd was frolicking somewhere in the area. I sent a report to the headquarters and decided to go even further east to see the second seals. Besides, I was curious what Astrid had to say to me.

- Have you heard anything about Zielenica, the daughter of the king of the Baltic? Astrid asked.

"I read at Fenikowski's, if I remember correctly," I replied, "back in elementary school.

-Exactly. Zielenica was the daughter of the king of the Baltic Sea, who was fished out in nets and delivered to Trzęsacz. Or more precisely, she was imprisoned in the local parish church and forcibly baptized. The truth was that the local pharosh had fallen in love with her and wanted to keep her for himself at all costs. Unfortunately, Zielenica did not withstand captivity and died of longing for the sea. She was buried in the consecrated ground near the parish church and it was then that the king of the Baltic claimed her. He began to take the soil piece by piece and took almost the entire parish church and the cemetery where the earthly remains of Zielenica were buried.

- And Zielenica is not dead at all and I have it in front of me? I asked in a mocking tone.

- No, that Zielenica died and was indeed buried in the Trzęsac cemetery – she replied calmly – but don't forget that we live a little differently than you.

It was difficult to digest everything. There must have been something to it, because she really had amazing abilities, but did it mean that she was...

"So I'm supposed to believe that Mermaids, Tritons, Dryads, Naiads, and other sea goddesses really exist?"

"That's obvious," Astrid replied calmly.

- And you're a mermaid? I asked.

She laughed merrily.

- Come, you learned disbeliever! She exclaimed.

She took off her backpack and I grabbed my hand and pulled me into the water. I threw off my backpack and holding hands, we ran into deeper water. She stopped and took my hands. The water reached our chests. She looked me in the eyes.

"Now hold my hands and watch," she said.

She lay flat on the water and after a while her legs turned into a strong, fish-like tail covered with golden scales. No, not fish, but dolphins. The caudal fin was located horizontally. She swung it hard and after a while she had two legs again, which she lowered to the bottom and stood in front of me. We looked into each other's eyes.

"It wasn't hypnosis or anything like that?" I asked consciously.

She laughed again.

"You have my word for it," she said, "that you don't.

"And what if I tell everyone that you are a mermaid?" – Told.

She giggled.

"And try it, Kasia, try it," she said, choking on laughter. "But who will believe you?"

Well, yes – I thought – he is absolutely right. Nobody will believe me.

"Not true," she replied to my thought, "there are people who know about our existence and prepare other people to meet us...

Unexpectedly, she put her arms around me and kissed me passionately on the lips.

- ... And from now on, you are one of them," she finished.

And despite the cool water, I got very hot.

# IX

We dragged ourselves slowly home. Astrid was tired because, as she explained to me, moving in conditions of increased gravity is a serious nuisance for aquatic creatures. This did not surprise me. A moment later, I was surprised by something else.

We approached the fence and I opened the gate.

Kuki was not there. I called him. He did not run or speak.

-Kuki! I shouted.

A dead, tense silence answered me.

"Wait," Astrid concentrated for a moment. "He's there, in the bushes, and he's unconscious.

We ran in that direction. In fact, Kuki was lying on his side, he was motionless. Astrid lifted his head and put him on her lap. The dog opened his eyes and tried to lick her hands. He was very weak.

I quickly ran my hands over my limbs and ribs. The bones were intact. I felt his head. There was no reaction to the pain. The reason must have been different. Kuki slowly got up on all fours, but he was still weak.

"Kuki, lie down," I ordered him.

We got up shaking our knees off the ground.

- What was that? Heat stroke? I asked.

"I don't know, you know better about it," she replied.

- And you don't? – I asked, astonished – after all...

- Kasia, I'm not a doctor or a veterinarian. I can only strengthen the action currents of the nervous system and "recharge" it, as Kuki is doing now. I could have woken him up from his state of bewilderment or unconsciousness, but I can't tell what caused him, do you understand?

I nodded.

"I'll bring him water," I replied and headed home.

I put the key in the keyhole and tried to turn it. I met with resistance.

"What's wrong, fuck," I growled and tried again.

The effect was the same. , I pressed the handle and the door opened. They were open.

I felt a sudden cold.

We had an uninvited guest or guests.

- Oh fuck! – I thought – that was all I was missing.

- Astrid! – I called – Aaaaastriiiid!!!

"I'm here, don't tremble like that," she said reassuringly, "what's going on..."

She understood on the spot.

- What do we do? She asked in a low voice.

- I'm going to bet that our "guests" have already given up on here – I replied – I'm calling for cops...

We were waiting for them when I came up with the idea to look around the house. We searched the garden using a centrifugal system.

"Look," Astrid pointed to something that was a few steps away from us.

I moved in that direction and after a while I was holding a gas pistol case on a pen in my fingers.

"American," Astrid muttered, looking at its bottom. "A pistol or a revolver?"

"A pistol," I replied, "a revolver does not throw empty shells.

I put the shell where it lay.

Further searches did not yield any results. We sat down in front of the house again. Kuki was already fine, but he was clearly scared, he lay down at our feet and did not move a step.

After a quarter of an hour, a navy blue and silver police car stopped in front of the house. Two uniformed men got out of it and, to my delight, Sergeant Malicki. I quickly told him what we had seen and what had happened to Kuki. He just nodded.

- We will have to go in there – said one of the policemen, aspirant Kowalczyk – ladies will stay here. All three drew their weapons and entered the house. After a few minutes, they left.

"There was no one there," said Malicki reassuringly, "but you must see if something has disappeared..."

We checked, or rather I checked. On the surface, everything was fine. Whoever our guests were, they left behind an exemplary order. Whatever they wanted to find, they found and had time to clean up. It was almost six in the afternoon...

"I don't think they clean up here," said Kowalczyk, "they're professionals." They left no traces.

"But I know what they took," I said, suppressing my anger, "and I just don't understand why the hell they needed it..."

- And what took? - tried Malicki?

"My latest purchase," I replied, "a 1 TB external computer memory.

- What did you have? Malicki asked.

- A few family photos and nothing more. I started using this only a few days ago. I didn't have time to load more...

- So it was almost empty?

I nodded.

"But don't be so happy," said the aspirant, "because I'm afraid that someone has uploaded the contents of your computer's disks D and E to this memory and run away."

- Well, there was over 150 GB... - I replied.

- What was there?

- First of all, photos and private correspondence – I answered.

- Nothing that concerned your company? Malicki asked.

"No, or at least nothing like that about Weddell's seals," I answered.

"Hmmm..." he muttered, "it means that he will try to break into your Headquarters again."

- But what for? – I asked – after all, you already have these materials and cargo, so what will the data we have give them?

The sergeant smiled.

"It's obvious," he said thoughtfully, "with this data, someone can try to take control of your herd and train these seals to smuggle ashes across the Baltic Sea." Someone has already found out about this method and the competition is starting to work...

* * *

We were lying next to each other, holding hands.

- Do you have a boyfriend? I asked.

"No," she replied, "it's a little different here than yours." Do not forget, although I am a human being like you, I am descended from human beings who have been genetically modified to live in water and on land. And you also have modified genes. That's why you feel so bad around people.

It was true.

- When did it happen? I asked, intrigued to the extreme.

"Oh, a long time ago," she answered, "about twenty thousand years ago... Or more precisely, in the times of the greatest heyday of the Atlantean Empire.

-Kidding? I asked with a laugh.

"No," Astrid said dead seriously, "Atlantis really existed, and Tsingalai is tangible proof of its existence!"

# X

I fell silent. What a crazy night.

"Tsingalai?" I finally asked.

"Our headquarters," she replied, "is in the South Pacific.

"An island?" I asked, curious.

- You can call it that... I won't explain it to you, because I'm afraid you won't understand. Don't be angry, but this is a higher school of driving...

"Sure, I'm not angry.

But it wasn't important.

"Do you interfere in our affairs, you know, in the affairs of humanity? I asked.

- Of course, if your mindless activity threatens the security of our existence, it is probably obvious.

"You won't say that the Titanic is your job, are you?...

She snorted with laughter.

- Well, no, it was someone else's intervention, but a K-129, it was our, let's call it that, intervention... - she said mysteriously - I don't know if you know, but we had to do it, because if this action was successful, Honolulu would evaporate from the face of the Earth, and World War III would inevitably break out between China, the USSR and the USA. With all the ecological effects of this: nuclear winter, contamination counted in terabecquerels, and other "pleasures" – she said it with a clear sneer.

-What???

- Exactly, Kasia. We had to do it. By the way, "Thresher" is also our work.

- "Thresher" too??? – I exclaimed in amazement – after all...

"They had torpedoes with nuclear warheads on board, they wanted to fire one at several target ships gathered in the open ocean. The whole operation was ultra-secret and therefore there is no mention of it anywhere. The contamination from the explosion of the torpedo warhead would be spread throughout the North Atlantic...

"What about the USS Scorpion?"

"And it wasn't us," she replied calmly, "it was the Israelis who sank this ship in retaliation for the sinking of the Israeli submarine INS Davar by the Americans during the Six-Day War."

- Are you watching us? I asked, although I already knew the answer.

"Of course, you are a threat to us, so we are guarding you.

Oh, so that's where all those mysterious "shadows" floating behind Russian and American submarines come from – I thought.

There was a moment of silence

"Okay," I said, though I had a hard time accepting what I heard, "tell me why you said I was a mermaid too." After all, it is impossible. I never felt...

She looked me in the eyes.

"You're a mermaid, but you've only known that for a few hours.

- But I never...

- ... Have you tried? She asked a bit mockingly.

- Nnno no... - I replied - I didn't try.

"Exactly, so tomorrow we'll try, and now it's half past two."

It was easy for her to say... - but youth finally won and about three o'clock I finally fell asleep...

I opened my eyes and my eyes fell on the window, behind which swirling inky clouds. It flashed and there was a thunderbolt. I looked at my watch, it was ten to seven. I was about to jump out of bed, but luckily I remembered that I had a day off today and I didn't have to hurry anywhere. [...]

However, we held hands and looked into each other's eyes.

"You feel very lonely," she said quietly, "someone hurt you or you have bad memories."

- How do you know? – I asked, amazed – do you read my thoughts?

"No, but I can feel your emotions. And they are negative.

"You're right," I said quietly, "I have negative emotions.

- Disappointed love?

"Not only..." I replied, looking at the storm raging outside the window, "I had someone I lost.

Robert was an officer of the Border Guard in Karpacz and my greatest love. My only man, so different from the depths that surrounded me. We met and wanted to get married. Nothing came of it, during the gang war in Gdańsk he blew up with his car. The bomb was planted by the drug mafia...

- And what happened to him? Astrid asked.

- He had, eh... a car accident... - I replied.

"Did you love him very much?" –Asked.

I nodded and felt tears in my eyes and a wet nose.

"You know," I said, swallowing my tears, "I was hoping that maybe in my computer I would find a sign from those mafiosi like 'we're going to kill you, bitch' or something like that, and here is nothing, he sneezes with water.

"Well, everything is still ahead of us..." said Astrid.

Suddenly, something came to my mind.

- Tell me, what is your mission? I asked suddenly. "Why are you interested in seals?"

She smiled.

"Can't you guess?"

I shook my head.

-Truly?

I thought about it.

-Smuggling? But this is common and too much played for the Sirens to deal with it...

"And didn't you think that this seal was radioactive?" She asked suddenly.

- Well, yes, it did. I even thought that it was kept in some nuclear weapons warehouse or in some abandoned civilian or military nuclear installation in the Königsberg Oblast...

- Or maybe these seals smuggled not only drugs? Astrid got out of bed and opened the window, letting in cool, fresh air. For a moment she stood stretching and flexing delightfully. I wanted to jump out of bed and drag her back to it.

"You won't tell me that..."

"But I'll tell you, I'll tell you," she replied, "that's what it's all about. The thing is that just such a seal fell into our hands. It had a small container with the radioisotope polonium-210 in it. Of course, radiation would kill it anyway, but on the black market such materials are expensive and the loss of one seal is a piece of cake compared to the profits. Do you grab?

She lay down next to me again.

"It started back in 1990, when the USSR collapsed and it was not known what to do with the plutonium-producing reactors for Soviet submarines. They were slowly stolen by the mafia and sold to the West. In pieces. Poles, Slovaks and Hungarians quickly caught on to it and used an effective border blockade against this kind of contraband, as you know. It was the same with Finland. The nuclear mafia therefore found a route through Moldova, Romania and Bulgaria, but it was quickly cut off there as well when Bulgaria and Romania joined the EU. Well, we had to come up with something, and it did.

- What?

She sighed.

- Initially, the cargo went on board ferries from Estonia to Sweden. Everything came out – for us, of course – after the disaster of the MF "Estonia". Understand? There were tons of them! A similar load is said to have been carried on board the MF "Jan Heweliusz". But this is not true, because we have checked it. I was in its wreckage right after the catastrophe in 1991 – there was no trace of radioactivity there... Only the examination of the wreck of the "Estonia" showed that there was more than half a ton of nuclear fuel there. And this is really a lot of money.

- Oh my god – I moaned – this is really something to fight for and kill...

- And you see. Now I ask you to join our forces.

- But where do we start?

She thought for a moment.

- From what? And from the beach volleyball tournament, which is on Sunday. I even signed us up and paid the deposit," she smiled mischievously. – It will be interesting, because we will play with the Krukowski sisters from Olesno, and they are the national champions for 2010...

- Is this your plan? I asked. "And besides, how can you be sure that they will take the bait?"

- They will surely swallow it, because in the online folder of the competition I listed our specialties - she replied. "And yes: you're a marine biologist and seal specialist, and I'm a nuclear physicist.

I snorted with laughter.

- Are you really an atomist physicist? I asked with amusement.

"Yes," she replied, "I have a master's degree in nucleonics, a diploma from the Sorbonne. Simply?

-With confidence. Shall we get up? I asked. […]

* * *

For the rest of the day, we prepared for Sunday's competition. In the sports store we bought identical white and blue sports and beach outfits, flip-flops and dark glasses. We liked the black bikini better, but we knew from experience that they would warm up to the sun, so we let it go. Besides, our new outfits were blue on the bottom and white on the top, so we looked just as attractive in them.

"Not bad," Astrid said, looking at herself in the mirror.

"Of course, when you have such a figurine, you are good at everything," I said with a slightly malicious intention.

- You have to take care of yourself! - she declared and forcibly put me in front of the mirror. "Look at you!" On his head - a raccoon. No makeup. Clothes - horrible! I won't even mention the shoes - probably from before the war. The first one! And you want to find yourself a peasant!? Such a chupirad!? ...

"Uh, there," I muttered, confused, "no exaggeration.

"Yes, you're pretty, you have original beauty, but it won't last forever. It passes. Your clock starts ticking...

-What about you?

"I'm different," she replied, "in Tsingalai, the aging process is slower, but it does. Time spares no one, not even those who travel in it...

- Another revelation – I thought – they travel in time!

"But I'm a Mermaid..." I said out loud.

She smiled.

- You are, but this effect doesn't work outside of Tsingalai...

## XI

The sun was pleasantly warm, but the fresh sea breeze gave goosebumps to the exposed parts of the body. We played with the Krukowski sisters and lost, which was not difficult to predict. But first we defeated about two girls from Katowice, then we gave to the Warsaw-Łódź couple. Unfortunately – the Krukowski sisters were unbeatable, and we lost point by point. After the next set, we sat next to each other, greedily drinking water.

- Do you see anyone? I asked.

"For now, a bunch of guys are staring at us here..." she replied.

I took a healthy sip of water and looked around the audience. A normal audience – girls and boys in tempting swimsuits, a few staid elderly people and married couples with children. But that's exactly how it was supposed to be. Whoever the mafia's competitors were, they had to blend in with the crowd – like Malicki's spies.

- Funny situation – I thought – they are hunting us, and Malicki's people are hunting them. But we were also hunting for anyone who could give us a shred of information on the topic we were interested in.

"Look at those couple," I said, "the ones standing next to the lifeguard's turret."

Astrid slowly turned her head and threw it out of the corner of her eye.

"That bleached blonde beast?"

I nodded slightly in confirmation.

There was a beautiful woman of about thirty-five or thirty-eight years old with a man with a forbidden mouth. I wouldn't have paid attention to them if it hadn't been for the woman's persistent gaze fixed on us. The guy was clearly bored and looked like a blasé Gestapo man... That's right. She was as slender as a reed, she held herself upright. The body, modeled by many hours of exercise, emanated energy and health. Her face, covered with delicate makeup, had nice, delicate features. The eyes were hidden behind dark glasses, but you could see piercing blue eyes from behind them. She wore a floral thong-bikini covering the dots of her shapely, tanned body.

"Uhm, it could be them," Astrid replied with a bored face.

We lost two sets and we didn't want to play the third. Patrycja and Jadwiga Krukowski were really good at these blocks and all that was left for us to do was to defend ourselves to the end and lose with honor...

The end of the break. I got up and went to the pitch.

The referee's whistle. The serve of the younger Krukowska. Rebound, second rebound and cutting. A block by both Krukowskis and the ball landed on our field. One to zero.

And then there were two, three, and four... With five, I got furious. And your impatience!

First, I won a serve for us. Then I started hitting the curveballs, shooting at the lines of their field. I equalized to five, and then we finally got the advantage. Finally, we won the set. But the Krukowskis gave us a hard time the next time. We left the pitch lost, but full of satisfaction. We took second place.

The event was coming to an end. I was standing with Astrid on the box with the cup and diploma in my hand and I wanted to laugh. We took second place. A fluke. I didn't expect something like this. We waved to people and I was finally able to go down and stop smiling at the cameras. I looked in the crowd looking for a familiar couple. They were gone. Neither a bleached blonde, nor a guy with the murder of a Gestapo man. I felt disappointed. So a miss?

And yet we didn't, because when we sat down in a summer restaurant and waited for the dishes we ordered, a guy came up to our table, at the sight of whom I felt a pleasant tickle in the tops of my breasts. A tall, blue-eyed blond man with a face... That's right – a cherub. Angel face. And this construction...

- Can you spare me a few minutes of conversation? He asked with an endearing smile. He had a strange, hard and guttural accent, but his Polish was almost idiomatic. However, I sensed a foreigner in him.

"With pleasure," Astrid replied, "what do we owe her to?"

- I saw you fighting on the beach – you were wonderful. You lost to the Krukowski sisters, but better than you did not cope with them, so your defeat is not so severe, but it can still turn around... - he said mysteriously.

- Hmmm... Thank you," Astrid said.

-Me too. What do you mean by the reversal of the situation? I asked.

He smiled charmingly.

- Today you were not lucky on the beach, so you may be lucky now. I have an interesting proposal for both ladies.

I made a surprised face.

- Oh, and what an interesting proposition is this? Astrid asked.

"Work in your learned profession," he replied, "we need people like ladies.

There was a moment of silence.

- I won't certify myself – I said, taking a red scarf out of my bag and tying it around my neck, which was an agreed sign for Malicki's people – how much will we earn?

Yesterday I agreed with Malicki that if we were contacted by mafia envoys, I would tie a scarf around my neck. I chose red because it reminded me of a color that heralded danger. In the event of making contact, two groups were to observe the delinquent or delinquents and ensure our safety. So far, we have not seen any spies, but it could have been anyone from the swirling Sunday crowd of holidaymakers and patients.

Blondas grinned.

"That's what you call quick decision-making," he said with an innocent smile. "To start with, three thousand a month plus a bonus of five thousand for each success at work.

I looked at Astrid.

- Three thousand zlotys per month? I said doubtfully.

"I'm sorry, I didn't tell you, I meant three thousand euros.

I was stunned.

That's almost eleven thousand zlotys – I thought – not bad. But this is a fraction of what they obtained from smuggling and trading in drugs and isotopes... And those seals... I guessed that I was supposed to train them to smuggle this "treify commodity". And what was Astrid's role?

I smiled sweetly.

- A charming gadget, sir... Sir..." I paused.

"I'm sorry and I ask for forgiveness," he said, smiling sweetly, "I should introduce myself to you, I'm Algirdas Barnatovičius and I'm from Klaipėda," he stood up and bowed low and gracefully.

- We are very pleased and... apology accepted," I replied.

"And I forgive you," Astrid said in the tone of a queen.

For a moment, we all laughed carefree.

"And as for the bells and whistles, I assure you that I'm not a gimmick," he reached into his pocket and took out two folders. "Our company exists and offers such work.

I looked at the colorful cover of the plastic bag – the name Polar & Subpolar Shipping Co. Ltd. didn't mean anything to me.

- Is it some kind of shipping company? I asked.

- Yes, Dear Madam, this is a company providing maritime transport services, quite unusual because they are polar and polar, and besides, we intend to put nuclear-powered ships into operation. The ladies will find out everything on the spot from our employer.

- And who is it? Astrid asked.

"A certain rich and influential businessman from the Far East, but he is not an Asian, but a European," Barnatovičius replied. "Anyway, you will meet him tonight, because he has a habit of making important strategic decisions for the company only on moonless nights, and he will be like that today.

"An interesting custom," I replied.

"Yes, don't the parliaments of some countries meet at night?" replied our Cicerone. "Who knows what, but you should know it best, because the Scandinavian *things* took place at night at the sacred stones.

"Of course," Astrid replied, "you're right, so we'll meet...?"

- Today, on the beach at 11:00 p.m. A motorboat and I will be waiting there. Do we have an appointment?

Despite my resistance, I nodded. The case looked very interesting and dangerous. I realized that we were dealing with a crime syndicate that would not hesitate to send us to the bottom of the Baltic Sea with a bullet in our heads and concrete socks.

# XII

The dark strip of land slowly disappeared below the horizon.

As agreed, the motorboat was waiting for us on the beach from the sea. The first stars were hatching in the bright blue sky. Arcturus' orange eye was burning, the bright Summer Triangle was pouring in from the east, and Antares shone bloodily in the south. The sea was calm and quiet, all storms were probably raging in other regions of the world. We were sailing in the exact direction of the Polar Road, and therefore straight north, towards international waters beyond the twelfth mile.

At least twenty-four kilometers, I thought, far away.

I caught myself thinking about running away before anything started... And for the time being, we were chattering merrily about anything and laughing at anything, while Barnatovičius had an inexhaustible supply of jokes and good humor, so we had a great time.

The sea was dark and quiet, only somewhere on the horizon I could see the lights of ships standing in the distant roadstead of the Tri-City and in front of us ships sailing from and to Kaliningrad. I looked up at the sky again and found that the Polar Woman had moved slightly towards my right hand. We turned north – north-west. After a few minutes, a massive silhouette of the ship appeared in front of the bow.

"Well, here we are," Barnatovičius said cheerfully, "this is one of the company's ships.

There was something disturbing about it, and after a while I realized that it was not lit like other ships I had seen on the horizon. Even the position lights were not lit – red on the port side, green on the right side and white top lights.

And they should.

- Ghost ship – I thought – a modern version of the Flying Dutchman...

I shuddered involuntarily.

I could sense some tension emanating from our Cicerone.

The helmsman circled the dark ship and I had a chance to take a close look at him. It was a large trawler-processing plant with a characteristic ramp at the stern, which was closed with something like a gate opened from the top. It was all strange. The ship, like our motorboat, was painted with dark, almost black paint. At the stern was its name Polaris Stella and the name of the port of Punta Arenas.

Punta Arenas? – I exclaimed in my mind – that's in Chile! Indeed – that I didn't pay attention to it either! The motorboat had the Chilean flag, white and red with a blue field with a white star in the upper left corner. A bit similar to the Polish one, but not Polish...

- Chilean ship? I asked with an innocent face.

"Yes, one of our fleet," replied Barnatovičius, "as you have rightly pointed out, it is one of the ports on the route to the

South Pole. We operate in these regions of the Earth, so what is amazing about it?

- Not at all, but I didn't expect...

- ... flag of Chile? – he asked with a smile – and most of the ships have the flag of the Virgin Islands or the Cayman Islands, i.e. cheap flags, so there is no reason to be surprised, Miss Kasia.

We reached the gangplank. A faint light came on, in the light of which we boarded. The ship still gave no sign of life, but that didn't mean that there was no one here, quite the opposite. Suddenly, we were surrounded by black-clad figures. I looked at them and was dumbfounded. They were people very similar to our guide. Similar? – to say the least – they were identical. Like identical brothers. How... Clones?

Barnatovičius said something to them in German, of which I understood only the words *der grosse Chef*.

"Please, sir, give me back your mobile phones," he said in a cold, commanding tone, "our boss doesn't like such devices."

We took our phones out of our bags. Barnatovičius put them in his pocket. One of his clones searched us with a metal detector, and the other with a radio wave scanner.

- *Sie sind klar* - we heard and after a while we all entered the superstructure.

Unlike the deck, it was bright here. I looked at the portholes and understood. All of them were painted over with black paint.

What a strange ship? – I thought – what hellish precautions?

On the other hand, everything was obvious, after all, the shipowner did not want to have problems and therefore did not enter any port. The ship had to be darkened to keep it out of sight. Outside, during the day, it presented itself as another trawler-processing plant, hundreds of which sail the waters of the oceans. Nobody paid attention to it, and the name and the flag? – all it took was a bucket of paint, a brush and today's name would disappear into oblivion. The history of piracy has known such numbers. The motorboat we arrived in was a kind of tender. The second – larger – had to be somewhere nearby. Somehow, they should bring water, a bunker, spare parts, and so on. The ship was diesel, not nuclear, so I couldn't imagine that it would be delivered to it in canisters...

Maples in black led us to a door with the inscription "Capitano". Barnatovičius knocked.

"*Komm herein*," we heard from behind the bulkhead.

He opened the door and ushered us into a tastefully decorated living room, divided in the middle by a cream-colored sliding partition. A few armchairs, a table and a bar. Standard equipment, but everything in good taste. In one of the armchairs sat our friend, a guy with the murder of an old Gestapo man. When he saw us, he got up from his chair.

- *Herzlich wilkommen meine liebe Frauen!* – he said – I warmly welcome my ladies!

I wouldn't say that I was delighted to see him. Neither did Astrid.

- yes... *Sie sind am hochsten Chef hier?* "Are you the biggest boss here?"

He grinned and nodded. Barnatovičius quietly left. We were left alone with this unpleasant guy.

"Oh, *nein* ," he replied, "I am only doing the honours of the house. *Setzen Sie bitte.*

He has a smile like Godzilla – I thought.

"I'm sorry, but my German is rather poor," I said, "why don't we switch to Polish or English?"

He smiled again like a tyrannosaurus. Very hungry *T. rex...*

"OK," he said, " *no problem.*

I hate waiting, especially for interviews.

Suddenly, something sounded and the partition parted. We looked curiously and to our amazement we saw an armchair, and on the armchair... - an unknown blonde from the beach sat enjoying our amazement.

"Kurt, introduce me," she said haughtily.

Kurt jumped up and hurriedly introduced us to the boss.

- Dear ladies, I would like to introduce you to Mrs. Aphrodite Stavros, the owner of Polar & Subpolar Shipping Co. Ltd.

I looked at her greedily. In fact, this name suited her like few others. Despite her age, she was beautiful and attractive.

And, as you can see, terribly dangerous.

There was an awkward silence, which was broken by Mrs. Stavros.

- Are you the ones who want to work for me? Please present your CV.

We nodded and presented our papers.

"Okay, so one more formality," she said when we finished and pressed a button.

After a while, I heard some footsteps in the corridor and the sound of the door opening.

"Hello Walter, do you recognize my guests?" She asked someone who was standing behind us.

- Of course, madame – we heard a familiar voice – these are two agents of the Polish special services.

It was the voice of Sergeant Malicki.

## XIII

I slowly turned my head. Malicki was standing dressed in the uniform of a Border Guard soldier. I could sense the terrible tension he was subjected to. Tension and something else that

I didn't have time to catch, because for a moment I let myself be carried away by my nerves and felt disgusting fear, but above all burning hatred.

"A traitor," I thought, "and a vile son of a bitch. I was so fooled. He was the one who cooperated with them. He was their plug in the Border Guard.

I gave him a look full of hatred. Behind him came two clones of Barnatovičius with Heckler & Koch submachine guns in their hands.

- What to do with them? Malicki asked.

"Smash," said the old Gestapo man. " *Selbstverständlich...*"

I cooled down. It won't be so easy for them with me. They won't shoot us here, and outside I can always jump into the water. I preferred to drown myself than die at the hands of such scoundrels...

I glanced at Astrid. She didn't look scared at all. Quite the opposite. She sat calm and relaxed. What's more, an ironic smile crept onto her face.

"Not yet," she said with a hint of amusement in her voice.

"By *the way*, who sent you here?"

Astrid smiled contemptuously.

- Your buddy is uninformed. She's from the Internal Security Agency," she nodded at me, "and I'm from the CIA." And I have a specific proposal for you.

- Do you have a proposal for me? Mrs. Stavros was surprised, "either you're insolent or...

- ... or you will listen to me and think about our proposal, because it is irrefutable," Astrid said calmly, "because we know what the password wrxsp65432190wz means and to which account it belongs. I'll tell you more – we're able to empty all your accounts in the US and Switzerland and Tokyo, Tananariwa and the Cayman Islands, and let you go with your bags, so?...

A cloud appeared on Mrs. Stavros's beautiful face. I sensed fear emanating from her.

"Come out," she said to the men.

They left without a murmur. We were left alone with the head of the most powerful gang on two continents. Maybe even three...

"What do you want?" Mrs. Stavros asked.

"Well, you'd better now," Astrid said, "the CIA is politely asking for help with our operations in the Middle East." We want to hunt down some of the guys from al-Qaeda who have slipped away from Pakistan and Afghanistan. We know they are in Malaya, but we can't get them there.

- And what do I get out of it? – asked Ms. Stavros.

"Untouched assets and liabilities, gracious lady," Astrid replied, "and the friendship of the American people, and that's not a small thing.

The phone buzzered out. Mrs. Stavros picked up the phone. She listened to someone on the other side for a moment, and then she said something in a language we didn't understand. We only understood that we gained time. She shouted something and Kurt, Malicki and two bodyguards burst into the parlor, followed by Barnatovičius.

"Take them to the stern," she pointed to us, "and smash them there." I don't believe these bitches.

- And what happened? Kurt asked.

"There are three or four helicopters going here," she said.

I don't know what she said next, because both clones twisted our arms and led us out of the parlor.

"Something didn't work out for you," I muttered, "and Malicki betrayed you.

- You don't know much. Don't judge by appearances," Astrid replied.

The clones led us to the aft deck, which was a ramp on which nets were pulled onto the deck of the trawler. We were pushed hard and walked a few steps towards the swing gate. On board were our familiar seals. They raised their heads at the sight of us. I thought I was going to die among the animals I was caring for, and I closed my eyes.

And then events gained momentum. I heard the metallic crack of a weapon being reloaded. I was just curious if I would hear a shot, if my brain would fall apart before the impulse reached my ear to the hearing center. It was idiotic, but I couldn't think of anything else.

And suddenly two shots rang out. My heart leaped into my throat. I was still alive...

"Will you be standing there for a long time?" – I heard Malicki's voice. "Quickly, open the gate and release the seal!"

I turned around. Malicki stood over two motionless silhouettes with a smoking pistol in his hand.

"You traitor..." I growled.

"Spare yourself, they'll be here soon," he said coldly, but I felt that he was as tight as a string.

Suddenly, the roar of aircraft engines was heard from the starboard side, and the black helicopter shone its powerful searchlights. Bursts of machine guns rang out. More searchlights flashed and the missile slammed into the superstructure. There was a huge bang and a hail of shrapnel flew onto the deck.

-Faster! Malicki shouted and rushed towards the nearest entrance.

He didn't have to repeat. We ran towards the stern. The animals, terrified by the bright light, the roar of engines and the roar of gunshots, thrashed around the entire deck. I reached the switch to the gate opening mechanism and pressed the green button. The wicket slowly began to rise. Astrid got me.

- Do you have your whistle? –Asked.

-No! I shouted back. "But wait, I'll try something else."

I took a deep breath and whistled on my fingers as much as I could. One short. Break. Three long ones. Break. Long, short, long, short – ESC. *Escape* – run. I repeated once again – the seals understood and began to slide off the deck into the black water.

- Let's run! Astrid shouted.

"But..." I didn't have time to finish, because Astrid pushed me with all her might. I lost my balance and fell into the water in the wake of the seals. I choked on the brackish water and felt the choking weight of the fluid in my lungs.

"It's over," my feverish brain ran, "they didn't shoot me, now I'm going to drown."

Instinctively, I inhaled another portion of water, to my amazement I found that I breathed water like air. My body went numb from the waist down, but I only swung my legs for a moment and floated to the surface. I looked and I was speechless, my legs were covered with silvery scales. Suddenly, Astrid's joyful face appeared next to me.

- What a nice tail! –She said.

"Thank you," I replied, "why didn't you tell me?"

- But you knew! – she replied – did you forget?

"I forgot, that's a fact," I sighed, "what are we doing?"

- We are running away from here. I'm worried about Malicki. He did not betray him. I hope he can escape.

- Who did he work for?

- For the Border Guard, it is obvious.

- But these are not Border Guard helicopters.

- No, it's UNACO. At last they caught up with Madame Aphrodite Stavros. We are getting out of here.

Meanwhile, helicopters circled around the ship, laying it down with fire from cannons and machine guns, and air-to-water missiles.

We followed the herd and after a while we caught up with them.

"Lead them to land," Astrid said, "and I'll swim behind them so they don't get distracted."

- OK. – I replied and pushed myself to the front.

We were a good mile away from the scene of the battle, when suddenly I felt a shockwave lash all over my body. I poked my head out and heard a huge bang. I turned around and saw the black trawler disintegrate in a huge fireball of explosion. After a few seconds, the sphere dimmed, turning into a huge post-explosion mushroom quickly rising into the starry sky.

I started to work my tail hard. There were still twenty-eight kilometers to land.

* * *

Water and sand. Sand and sky.

Blue, white and gold.

The sun's heat penetrates me through and through.

"And you avenged Robert's death," Astrid said.

We sat on the sand, watching the sun, dragging its golden coat, slowly sinking in the Bay of Gdańsk.

I just nodded in response.

"The taste of revenge is not sweet at all," I replied.

-Bitter...?

"Uhm..." I nodded again.

She put her arm around me.

- What about Malicki? –Asked.

"He is alive, the explosion battered him, but people from UNACO fished him out of the sea and delivered him to a hospital in Gdańsk, by the way, together with Mrs. Stavros and half of her gang, the lion's share of the Asian police have arrest warrants on them. Walter will be fine. Oh, and he got a promotion and immediately to an officer. He is now a second lieutenant of the Border Guard. A promotion from the very top with the president's signature, and by at least ten degrees. By the way, the commander of the UNACO team is a girl, a pretty beast. Her name is Mira. She also visited him.

"It's nice to think you're a friend of the hero," laughed Astrid.

"Of course it's nice," I replied. "Maja doesn't leave him even for a moment, so I'm calm about him.

We looked at the setting sun again.

- What did they actually want here? What are these clones? I asked.

- What do you know about the Andean Fortress or the Fourth Reich?

-Nothing.

- Exactly. Not many people know about it like the Illuminati or the Rosicrucians. These are the descendants of the Nazis who fled through the Vatican to South America. I understood everything when I saw the name and home port of their ship. What did they want here? Of course, they bought weapons and fissile materials in Europe on the left. Most of the special services do not know about their existence, and if they do, they tolerate them, because – as in Poland – they have strong connections with the Church, and as you know, in Poland the Church is an untouchable sacred cow...

"Okay, but those clones?

- It's obvious, they were produced. They are ideal soldiers of both sexes.

I shuddered. The thought of an army of clones, sadistic assassins was not pleasant at all...

"And how do you know that?" I asked, intrigued.

- Do you know Daniel Laskowski? This is a guy who cut his teeth on fights with them. I talked to him about when he was with us.

"With you?"

- W Tsingalai.

I sighed. It was hard to believe in all this, although on the other hand, the events of the last few days showed that the world is not as simple as it seemed to me. I understood that the age of innocence was over and that now I would have to consciously participate in all of this, knowing the whole truth.

"I'm worried about our world," I said a little hesitantly.

"And I'm worried about you," Astrid said cheerfully, "what are you going to do now?"

"I'll go back to my dear seals," I replied, "but first I'm going on an overdue vacation."

Astrid smiled.

- Where are you going to spend it?

- Because I know? Maybe I'll meet my parents. Maybe I'll go somewhere... I don't know yet.

Astrid's eyes glowed green in the setting sun.

"My dear, you are a mermaid, so I suggest you go where you should go in the first place. There is an island in the South Pacific that does not exist. Tsingalai. This is your homeland.

"And will you go there with me?" I asked.

Astrid's fingers found my hand.

"But how do we get there?" – I was worried.

"Don't worry about that, you'll see soon," she said with a mysterious smile.

And I saw. But that's another story.

# CHAPTER 28. SOMEWHERE IN THE MIDDLE OF THE TRIANGLE

### December 5, 8:00 a.m. EST

A gray plane undulating in all possible directions behind the panoramic glass of the bridge, white crested birds and a gray, cruel sky. The deck sways and vibrates. A storm in the Atlantic. Something I hate like hell. He throws the boat like a pea in a box, all doubts come under the throat. Half of the staff is sick.

- *Meine Herren!* – I hear the voice of Captain Helmut Mehner behind me – what good news do you have on this beautiful morning?

- A beautiful fucking morning, a typical German sense of humor – I think.

"As you can see, captain," I answer and hand him a map with a plotted course. "We are at 30°02'00" north and 070°00'06" west, course 265°, we are going a little ahead.

The old man was an old-school captain, and calculating tenths, hundredths, and thousandths of a degree from GPS data made him furious. For him, time stopped at the sextant and the astrolabe...

I poured him a cup of coffee and handed it to him. He thanked me with a nod.

-Weather? Captain Mehner lit his pipe and glanced at the monitor of the on-board computer.

"Nasty captain. The wind is getting stronger and stronger and from the south-west – I replied – the wave promises to be at least eight. And we already have five-six. We make only five knots. A hurricane is coming, and it's ten – eleven.

The old man nodded.

- What's next to us? – he asked another question, puffing from his pipe.

He asked about the ships passing by.

"To the north of us, the freighter 'John Willmann', a Briton, fifteen miles. To the southeast, the cruise ship "Serenade of the Seas", twelve miles, goes from Nassau to Hamilton. Two miles away, a Norwegian "Nordheim" and a Spaniard "Leonian" are also going to Miami. And behind us was a twenty-two mile Russian "Volgobalt-315" from Hamilton to Cuba.

The old man raised his eyebrows.

- Volgobalt?

I nod my head in agreement.

- After all, these are not oceanic vessels.

"Well, they are not," I shrugged, "but as you can see... Anyway, it's their business, they can get into trouble, if necessary, we can reach them in four hours.

"I'd rather not..." the old man shook his head.

"Me too," I replied, because we were both thinking the same thing. We would rather not have castaways on the side...

The captain thought for a moment.

"Give me a little more to the north, just in case..."

" *Aye, aye,*" I answer, "helmsman, please give five steps to starboard."

The helmsman turns the wheel.

- First of all, there are five steps to starboard.

- Keep it up.

- Keep it up.

- What about the left-hand pump? Mehner glanced at the weather reports.

"Chief and his men made it at night. It runs like new.

Chief Arthur McArthur was a mechanic from Glasgow and a master of his trade. The crew liked him for his good humor and great knowledge of all the devices and machines that he loved and caressed, unlike the grumpy Mehner.

"All right," the captain visibly cheered up. "We have to get to the cover of the land as soon as possible. I'd rather not risk a disaster on the high seas, and we both know why.

The old man was afraid of what each of us feared when going on this cruise. The entire crew had to sign a pledge to remain silent, but only the captain and I knew exactly what we were carrying our MV "Caribbean Pearl" from Hamburg to Miami... The crew could only guess that the cargo was extremely dangerous. What if she knew? The case was TOP SECRET. Hamburg was the port of departure as Miami was the destination, only on paper, because in fact we were going from Brest to Galveston, where the processing plants of the pig we were transporting were located.

"We are a long way from land, and I would rather not wait out the storm in Bermuda," said the captain. "Besides, I don't want to answer the stupid questions of their customs officers.

- Me too, captain.

I took a huge sip of my coffee and looked out the window again. The wind was getting stronger, the wave was slowly rising. We were rocking quite well. The "Carribean Pearl" was short but bulky, like a Hanseatic cog. She was one of the first ships launched by the Norwegians after the war, adapted to sail in the Baltic Sea and the seas of the North, and not in the subtropical waters of the Atlantic, where it was difficult to find ice fields or even ice floes that could be crushed by her reinforced bow. The short, bulky hull had a characteristic that the ship swayed on the water like a buoy. But it was inconspicuous in ports around the world and therefore ideal for transporting special purpose cargo, which we had been transporting for some time from the European Union countries to the United States and back. Of course, not for ordinary rates, but three and four times higher. Well, because the load was also uninteresting. More dangerous than a whole pack of rabid sharks. Or sperm whales, not to mention killer whales...

"That would get us out of *Xavier*'s way.

*Xavier*, it was this tropical hurricane that went from the Gulf of Mexico to the waters of the Atlantic. He had the strength of the famous *Katrina* and now he was pushing through the Florida Strait to the north-northeast. Exactly in our direction.

"Not a bad thought, Mr. One," the captain looked at me with appreciation in one eye. "But then we have to storm in the very center of the Bermuda Triangle.

I looked at him in amazement, and the helmsman laughed.

"You don't believe in these fairy tales, *Herr Kapitän, nich wahr,* do you?" –Asked.

"Fairy tales and not fairy tales, Mr. First," he replied with undisturbed calmness, "the sea has this thing that you can find everything in it. From amber and manganese rolls to Mermaids and even Godzilla, not to mention sea snakes.

- I'll agree with the first one, and with the second... Somehow I didn't see them – I muttered looking out the window, where heavy waves were rolling – and I've been swimming since yesterday.

"Well, don't be surprised when you meet one," the old man looked at the map, "we're going to follow your advice first, right in the middle of the monster's mouth, and pray that it doesn't swallow us..."

\* \* \*

Cargo control, that was my job. Bumping up the gangways, I went down to the hold, where on thick, wooden pallets there were thirty gray containers that reminded me of huge coffins. There were no inscriptions or markings on the smooth surfaces. Even symbols or warning pictograms. And yet they should be if it was a normal ship and a normal cargo. The thing is, it was neither a normal ship nor a normal cargo. Even the crew was not normal. A collection of people from different countries, very carefully selected into one team. Theoretically, it should not work, but it worked well and precisely and since 2002, when our services were first used – or rather, not, we were called to provide these services...

"Caribbean Pearl" was swaying more and more on the wave. Bumping into the bulkhead, I walked around the hold and checked every belt and every nib securing the load. We were supposedly told that the cargo was safe, but it was not sugar or bananas. I took the meter out of my pocket and walked around all the containers again. At the third time, the meter chirped. I finished the inspection and approached the "three" again. I took the "iron" out of the tool compartment and turned it on. After a few seconds I had a reading. It wasn't much, but it wasn't good either.

I went to the phone and turned onto the bridge.

"Captain, we have a small leak. Normal, but... You know, the devil doesn't sleep," I said into the microphone.

" *I* ," he accepted it succinctly, "how much of it is there?"

"Forty-two units," I replied.

- Well, it's not bad – he replied. "Which number?"

"Three," I replied.

He was silent for a moment.

- And the others? –Asks.

- OK, tres bien and zehr gut – I replied.

"Then shut the hold and go in there as rarely as possible," he said at last. "Oh, and keep people away so that no one hangs around there." Besides, go to sleep, for now, because the next day will give us a hard time. The announcement from Nassau says about ten.

I knew that much myself. The deck under his feet was swaying more and more dangerously. I ordered the storms to be hung on the deck and to see that all hatches were closed. Climbing up the steep gangways, I thought about collapsing on the bunk and sleeping off my eight hours. I was immune to rocking, but it dulled me and I always felt sleep-deprived during a storm. I looked at the barometer – the pressure was falling on my face. It was eight-fifty when I finally stepped into my cabin. Tired as a dead dog, I threw myself on the bunk and fell asleep without even knowing when...

**December 5, 5:13 p.m. EST**

The ringing of the phone brought me back to reality from the abyss of dreams. I looked at my watch and picked up the phone, which was the pinnacle of my acrobatic possibilities – the ship was tossed on the waves, like a float when a huge fish is hooked.

-Halo! I said into the microphone, overcoming the resistance of my throat. "What's going on again?"

"First sir, come to the bridge," I heard the voice of the watchman, Frank Bannister, our third officer, "only quickly, we're in trouble!"

I jumped to my feet and ran to the bridge and dressed on the run. After two minutes I ran into the bridge wondering how many bruises I had made by hitting myself with my whole body in the bulkhead...

"What's Frankie?" I asked, reaching him and grabbing the first handrail I could find.

"Look here," he said, pointing to the greenish screen of the radar, "what do you see?"

I looked.

On the dark surface of the radar monitor, I could see concentric waves that were normal in a storm, and somewhere to the west of us was a huge patch of a cruise ship, which seemed to be adrift or moving so slowly that it was imperceptible. The second, smaller one was on the countercourse.

- What's going on? I see nothing but these two boats.

"Well, now look over there," the third pointed something behind the glass towards the stern.

I looked and felt myself numb.

The ocean in front of us resembled an unconscious churn of waves driven by the wind from the southwest. I looked to the sides, and I saw the same landscape. But from behind...

It looked like a huge furrow, at least a mile wide and as long as the horizon could see. I couldn't see its depth from that position, but it must have been enormous. And she was slowly approaching us. Maybe it seemed to me that slowly, because in such moments time stretches like bubble gum...

- *By God...* Mr. One, what do we do?

"So far, a good impression," I muttered, "comes from behind, we have a chance." Stay the course, let THIS take us from the butt...

-Helmsman! Stay on course – I instructed the helmsman and leaned harder on my feet.

" *Oui mon Capitain* ," replied Loic Breitone, a tall boy from Normandy, "I'm holding two-six-five!"

- What could it be? – wondered the other.

"To my mind, it's a soliton wave," I muttered, "the kind that supposedly finished "Thresher" in the sixty-seventh...

"Third, boss," Loic corrected me.

- Uhmmm... - I nodded - that's right, in the third one, and by *the way*, THIS will be here soon.

- We are not announcing the alarm? Loic was surprised.

I shook my head.

- No, it's too late. I'm afraid there would be more casualties if I announced it now...

I didn't finish. The sea crevasse caught up with the "Caribbean Pearl" and began to pull her into its watery abyss. The stern of the ship sank suddenly into the abyss, and the bow went sharply upwards.

- Take care! I shouted, maybe unnecessarily, because everyone grabbed what they could to stay on their feet.

I looked down, the stern of the ship slowly approaching the bottom of the valley of this unusual wave. It whistled in the pipe.

- Bridge, what's going on? The chief's voice came out.

- So far everything is OK. – I replied – get ready to drive the other way.

"A superwave? – it was more of a statement than a question.

"Something like that," I replied, and then I plugged the pipe, because masses of water fell on the stern when it reached the bottom of the wave. The "Caribbean Pearl" slowly straightened up, and after a while the stern rose almost to its zenith. I blew into the pipe.

-Machine! Let's start the ride in the other direction!

- OK, let's hold on!

The ship creaked all its bindings again as it began to climb the slope of the Extrawave.

After a minute it was all over. The sea around us was foaming and undulating again, and the Caribbean Pearl was swaying like a cork on a wave. In a word, everything returned to normal.

"Call the old man," I advised the third, "and I wasn't here." I go to inspect the cargo and let everyone stay as far away from the cargo hold as possible.

- OK, Mr. One!

"Well, have fun," I said. "Oh, and broadcast CQ's warning about this wave. Someone might be in damn trouble, I thought of the cruise ship.

I got off the bridge and walked towards the hold, bumping mercilessly against the bulkhead and the stairs of the gangways. After a few minutes, I found myself among gray containers. I looked at them carefully – they looked intact. Going up and down that infernal elevator didn't damage any of them. I breathed a sigh of relief. Just in case, I took the detector and approached the "three". I turned it on and groaned—a red light the size of a large ant's head glowed in warning. I looked at the scale – there were already 136 microsieverts per hour and this was beta/gamma radiation. It seemed that we could have problems, and it was us. Somewhere the biological shield of the load of spent rods from French and German nuclear reactors carried by us, which were going to be processed in the States, was released, and now this filth – extremely "hot" and toxic could also threaten us. The radiation warmed the damn containers and it was warm in the hold. About 30 degrees Celsius. I picked up the phone and dialed the captain's number.

"Mehner, I'm listening," said the Old Man's voice.

"The first one from this side," I replied, "unfortunately, captain, I have bad news.

" Me?

- *Jawohl*, the "three" still has a leak and it's already one hundred and thirty-six units. In addition, the load starts to heat up. It's because of this damn wave...

- And the negligence of the cargo owner. Phènix d'Or didn't properly secure this shit and now we have a problem.

- What do we do? We are still closing the cargo hold for the crew and maybe we can ventilate it? It's only fifteen degrees outside, so it's going to cool down a bit.

- Not while it rains. Water can get into the container and...

Sure, there could have been an unexpected chemical reaction, the end of which could have been a big boom like in Chernobyl and Fukushima...

- OK, in this case we wait for the weather. I hope that the biological shield of this *scheiss* will endure. I close the stall and evacuate from here.

"Do it," Mehner said, and hung up the phone.

I left the hold and closed it on deaf ears. I entered a new code into the lock of the entire hydraulics opening the covers, in case anyone wanted to get in there and into the entrance hatch from the superstructure side. And then I went to my room.

### December 6, 00:30 EST

I lay on the bunk and tried to sleep. The events of yesterday did not leave me alone. Our "Caribbean Pearl" was a special ship for transporting extra-special cargoes – most often nuclear fuel from the USA to France and Great Britain, and nuclear waste and spent fuel rods in the other direction. Under the agreement of April 2012, all old-type nuclear power plants in Europe were decommissioned and replaced with plants from ecological and renewable sources – as was done in Germany, or nuclear power plants of a new type and built in seismic areas. Initially, the case was dealt with by UNSCEAR, but after several corruption scandals in Poland, the European Commission started reforming itself and focused on the energy security of the entire EU. As a result, north-western Poland and the adjacent districts of Germany became the energy center of Central Europe. Twenty powerful nuclear power plants were built there, taking water from the Oder and the Baltic Sea. The second energy bonanza was north-western France, where on the Breton Peninsula the Anglo-French consortium Golden Phoenix - Phènix d'Or Co. Ltd. was built, only six, but gigantic nuclear power plants with a capacity of gigawatts. They supplied electricity to almost all the countries of the old twelve except Greece, which received electricity from the Eastern Bonanza.

Of course, such a juggernaut absorbed tons of enriched uranium and thorium. Some of the nuclear fuel was supplied by the EU, but a third came from the United States, South Africa and Australia. And then the American corporation John Dante Goldman Uranium Mining and Power Co. joined Golden Phoenix - Phènix d'Or Co. Ltd. The Americans had their own energy base based on nuclear power plants utilizing the AP-1500 and the latest AP-2400 reactors. In Europe, the Super Phènix and Ultra Phènix reactors were in operation, also with a capacity of more than two gigawatts each. The transport of this "hot" commodity was carried out only by sea, so as not to expose itself to attacks from various types of terrorists, extremists and other freaks who already saw themselves in the role of masters of the world sitting on bombs. It took place through such crypts as the "Caribbean Pearl" – small, unobtrusive. In the manifestos and customs bills of lading, "general cargo" was mentioned. And only a few insiders knew what was really being transported. Governments didn't ask many questions, everyone was happy – even the protests of environmentalists subsided when it turned out that the Super Phènix and Ultra Phènix technology is 99.999% safe and cannot be repeated by Three Mile Island or Chernobyl or Fukushima. Even in the event of an earthquake with a magnitude of 9 on the Rychter scale or a nuclear explosion in the immediate vicinity of the power plant. In addition, these reactors recovered some of the nuclear fuel and thus "burned" less uranium, thorium or plutonium. Now, on this voyage, we were carrying thirty containers from the power plant in Le Havre, in which the fuel rods were to be located. Worn rods, of course. Packed in several layers of lead, cadmium and something else that was supposed to protect against radiation. And yet it did not protect me and the "three" worried me. Radiation meant trouble. And this is what we all wanted to avoid. At least the Old Man and me.

Someone quietly opened the door and slipped into my cabin. Probably Royas, our second mate, who must have run out of whiskey and borrowed a bottle from me.

-Miguel! – I said loudly without opening my eyes – don't forget to give it back!

"Robert, it's me..." I heard a quiet whisper.

I opened my eyes and my gaze fell on a young woman sitting crouched next to the koi. Delicate facial features, long hair of dark honey amber and wide open green eyes. That hair was her only garment, from which drops of water dripped onto the carpet.

"It's me," said Janta, "do you recognize me, do you?"

I got up and sat down on the bunk.

- How did you come here? –Asked. "After all...

I got up from my bunk and she from her crouch, and she just threw her arms around my neck. Instinctively, I took her to me. She was still wet, so I released her from my grip and gave her a bath towel. She calmly wiped her model body of a professional athlete.

- What are you actually doing here? I asked again.

"Aren't you happy to be with you?" – she asked, looking at me from under her eye – because I'm so happy...

I sighed. It was so unexpected that I didn't know how to react.

"I'm glad, of course," I said hesitantly, "but you showed up so... unexpectedly that...

She smiled, flashing her teeth.

"Of course, I understand," she said, "first give me something to wear."

I gave her a shirt and Bermuda shorts. She put them on and sat down next to me. I put my arm around her and she snuggled up to me. It was all too good to be true. Although...

* * *

Janta... I learned this unusual name during my last vacation in Denmark. I hid in some damn asshole near Lemvig. Peace, quiet, warm April and beautiful surroundings... And it was then that I met her for the first time. Janta. At the bathing beach in Ferring. She came out of the sea in a blue bikini and just came up to me. Anyway, the beach was almost empty and there was no one in sight except me.

" *God dag* ," she said with a charming smile.

" *God dag* ," I answered. "Unfortunately, I don't speak Danish.

- It doesn't matter, neither do I. Are you here on holiday? – she asked in English as if we had known each other for God knows how long ago.

"You can call it that," I muttered, a bit surprised by her brusqueness.

"I'm sorry, but I didn't know how to start this conversation," she smiled at me, "to make it come out as natural as possible.

I looked at her in amazement.

"Oh yes," she continued, "I'd like to talk to you about a few topics that interest you and me.

- Don't you think it's a bit too fast? I expressed my doubts.

- And what are you waiting for? – she countered – we have one life, and a short one. My name is Janta, and you?

"Robert," I replied, "Bob for friends."

"OK. Bobby, Bobik?" Can it be?

- If you are a friend, you always...

And so we talked, basking in the April sun, which was already scorching healthily. And when the sun hung over the misty horizon, I got up from the blanket and walked towards the car.

- Are you Polish? She was amazed at the sight of my car and its license plates.

- And this is something bad? I countered.

- No, there are a lot of Poles here. And by *the way*, can't you eliminate unemployment in your country, and you have to drop everything and leave God knows where?

I sighed. How many more times will I have to answer this question and explain to Europeans that Poles are brave in wartime, but hopeless in peacetime...?

- How to tell you – I thought for a moment – Poles are wonderful, wise and willing to sacrifice in the name of ideals and faith only when they have a whip over their back and a bayonet on their throat. But when they can decide for themselves, then they usually lose to themselves.

She nodded.

"This is a rather concise, but very accurate assessment of your nation.

- But that's how it is.

- And that's why you left Polish?

- Exactly, besides, I can't live in such a strongly cohesive country.

- In which one? She asked with utter amazement.

- Klechized. Possessed by priests.

"Oh, I see. And I'm not surprised by you. With such views, you have nothing to do there...

She walked me to the car and then returned between the dunes. The next day I met her again. She came out of the sea as if out of nowhere, sat down next to me and we talked about everything and nothing. I expected some questions about my work, some camouflaged allusions or other attempts to probe me before recruiting me for secret cooperation, but there was nothing like that. Finally, I couldn't stand it out of curiosity and asked her a question:

- Where do you actually live?

"And what do you mean?" She replied with a mysterious smile.

- Well, where is your home, work, family and so on...

"There," she said, and with a movement of her head she pointed to the sea.

- What does there mean? – I asked – across the sea? Are you English? A Scottish woman? Irish? Icelandic?

She laughed.

"You won't believe it if I tell you," she replied.

- A Dane? – I continued – German?

-No. But what I am going to tell you, I trust to your honesty and discretion.

I felt my eyebrows lift.

- Is it such a secret?

"That much," she replied seriously, and there was no hint of cheerfulness or defiance in the green of her eyes.

I thought for a moment.

- OK, what is this secret?

She looked discreetly to the sides. There was no one in sight, only somewhere in the distance some anglers were whipping blue waves with their lines.

"Do you believe in the existence of intelligent races on our planet beyond humans?"

The question was so unexpected that I felt a complete squirm of the excavator. A *full-blown one.*

"Wait a minute," I replied in an uncertain voice, "you want to say that you..."

She nodded.

- I'm a mermaid. Janta is a name derived from the Slavic amber. In Russia, we are called Rusalki. In Anglo-Saxon countries, Sea Maidens – *Mermaids.*

I shook my head.

"Nu, I don't know what you want," I said in Russian. "You don't Rusalka and you don't Morskaya Dieva..." Zatiem, show me your fish, tassel.

"You don't have to believe it, but that's how it is," she replied in Polish and laughed.

- Dziadek, a co?

- You have clear pronunciation, no raids with peeing and coughing. Literary.

She spoke clearly, without an accent. But this proved nothing. Languages can be learned...

"Okay, can you show me some direct evidence?" – I asked in Polish and was extremely curious if he would understand.

- If by direct proof you mean a fish tail, then of course yes. Come with me," she said, and got up from the blanket we were sitting on. "Will you finally believe me when I show you?"

Her Polish was impeccable.

"Come on," she shook my hand.

I stood up and took her hand. She was warm, delicate, feminine. Normal.

And yet.

We went up to our chests into the water, which was cold as it is at this time of year. Janta took my neck with her arm and lifted my legs so that I could take her under my knees.

- Watch now! –She said.

And before my eyes there was a transformation. Her legs, covered with smooth and tanned skin, were covered more or less to the waist with a fine, silvery scale. Instead of feet, a wide, bluish, crescent-shaped fin appeared. It was not vertical like fish, but horizontal like dolphins. Blue panties and bra slipped from her body, and my eyes picked out nice, shapely and firm breasts. I felt stupid.

Janta wagged her tail and stood back next to me. She slowly put on her bikini.

"How are you..." I mumbled, slightly stunned.

Janta's eyes laughed. She took me by the neck and kissed me on the lips.

"Now you believe me?" –Asked.

"I believe because I have seen and touched," I replied, snapping my teeth.

She gave me an amused look.

"Sure," she said lightly, "we're going out because you'll catch a cold." You also changed the color, to blue – pale.

Indeed, I was trembling terribly. The water had to be about ten or twelve degrees and no more. Numb from the cold, I went out to the beach. Janta followed me step by step, then took a towel and began to wipe me intensely. It dried up on its own in no time.

- Do you speed up your metabolism and warm up your body? – I asked implicitly.

"Evolutionary adaptation," she replied, "is done by itself, without my consciousness. A defense mechanism, as you prefer.

I nodded. At least I understood that.


And suddenly I realized that I had undergone some kind of initiation and entered another, completely unknown dimension of reality.

"That's right," I heard her voice, "it was an initiation.

- How is initiation? – I asked – for what? Wait, are you reading my mind?

- You have read Lloyd's "Married to a Mermaid", have you? Something like this was and still is possible. And as for mind reading, I feel it more than I read it

I rummaged through my memory. And I remembered.

- Yes, I remember, there was something like that. But what does it mean?

"Well, only that you're my fiancé," she replied. "After all, I don't undress in front of just anyone and I won't give myself to just anyone but you.

The jaw slammed against the sand again.

- Uh... What? Who?

"My fiancé," she replied calmly, "I chose you, and I don't think you should think long about it.

I sat down on the blanket. It was, to put it mildly, very unexpected. Two days of acquaintance and something like that!

Janta leaned over me and kissed me on the lips again. Her lips were warm and moist. Normal, like a normal woman.

- Sleep on it. And until tomorrow. I hope you want to meet me again," she whispered in my ear and slowly walked away towards the sea.

She was moving further and further away, disappearing in the waves, until finally another wave covered her and Janta disappeared from my world. And I was left on the warm sand with confusion in my head. I spent the rest of the day at the

Easter festival in the town and tried to have fun with the locals and tourists, but my thoughts were with Janta and her strange proposal.

- Do you remember? I heard her voice.

I came back to reality. Janta in my checked flannel shirt and colorful Bermuda shorts looked like one and a half misfortunes. Her look was also unhappy.

- Well, I remember – I replied. "You didn't show up then, so I think you changed your mind." In short, you set me up.

She shook her head.

- It's not like that. Something happened that interrupted me and I couldn't meet you, although I really wanted to.

I raised my eyebrows.

- What happened, what was it?

Now she was amazed.

"Don't you remember?" Catastrophe in the English Channel!

Well, yes, I forgot. The next day, in the English Channel, near Bouglone, the huge tanker "Europe Exxon Express" exploded with half a million tons of oil on board. "3E" or "EEE" as it was called collided with the shuttle to Dover and literally blew it up. More than one hundred and fifty people died on the ferry and twenty-four on the tanker. Some of the unburned oil went to sea. The spot was at least two hundred square kilometers in size. The media hailed this catastrophe as "bloody Easter", and tankers had to sail around the British Isles from the west from that day...

"Indeed," I muttered, "I forgot about it. But that's not what you want to talk to me about?

She shook her head.

"So I'm listening," I said, pouring her a glass of Jackie Daniels on two fingers and throwing in a few ice cubes. Janta took a glass and took a sip of some amber liquid. She coughed.

And I was all ears.


### December 6, 01:00 EST

- What are you carrying now, on this cruise? –Asked.

"The same as always," I replied, "general cargo and machine parts.

She looked at me like I was a fool.

- That's not what I'm asking – she replied – what are you REALLY carrying?

"According to what we were told in France, we have used fuel rods from the Le Hauge power plant on the side.

She nodded.

- Have you checked the cargo?

I shook my head.

- I don't advise you – I muttered – it's "hot" and besides, it's enclosed in a biological shield that can only be opened in processing plants, so what?

She ignored my question.

- Are any of the containers hyperactive? – she asked another question.

- Hyperactive?

- Oh dear, doesn't it sometimes emit radiation?

"Ah, that's what you mean, yes. One of them, number three. And what?

She looked up at me and took a long sip of whiskey.

- Fucking hell, that's what I was afraid of – she cursed in Polish – that's what I was afraid of, damn it...

I poured myself a huge shot of Jack Daniels and added ice. It seemed that the real emotions were just beginning and I was done with sleeping until dawn. I took a sip of the burning liquid, stared at the ceiling and whistled through my teeth "Whiskey in the jar..."

"Don't worry," I replied, "after all, it's a bit of beta or gamma radiation..."

She looked at me so that I felt cold.

- And neutrons?

- Never, mom tylko detector G-M β/γ.

- Well, yes. Do you know what you REALLY have on board?

"Well..." I shook my head. "Well, I don't know.

-Exactly! You don't know. Well, I'll tell you! She exclaimed. "You have thirty neutron warheads here, with a power of about a hundred – one hundred and twenty kilotons each. One or even two of them are unstable and as you can see, the radiation has pierced the biological shields.

"Well, no..." I groaned, "are you serious?

"No, I'm joking," she grumbled, "seriously, of course!"

- But what is it all about? –Asked.

- As far as we know, it appears that the French decided to get rid of compromising gadgets and sent these toys to America. Officially, France did not have neutron warheads, but as you can see, this was not true.

- Wait, but the French don't...

"Of course I do, and I'll even tell you where!"

- In Mururoa?

-Also. But above all, in Reggan, Algeria. That's where it all began. This was the place where the French launched their ballistic and space missiles, and also detonated four nuclear charges. Back in the 60s. It was called *Gerboise* – desert jumper. First it was *Gerboise Bleue* – seventy kilotons, then *Gerboise Blanche* with about five kilotons, next was *Gerboise Rouge*, also under five kilotons, and finally *Gerboise Verte* with only one kejti... Two of them were fired over soldiers in full armament. Such a French edition of the American *Big*

*Smokey*... Then Algeria gained independence and the French moved from there. The missiles went to Kourou in Guyana, and the nuclear warheads went to Mururoa. Do you grab?

I nodded.

- At the beginning of the 1960s, the military of that time was not yet aware of the possibilities of small nuclear explosions and their use to destroy tactical targets. And the French were immediately surprised that when a certain amount of beryllium hydride is added to the lithium hydride mixture, the neutron flux increases. And they have already tried it on Mururoa...

"That means these thirty warheads...

- … you have it on board," she finished.

I looked at her. A beautiful young woman and such terminology. - Fuck, what a time - I thought - such girls should love and be loved, not deal with this madness...

- And what about the other hold? –Asked.

"Some machine parts," I answered, "to tell the truth, I don't know what they are. There is nothing in the papers except this concise statement. I was interested in the tref load.

"So it can be anything," she concluded. "I'd like to see it.

- Hmmm... - I muttered - and you wouldn't want stars from the sky?

She smiled with an effort.

- Believe me, but no. I want to see what you have in the other hold.

I thought for a moment.

- OK. – I replied after a few seconds – it can be done.

We got up from the berth. Of course, Janta couldn't walk as she stood, so I gave her a bright yellow oilskin with a broad-winged storm hat and high rubber boots. I opened the door and looked around the hallway. There was not a living soul to be seen until the companionway. I quickly walked over to the gangway and glanced down. There was no one on the gangways. The ship was less rocking and you could move quite quickly without attracting anyone's attention. The storm was subsiding and you could feel it. The howling of the wind outside was almost inaudible. The hurricane went further north.

In two weeks it will be windy and rainy in Poland... - I thought a bit senselessly considering the situation I was in.

I nodded my hand and Janta was next to me in no time.

"We're going down, just quietly," I whispered.

We quickly slipped across the four decks and found ourselves in the corridor leading to both holds.

- Where do you have these containers? She asked in a whisper.

"In the number one hold," I pointed to a massive hatch. "But we're going there.

I pointed down the hall.

- To hold number two.

-Yes...

We set off and after a minute we were standing at the second manhole. There was no combination lock here, so I opened the hatch without any problems and entered the hold. Janta followed me. I closed the hatch and turned on the charge lamps.

The entire space of the cargo hold was filled with large crates standing on wooden pallets. What they contained was almost perfectly visible from behind the rolls of translucent plastic foil.

"Well, you have your machines," I said, "and what do you think?"

Janta approached the first of them. She looked at it carefully. Then to the second, third and another... Finally, she stopped and waved her hand at me.

I approached her and she pointed to the inside of the crate.

I glanced in that direction and was dumbfounded. There were some huge coils of tubes and wires that looked like fragments of some gigantic transformer or rather an electromagnet...

- Do you know what it is? She asked me in an undertone.

"Damn," I replied, "some kind of transformer?" Converter?

She shook her head negatively.

"No, although in a way you're right, of course," she replied.

I had had enough of it.

I grabbed her shoulders and turned her to me.

"Listen, mermaid," I growled in her face, "Tell me, what's going on here?" You show up uninvited, trying to intimidate me with stories about N-bombs. What are you playing? I want to know what stakes I'm risking my neck for!

She looked sadly.

"Don't you trust me?" she asked quietly.

"No, because you're not telling me the truth.

"But I told you," she replied, "there are really these neutron warheads..."

- And here? – I hissed with the rest of the passion that tormented me.

"You won't believe it if I tell you," she replied.

- Well, at least try!

She gently freed herself from my grip.

- If you want to know, then listen. Here, in front of you, is the *rel'sotron*, the magnetic cannon, anti-aircraft and anti-satellite weapon of the 21st century.

December 6, 02:00 EST

I cooled down. Janta embraced me and so we hugged each other like two crying mothers over a shitty child. We were back in my cabin and the terrible reality was slowly sinking in. Someone used our transports for their nefarious purposes. Someone dreamed of wars and revolutions again. Someone wanted to cast the flame of war on a somewhat stable world again.

"What the hell is this cannon?" –Asked.

She smiled.

" *Rel'sotron?"* Oh, this is a very sophisticated technique. In short, solenoids through which electricity is passed are able to eject pieces of metal from their interior. Do you grasp the principle?

- Of course it is.

-Exactly. Now such a solenoid acts as a cannon throwing projectiles at a speed of about Ma 7, which is more than two kilometers per second in the atmosphere! And which is cooled with helium to a temperature of only one or two Kelvin, it can eject projectiles at a speed of over 12 km/s. And as you know, this is the Second Space Speed... Understand? You can shoot down ANY orbital vehicle! This is not Babylon the Great. Something like this really exists and... he's on this ship.

We sat down on the berth. All drowsiness is gone. I made Satan and poured it into cups.

- Who the hell wants to play war? –Asked.

"Don't you know?" – she asked with a slight amazement – the whole world is drumming about it.

- I don't listen to the radio and I don't watch TV – I muttered – who?

- Generals Hector Zargoza, Alonso Esteranda and Santiago Dourano of Cotaricana. Three far-right generals overthrew the government of President Apollon Diaz. The coup was perfectly prepared. The special services of Diaz, as well as Panama and Honduras, did not expect or suspect anything. The army renounced obedience to the president, and then moved on Nounas. Diaz fled to Belize at the last moment, and after twenty-four hours, all opposition and resistance was liquidated. Zargoza simply ordered anyone who opposed him to be smashed. Apparently, there was a massacre in Nounas, but this is known only second- and third-hand, because the borders were locked and journalists were expelled at an express pace. Internet and all other connections were either interrupted or blocked. Zargoza decided to oppose any intervention, especially the American one, and that's why he needs these bombs and a magnetic cannon...

She lay down on the berth. She must have been tired.

"Wait," I said soberly, "if there's such a gag and hat for everything, where did YOU get this information?"

"Your services don't have them, but ours do," she replied. "And I'll tell you more. Someone else is behind all this.

I raised my eyebrows. If the Syrena had their services in our company, they worked much more efficiently than ours... - I'm starting to be afraid – I thought.

-Who? China, North Korea? Maybe Kuba?

She shook her head again.

- No, none of them. This is not the shade of villainy. It looks more like Hitler and his damn delusions than Castro or Kim...

"So?"

"An Andean fortress," she replied. – That is why the Americans took up this issue. They don't want to have a Führer at their side, who, as you can see, has already found a source of arms supplies...

- … from France," I finished almost in a whisper, "you can't believe it...

- Not from France, but from Canada. Do you know what AQL is?

-No.

- Quebec Liberation Army. A bunch of freaks dreaming of separating Quebec from Canada and joining it to France. It has more followers in France than in Canada, so now you understand that French footprint. They got them these warheads, a cannon and a ship. Now listen: we must not allow these goodies to fall into the hands of these criminals from Cotaricana!

I finally started to think, because caffeine activated my gray cells.

"Rather, their principals at *Festuung Anden* ," I said. Sink this boat with a load, it's out of the question. Give it to the Americans?

"Yes, as long as no one from Galveston is in the service of THOSE people, and everything indicates that they are.

- Hand over to the British? – I thought – we have two days to Nassau in the Bahamas.

She thought about it.

"That could be done, as long as the crew doesn't bother you," she said thoughtfully.

- We're going between Eleuthera and Gran Abaco going straight to New Providence, so I'll try to get our boat on the reefs somewhere north of Eleuthera. There are plenty of shoals and reefs there, so it may work. But that's not all. We need to publicize what we have on board. I don't have any contacts with the media or Greenpeace, so maybe you...

She nodded.

- My friend from Bermuda will take care of that. Professor Milczarek. I don't know if it's a name or a pseudonym, but he's the only one who can help in such a situation. Oh, and one more thing. Your ship is being followed by another ship that is following you. This is a camouflaged seagoing vessel that is armed. Such a *Q-ship*. For now, they have lost you, but you may be in trouble when they find you, and they will.

- Do you have a vision of the future? –Asked.

"No, but they have a very strong and very strong radar..." she smiled.

- Is this the "Volgobalt"? So I have to put our vault on the reefs right next to the entrance to the port in Port Nassau – I replied – there is simply no other way out...

"Exactly, those Russians from the Volgobalt were murdered and the bodies thrown overboard as soon as they left Hamilton. The sharks have taken the corpse and now there will be one more legend more about the evil powers of the Bermuda Triangle...

"Well, now I'm starting to understand what's going on here..." I muttered.

- So how do we proceed? She asked, getting up from her seat.

"In two days, I'll land our ship on the Devil's Reef on the approach to Port Nassau. It is only two miles from the port. At the same time, the media must announce the cargo that is on the side, with particular emphasis on the radiation from the unstable N warheads. And upload everything to the Internet.

- And what about the "Volgobalt" and the pirates on board? –Asked.

I smiled.

"Then let's leave it to the Grey Chimney Company[64], after all, pirates are their job..."

**December 6, 12:00 p.m. EST**

I took the watch and was now stuck on the bridge. My head hurt a bit after a sleepless night, but that was the least of my worries.

At three in the morning I went down to the stern with Janta, from where she jumped into the still rocking ocean. To say goodbye, she made a stand in the water and wagged her tail at me. I followed her with my eyes and went to use the remaining four hours of rest. Over the last 24 hours, we had only done fifty miles in the direction of the Bahamas and we had to catch up with the delay. I told the machine to give it "half ahead" and our speed jumped to eleven knots. Łajba could squeeze out even eighteen, but with a flaut. Now there was no chance to achieve more, because the ocean was still rocked by six. But the further south it went, the better it was and the swaying was less tiring. The crew got down to ordinary, routine work. All in all, everything was returning to normal.

---

[64] British Navy – Royal Navy.

The weather report from Nassau also did not herald anything dangerous. The hurricane was raging somewhere near Washington, D.C., and here the sky was getting clearer and clearer with each passing moment, until the sun finally shone. The spectra of the waves disappeared on the radar, and again we could clearly see the sharp echoes of ships walking in the Triangle, the south-western side of which we were approaching with every turn of the propeller. Behind us we could see the echo of "Volgobalt", which followed us trail by trail.

### December 6, 6:00 p.m. EST

- How much have we done? Captain Mehner asked.

"Another hundred and fifty miles," I said, "we're turning fifteen knots now.

"Keep it up, Mr. One," the old man was apparently pleased.

I couldn't say that about myself. He put the phone down and I sighed.

I didn't tell him the most important thing. The Volgobalt was still behind, and for a fixed distance of eight miles. I gave it "small" twice and he slowed down twice. I gave "the whole one" and they also sped up. One thing was obvious – Janta was not lying. We were followed and I was just curious when they would try to get us...

### December 7, 01:00 MSK, Moscow

The office of the commander of the naval forces of the Russian Federation, Admiral Vyacheslav Sokolov, was dark with smoke. Outside the windows in the evening sky of Moscow, another snowy squall was flashing by. The frost was getting stronger and the streets were slowly getting drifts. The meeting was over, there was one more point to discuss.

- And we have the last point – the admiral reached for another pile of papers – captain, please report.

He pointed to the first-rank captain Matvei Aristov, who stood up and walked over to the screen. The light in the office went out.

"Let me start by saying," he began, "that in an unknown way and in not very clear circumstances, thirty neutron warheads with a power of thirty to one hundred kilotons each were stolen from our Missile Troops base. Most likely, the perpetrators are Chechen separatists or terrorists associated with Al-Qaeda. There is also Al-Ansar al-Islam, Al-Gevra al-Naum or a related group, or one of the mafia groups operating in the area of the base in Ust' Uluk. Our counterintelligence is working on it.

"The Islamic separatists are out," said Deputy Vice Admiral Sergei Polyesky, "first of all, they would use them against us...

"We do not rule out any possibility," said Aristov, "and this is one of many. Personally, I would bet on the mafia. One neutron probe on the black market costs well over ten million euros.

- Not dollars? Someone asked from the other end of the meeting table.

- No, after the recent declines on the stock exchanges in New York, London and Berlin, the criminal underground switched to settlements in euros or Swiss francs, and in the Far East in yen. The world is changing, gentlemen... Thirty warheads is about half a billion euros. The question is: who has the money to pay so much for it?

- Only the mafia?

"Or someone who wants to use this weapon very much in case of aggression, someone who has a bayonet on his throat," Aristov displayed the first slide. "As you probably know, comrades, there has been a coup in Costaricana. Its scenario is exactly reminiscent of the events in Chile in 1973, when the government of Salvatore Allende was overthrown by General Augusto Pinochet and Admiral José Caesar Mendoza.

- So the order of this theft was the military junta from Cotaricana? The same voice said. – But despite the name, this country is as poor as a church mouse! Half a billion euros is the value of their entire GDP for ten years...

There was laughter.

- And yet it is all correct. The warheads were stolen by someone and delivered to France. And one more thing, a working model *of the rel'sotron* was stolen from us. Real and working DEM from *Project Fonar*. Those who are not familiar with it must know that it is an electromagnetic weapon that throws projectiles at a huge speed of over 12 km/s, which allows us to shoot down any artificial satellite of the earth from its orbit. The American equivalent is called *railgun* and has similar performance, but ours is better, because we used liquid helium to cool the magnets, which allows for reduced energy consumption and increased muzzle velocity. We know this for sure, because our people at the IAEA learned that they were loaded onto the ship "Carriban Pearl" and sent to Galveston on December 1. Routine procedure for transporting nuclear fuel and spent rods to processing plants in Houston. But something unusual happened, namely: on the fourth of December, our ship "Volgobalt-315" was most likely attacked and hijacked in Bermuda. We don't know what happened to the crew, our agents in Hamilton don't know anything about what happened to them yet.

- It's the Bermuda Triangle! A voice called again from the other end of the table.

"Comrade Captain Tkachenko of the second rank," the admiral raised his voice while trying to stifle a laugh, "please refrain from unscientific comments!"

"Yes, comrade admiral," Tkachenko snorted and became silent.

For a moment, the mood relaxed, but curiosity quickly returned. The laughter stopped.

- And what next? Poliskyi asked.

"Our satellite intelligence is observing the Volgobalt, which is sailing eight miles behind the Caribbean Pearl. We have no reconnaissance of the situation on board, but it seems that our crew died or were forced to work for the kidnappers. Anyway, something will have to be done about it, so that the Americans don't hang dead dogs on us again. The political implications, comrades, may be the worst. Besides, the president and the prime minister are pushing to finish this matter as soon as possible, before a serious crisis begins. That's why I suggest you do it like this...

**24 hours later, in the waters of the Bermuda Triangle...**

- One more day and we'll be in the Bahamas – I thought as I put our position on the map. Again, I had the evening sky outside the window, which was quickly running like a dark blue of night. I thought that it was already night in Europe, cold and snowy. At home, kids are waiting for Santa Claus or Christmas Star... I smiled at this thought and memories.

"Mr. One, look at the starboard side. At five o'clock – I heard the voice of Ferro Vojtaššak, a sailor of Slovak origin on watch – I think we have a problem. Is it some kind of "nuke"?

In fact, a small, but intensely dark, almost black cloud was approaching quickly from the north-east. It was connected to the sea by dark bands of whirlpool illuminated by the purple light of lightning and in fact resembled a huge mushroom, as after an atomic explosion. It was still far away.

- Oh! – I thought – what else will happen to us?

"We'll try to get out of TEMU's way," I said, "the rudder is right to the side, the course is three hundred and thirty."

- It's three hundred and thirty!

I moved the handle of the machine telegraph to "full speed ahead".

I blew into the pipe.

"Engine room," I heard the chief's voice in response.

"Chief, add some revs, we have a little problem here.

- How small? The chief asked.

- A rainy squall plus a thunderstorm sixteen miles away and heading our way.

"We will not escape, but I will try," he said, "and I will give you the whole one."

The machines started sharply and the ship began to circulate. On the radar you could see an echo of this SOMETHING. I looked at the log, which began to climb up as the ship's diesels revved up.

- Don't you think that this is an almost full-metal reflection? Ferro said.

I nodded. The echo of this SOMETHING was one bright spot on the greenish screen of the radar...

- Maybe there is something to it? – I wondered – some UFO?

Ferr's eyes lit up.

- Do you think so too?

- I don't know, but I have heard about several strange accidents in such circumstances. Even at the beginning of aviation, there were reports in the press about encounters with planes with something similar and not much different from clouds. When our machines fell into such "clouds", their instruments broke down, pilots lost their orientation and, as a result, with flying apparatuses, as airplanes were then called, crashes and disasters occurred, and sometimes they simply disappeared without a trace. One such incident took place in the USA in 1942. The airship "L-8" piloted by Cody and Adams took off from the base in San Francisco on a patrol flight along the coast. The manoeuvres of the aircraft were followed by many people from fishing boats and ships standing in the roadstead. Everyone saw the airship fly into one and only cloud passing in the blue sky. And as it turned out later, it was at this moment that radio contact with the airship's pilots was lost. And then something strange happened – the airship did not come out of this cloud! After several hours, an airship was found, which was on the coast. The parachutes were in their places, the radio station was operational, the engines were in working order, only both pilots disappeared. And it only remained a mystery how the airship could land on the beach completely undamaged...?

-Truly?

- Apparently yes. Anyway, the Americans called this airship *The Ghost Blimp* – a ghost balloon.

- Supposedly such an overhead Flying Dutchman?

-Exactly. A similar case occurred in 1930 at the Christi Corps in Texas. This time it was a plane that exploded after it flew into a cloud. The bodies of the pilot and passenger were never found, although the remains of the machine were smeared over a kilometer and a half...

- And here?

- Oh, it was very interesting here. First, the famous Charles Lindberg had problems during the flight from Havana to the Bahamas. That was in 1928. Then there was the story of flight number 19, from December 1945... These hazy objects, some experts believe, are being manufactured by aliens in order to mask the presence of UFOs during this "human hunt." And it happens most often in places where "hunters" have the least chance to enter the field of vision of inconvenient witnesses.

- Mr. so on serio...?

- Whoever wants, let him believe, who doesn't want to... - I didn't finish, because I was touched by a sudden thought.

I looked at the radar monitor. The "Volgobalt" trailing behind us disappeared. It is just as if he dissolved in a cloud. I looked through the binoculars. In the opal circles of the binoculars, I saw strange, purple lightning and pouring streams of rain. The sea under the strange cloud was smooth as oil. I still haven't seen "Volgobalt". He had apparently turned south, or simply hidden behind the rainy storm zone.

- What are we doing first, Mr. First? Vojtaššak asked.

I thought for a moment.

"We're back on the old course, it doesn't look as dangerous as it seems," I said, "and please tell me the position."

" *Aye-aye, sir!"* Vojtaššak spun the steering wheel.

I turned the handle of the machine telegraph "half ahead" and the vibration of the machines subsided. I opened the journal and made an entry for 6:35 PM EST.

"We are at 26°26'41" north and 075°49'12" west," Ferro said. "And on top of that, we have four thousand seven hundred and sixty meters under the keel.

I thought that it didn't matter to us in the slightest, but it could matter to Janta and her compatriots. Something had to be done with the bard we had in the holds. At the same time, this crap was radiating more and more. I wondered if the Mermaids had something to do with this "nuke"...

December 8, 00:45 EST

I dreamed that I was in some grey-green space full of steadily swaying brown shapes, in which from time to time bluish and greenish lights were lit, like fireflies. I heard some indistinct voices, as if from behind a thick layer of water. I pricked up my ears, but those voices said something completely incomprehensible. I wanted to look around, but I couldn't, something was restricting my movements. The voices became louder. Suddenly, I saw a strong flash, I jerked hard and... I opened my eyes, into which the glow of the bedside lamp was shining.

I was lying on my back on my bunk, among the dug sheets, and Janta was sitting at the edge of my bed, looking at me with her green eyes.

- Is that you? – I croaked – what happened?

She smiled.

"I have come to you," she replied, "is that not reason enough?"

I sat down next to her and she put her arms around me and put her head on my shoulder. She was naked, and her smooth, silky skin exuded warmth. Her hair smelled of sea salt and something else, like a delicate but incredibly sensual perfume. We sat there for a while until I sobered up from the rest of my sleep and realized what was happening.

"How did you get here?" –Asked.

-Normally. I jumped from the wave onto the aft deck, then went into the superstructure and onto the second deck to you. It's not difficult, after all, I've been here once before...

-???

"Well, yes, and besides, I can always find you. There is a special bond between us that allows me to find you even at the end of the world.

- Oh, so this is the famous attachment of the Mermaid to a man?

She nodded and laughed.

"Just so you know. Thanks to this, our species survives. Yours too, but in your country it has been dulled by civilization, religion and other nonsense that you bother with. We live closer to Nature and..." she stopped, as if she realized that she had said too much.

I decided to pull her tongue.

- … And what? –Asked.

- And we draw our strength and possibilities from her. Nature doesn't lie, you just have to be able to ask it the right questions," she said in the coldest blood and smiled mysteriously.

"Uhmmm..." I replied, raising an eyebrow significantly. It was obvious that she dismissed me.

"And that's the way it is," she said and kissed me on the lips. Slowly, with sophistication. And I...

- All Mermaids love like that? –Asked.

She smiled and hugged me with her hip and side.

- Yes, yes. Anyway, all your writers write about it. A mermaid in bed, that's what all real men dream of. But only a real man can make love and satisfy a mermaid. Sex with a mermaid is not a sport for dead people.

We snorted with laughter. And then we both slid into the warm blackness of sleep without visions or delirium.

### December 8, 06:10 EST

We stood on the aft deck covered with a windbreak.

"So you're going to run this vault aground?" –Asked.

"Yes, this is the only way to get it done without arousing suspicion," I said, "I'll have to ask you for help." A magnetic compass must go crazy for a few minutes. I will neutralize the gyrocompass and this is the only way to do it.

She thought for a moment.

"Okay, then, it can be done," she said, "you will bring the boat to 25°31'08" north and 076°53'47" west, to the shallows off Harour Island. Just don't make a mistake.

"Oh, that's the least of our worries," I muttered, "our biggest worry is there," I pointed overstern.

"Oh, those," she said, "well, we're going to make one more demonstration of the terrible and mysterious forces of the Bermuda Triangle."

And she giggled cutely.

"I'm falling, it's getting light," she said, then took off her coat and shoes, kissed me on the lips and jumped over the railing in one leap.

A dozen or so seconds later, on the crest of the approaching wave, I saw a shiny silvery tail. I breathed a sigh of relief and, taking my storm jacket and boots, I entered the superstructure.

### December 8, 4:45 p.m. EST

On the southwestern horizon, only a slightly darker strip of land finally appeared. Almost simultaneously, the inscription "Northern Eleuthera" popped up on the GPS locator's screen.

"Finally," I heard the Old Man's voice behind me, "we've even made a little bit of time.

"I was afraid that we would be later, but as you can see..." I replied, looking at the radar screen, on which the contours of Eleuthera were clearly drawn, or rather its two islands on the northern shore: Harour and Russel Island. To the northwest, too, the vague contours of Great Abaco loomed.

"Maybe we should go more north, it's deeper there," I said again, "more than three kilometers. After all, this is the Grand Bahamas Canyon...

"Yes, but we have to catch up for about half a day, Mr. One," Captain Mehner looked through the binoculars towards the shore.

That suited me. We were less visible against the background of the shore, and our friends from the Volgobalt could easily lose us even on the radar.

- What do you think of this ship? The old man spoke suddenly. "We are being followed almost by trail. Now he is only two miles away from us...

- Maybe we just do them as a pilot? I gave him the first thought that came to my mind.

" *Nein*, they've been following us all the time since Bermuda," the captain shook his head, "I don't like that, Mr. One."

"But they disappeared for the time of the passage of this... This...

"I know, I read your post," he muttered. – A local storm, uh, khe, you called it nicely!

I responded with silence that lasted a few seconds.

"And they," I nodded towards the stern. –Pirates?

"If only ... - he muttered - if I were you, I would start praying that they would only be pirates...

- Is that that it? I muttered, raising an eyebrow. "Aren't you exaggerating, Captain?"

He shook his head and exhaled a fragrant cloud of smoke.

- You see, the Russians sail to Cuba and Venezuela, but along southern routes, bypassing the Bahamas and the Keys from the south, to Santiago de Cuba and Manzanillo. They don't venture here. And they, as you can see...

- Actually, I don't like it either... - I muttered. "So we'll go hiding by the shore?"

"*I, natürlich,*" the captain began to observe the sea again. "Look at our cargo, OK?"

"*Aye-aye, Captain,*" I said and stepped off the bridge.

I quickly crossed the companionway and found myself in front of the hatch to the number one hold. I entered the code and the lock snapped off. I went inside and reached for the light switch. I snapped it and the hold was flooded with a sharp light.

- Oh, jam! - I blurted out in Polish.

Containers with warheads were scattered all over the deck. The nibs cracked, and the webbing straps wore from the ship's movement caused by the high wave. But that was not the most important thing. One of the containers broke and a conical object with Russian markings slipped out of the inside. I went numb. Janta was right, these were neutron warheads, but not French but Russian!

Suddenly, several facts merged into a terrifying whole...

I picked up the phone.

"Captain, we have a serious problem here," I said in a calm voice, "could you come downstairs?"

There was silence for a moment.

"We also have a problem here," Mehner blurted it out into the microphone, "so come here."

He said it calmly, but in such a tone that sent shivers down my spine. I also measured the radioactivity, fortunately it did not exceed the norm, only the three were radiating as usual.

I left the hold and, taking two steps each, rushed up. I ran into the bridge and fell to the captain.

"I'm here," I panted, "what's going on?"

"Look," he said, handing me the binoculars and nodding his head to me in the direction of the stern. "Our friends have guests.

"And straight from the sky," said Loic Breitone, standing at the helm.

In the field of view of the binoculars, I saw the Volgobalt stand adrift, and three large helicopters were hovering over it, dark and without any markings. The helicopters were standing in a hang, and tiny silhouettes were sliding down from them to the deck on ropes...

"Looks like an attack by SAS or SEAL commandos," I muttered.

"It doesn't look like it, because it IS a commando attack," said the captain, "and worst of all, they are going to pay us a visit as well."

In fact, one of the helicopters moved towards us and was quickly approaching our ship. We looked at him and...

- *Scheisse* – Mehner hissed it through clenched teeth – it is a Russian assault "Mi-8" or "Mi-10" in the naval version. They are Cubans, Venezuelans...

- … or the Russians," I finished for him.

The helicopter hovered over us and three armed men quickly descended the rope. I looked at their weapons – they were AKS-74U submachine guns with a caliber of 5.45 mm.

"But the Russians," I thought with satisfaction.

Something else caught my attention – the hovering helicopter was very quiet, you could hardly hear its engines, and it should be making noise like hell... Apparently, the Russians have invented some way to silence the operation of engines almost to a minimum.

Meanwhile, three commandos ran into the bridge and two of them immediately took us at gunpoint. The third, to our amazement, approached the Old Man and saluted elegantly.

We did not expect this.

"I am Captain Sergei Porshnev of the Russian Navy," he said in flawless English, "and I demand that you hand over the things you have in your holds." They belong to the Russian Federation and are owned by our government. They were stolen from us, and Mother Rossiya doesn't like to be robbed. Not to mention the fact that our batiushka Putin was very *confused* when he found out about it.

We were stunned.

How did they know? – I was pounding in my head. "Maybe they caught Janta?"

"Welcome on board, Commander," said the Old Man calmly. "You can lower your weapons, you have no enemies here. And as for the cargo, take it. Oh, and please give me a receipt, if it doesn't cause you any trouble.

Porshnev nodded.

"Thank you," he said, "I hope everything goes smoothly." And as for the receipt, well, we don't. I am not authorized to issue them, but since you insist...

He took his pistol out of the holster and fired twice at the dome of the magnetic compass. He blew into the barrel and put it back in the case.

"You will say that the vile Russians terrorized you and took their *pears*," he smiled apologetically.

We stood motionless. The roar of gunfire made our ears ring.

- Okay, Volod'ka, we'll take what's ours and get out of here! He said it into the microphone of his walkie-talkie and two of his companions holding us at gunpoint came out of the bridge.

The net was lowered from the helicopter, into which the contents of the first cargo hold were loaded. The second helicopter, which flew from the Volgobalt, quickly took the contents of the second one. After a quarter of an hour, we were alone. We couldn't believe that the Russians took their toys and left without hurting us...

December 8, 10:00 p.m. EST

We were standing in the roadstead of the port of Nassau, or rather in the area between Rose and Paradise Island, where we were put up because of fears of radioactivity, which didn't make any sense, because there were motorboats and sailboats hanging around there all the time, which could be contaminated. The port authorities probably wanted to calm their conscience and not to start panic in this paradise...

I stood on the top deck and looked at the nightlife of the city. Somewhere in the southwest there was an occasional flash, and not at all for the weather. Another storm was approaching, and the barometer was falling head over heels again. Another storm was coming, already called *Yetta*.

Tomorrow, an investigator from Golden Phoenix - Phènix d'Or and the Americans from Uranium Mining and Power were to fly in from Galveston, who were to interrogate us about the transport of tref goods - more treif than usual. I wondered if they would try to put all the blame on us for what had happened in the last few days, or if they would look for a scapegoat somewhere else?

I sighed and spat over the railing. A bit for fanfaronade, a bit of bad charm. I turned and was about to enter the superstructure when I heard a soft splash of water and a voice calling my name. I went back to the railing. From the water from the ocean side, the graceful head of the Mermaid emerged. My Mermaid.

"Janta?" What are you doing here?

"I wanted to make an appointment with you," she replied, "how about a meeting on the beach on Rose Island. There are the fewest people there, and I would like to meet you. From the ocean side, OK.?

- Did you miss it? –Asked.

"Very much," she replied, "when will you come?"

"Let's say at four o'clock in the afternoon. But what about *Yetta*?

She waved her hand dismissively.

- Don't worry about that, it will go sideways, we won't even feel it. I take you at your word," she replied and dipped in, and then, as usual, she waved her tail at me goodbye like a dolphin.

And she disappeared into the depths.

I returned to the bridge. I wandered around the decks, and then rushed the watchmen to close all the hatches and portholes. Could it be that the Sirens have some way to silence or direct a tropical hurricane elsewhere? Nevertheless, I didn't want to fight with some local thugs or local pirates and thus increase the number of victims of the Triangle...

**9 December, afternoon.**

"I'm off, so I'm sailing to Rose Island," I told the Old Man. "Maybe I'll finally find myself a Mermaid...

"And go, go," Captain Mehner shrugged, "just come back before twelve." I'm also going ashore with the chief and I'll not be back until the morning. Only the watch on the bridge and in the machine remains.

"OK," I replied, "I'll take *the Zodiac.*"

I left the Old Man's cabin and went to starboard, where the motor dinghy was rocking. The second was a communication tender with the mainland and was on the port side. For a moment I considered taking a walkie-talkie, but finally I waved my hand at it. After all, I also deserved something from life.

I bounced off the side and started the engine. At first I headed towards the beach, but then I turned north and headed for the strait to sail around Rose Island from the north. I still had a quarter of an hour before the appointment. The weather was sunny and quite calm, only in the west you could see a dark tire of clouds. Yetta was raging there, harassing somewhere in Florida and its inhabitants...

I circumnavigated the Isle of Roses from the north and *the Zodiac broke* out into the wide water of the Atlantic, but I directed it towards White Sand Beach, its deserted section at the height of the promontory near Fruit Garden. Fancy villas and holiday resorts were on the other side of the island and no one could disturb us, besides, the December storm that was to come to these parts effectively scared away the visitors. I swam slowly, carefully looking at the water. And suddenly, a little to the right of the bow, the water foamed and the tail rose above it. It was Janta who directed me towards the beach.

I swam to the shore and dropped the anchor, and jumped into the warm water. This was what I loved the tropics for – warm, crystal clear water all year round.

-Halo! – I heard behind me.

I turned around. Janta got up from the water, and next to her was another girl a little like her, only a little younger?...

- Hello... – I replied hesitantly – ... I see you took the chaperone with you?

They laughed.

"No, although maybe I should," Janta replied. "Get to know each other, this is Robert. Bob, this is Marietta.

"Hi Bob," Marietta said, shaking my hand, "I'm her cousin, so we're a little alike."

She answered the question I didn't ask, I thought, so they can read minds after all?

We got out of the water onto a narrow strip of beach, beyond which there was a strip of low bushes and grass, and then palm trees.

"Why don't we go to Gilligan Island?" – I suggested.

- To Sandy Cay or Honeymoon Island? Marietta raised her eyebrows, "thank you, too much of the audience." I prefer here.

"And here you can make a fire," said Janta, pointing to the dry palm leaves and branches lying beyond the white sand of the beach. "As far as I know, this part of the beach is public, so no idiot will attach himself to us...

After several minutes, we sat down by the burning fire.

"It's a pity we don't have something for the grill," I noticed.

"Well, you're right, we didn't think about it. Anyway, it's also fun that way," said Janta.

"It's going to get dark in a few minutes," Marietta said, "so we'll be happier by the fire, and I'm not hungry."

"Tell me, how did you do with those guys from Galveston?" Janta asked me.

"Not at all," I replied. "They came, questioned me and the Old Man and Radzik. They didn't even have dinner with us and disappeared somewhere to hell.

"Aren't you surprised?"

"No," I said, "They're big guys, *white collars*, but the whole thing is stinking from A to Z. They asked us, they asked us, and none of them even noted what we told them. It seemed that they had ready answers to every question and this whole "interrogation" was an empty formality that they had to do before they moved out.

Janta frowned.

"I don't like that," she said.

- Me too. But...

And suddenly I understood what she meant.

"Well, no, do you think we'll be the scapegoats?"

"Exactly," she replied, "and they may be preparing something for you, some surprise."

- What kind of language, for example?

- A mine on the farwater, a torpedo to the side, pirates on board...

- I'm already scared... - I muttered - aren't you exaggerating?

She raised her green eyes to me.

"No," she said firmly. "And I am of the opinion that you should not return to the ship.

I was amazed by her firm tone.

- Uh, there. But you must be exaggerating a little," I said, "I don't think they'll dare to peek us so close to the port."

- And how dare they?

-Exactly? – Marietta unexpectedly supported her – believe me, such things did not happen in the Triangle!

"But these are all supposedly fairy tales, not even an honest myth," I said in a tone of gentle persuasion, "so don't scare me with them!"

"What do you think," Marietta got up from the sand and brushed off her legs and shapely bottom.

She walked over to Janta and sat down next to her, and after a while their eyes met mine. Janta stood up and knelt down. Her hand went to her side and in one movement she undid the ribbons and slipped off her bra.

"OK, but we won't let you get on your ship so quickly," she said.

The wind began to blow from the ocean. For now, it was light, but the wind was getting stronger from quarter to quarter of an hour. I looked at my watch. It was almost a quarter to nine.

"You'll have to sail away," Janta said with regret in her voice, "which is a pity, because I still wanted to...

"Me too, but I need to see what about the ship. Maybe I'll muster tomorrow," I said, referring to Janta and Marietta's warnings.

At the same time, I felt a strange anxiety. I quickly pulled myself together. Both Sirens were also restless.

"Get on the *Zodiac*," I said, "I'll drop you off near the reef."

They nodded and took a seat in the dinghy.

I started the engine and jumping on the growing wave we turned off White Sand Beach. After passing the headland, the wave calmed down a bit, and in the darkness you could see the white foam of the crashing element on the teeth of the reefs. After a few moments, Janta held out her hand.

"Drop us there," she said, "and get out of here." Look, this ship of yours is almost dark. It doesn't mean anything good...

She was right. The "Caribbean Pearl" stood silent and dark, swaying to the rhythm of a dead wave. Only the trap lamp was on and nothing else. Why were all the lights turned off?

"Slow down," Janta said and stood up. Marietta too, and after a while they both jumped overboard.

I didn't wait for the words of farewell, but turned up the throttle and headed towards the boat. Two cables before entering the gangplank, I reduced the revs to a minimum to swim to it as quietly as possible. I sailed around the crypt. The second tender was not there, which meant that the crew was still in port. But what about watches?

I swam to the gangplank, turned off the engine and moored the *Zodiac*, and after a while I jumped on the platform and tiptoed up the gangplank. I stepped out on deck and looked around the deck. A living spirit. There was no gangway, and the hatch to the superstructure was wide open...

December 9, 9:20 p.m. EST

I felt like the sailors who discovered the Mary Celeste drifting. I felt uncomfortable. Sneaking I went to the bridge.

"Is anyone here?" I threw the question into the darkness, not counting on an answer. And yet, in the darkness there, I heard a soft moan. I groped for the hiding place and took out a fluorescent lamp. I broke a plastic stick and the sternum was flooded with cold bluish light.

I looked at the deck. Loic was lying under the steering wheel in a pool of blood, which was black in this ghostly light. I fell to him.

"Loic! – I shouted – What happened here?

He opened his eyes and looked at me. He wanted to say something, but only a whisper came out of his mouth. I leaned over him.

-This... They'll come back here..." he whispered.

- Who was that?

"The Spaniards..." he whispered and lost consciousness.

I looked at him more closely. He got two bullets in the stomach. He lost a lot of blood... Was he raving? Was he raving or not? What kind of Spaniards? "I had a hurricane of thoughts in my head. "What happened here???

I quickly ripped off my shirt and made makeshift jerks that I stuck into the wounds. That was all I could do.

Loic was on the bridge – I counted – in the Thor Jurgenson, a taciturn Dane, and Fero Vojtaššak was standing by the gangplank. I didn't find him anywhere, it could mean that he was already dead. The attackers killed him first and threw his body into the water.

I ran down to the engine room. As I expected, Thor lay almost cut in half by a burst fired at close range, his suit bearing traces of osmalin from burnt gunpowder. I slowly walked to the hold. To my surprise, hold number one was locked. I opened it and walked in.

At that moment, I felt someone's presence behind me. I turned around in a flash, and almost instinctively shielded myself with my hand from the heavy crowbar that nearly smashed my skull. I deflected the blow and grabbed the attacker's hand. In the light of the lamp, I saw Vojtaššak's terrified face.

"Calm down, Ferro," I said in a calm tone, "it's me."

- First Sir!

- What happened here?

From Vojtaššak's incoherent story, I learned that just after darkness fell, a motorboat without any markings docked on the gangplank, from which some Spanish-speaking people armed like SEAL commandos got out. Vojtaššak tried to stop them, but someone hit him suddenly on the head and he lost consciousness. He woke up lying at the base of the gangplank at the hatch to the hold, which was not locked. He crawled into it and closed the hatch, then waited for them with a crowbar in his hand.

"What about Loice?" – he asked at the end – and with Thor.

"Thor is dead, Loic is badly wounded. If we deliver him to the hospital on time, he will lick himself.

- *Sakra!* This is what we are doing, Mr. First," he concluded with a question.

I thought for a moment. The situation was awful, but they had to be saved.

- You will take *the Zodiac.* We'll load up the Loic and deliver it to the Nassau Hospital. Then you will find the captain and tell him everything. He will know what to do next.

- And you?

"I'm staying here, someone has to guard this boat. Go!

We left the hold and immediately went to the bridge. Loic was still alive. We moved it to *the Zodiac.* I told him to swim and threw away the mooring. As I had instructed, he turned forward on the little one, and only when he was half a mile from our ship did he speed up and disappear from my sight. I was left alone.

I breathed a sigh of relief. At least these two were safe by now.

I went to the engine room and started the generator. A light flashed on all decks. I covered Jurgenson's body with a piece of tarpaulin, then went to my cabin and opened the compartment where my faithful friend – a *desert eagle .50* and six magazines – were located. I remembered one night in Kosovo when we were surrounded by Serbs. I lost four teammates then, but I shot myself and the rest of the guys the way out with this pistol...

I loaded it up and secured it. I was ready to receive guests. I only hoped that Ferr would be able to get Loic alive to the hospital and that he would be able to warn the crew. She was supposed to be on the side until midnight, so...

### December 10, 00:30 EST

The uninvited guests arrived shortly after midnight. There were ten of them, a whole team of guys armed like commandos, but who probably weren't commandos, judging by their behavior. They drove up to the gangway at full throttle and disembarked on the deck, immediately scattering all over the ship. This meant that they were either so confident that they didn't think they would encounter resistance, or so stupid that they abandoned all caution. This was a very fortunate circumstance for me. In both cases, it gave me the advantage of my own pitch. I waited another minute for them to disperse throughout the ship. They were pounding and pounding so that I could easily locate them...

I walked down from the upper deck to the bridge, where two thugs were carefully examining the pool of blood that Loic had left behind. I didn't play with ado, but smashed the skull between the eyes first of the one who was standing closer to me, and then I snatched it out of the other who was trying to raise the uzi to his hip. I hoped that the shots would attract others and I lurked at the entrance ticket.

And sure enough, three more were running up the hill, babbling something in Spanish and aiming at all corners with their uzis with long silencers. The first of them saw me literally at the moment when I put a filling in his sternum and adjusted his head. Splattering his brain and blood onto the bulkhead, he slumped on the deck.

Three less, I thought.

The other two stepped back.

And that's what I meant.

I jumped across the entire width of the corridor, opened the door and ran up the gangplank to the aft deck, then I circled the superstructure and lurked behind the corner with a view of the front deck. I heard those from above shouting something to their colleagues who jumped out of the now open hold. And it was their mistake, because against the background of the illuminated deck they looked like targets at a shooting range. The four ran to the gangplank leading to the bridge.

I aimed at the last of them and sent him a pill. The impact of a half-inch bullet is terrible. In this case, it stopped and threw a ninety-kilo man against the deck.

- *Holá, amigos!* I shouted and ran to the stern.

Two of them ran towards me, and the third towards the other aisle to approach me from the other side.

"Amateurs," I thought. "They didn't even bother to do a reconnaissance.

That road was blocked by a pile of crates of provisions. The guy would have to go through them, or turn back. After a while, I heard a bunch of curses from the other side. I felt a mocking smile twist my face.

I jumped behind the winch and crouched down waiting for them to come. Two thugs were sneaking around, aiming at every suspicious shadow. When they came ten paces, I whistled. They stopped, looking around in all directions.

My *desert eagle* thundered twice, sending both of them straight to hell. I had half of the killers' commando out of my mind. I changed the magazine and quickly jumped into the hatch leading to the anchor key. Now I was going to shoot those who were looting in the hull. Two were on the bridge, the third on the deck, so two were certainly in the aft part of the ship, where the engine room, the magazines and the chief's workshop with his cubicle were located.

I heard the muffled claps of gunfire and the clatter of bullets hitting the deck plating overhead.

- But they are amateurs... - I thought again. "Professionals would never behave like that. Professionals would try to approach me and shoot me. They, in turn, behaved like children who were given a gun in their hands and told to play scavenger hunt...

Nevertheless, I kept my guard. Amateurs or not, they were still dangerous. The advantage of my own pitch and the element of surprise protected me only partially. They were still outnumbered – five to one.

I opened the hatch to the deck and took a look. There was no one there. From it led the road to the engine room, and from there to the hold and to the bilges. And also upwards, on the bridge. My opponents were not there. I did not hear them at all, but the sounds of their footsteps came from above. After a while, I heard them activate the winch pulling out the anchor chain. They hoped that I would be in the puddle room and that the moving chain would crush me, or flush me out of the room outside – that is, on board. I quickly ran to the gangway and looked around quickly. No one in sight.

Running as quietly as I could, I got out to the entrance to the top and after a while I was at the exit to the front deck. I could do two things – hide somewhere in the superstructure, or jump outside and get into a shootout with bandits. There was also a third option – to jump out to the watch and swim to Nassau. But I could shoot myself in the head right away. They had a boat...

Immediately... boat! – a shadow of an idea loomed in my head – how about jumping in, starting and drifting away? There they left no man in his stupidity... It's worth a try!

I quietly came out of my hiding place and walked to the railing. The boat was next to the gangway and there was no one in it. I was about to run up the gangplank when something strange happened. Right next to the gangplank appeared a rod protruding vertically from the water. After a while I heard a muffled phew... and a black, rounded shape appeared at the side of the Caraibean Pearl, and after a second a hatch opened, from which several large men fell out. Four of them ran into the gangplank, the others climbed to the railing. There were weapons in their hands.

- *Hands up!* – I heard behind me. – *Freeze!*

I put my gun on the deck and slowly raised my hands.

- Where are the rest? – the question was asked.

-Aft. There are five of them.

- *Give me the rebiate* – I heard in response.

Russians!? – I thought – damn fast and efficient Russian commandos. What are they doing here?

I heard screams and bursts from machine guns behind me. The Russians did not use silencers and the sharp clamor of Kalashnikovs carried through the water. Immediately minutes later, they returned and put the bodies of the dead in the spoor.

One of the Russians, apparently the commander, came up to me.

- Who are you? He asked sharply.

I introduced myself to him. He looked at me more kindly.

"We had to clean them up," he grumbled, "they were the ones who killed our people on the Volgobalt a few days ago in Bermuda. And where is your crew?

- On land. They killed our watchman and seriously wounded the other...

He nodded as if he knew.

- How many of them were there?

-Ten. I killed five myself, the rest you ...

He looked at me appreciatively.

" *Molodets*," he muttered. "Where did you fight?"

- I was in Kosovo, then in Croatia.

He nodded again.

"Okay, the *housekeeper,*" he said, "we're going to get them too." We have to identify them, and what's wrong is not us. Give him back the gun," he ordered the commando guarding me.

- Thank you for your help – I replied – I don't know if I could manage on my own.

- *I'm thinking.* Oh, and one more thing. We weren't here, do we understand?

He whistled on his fingers and after a while the Russians got together and disappeared into the darkness of the night. It gurgled overboard and the midget slid into the dark waters. After the visit, all that was left were blood stains and piles of bullet casings scattered here and there.

Who notified them? How did they know that Costa Ricans would be here again? – I thought sitting on the deck. – And the most important thing: why did they leave a living witness, that is, me? After all, they had to reckon with the fact that I would reveal to the authorities and media that they were here...

I went to my cabin and went back to the gangway with a bottle of Jack Daniels. I drank and reflected on what had happened to me during those days. And so, struggling with my thoughts and struggling with an almost empty bottle, I was found by the crew, who returned from the mainland around three in the morning.

### December 10, 4:00 p.m. EST

I woke up with a dry throat and a terrible headache. The monstrous hangover was taking its toll. Semi-conscious from pain and general weakness, I found Alka-zeltzer and mineral water. I threw two pills into a glass, poured mineral and bubbled them, and then drank it in a sprite. After a few minutes, I felt the caffeine and vitamin C contained in them start to work and the hurricane raging under my skull slowly decreases its strength and I can think relatively normally...

I got up, dressed and dragged myself to the bridge. The old man was not there – maybe he was sleeping off the night, or maybe he was explaining himself to the port authorities. Frank Bannister was on the bridge.

"You don't look good, Mr. First," he remarked when he saw me, but you deserved it after everything that had happened here.

I shook my head and asked for a coffee for my breastbone. After a few minutes, the steward brought me a whole jug.

- How did you get here? I asked, wincing at the sound of my own voice.

- Simply, in our boat. And what was most interesting, there was a girl standing on the quay and she said that the gentleman sent her because there was no communication with the ship and that we should all wait on the quay. The old man got mad and went to the captain's office with a row. In the captain's office they said that they knew nothing about us... Normally a Czech film.

- And what next?

- And then the Old Man saw *the Zodiac* and the traces of blood when he came back. He made a fuss with the port police and told them to look for all of you, because he didn't know who had arrived. He thought it was you, but then Ferro came and everything was cleared up.

"And what about Loice?"

"He underwent two surgeries and is alive. Serious but stable condition.

"She'll lick herself," I muttered.

- And what about that girl who stopped you?

-Faded. It was as if she had jumped into the water.

- You mean she jumped or not?

-No... how to say it – the third one got tangled up – she walked along the quay, and when she disappeared, we heard a splash from the other side...

- And what did she look like? I asked, because I finally realized what Bannister was saying.

"Blonde, about twenty-five years old, green eyes, tall, very pretty...

- Janta! –I thought. "She was the one who saved the crew...

- Well, it was interesting there.

- And how did you manage here? You beat ten thugs to death...

"Only five..." I grumbled.

-Like this? – he was surprised – after all...

"Exactly," I replied, "the other five were destroyed by Russian commandos. SPETSNAZ of their *marvoi*. As good as the SEAL boys... They were settling scores for their boys from "Volgobałt". It's a pity that Thor didn't survive... But – but, where's the captain?

- On land, you explain yourself to cops and company representatives.

- What else robimy does? Chyba płyniemy in the house?

- And God deigns to know. I think the old man will bring some directives from the company, we'll see.

At that moment, we heard the sound of engines running and *Zodiak and the* captain hit the gangplank. After a few minutes, he ran into the bridge.

"Mr. Three," he began without preliminaries, "clean up this brothel on the deck.

Frank nodded and began to hurry the crew to work.

- Oh, the first one! "Are you good for anything?" cried the Old Man when he saw me?

- *Jawohl!* I am – I replied getting up from the navigator's chair.

- So *sehr gut!* – he replied – to prepare the ship for the sea. We go to Tampa for some hot filth and we have a Coast Guard escort all the way back to the Bahamas.

"Oh, to Florida," said the third, "I haven't been there for a long time!"

- Well, don't be happy – the captain's face was cloudy – we take the cargo and go to... to Le Havre. There we will be questioned by at least five French interviews and, in addition, a commission from the company. Not to mention NATO intelligence...

## December 10, 24:00 EST

We were leaving at twelve o'clock at night. The ship gave up its moorings and with a fairly low wave for December, we were heading towards Florida. I was happy to go to Miami, but for some reason the Americans chose Tampa – a port located on the western side of the peninsula. Apparently, the nuclear fuel cargo was to arrive by land and then be loaded onto the Company's ship and sail to Europe. During the flight across the Atlantic, nothing – except for the nasty weather – threatened us.

## December 12, 22:30 AST

We reach the quay of the port in Tampa. Dim lights, on the quay of a living soul. The mooring workers leave as soon as they can. I don't know what they were told, but probably nothing flattering... I look through binoculars at the waterfront and find that it is carefully guarded by MP. That is why there was no welcoming committee of customs officers and clarers. Even immigration officers. We were treated like a ship of plague victims!

Loading the containers with plutonium was equally quick and efficient. Apparently, no one wanted to come into contact with us, and neither did the ship – maybe they were afraid of radiation, or maybe some terrorists from Cotaricana? Hell knows...

## December 12, 04:50 AST

We leave Tampa. With us a large Hamilton-class patrol ship armed like a light cruiser – an automatic 127 mm gun, anti-aircraft guns, torpedoes and missiles capable of destroying everything that stands in our way.

And us, too, if necessary – a nonsensical thought is pounding in my head.

Although after what we have been through, everything was possible... The old man has put the ship on its course and we are going half ahead towards the Florida Strait.

In a week we will be on the other side of the Atlantic – I think and look forward to Christmas on land. "Maybe I'll go to Switzerland for skiing?" Or to Zakopane? Although it is getting more and more expensive there, and the level of service is mediocre...

December 13, 11:00 p.m. EST

I'm lying on a bunk. And I try to fall asleep. We have the Bahamas behind us and are slowly moving away from the American continent in a subsiding storm. I count rams, I predict the multiplication table, but sleep does not come. Something is bothering me. I have the impression that I have forgotten something extremely important, or maybe something extremely important will happen soon...

A damn state of inner anxiety. To say little – this is fear. Fear of the unknown? I wonder if my intuition or reason is telling me that. I can't stand it – I get up and get dressed, and then almost run to the bridge.

It's eleven o'clock at night on my watch, and I sweep my eyes around the radar screen—it's set to a range of twelve miles and empty. There is no greater echo beyond the shadows of the waves...

- What's going on, Mr. First? – asks Jim Archer, the youngest member of our crew, worried.

- Where are we? – I answer without giving him an answer. My anxiety is contagious to him as well...

- 27°27'47".47 north and 070°07'42".30 west – he answers, and I see his face turn pale. "My God, Mr. First, we are...

- ... in the middle of the Bermuda Triangle – I finish for him. "Are you afraid?"

Jim swallows and I pull myself together.

- So many sevens, nothing bad should happen to us – I say soothingly.

- I don't believe in superstitions – Jim also breathes a sigh of relief.

- Neither do I, but God guards the guarded – I translate the Polish saying into English – it's like with you: warned – armed!

We laugh looking into the darkness of the Atlantic night.

## December 13, 11:59 p.m. EST

"So, it's midnight in a minute," Jim stretched like a happy kitten, "go to bed first, sir." Tomorrow will be a hard day, because I have a feeling that this storm will not leave us, and the Azores High will probably stop it in these waters...

"Oh, no," I answer, "the Azores are too far away, and this storm will go on its usual course: to Iceland, and then it will turn east and south-east and go to Central Europe. In two weeks there will be a thaw there.

- And you won't ski...

"Well, no," I shrug, "maybe I'll go climbing?"

I looked at my watch, twelve popped up on my binary reader. It was exactly midnight. What happened next resembled some kind of nightmare combined with horror.

At first we felt a violent shock, as if the ship had hit some obstacle. But we had more than four kilometers to the bottom, and hundreds of miles to the nearest land... Then the light went out and at the same time we heard a dull bang.

-Hold! – I heard Jim's voice – Mr. One!

I jumped to the window and went numb with terror.

The hold resembled the entrance to Hell, or at least the crater of a volcano. Its lid was torn out and hung over the railing. The heat of white flames emanated from inside. It must have been a thousand degrees, if not more. I don't know what it was, but extinguishing it with water was pointless.

Besides, radiation... A uranium oxide "lozenge" in a zirconium casing will not be extinguished with water, because each attempt to extinguish it only starts a fire and increases the possibility of a chemical explosion of a mixture fulminating hydrogen with oxygen from the atmosphere... .

- "Leave ship" alarm – I gave the command and pressed the alarm siren button. Fortunately, it had an independent power supply and in all rooms there was yodeling of its signals.

A moment later, we felt another shock and the lid of cargo hold number two blew up, from which bright flames shot into the sky. I thought that this is what burning tankers from Arctic convoys must have looked like when they were hit by German torpedoes...

I heard another bang and glass fell from everywhere. I felt a powerful blow to my crown and sank into boundless blackness...

## 24 December, morning

I opened my eyes. The harsh light of day hit her pupils mercilessly, so I closed her again and waited for her to get used to the light.

"The patient has woken up," I hear.

I open my eyes. Sitting next to me is a nurse with a strangely familiar face. I strain my brain, but I can't remember who started...

"Don't you recognize me?" – he asks.

I shake my head.

- Amnesia – I hear a strange voice – post-traumatic.

The doctor's face is shown in the field of vision.

- What is your name? – he asks.

I strain my memory again, realizing at the same time that I don't remember this...

"And now you need to sleep again," I hear the doctor's voice and feel the needle prick.

The world has departed from me in expanding blackness...

## Bermuda, two months later

I am completely back to myself. I remembered everything that had lurked somewhere in the recesses of my memory, and Janta was not far from me. I was visited by crew members who were able to walk after what happened to us in the middle of the Bermuda Triangle. According to their accounts, I was able to reconstruct what had actually happened on board the Caribbean Pearl on that fateful night of December 13/14 of last year.

Explosion of thermite bombs planted in two cargo holds. It was supposed to look as if the ship literally sank under the water, burning. Someone must have liked a good job. The crew was saved only because we managed to activate the alarm. If it wasn't, half of them would die, and the rest would be eaten by sharks or other voracious fish.

We were lucky. The explosions and fire were spotted by a spy satellite, which transmitted an image of what was happening to the NORAD operations center. The temperature of the explosion was so high that the operators thought that missiles had been fired at the United States. As this phenomenon could not be identified, and no rocket flying for America was seen, a reconnaissance plane was sent from Miami to find our lifeboats and rafts, and in turn a rescue ship was sent to pick us up and take us on board. This is what our survival looked like. Of course – as on this kind of occasion – the tabloid press began to use it to the fullest and I cringed with laughter when reading the nonsense that was written. Of course, there was also the other side of this scandal.

On the other hand, the case of the activities of the John Dante Goldman Uranium Mining and Power Co. was based on the Senate, whose committee decided to take a closer look at this company and its activities – including cooperation with Golden Phoenix - Phènix d'Or Co. Ltd. An investigation was launched, during which twisted business with the regime in Costarican, connections with terrorists from the AQL and mysterious neo-Nazi organizations in South America began to emerge. There was a riot, compared to which the Iran-Contra affair is a small beer, not even a small piece of cake, and Ollie North is a pathetic amateur. The *nuke-ships scandal* – as the tabloid press dubbed it – was spreading in wider and wider circles...

All this happened while I was lying with my head smashed in the hospital in Hamilton and coming back to myself. Finally, I was discharged from the hospital and I was able to be released. Janta came to pick me up and waited for the nurse to give me all the documents. With a pile of papers under my arm, I finally went out in front of the hospital and fell into Janta's arms.

- What are you going to do with yourself when you are healthy? She asked after exchanging welcome hugs and kisses.

- Install myself somewhere and come back somehow... - I started and I realized that in fact I had no one to go to, where and to what.

- Do you have nowhere to go back? Janta asked, but it was actually a statement, "Where is your home, sailor?"

"Four kilometers under the ocean water," I grumbled, "I could go back to London.

- Do you live there? She was interested.

" *Ad interim*," I replied, "temporarily. I rent a cottage in Felixtowe.

"Do you have anyone there?"

- But you know very well that you don't...

"I'm sorry to question you, but I want to know where I stand.

I stopped and looked at her in amazement.

"Do you mean that...

- ... that whatever you say, I will say yes," she replied.

We snorted with laughter.

"I didn't even give you a ring," I said regretfully, "for a romantic mermaid, you're very matter-of-fact."

"Because I am," she replied, "I love you, so why can't we be together?"

- Well, yes, but where are we going to live? Probably not in Felixtowe. A nice city, by the sea, but I don't know if you would feel comfortable there. And I'm not fit for the ocean.

She laughed.

"And who says that," she said at the end, " *marinacha!"*

- Well, OK, we'll live on the boat – I suggested.

"No, in Tsingalai," she said.

- Uh, where?

"In Tsingalai, I'm talking.

- What is it?

- This is the place where the largest cultural and administrative center of the Sea People is located, something like your capitals of countries. Of course, it is adapted to sustain the life of oxygen-breathing beings like you. And so do I, of course.

I shrugged.

- I hear it for the first time.

She smiled mysteriously.

"I'm betting it's not," she said, "and you may have even dreamed of this place."

- So where is it?

- In the South Pacific. Marie Therese Reef.

-There??? – my eyebrows went up in amazement – after all, there... Wait, wait...

She laughed again.

"Of course, do you remember Verne's 'The Mysterious Island'?"

- Of course. These are Lincoln Island and Tabor Island.

She sighed with feigned compassion and relief at the same time.

-No... Surprised! But we'll talk about that later. Now go to the beach. I missed the sun and water.

Me too. I told her that, so first we went to the Grape Bay Beach Hotel, where Janta had installed herself, and from now on I did too.

- How did you register us? I asked, surprised.

"Don't you know?" she replied with a mischievous smile, "as usual in such cases: Mr. and Mrs. Smith." The end, period, *the end.*

- And the costs of stay? This is one of the more expensive hotels...

"What do I care?" she shrugged, "while the nuke-ships investigation is ongoing , Uncle Sam is paying for our stay here."

Well, that was acceptable.

"What do we do, Mister Smith?" She asked, after I had settled into our room.

"First, some dinner, just not pizza or other fast-shit, and then the beach," I suggested.

-Very well. Then we will lie by the pool or on the beach, it's only a hundred meters away, and finally talk. I'll tell you a story that concerns my ancestors and the shipwreck of a passenger ship in the Atlantic. It's a mystery that I can't solve.

And probably no one, so maybe you can give me some advice...?

-I?

"Of course you," she said with a mysterious smile, "are you *a marinacha* or not?"

I nodded.

- So let's go for a bite to eat, and then I have to buy myself a fancy bikini. Let those babsztyls who are groping you with their eyes see that they have no chance...

- Eh, these women – I thought – whether mermaids or aliens, they are always the same...

She looked at me.

"Guys," she snorted, "always think of only one thing!"

I looked at her.

"And didn't it occur to your pretty head that this is what this world is based on and around it?"

"Sexist talk," she laughed and pulled my hand, "come on and don't whine!"

And we went together to a restaurant, where we were given normal, European food. Fortunately, from French-Italian cuisine, not English, which I feared. We ate what they gave us and Janta rushed to the hotel shop. After a while, she returned with three costumes in her hand. Two were in some colorful spots that hurt your eyes in the subtropical sun, the third was smooth and green.

- Which one do you like the most? –Asked.

"Green," I said, "fits your eyes. They are also green.

She smiled.

"Actually," she grumbled, "he's the most tempting of all.

"Women love to undress," I said, "and not for other women.

She stuck her tongue out at me. Then she went to the toilet and came out of it already in her outfit. She was stunning.

"You're stunning," I said, "you look like a Water Nymph."

"And you, like a pale man," she said, "come to the sun, at least it's free here..."

"Anyway, you look like wow... Even double wow!

"I'll tell you our secret," she said in a stage whisper, "I love undressing, because nudity is our natural state. Only Poles are born in horned caps and with a sword in their hand. The rest of the nations are born normally, i.e. completely naked. Understood? And now come, the sun and the water await. Go change your clothes at last, oh, I bought you swimming trunks...

And so we went to the beach. We sat next to each other. Janta snuggled up to me, and I put my arm around her. We both looked at the sky, where sunlit clouds were wandering.

"What is this sensational story you want to tell me?"

- It concerns my great-grandmother, who, like me, went stupid and fell in love with a man. And, of course, she followed him into the world...

"What a beautiful beginning," I grumbled, "do you want to bring me down at the very beginning of our, eh..., relationship?"

She giggled cutely.

"Not to bring them down, but to dominate," she said calmly, "but as I know you, I know that you will not give in." And when will you propose to me?

"Tomorrow," I replied, "today I don't feel like going to the shops.

She clung to me tighter and I kissed her on the lips.

"But tomorrow," she said when I let her catch her breath.

"OK, you have my word," I replied, "and now your story..."

And so she told it, and when she finished it got quite dark, and I had the impression that I had been hit in the skull by a beam again. But that's a topic from another ballad...[65]

**CR**

---

[65] The rest of this story can be found in the book entitled "The Mysteries of the Titanic and Other Tragedies".

# Chapter 29. Daeghtine

**30 V - afternoon**

The sea is murmuring. The setting sun illuminates the dunes with a strong, reddish light. We lie on the dry sand and kiss. Somewhere far away you can hear the cry of seagulls. I look into Berenika's face and keep wondering how lucky I am to be the partner of this extraordinary woman. After all, Berenika is not an ordinary girl, but she is a mermaid. A human being inhabiting the ocean, whom I met thanks to an incredible coincidence. Together we experienced a great adventure with whales and the ISS station. Together we met people from the Future and beings from other worlds. And then we went through life together. It was not easy for us. We are human beings from two worlds... But this is the least important.

We are happy. And that's all that matters.

I take Berenika in and we lie with our eyes closed, cuddled up in a shallow hole.

Suddenly, Berenika tenses up. I can feel the muscles of her strong body tensing.

-Hear? – he whispers in my ear.

"No," I answer, pricking up my ears.

Berenika has much more acute senses than mine. He can see in the dark and hear infra- and ultrasound. Mermaids have these adaptations to life in the deep...

"It's getting louder and louder," he whispers, "you're about to hear it." Such a whistling rumble at a low frequency.

I strain my ears. In fact, after a few seconds I hear the sound that Berenika described so precisely, some low, whistling rumble.

- What is it? A submarine?

"No, it's too loud even for a nuclear power plant," Berenika shakes her head. –See!

-Where? – I ask, but unnecessarily. A clear sky and excellent visibility at once begins to be covered by fog that comes out of nowhere. At least I thought so. The fog quickly thickened and visibility dropped to several meters.

"Do you see anything?" –Ask.

Berenice shakes her head. The fog swirls and slowly begins to thin. After a minute or so, everything returns to normal. Again, the sun illuminates the sea, the beach and us.

- What was that? Berenice asked this time.

I felt my eyebrows rise in exorbitant amazement. Who's who, but she should know best.

"Something like this has been seen in the Bermuda Triangle, but not in the Baltic Sea. And it always heralded trouble," I said, sweeping my eyes over the horizon on which the ferry to Sweden was slowly moving.

- I don't know what you mean by "trouble", but I sense that something has changed in our environment...

- In general or especially?

She sat down on the sand and looked around.

"In general," she said, "it has to do with the Station.

I guessed.

- Do we have guests?

"A guest," Berenika clarified. "And that's her. Woman.

It was starting to get interesting. I didn't expect anyone, neither did Berenika. Not from our circle of friends. It could only be Sylvia-Kadumé or... Urszula?

- Anyone you know? I asked, just to be sure. She nodded.

"I'm feeling trouble," she said.

"Sure," I muttered, "trouble is my specialty...

We laughed. We were too happy to worry about them. Until then.

She stood up and brushed the sand off her shorts and T-shirt. I also got up and we both headed towards the Station.

Located in the old watchtower of the Border Protection Forces, our Marine Animal Rescue Station was designed to save all kinds of marine mammals in the Baltic Sea – from porpoises and seals to whales, which sometimes came here from the Atlantic and the North Sea. It employed a team of six volunteers and permanent scientific staff. About twenty in total, and up to thirty people in gusts. After last year's action, we managed to save Megusia from the fishing net – an almost thirty-meter long Megalodon shark, which had strayed to the Baltic Sea from the equatorial waters of the Atlantic. Thanks to this, our stations became famous all over the world and for some time we couldn't get rid of journalists. But fortunately that was in the past, today we worked normally and only from time to time someone from the "wide world" came to learn something about Baltic animals or megalodons. Most often sensation hunters or scientists. For normal hamburger ruminants, the topic ceased to exist...

In front of the Station building stood a large, silvery-gray van with no inscriptions on Swedish plates. Next to us, on a bench, sat a young woman with her back to us. At the sound of our footsteps, she turned her head, and after a while, amid shouts of joy, we embraced Úrsula cordially.

"Did you come in that cart?" Berenice asked.

Ula smiled.

- Sort of - she replied - only parking didn't work out very well for me...

I looked at the van – it was standing on the lawn as if a crane had put it there. There were no wheel tracks.

"Let me guess," I said, "you put it up right after you flew out of the well of the time-frame?"

Ula nodded.

- And the cloud was artificial? Berenice asked.

-Was! Ula nodded in the coldest blood.

- Ha, ha – I knew it! Berenice said. "This is your tactical camouflage...

"But at least no one saw me park in front of the Station," Urszula cut off. – By the way, I hope you will give me hospitality for a few days? I have a very urgent matter to deal with in YOUR place and time. OK.?

We nodded, it was finally getting interesting.

### May 31 – morning

I woke up first. I got up and looked around our bedroom. Ula and Berenika were still asleep, the third volunteer, twenty-three-year-old Grażyna, was on duty all night. In the second bedroom slept two sisters, Ana and Ineza from Almería, and Helga Holgersen from Skagen. All of them were students of the University of Gdańsk and were doing summer internships. Berenika and I were the oldest volunteers here, so we had to keep an eye on them so that they didn't miss something important, which was especially true of the Fuentes sisters, who were terribly scatterbrained, as Latinas are. Helga, on the other hand, was a monster of accuracy, which was sometimes irritating, but only because her perfection was stinging in the eye.

I shuffled to the bathroom and after a while I was standing under the warm streams of water. I got out of the shower and wrapped a towel around my hips. Then I took out a shaver and foam from my make-up bag and started shaving. At one point, I felt a cool gust on the bare skin of my back and Helga materialized behind me, wrapped only in a fluffy bath towel. She smiled seductively.

" *Hi*, Walter," she said, cuddling up to me, "how did you sleep?"

"It used to be better," I replied.

"You would certainly be better off with me than with that mermaid of yours," she said, bending over and exposing her shapely breasts, "I'm warm, and she's not." Brrr...

-Jealous? I asked, picking up the rest of the stubble from my cheek.

" *I, det er jo klart* ," she replied, "it's clear, don't forget that I'm here *especially for you...*"

"You have my word that I still remember," I said.

She slowly turned away from me and with a studied movement took off her towel and slowly turned around naked so that I could have a good look at her. I smiled. All Helga. She had a harmonious, but at the same time strong, athletic body covered with an evenly golden tan. She could play Valkyrie or another goddess from the Scandinavian pantheon of female deities. My Mermaid was a chucher next to her...

Swaying her hips seductively, Helga stepped into the shower and indulged in the pleasure of bathing. I washed my face, smelled of aftershave, sprayed with deodorant, and left the bathroom.

I made myself a coffee and drank it while watching the next day get up. The sun was slowly rising, shining through the veil of fog. The orange disc slowly climbed upwards. The sea, invisible through the fog, could only be seen along the orange sun trail. A wonderful spectacle that I have always tried to contemplate alone...

But not today.

Helga walked into the mess hall and poured herself a cup of coffee, then stood next to me. It was warm and smelled of some pleasant, sensual smell... What was it? – I thought for a moment – Chanel? Soir de Paris? Prêt à porter? A delicate smell was visible through the aroma of coffee.

I looked away from the window and looked at Helga. For a moment, I contemplated her right profile. She was looking out the window and pretending not to see my gaze. I wanted to laugh. Suddenly, Helga stretched out her hand, pointing to something outside the window.

- *Der!* "Walter, there!" she cried.

I looked away and looked in the direction indicated.

On the orange-yellow trail from the sun there was a bright, sunny reflex, but it was not a reflex. It was something more material. We stared at it for a few seconds.

"Close your eyes," I said and squeezed my eyes shut.

Just in time. A powerful stream of bright light splashed into our eyes. Helga screamed, because it must have blinded her. After a few seconds, everything returned to normal. I opened my eyes. Above the trail and slightly to the left of the sun, a fairly strong orange light was burning, which slowly rose and moved in the sky in a northerly direction, over the open sea, darkening at the same time.

- W-what was that? Helga looked at me with a kind of horror in her eyes.

"UFOs," I replied.

- Men... - she moaned - UFOs do not exist!

I smiled wryly.

" *Oh, really?"* "And what was that?" Witch on a broomstick or maybe Harry Potter?

She slowly cooled down from her amazement.


And horror.

Her eyes narrowed. She turned pale under her tan.

"You knew," she whispered, "from where?"

I shrugged.

- I used to deal with it, and professionally. Before I became a ufologist, I was an analyst. I worked for the services.

- For NATO? In this regard?

I nodded in agreement.

- But how did you know that ... that it would fly out of the water?

I finished the rest of the coffee and washed the mug, then opened the fridge.

- How did I know? –Ask. I have already seen it once on a ferry from Sweden to Polish. That was in June a few years ago. We were returning to Polish from a meeting with the Swedes from FRA and FOI by ferry to Świnoujście. And almost in the same situation. We ate breakfast. The ferry was going in the fog and only the trail from the sun and the sun itself was visible. And it was then that I saw first such a moving reflex, and then there was a blinding flash. Only that something disappeared above...

- And what, something happened later? "Helga was herself again, a cool and matter-of-fact Scandinavian. "What happened next?"

"Well, nothing," I replied, "until today...

I tactfully passed over the spectacular collapse of the ruling Order and Fairness party and the meeting with Kadumé, who was an alien after all. Only six people knew about its existence, one of whom was a Mermaid, the other a visitor from another time, and the others had their memory erased and modified so that they remembered only as much as they should.

- Hmmm... I don't believe you somehow," Helga thought for a moment, "but you met Berenice, and she's a mermaid." And who is Ursula?

"A friend," I replied, "stopped by for a few days. He has something to do here.

Helga smiled brightly.

"If we were you, you should have a good rest, because we'll torture you, *på død* – to death..."

And she left.

### 31 V – afternoon

We were lying next to each other on bath towels, frying in the sun. Helga was on duty and both sisters went to Władysławowo, so we had twelve hours to deliberate. The warm sun made me lazy, the sound of the sea put me to sleep. And yet we didn't want to sleep. We lay down so that Urszula was between us and we waited for her words like vultures on a fall. But she was clearly pleased to expose ninety-eight percent of her body in a colorful thong-bikini to the sun. And she was silent.

"Ula, maybe we can finally find out what brings you here?" Berenice said, looking at her from behind her almost black glasses.

Úrsula stretched delightfully in a way that made you shiver.

- Uhmmm... - she murmured - give me a moment of happiness and warmth...

- Are you on vacation or on a mission? Berenice said it with some unkind intention. Murder lurked in her eyes.

Ula sat down and smiled at us.

"All right, my dears," she said, "if you are so impatient..."

"We are," I answered, "so we are listening.

Ula stared for a moment into the bluish distance.

- What do you know about the extinction of the Dinosauroids?

We looked at each other. Berenice raised her eyebrows.

"You mean the sentient reptiles of the Mesozoic?" –Asked.

Ula nodded.

- Exactly. What do you know about it?

"As much as the Alvarez theory," I replied. "Sixty-four million, eight hundred thousand years ago, the asteroid Chicxulub hit the Earth, causing an ecological disaster. It was the turn of K/Pg, Cretaceous and Paleogene.

"That's right," Ula lay down on the towel again, facing the sun, "but Chicxulub was the biggest one." Apart from it, there was also the Silver Pit and a dozen others. They simply fell like the debris of Comet Shoemaker-Levy 9 on Jupiter in 1994. The sentient lizards inhabiting the Earth – Dinosauroids – predicted the catastrophe and decided to wait it out. To this end, some of them entered the planetary underground, and some hid in the mountains. Most of them did not survive the cataclysm, and those who did did regress to the level of, hmmm... *Homo sapiens neanderthalis...* Later, they became extinct and only some survivors hiding in the cave complexes of Mato Grosso or the Rocky Mountains survived to YOUR times.

- And in the Himalayas? Berenice said.

"They haven't been there yet," replied Ula, "the Deccan has just collided with Asia."

"Did you see that?" I exclaimed involuntarily.

"Personally, no," she replied, "it's a process stretched over millions of years, but I saw the beginning of this process. And it wasn't that exciting at all...

"Okay," Berenice said this time, "tell us, what is your mission?"

"Yes," replied Ula, "history likes to repeat itself. In the 20th century, the Earth is expected to collide with the asteroid 2133 TU1784. Actually, it is not even an asteroid, but something like a conglomerate of small cosmic bodies bound by the forces of gravity. Something like the Chicxulub asteroid. Understand?

We nodded.

"OK, then the Dinosauroids..." said Berenice hesitantly.

- ... They almost died out because they assumed that a series of thermonuclear explosions would blow the asteroids into fragments. And so it happened, because it was something like Daeghtine.

"Daeghtine?" I asked, although I guessed the answer.

- Asteroid 2133 TU1784, that's what it's called.

"And what next?" asked Berenice, not hiding her curiosity.

Ula smiled unhappily.

- Well, that Daeghtine will strike in the Black Sea region, more precisely in Odessa. You can sing the rest.

- OK, but what do we have to do with it? I asked, intrigued to the highest degree.

"You will have to make preparations to repel the attack have to start this year.

31 V/1 VI – evening-night

We sat at dinner, but we ate somehow sluggishly. That is, both sisters were eating portions of grilled flounder, which they bought in Hel. Somehow our appetite was gone, and finally I got up from the table and dragged myself to the duty room, where I relaxed Helga.

I sat in the armchair, staring blankly at the computer monitors. The case looked idiotic, to say the least: an employee of a historical institute from the 26th century came to the 21st century in order to prevent a world catastrophe that is yet to happen in the 20th century. If it wasn't for the fact that I know Urszula, I would say that this is some kind of crazy nonsense.

And yet no. Ula showed me all the documentation, which – if it wasn't an idiotic joke – looked real. According to it, one of the wandering planets approached our Oort Cloud, from where it knocked out a dozen or so "crumbs" of matter from its orbits through the gravitational influence. Of course, these "crumbs" had a mass of millions of tons and a collision with them caused a repeat of the turn of the Cretaceous and Paleogene – the total annihilation of most organisms on our planet, after which life will have to start almost from scratch...

Of course, the only man we could count on for help was Professor Pomian – my boss and employer, whose assistant I had been for several years. He was the only one who seriously believed in the existence of what he called parallel terrestrial and extraterrestrial beings. He was a Nobel Prize winner, which was a very favorable circumstance, but at the same time such a controversial figure that by some he was considered by some to be – to put it mildly – a madman, a charlatan, a swindler and a fraud. I had a terrible desire to call him and bring him to Hel so that he could listen to Ula himself and read her documentation. That would be the best way out of the situation we found ourselves in, because I had no doubt that Ula was telling the truth.

It was necessary to act, because this cursed asteroid actually resembled a bag full of stones. The use of nuclear weapons would do nothing – the energy of the explosion would be absorbed by the solids, and the force of gravity would glue them back together into one object. The result is known. And even if Daeghtine were broken into smaller fragments, the scenario of July 2004 on Jupiter would be repeated. The Earth would receive a series of impacts from lumps whose impact energy would be thousands, if not millions, of megatons. By the way, I found out that the word Daeghtine doesn't mean anything, it's a name that was computer-generated, because the range of names of gods, famous people and heroes has already run out, so the names of cosmic objects have been generated so that they are easy to remember and pronounce.

It was midnight when Berenika appeared at the door of the duty room. Barefoot and with my shirt on my back. Without a word, she sat on my lap. We embraced each other and sat there for a few minutes without saying a word. I was happy that she was with me and it was right now, when I was sitting in the duty room and fighting with my thoughts... The warmth of her body was soothing and her presence calmed my nerves.

- What are you going to do about it? She asked in a whisper.

- With what?

- With what Urszula told us.

"It doesn't look bad," I replied, "first of all, I'll call Professor Pomian in the morning and ask him to come here and talk to Urszula in person, and of course look at her documentation." And the rest is not our business. He has influence in the world of science and politics, so he will manage.

- And if not?

I smiled.

- You don't know Pomian. There is no more stubborn Aries in the entire Zodiac!

- Is he an Aries? –Asked.

- Yes, and from the year of the Sheep. In a word, Aries squared!

We laughed and immediately got over all our fears.

I looked at my watch – it was one o'clock.

"Go to sleep Berenice, I have something else to do here."

I kissed her and she got up from my lap and went to the bedroom.

I was left alone.

First of all, I wrote a lengthy email to Professor Pomian, in which I explained the problem to him and asked him to come to our Station as soon as possible. With a flick of a key, I sent the letter into electronic space, and I leaned back in my armchair, watching the sky light up in the northeast.

2.VI – morning

Nothing interesting happened all day yesterday. I passed the duty to Ania and then I slept through the late night. And so I spent Children's Day.

And the next day, Professor Pomian appeared at the Station. His black Volkswagen parked next to Ursula's timeplane, and he sat on a bench and exposed his face to the sun. Whoever saw it would think it was some kind of holidaymaker who had come on holiday. Dark glasses, a Hawaiian T-shirt and shorts would have fooled many people, but those in his knowledge knew that behind this carefree outfit and dark glasses there was a stout and brilliant mind. I thought that Ula had perfectly selected him for this job.

After a short welcome and breakfast, we went to the beach. And again, like two days ago, Úrsula told him about the whole matter. He listened attentively and from time to time asked a question that clarified her story. When she finished, the professor looked around and spoke in these words:

- Who knows about it, except you – he looked at me, Ula and Berenika.

"Only them," Úrsula replied.

- That's good, and let it stay that way. I know a couple of high-ranking people in the UN, Russia and the USA to whom I will present this. Where is this facility now?

- Daeghtine?

"No, the damn planet that will cause Daeghtine to go out of orbit. Does it have a name?

- Oh, yes. It was called Nemesis," Úrsula replied, "in honor of the stories of twentieth-century astronomers and astrologers...

We all laughed, as if the cosmic threat had disappeared.

"A strange man is," I thought, "it is enough to name what threatens him and he feels as if it provides him with security.

"And why is Daeghtine so dangerous?" After all, you can smash it somehow? – said Berenice, who had been silent so far.

Úrsula sighed.

"You see, it's not a uniform lump of stone or metal," she began her lecture, "but a conglomerate, breccia, if you prefer." It consists of several solids connected by gravitational forces. A nuclear explosion will cause its energy to be absorbed and dissipated by lumps, which will then slowly come back together anyway, you understand? It's like shooting a bag of stones with an air rifle. I told you - don't you remember?

Berenice nodded.

- There is one more thing you do not know. The fact that these damn lumps can fall to Earth is still a small piece of cake. Mr. Pikuś. The real problem is that they are stuffed with radioactive isotopes from half of the Mendeleev Table. And no one knows why. Perhaps it is some ruin of an artificial creation of one of the ancient space cultures, no one knows. We organize an expedition there, but the problem is that apart from jumping into space, we have to make a jump in time. And this costs a little. And the laws of economics apply to you, to us, and to the XXX century...

"How do you know that?" – asked the professor.

"We studied the effects of the impacts of these lumps a year after the catastrophe. The Earth was dead, not because of the release of kinetic energy from the impact, but because of the contamination. Understand – two of them hit the oceanic plates in the Pacific and Atlantic. There, the Earth's crust is relatively thin, about five to ten kilometers. Understand? What everyone feared the most happened – millions of cubic kilometers of magma poured out through these two bullet holes. This changed the composition of the atmosphere to such an extent that the mega-greenhouse effect began. The synergistic result was that the Earth began to resemble Venus after the impact of its moon - Neith: the temperature at the surface rose to two hundred and fifty degrees, the pressure increased to one hundred atmospheres... In a word, the planet was not suitable for life at all, which, by the way, became extinct... And on top of that, radioactive contamination with long-term radioisotopes, which will take several million years before they decay to a viable level. In a word, the hell in which the ancients believed.

- Even extremophiles will die??? Berenice exclaimed.

Ula nodded.

"They too, unfortunately," she replied.

We all fell silent. The sea roared, and we suddenly realized on what thin threads the fate of all Humanity hung.

And ours too...

2/3.VI – night.

The professor left in the evening, taking with him the documentation provided to him by Urszula.

We are now lying side by side, looking out of the window, behind which the forest is silvered in the greenish, quivering light of the bitten moon. On the next bed, Ula sighs. Berenika hugs me tighter. Grażynka also does not sleep. We listen to the sound of the sea.

-Walter? – I hear Grażyna whisper. – Is what you were talking about... Will it really happen?

"But you have heard," said Úrsula, "this is what will happen if we do not prevent it NOW.

A moment of silence.

- But how is this possible? Are you traveling in time and can't deal with this stupid asteroid? Grażynka sobbed.

I sighed.

- The problem is that it is not. But our actions will NOW change the reality in the 26th century and prevent tragedy in the 20th century, do you understand? The sooner we get down to it, the better. According to the principle: *warned* –

*armed!* – warned – armed, as the English say. We will simply change Reality. Anyway, there is no other way. But we have time now – two generations of the 21st century, twenty-six generations to the 20th century. Powerful mental and technical potential at your disposal...

- ... and chronography – Ula caught my word.

- And chronography. So there is a chance that we will successfully defend our planet and not share the fate of the Dinosauroids," I finished.

- By the way, I don't understand what mistake they made that they did not protect themselves from the misfortune, from the catastrophe that swept away their world? Berenice wondered.

"They did not take into account the effect of absorbing the energy of the explosion by the components of the asteroid," Urszula explained. "Besides, they put everything on one card, on one powerful shot. Yes, the shot was precise, but it blew the space stray into several fragments, which bombarded the Earth like Jupiter's comet S-L 9 in 1994.

- And you didn't want to help them to survive? Grażynka sobbed. – After all, they were also rational beings.

Ula laughed softly.

- We tried, but understand that they did not take our warnings to note at all. Besides...

She fell silent. There was silence.

-Besides... what? Berenice asked after a moment.

- Only that THIS change in Reality would be even more drastic FOR US and mammals would never master any ecological niche. Understand? We simply WOULDN't exist.

We all fell silent. I felt the night chill from the window. The wind awoke and the pines rustled outside the window. I covered us with a blanket. Ursula was right, and only now have we fully realized the consequences.

- They didn't have chronography? Berenice asked.

"No," said Ula. – And what is most interesting, they understood time in a completely different way. Not as a process, but as such... extended duration. That's what they called it. Maybe it was due to their reptilian way of perceiving? I do not know. They had a completely different philosophical system and a completely different understanding of our world. That is, they knew the laws, our world and the laws that govern it, but they interpreted them differently. I think we could learn a lot from them...

"Were your people there?" I asked, extremely interested.

"Of course," she replied. "First of all, we had to find out what was the cause of all five episodes of the Great Extinction and these were the goals of the first expeditions in Time.

-Truly? And what did you see there? Grażynka stopped sobbing and her voice sounded almost childlike interest.

"Your scholars were not wrong about the Great Bombardment. In Ordovician, the Earth was indeed hit by a stream of gamma rays, which annihilated life in the oceans to a depth of thirty meters. Fortunately, there was nothing on land yet. The most interesting was the Perm Episode. It was caused by volcanism, but the primary cause was the impact of an asteroid in the area of today's Tunguska Hills. The energy of the impact pierced the continental crust in this part of Asia, then about twenty kilometers, and a fountain of magma splashed from the asthenosphere. We know the effects: a change in the composition of the atmosphere, a change in the albedo of the planet, the greenhouse effect and then global cooling. As a result, ninety-five or even ninety-nine percent of species went to hell... There is one conclusion: the greatest danger is there," she stretched out her hand, pointing to the ceiling.

"In space," sighed Berenice.

-Exactly! – Ula concluded. "In space. Enough talking, let's sleep!

We fell silent and no one spoke until the lights of a new day appeared outside the window.

Then I fell asleep.

### 3.VI – afternoon

In the morning, Úrsula went back to her home. This time, without any side effects, she just got into her van and disappeared. No bang, no flashes, fog and other unusual phenomena. And everything slowly returned to the lazy holiday routine. It just got boring. Whales were swimming somewhere in the Atlantic, megalodons sank into the depths, seals were basking on a sunny beach where more and more people were walking. From the sea it smelled of salt far, from the land freshly cut grass...

I dragged myself back to the Station building, where Berenika had prepared breakfast for everyone. I ate tastelessly, just to get stuffed.

- What are we doing today? Berenice asked.

- I would like to go to Piaski on the Vistula Spit. I would like to see what is actually there under the layers of sand.

- And what could be there?

- And it is. Uranium ore. Admittedly, only from forty meters down, but some nests may be shallower.

-I don't understand... Where does this uranium-bearing layer come from in this area?

-Me neither. But when Urszula was talking about the construction of Daeghtine, it occurred to me that something like this could happen on a smaller scale in north-western Polish. Look: here there is a huge area of uranium ore occurrence - from Gdańsk and Piaski in the north - to Tczew in the south and stretches east to Suwałki. The found deposit is located in the vicinity of Krynica Morska. By the way, there are iron ore deposits in the vicinity of Suwałki. Just like in Western Pomerania, where post-meteorite craters have been found... - and therefore...

- I'll go with you! Berenice exclaimed.

- And I with you! "Grażynka appeared unexpectedly before us. –You are welcome! You are welcome! You are welcome!

- Do you know anything about it? –Asked.

She smiled.

"I've taken a course in exploration geology," she said with a mischievous smile, "because I once wanted to prospect for gold, and as a child I read a novel by Cooper and Curwood." By the way, there are about a hundred thousand tons of uranium ore in Poland, so the exploitation may be profitable...

All three of us laughed.

"Sure, you're coming with us," Berenice said.

- And you won't take me? Helga asked pitifully, who had just entered the room and heard Grażynka's last words.

- Do you know anything about geology? –Asked.

She shook her head.

" *Hey* ," she replied, " *men*... Walter and I saw *a submersible* UFO taking off from underwater. And this has to do with uranium!

- Do you think so...? Grażyna asked in an uncertain tone.

She nodded.

- I read it from Robert Douvall and Robert Hastings that UFOs often appear in the vicinity of *uranmines*, and that there are fossil works there... *You understand it?*

And of course, she went with us.

We drove through the Pomeranian landscapes. I drove alternately with Berenika, who managed to pass the driving test on the first attempt and did quite well.

I was thinking about all that had been said before. The uranium-bearing area had the shape of an ellipse reaching the Tri-City in the south-west and under the Sambia peninsula it reached deep into the Baltic Sea, which fit the theory of the uranium meteorite. This is what a spread ellipse should look like. It also seemed that its largest mass was under the Tri-City, because there is the most uranium there. Only the most important question is: when? For it is obvious that if it was a uranium meteorite, it could have fallen at any time, and its flaming debris melted into and penetrated into the earlier geological layers. To determine its age, it was necessary to analyse the amount of uranium to its decay products, and these could only be done at CLOR or AGH UST laboratories.

At noon, we entered the Spit and headed towards the Russian border. On the way, we looked at the local seaside forest from the north and the Vistula Lagoon from the south. I wanted to see the seals here, but it was impossible. The northern beach was behind the forest. Finally, we arrived at Krynica Morska and the Seal Patrol Station located there.

### 3.VI – evening

The meeting with the seal sealers came to an end. It turned out that they had also seen some strange light phenomena on the high seas several times, but what was most interesting, they were in the water, not in the air. This manifested itself in the movement of a bright, greenish-blue light, which after some time darkened and disappeared, as if the "something" that shone it was submerging into the depths of the sea, or gradually extinguished.

Another time, one of the girls saw a dozen or so "meteorites" that fell somewhere in the waters of the Russian part of the Lagoon. Then, while diving, she heard strange noises that were not associated with anything known to her. Perhaps they were Mermaids, but she wasn't sure. Of course, they could have been some trained porpoises or even dolphins, but the former were rarely seen here, and the latter were trained by the Russians in the Black Sea, and we doubted whether they would adapt to the sweetish and cool waters of the Baltic Sea.

Around nine o'clock we parted ways with the friendly crew of the Station and went back to Hel.

- It's a pity that we didn't take our motorboat – Grażyna noted belatedly.

- Well, maybe we could see something interesting? Helga supported her.

"And what do the Mermaids say," I asked, squinting at Berenice, who was sitting next to me, "after all, this is your living space?"

"Nothing," she replied in the coldest blood. "The problem is that we don't know ourselves. Aghartians perhaps, but I'm not sure. Neither did Laskowski's friends from the Andean Fortress. Their flying apparatus is too primitive. It seems that there is some other – third or even fourth force in it.

- Time Wanderers? Berenice speculated.

- *Vanderere and tid*? – Helga said skeptically – *I don't think so...*

"Me too, but I meant wanderers from the OTHER side of Time, from the Past," Berenice replied.

There was silence for a moment.

"You mean Dinosauroids?" Grażyna said slowly.

- Exactly! Berenika adjusted herself in her armchair.

"Eh, no," I muttered, "I would like the Atlanteans better."

Berenice shook her head.

"You can believe me, but we would know something about it. The Atlantean civilization was focused on biotechnology," Berenice said. "They were able to produce miracles with the help of genetic engineering. Centaurs, Chimeras, Harpies – it's all their work. And so are we.

- OK, but where are their remains? Helga asked.

"They're decomposed," Berenice replied. – It was also genetically determined. After the death of such a hybrid, it decomposed to zero, which is why only legends about them survived.

We fell silent. Each of us digested these revelations in silence. We entered Kosa and passed Kuźnica, when Grażynka offered us a swim in the sea.

"I don't have swimming trunks," I muttered.

- So what? Berenika smiled temptingly, "it will be more pleasant." What do you think?

The others expressed their enthusiasm, and I shrugged. After all, I didn't have to splash in the sea...

"Walter, lock this car and come on," Berenika and Helga held out their hands to me.

I locked the car and jogged after them, but they caught me and led me to the beach. Berenika immediately threw off her dress and panties, and then ran naked into the water. Grażyna followed her with Helga, as God created them. All three splashed around like little girls, and I looked at this beautiful spectacle full of ineffable grace.

I dropped my shirt and shorts and joined them. We sailed towards Focza Rewa and entered a sandbank. There was not a single seal there and we jumped into the water again.

- Shall we go for a walk to the continent? Berenice asked, "It's only one and a half meters here. You can walk on foot...

"Are you crazy?" *Naked?* Helga exclaimed.

Berenice laughed.

- Well, I forgot that I am the only one who swims like that. Return?

"Just a moment, it's so wonderful," whispered Grażynka.

[…] Berenice was the first to wake up.

"We're coming back, it's already dark.

I looked up. Vega burned overhead, Deneb shone beside her, and to the south of them crept the white light of Altair. It was about half past twelve. We waded in the water and after a while we went out to the beach. I shook myself out of the water like a dog, the girls wringed their hair out. All three of them froze at once. I looked at them, their faces facing east, and they expressed wonder.

- What's wrong? I asked, but unnecessarily.

I turned around and looked towards the Bay of Gdańsk. About half a mile away, a patch of white and green light shone in the water. Suddenly, it began to approach us, and then it made an incredibly tight turn, and with increasing speed it began to move away, towards the center of the Bay.

Suddenly, it shone white and jumped out over the water. It flashed a subdued whiteness, which suddenly turned red and a red ball now floated above the water. It hovered a few meters above the water for a while, and then with incredible speed it shot up and disappeared into the starry sky.

" *Finis*," I said in a voice that was not my own, "it's over, as they used to say in ancient Rome..."

### 3/4.VI – night

- Have you seen the same thing as us? – Latino sisters asked us after returning to the Station. "We saw the authentic OVNI! It was a white ball of light!

"Yes, we do too," Berenice said.

- What was she like? White? Grażyna exclaimed, looking at me.

"White," said Ana. "And what?"

- And the fact that we saw it, but a red one – replied Grażyna.

" *Oh, really?"* Ineza asked, "Are you sure?"

We nodded in unison and then told our side of the story, omitting the details of our night bath. They listened with emotion.

I collected my thoughts.

- OK, girls. I have a request for you: write down what you have seen in the smallest detail and we will send it to Professor Pomian. He will know what to do with it.

- Of course, except... - Grażyna began.

- ... of course, except for the circumstances known," Berenika finished.

Ana made curious eyes.

- What circumstances? –Asked.

"An evening swim in the Bay," said Helga, who had been silent so far, arousing general hilarity.

"Without clothes, by the way," Berenika added. Ineza gave me a lingering look.

"It must have been very interesting," she said. "I'm beginning to regret that I wasn't there...

When we finally went to bed, it was well after twelve. But sleep would not come.

-Walter? – I heard Grażyna's voice – are you awake?

"No," I answered. "Something wrong?"

"I'm afraid," she said.

-What? I asked, intrigued.

"Actually, I should have told you about it a long time ago, but..." she paused.

- Of course, I understand. Come to us and fight what you have on your liver.

Grażyna got up and lay down between us. Berenice embraced her to calm her down. Grażyna was silent for a moment, and then she told us.

It turned out that Grażyna also got her way, and probably the most of all of us. She also had her encounter not so much with a UFO, but with SOMETHING so strange that she couldn't even call IT a living being... It took place a few days ago, when she went for a walk along the beach towards Jastarnia. At some point, a tall, at least two-meter tall figure came out of the forest to meet her, who was moving in some strange, inhuman way. The figure was dressed in a white loose jumpsuit, and his face was partially covered as if by a surgical mask. At some point, the figure turned its gaze to her and Grażyna saw two strange, yellow-brown eyes staring at her with predatory interest. What happened next, she does not know – she only remembered pain and dark chaos... She woke up in exactly the same place where she had first spotted the Alien. She had a headache and her stomach went up to her throat, which went away after a few minutes. After the strange meeting, what remained was a feeling of fear and... dream. Dreams in which she wanders through some underground corridors in an incredibly greenish light, she meets some reptilian creatures who hypnotize her with the looks of their amazing eyes. She always wakes up mentally shattered and with a feeling of incredible fear...

She finished and sobbed, and finally fell asleep in the arms of Berenice, who also fell asleep.

And I had a sleepless night again...

**4.VI – morning**

I got up as soon as dawn began to break with the feeling of being shattered after a sleepless night. I quietly slipped out of the bedroom and went to the mess hall, where I made myself a devil and then unfolded my laptop.

I thought for a moment, and then I wrote a long email to the professor, in which I reported to him the events of the last day plus Grażynka's revelations. I added my guesses about who or what we are dealing with.

One thing I could be sure of, whoever they were, they came from our planet. In general, the Interterrans from Robin Cook's novels came to mind, but if they existed, there would probably be some legends or at least fairy tales left after them. Meanwhile, there were none, that is, I had not heard of any, so I counted on the professor and his contacts. They could also have been Dinosauroids, but there were no traces of them in the geological layers on the border of the Cretaceous and Paleogene, so I couldn't take them into account either, unless...

A crazy idea came to me, but it was possible in this crazy world. I left it for later. I looked at the window, which was already quite bright, and by clicking on the icon I sent the information for the professor into the blue space of the Internet.

I was so lost in thought that I didn't react to the movement outside of me until I felt the touch of a warm and tanned hand on my shoulder. I turned my head and my gaze met the gaze of Grażyna's brown eyes. She stood behind me in her thin dressing gown and looked questioningly at my computer screen.

- Who is it for? She asked quietly.

"To Professor Pomian," I replied, "maybe he'll come up with something."

She nodded.

"And you can't?" She asked with defiance in her voice.

I shrugged.

"I can, if you care so much about it," I said, "I am personally convinced that all this leads to some kind of contact with them.

- Is it a certainty or a hunch?

"A hunch, but with a high degree of probability," I replied.

She took a step forward, leaning against me.

"Tell me," she said quietly, "tell me if you and Berenice..." Are you and her a couple?

- Ah, that's what you mean... – I thought. -Honestly?

-Yes.

- Yes and no. Yes, we like each other, because in a sense we participate in one experiment. And no, because each of us has her own life: she in the ocean, I on land.

- But you sleep together? – that was a statement.

- Yes, we ONLY sleep, as if you didn't notice.

She smiled. She sat on my lap and snuggled up against me. Through the thin material of her dressing gown, I felt the warm touch of her body.

"I'm very happy," she whispered in my ear. "We're both alone, so...

She bit me gently on the ear and then got up only to throw off her robe and now cuddle up to me again completely naked. I embraced her and she leaned over me. Her lips parted and her dark hair fell over my face. She smelled delicately of some cosmetics and sleep. We kissed each other warmly.

"Let's get out of here," she whispered.

I shook my head and gently freed myself from her warm embrace.

"Don't you want me?" Why? She asked reproachfully. – What happened?

I sighed. How difficult it was to explain it to her!

"Not now," I answered, "not yet.

Her beautifully defined, almost black eyebrows rose high. She was amazed to the highest degree, and I was not surprised at her.

- But why? Am I not sexy enough? See! She said and turned around. She was indeed sexy...

"It's not like that," I said firmly, "it's that at any moment there can be contact with Them, and you will be the recipient of it!"

### 4.VI – afternoon

And yet I was wrong. The addressee was the whole of Humanity, and we were only a medium. A mailbox that was supposed to deliver an important message to people.

We ate dinner and at half past four out of nowhere Grażyna suggested sunbathing. Undressed, we left the Station and headed for the beach, when suddenly it happened...

First, Grażyna let out a quiet cry, and then I felt someone's eyes on me. It was a very unpleasant feeling. Berenika looked at me knowingly – she felt the same. And then Grażyna moved forward with some unnatural, automatic step, looking ahead with a glassy, blind gaze.

"She's in a trance," I heard Berenice whisper.

I thought that Grażyna was susceptible to hypnosis, but I didn't see anything nearby that would put her in this state, unless...

"She had it programmed for her previous meeting with them," I said. – A suggestion was imposed on her to take us out of the Station and direct us to the place indicated by them.

- So what do we do? Berenice's voice sounded with uncertainty.

And fear.

"Don't be afraid," I said soothingly, taking her hand, "if they wanted to kill us, they would have done it by now, and without all this ado..."

We entered the belt of dunes and Grażyna stopped. Her body became unnaturally stiff and her breathing shallow. His face turned pale and expressed nothing.

"It's here, they're already here," she said in a voice that was not her own, so that we shivered despite the hot day.

I pulled myself together.

"If so, let them show up," I said calmly but firmly. "I don't like talking to empty air.

Grażyna turned to me. An expression of stony calm froze on her face.

"Wish granted," she said in the same dead tone, "look there!"

Her hand pointed to the foot of the nearest dune. At the same time, the scorching air became thick and colorful, and after a few seconds, an astonishing figure finally appeared.

- This is a hologram – said Grażyna – forgive me, but otherwise we cannot contact you. The microbes in your time are not present in ours and vice versa. There is a possibility of bilateral infection.

I breathed a sigh of relief. At least I understood that. Meanwhile, I looked at the Alien. If anyone has seen Russell and Dale's reconstructions of Dinosauroids, they know what I'm talking about. The creature was about two meters tall, with a bald skull, four-toed hands, and three-toed feet. So she was undoubtedly reptilian. Her strong, strongly muscular body was covered with smooth, as if covered with tiny scales, grayish-greenish skin. The greenish-yellow reptilian eyes looked sharp and intelligent. Behind their veil there was apparently a stout mind...

"Who are you and where do you come from?" asked Berenice.

- I am a Dinosauroid, as you call us, and I come from the abyss of Time, on this planet, of course – answered Grażyna.

- So still! – I thought with satisfaction – they survived this cosmic Armageddon.

- Was it before or after the cataclysm that wiped out the dinosaurs? I asked another question.

"In our case, the concept of time does not exist," we heard in response. So Ursula was right!

- OK, then why did you come here? What is the purpose of your mission? I asked again.

We waited a while, and then...

The dinosauroid showed us a projection that showed that after digging the Vistula Spit, the water balance would be disturbed in deep layers of sands lying up to seventy meters deep into the ground, and in which there are nests of uranium ores, which, after flooding with water and slowing down neutrons, will turn into small nuclear reactors that will heat groundwater and contaminate it with decay products. A huge radioactive stain will be created, which will be a death sentence for all life in a large part of the southern Baltic Sea.

"But that's not all," the dinosauroid paused, "you're threatened by a radio-asteroid impact. But you probably already know that.

We knew it, but how did they know? Did they have their intelligence in our place and time?

"We know this because we can also move in space and time," he answered my unasked question. – We avoided the fate of our brothers by making a jump in Time. We have changed Reality and now live on the Earth that existed before it was covered by glaciers from the poles to the equator, in a relatively safe epoch for us.

- Cryogen!? – I was shaken by a vague guess. "But after all...

- No traces of our activity have survived to your times, because they were destroyed by glaciers and other cataclysms. That is why until today no one knew about our existence. Just as after the Cataclysm, there is nothing left of us that can tell you about our existence. To use a simile, in each case, cataclysms removed the last pages from the fossil record, as if someone were tearing the last pages out of a book.

I decided to ask him about what I had always been interested in.

- Have you come into contact with intelligent beings from other planets?

The dinosauroid hesitated for a moment, and then said:

"The cosmos is teeming with life. Life develops wherever there is a shadow of its creation. You will see for yourself. But we have not met them in the times we inhabit. They had not yet had time to develop, although life itself already existed at that time and at a high level of development..."

And the Dinosauroid disappeared. The hologram simply vanished into thin air. At the same time, Grażyna took a deep breath and the colors returned to her face. The body is no longer rigid. Suddenly, she sat down on the sand.

"Dizzy," she said. "But I'm weak..." I have to lie down.

So I picked her up and carrying her in my arms we returned to the Station. Entering the building, I looked at the clock.

It was twenty-four...

4/5.VI – night

In the evening, Grażynka felt unwell and went to bed. She felt shattered and exhausted. Berenika finally went for a swim on the open sea, and I sat down in the duty room and typed out a kilometer-long e-mail to Professor Pomian. I described to him the whole encounter with the Dinosauroid and what we learned from him.

Amazingly, my memory perfectly stored all the information that the Dinosauroid had given us. Apparently, there was some kind of tweaking of my brain, or modification of my memory, and Berenice's as well, and his ability to remember was multiplied. After an hour, I sent the letter and breathed a sigh of relief. My role was played. I could get down to normal work.

I swept my eyes over the screens of the Station's computers, but there was nothing suspicious on them. All the animals we had under our care were safe, and nothing new appeared from the side of the Straits. It became gray, commonplace and boring. Again I looked at the window, in which the stars were floating in the sky...

### 5.VI – morning

- Here, read! Berenika threw sheets of newspapers on my desk.

I looked at the front page, where the big title was striking: ARE WE THREATENED BY THE ASTEROID DAEGHTINE? - and then there was an interview with Professor Pomian, who warned about a possible collision with the radio asteroid Daeghtine, which could threaten the Earth in a few hundred years. The professor referred to the results of his research on the Vistula Spit, under which, according to him, there are traces of a radioasteroid that splashed there sixty-four million eight hundred thousand years ago, ending the era of dinosaurs.

I finished reading and there was silence. Other tabloids reprinted the interview without stupid comments. The surprise was total. We looked into each other's eyes and breathed a sigh of relief.

The reality has changed. The future of Humanity was secure.

And ours too.

\*\*\*

All the stories that have been quoted here are just fantasy and not even scientific. I just wanted to point out the possibilities of what we can find in the oceans, because the time of the greatest discoveries is still ahead of us... And what is most important – at any time we can meet beings from other planets, other universes or another Time. And who knows if they are not already happening...?

# CHAPTER 30. MERMAIDS ON WHEELS

Let's love the Syrenkas, there are almost none left. It wasn't a bad car, I still remember the smell of its interior. There's no history of the Polish People's Republic without the Syrenka. It was a native design, perhaps rustic, but now we produce nothing. I preferred it to the "Maluch"; it was spacious and had room for luggage. It wasn't that bad; when my friend went to Italy in a Syrenka in the 1970s, people at every gas station photographed it en masse...

The decision to start design work on the new Polish small-capacity car, the Syrena, was made in May 1953. The Political Bureau announced: "...a popular, time-saving means of transport should be built for official duties and leisure, intended for innovators, leading workers, activists, scientists, and prominent representatives of the intelligentsia."

*FSO Syrena 100 (Wikipedia)*

In June 1955, the prototype of the Syrena was presented for the first time at the XXIV Poznań International Fair. Its production began on March 20, 1957. The first Syrena model initially did not have a numerical designation, and only after the appearance of the next version, the 101, was the first model designated as 100. In the first year, 200 units of Syrenas were produced, their bodies made of hand-hammered sheet metal. The maximum speed was 100 km/h, and the average fuel consumption was 8.5 liters/100 km.

*FSO Syrena 101 (Wikipedia)*

The first modernized version, designated Syrena 101, was put into serial production in 1960. The power unit achieved 27 hp, allowing it to reach a speed of 105 km/h.

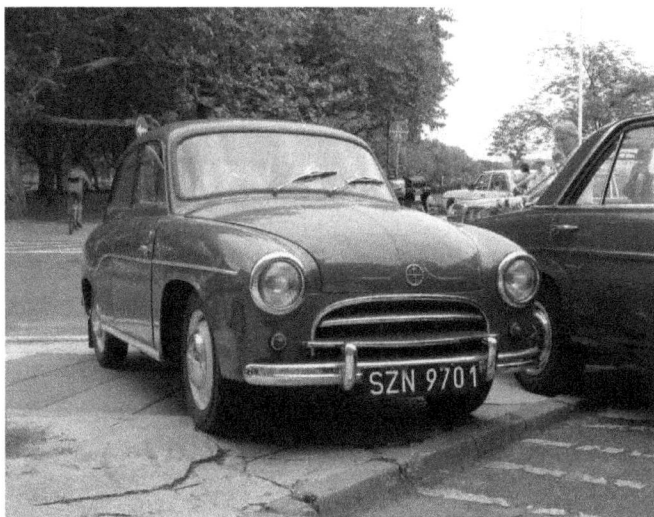

*FSO Syrena 102 (Wikipedia)*

The Syrena 102 was produced from 1962–1963. It differed from the previous model – the Syrena 101 – by having a shorter, differently designed trunk lid. The 103 model was produced from October 1963 to July 1966. Compared to its predecessor, the main changes were a modernized front (different air intake) and a new S-150 engine. There was also a 103 S version, equipped with a 40 HP Wartburg engine and a synchronized gearbox, which significantly improved the vehicle's performance. This version, colloquially known as "folksdojcz," was distinguished by double decorative strips on the sides of the body.

The FSO Syrena 104 model was produced from 1966–1972. It featured a new three-cylinder S-31 engine with a displacement of 842 cm$^3$ and a maximum power of 40 HP, as well as a fully synchronized gearbox. The Syrena 104 was the last model with "suicide doors," meaning they opened against the direction of travel.

*FSO Syrena 103 (Wikipedia)*

*FSO Syrena 104 (Wikipedia)*

The Syrena 105 was produced from June 1972 by FSO, and then, after the entire production was transferred, from 1972–1983 by FSM Bielsko. On August 30, 1972, FSM began production of this type of car. From 1975, the Syrena 105 Lux version was also produced, with the gear shift lever and handbrake lever on the floor. The Syrena 105 saw derivative versions: the Syrena R-20 is an agricultural pick-up, while the Syrena Bosto is a van. In 2013, a Syrena 105 unit was purchased in Poland by the crew of a British program.

*FSO Syrena 105 (Wikipedia)*

Fans of four wheels, imported to Great Britain, renovated in a dedicated episode of the show, and then sold for 8,000 pounds to the private Bubble Car Museum in Lincolnshire. A total of 521,311 units were produced from 1957 to 1983. Additionally, a great song by Andrzej Rosiewicz.

*Once a little Fiat fell in love with a Syrenka*
*He couldn't sleep at night because of her, he sobbed during rush hour*
*And he wiped his tear-filled headlight-eyes -*
*So much he longed for his beloved Syrenka*

*"My dear, ouch, oh, come io amo te" -*
*He remembered Italian from his father, still remembered a little from his father*
*When he first saw her, she was driving to Okęcie*
*He wanted to catch up, but didn't make it - she disappeared around the bend*
*But then at an exhibition he met her in Zachęta*
*He asked her if she would grant him happiness*
*All together: happiness*
*Once again: happiness*
*So right after the exhibition he invited her skiing*
*But they didn't go, because he wasn't broken in yet*
*So they just dropped by Fukier's for a little wine*
*In the evening they got drunk on gasoline*
*In a tiny, quiet gas station*
*For the first time she whispered "I love you" to him*
*When they were returning home, he was already kissing Syrenka*
*And then in front of the garage he asked for her hand*
*Syrenka, kissing Fiat's forehead tenderly*
*Replied: "Ask your mom for my wheel*
*Convince Mama Volga and Papa old-Fiat*
*How much you love me, that you will be like this for years*

*That you want to be so faithful to me, all the way to the junkyard*

*Tell them all this so nicely!"*

*So the next morning he called for a chauffeur*

*He ordered a bath, an inspection, and a hairdresser*

*At the "U Kalinki" flower shop he ordered fresh flowers*

*For Mama Volga, and for Papa...*

*He bought half a liter of fresh Super-Shell*

*And thus laden, he set off from Bielany on Sunday*

*He told the driver to go straight to Okęcie*

*The engine played cheerfully: "I'll be a son-in-law!"*

*All together: son-in-law*

*Once again: son-in-law*

*He stood before Mama Volga and Papa, trembling all over*

*He assured them that their feelings with Syrenka were hot*

*They had united and that this union would be perfect*

*But Mama Volga said he was too small*

*Fiat was too small, even though he stood on his tires, too small!*

*Because with in-laws you never know, oh, you never know*

*Sometimes it's good, and sometimes it's...*

*Ay daj bi bi daj; da bi bi da; di bi bi daj*

*Ay daj bi bi daj; da di di di di daj*

*Oh, ta joj*

---oooOooo---

Thanks to Stanisław for this text. It directly proves that, contrary to the views expressed in the West that Poland was a backwater, we had our own automotive industry and our own cars – maybe not like in the USA or the EU – but our own. And we should remember that.

KONIEC – KONEC – THE END